TRANSPORT IN EUROPE

The Artech House ITS Series

For a complete listing of *The Artech House Mobile Communications Library,* turn to the back of this book.

TRANSPORT IN EUROPE

Christian Gerondeau

Artech House, Inc.
Boston • London

Library of Congress Cataloging-in-Publication Data
Gerondeau, Christian, 1938–
    Transport in Europe / Christian Gerondeau.
      p.   cm.
    Includes bibliographical references and index.
    ISBN 0-89006-931-X (alk. paper)
      1.Transportation—Europe.   2. Transportation—Europe—Planning.
3. Transportation and state—Europe.   I. Title.
    HE242.A2G47 1997
    388'.094—dc21   97-9806
                                                              CIP

British Library Cataloguing in Publication Data
Gerondeau, Christian
    Transport in Europe
    1. Transportation—Europe.
    I. Title
    388'.094

    ISBN 0-89006-931-X

11564350

Cover design by Jennifer Makower.

Learning Resources
Centre

© 1997 ARTECH HOUSE, INC.
685 Canton Street
Norwood, MA 02062

International Standard Book Number: 0-89006-931-X
Library of Congress Catalog Card Number: 97-9806

10 9 8 7 6 5 4 3 2 1

▼▼▼

CONTENTS

v

ABOUT THE AUTHOR AND SOME RECENT TRANSPORT EVENTS

by Pierre Giraudet
Former Director General of the RATP (Paris Metro and Bus Transport Authority)
Honorary Chairman of Air France
Former Chairman of the IATA

The path traced by Christian Gerondeau in the course of his career is closely linked to the recent history of transport in France and in some ways in Europe.

Christian Gerondeau is from a family of engineers. His great-grandfather, grandfather, and father before him were all graduates of the Ecole Polytechnique, the best known of all the French "Grandes Ecoles" (higher institutes) of engineering, as is his son. Both great-grandfather and grandfather also graduated from the Ecole Nationale des Ponts et Chaussées, the world's oldest established school of engineering, founded in 1747 and celebrating its 250th anniversary this year. As was only natural at the time, both went on to make their career in railway engineering. His great-grandfather was responsible for the construction of a great viaduct on one of the lines through the Massif Central. His grandfather was general manager of the famous Compagnie des chemins de fer du Nord, up to the nationalisation of the French railway system in 1937 and today Eurostar passengers boarding for London at the "Gare du Nord" station just walk by his office.

On entering government service in 1962 as a member of the national corps of Ponts et Chaussées (literally, "bridges and roadways") engineers, Christian Gerondeau chose to concentrate on the hitherto little-known field of road traffic, a field he shows is still today widely misunderstood.

F.1 FIRST PUBLICATIONS

In June 1963, at the age of 25, he began publishing a series of documents on behalf of the Ministère des Travaux Publics, France's infrastructure ministry. The first of these documents, which described the unavoidable changes to French cities as a result of the spread of the car, was premonitory indeed, as subsequent events were to prove his thesis right more than 30 years later, as can be seen from the following quotations:

> *The increase in car ownership is going to continue from its present level of 1 car per 7 inhabitants up to a level of about one car for 2,5 inhabitants.*

> *This fact, together with the increase in our cities population and the improvement of the level of life is going to multiply car trips in such a way that it will not be possible for our traditional road network to cope with them. The creation of urban motorways networks is consequently unavoidable for every city over a certain size limit, which is certainly under 100.000 inhabitants . . .*

> *Then, to travel 10 kilometres will only need a few minutes. Land available for urban uses will be increased by a factor of 10 or 100, leading to a sharp decrease in overall densities and the easing of urban land costs . . .*

> *The great revolution of our cities has yet to begin. We have to organise us for it, and plan our road networks for the long term, even if their actual building is not going to be immediate . . .*

When the 5th National Plan was in the making, his series of documents was instrumental in ensuring the systematic inclusion of motorways in the overall planning guidelines laid down for French urban areas.

After a period spent working on planning and development, where he helped to implement these initial guidelines, in 1969, Christian Gerondeau published a book on urban transport, now out of print but still relevant in view of the accuracy of his forecasts.

Also in 1969, at the age of 31, Christian Gerondeau was appointed special adviser on infrastructure, housing, and transport to the then French prime minister, Jacques Chaban-Delmas.

For three years, he was able to put his ideas into action, instigating a series of decisions that were to make their mark on the nation's transport policy for the next quarter of a century.

F.2 THE ROAD NETWORK

As soon as he took up his new post, he was able to convince the prime minister that one of the most effective social measures that he could introduce would be a substantial increase in investment credits for urban road building to open up new areas for development and thus reduce the burden of land cost on the cost of new housing, whether private or social ones. As a result, the urban road building budget tripled.

The result of that decision was to maintain a high level of spending on urban roads over a number of years, which meant that the Paris region and major provincial cities in France were soon equipped with motorway networks that are the envy of some other European countries.

At the same time, Christian Gerondeau was one of the proponents of a policy that increased the annual rate of construction of intercity motorways from 100 km a year to 300, including by setting up a number of private companies.

His influence proved no less decisive in the field of public transport, through two major reforms.

F.3 CREATION OF THE PARIS REGIONAL EXPRESS NETWORK (RESEAU EXPRESS REGIONAL OR R.E.R.)

One of these concerned the Paris public transport system, which alone represents over half of all urban public transport in France. At that time, there were two rail networks in the Paris region: one was the high-density urban Metro system, unparalleled anywhere else in the world, run by the RATP (Paris transport authority), but serving only the region centre, including the city of Paris. The second network comprised some 40 suburban railway lines managed by the SNCF (French national rail company), running into eight different and unconnected terminals, which made for difficult connections between suburbs and city centre. By 1969, however, work had been under way for almost 10 years on the first regional rail link—line A—under the auspices of the RATP, designed to create an underground link between two former SNCF suburban lines, one serving the west of the capital, the other the east.

This was, however, a one-off project designed in complete isolation from the rest of the suburban rail network, and the costs involved were huge since the tunnels, running 30m below Paris, had the same gauge as those on intercity lines. As for the three new underground stations being created, their dimensions were described as "pharaonic" by the president of the day, Georges Pompidou, as they were just much enlarged copies of the traditional metro stations, which were designed to be built from the ground.

So he was quick to identify the disproportionate cost of the projected line A in comparison to the benefits to be expected from its configuration as an isolated system. He succeeded in convincing the prime minister to suspend work on the central trunk section, proposing later on the solution that was eventually adopted. He suggested that line A should become one of the major elements in an "interconnected" network to give the majority—not just two—of the suburban lines access to the heart of Paris.

This meant completely redesigning the plans drawn up for the two stations on line A still to be built. The Gare de Lyon station was reoriented by 90 degrees to allow for suburban trains one day to be connected to the future network. The station planned for the centre of Paris (Châtelet-Les Halles), where the old market of Les Halles once stood, was extended to seven tracks, becoming the "hub" of the Paris regional network: the three central tracks were reserved for the SNCF, and the four outside tracks for the RATP. The proposed new scheme also planned to link up the western section of line A with two SNCF lines serving one of the new towns created in the region, Cergy-Pontoise, and part of the existing suburbs.

At the same time, Christian Gerondeau suggested creating two other new lines. Line B, perpendicular to line A, would connect an existing RATP suburban line in the south—the Sceaux line—to the Gare du Nord network, which serves the northern suburbs of the Paris region and the Charles de Gaulle airport and is run by the SNCF. The other one, which was later to be called line D, would connect the southeast and north SNCF networks.

The extension of the Sceaux line northwards had indeed been considered earlier, but on technical and financial conditions that posed considerable difficulties. Christian Gerondeau embarked on a personal review of the plans of underground Paris to demonstrate that new technical solutions could make the project feasible at a far lower cost. The only "London-type" station of the Paris RER is to be found on line B (Station St Michel).

At the beginning of 1972, this revolutionary approach—a revised line A plus lines B and D—was adopted in its entirety by the French government, enabling work on completing the central trunk sections to recommence on an entirely new footing after three years of interruption. At this time, I was appointed chairman of the RATP and thus was privileged to help develop this programme and begin its realisation.

Such were the origins of what is today considered as one of the most efficient regional transport networks in the world, since imitated in other countries.

At the same time, Christian Gerondeau persuaded the SNCF for the first time to appoint a manager for the entire Paris suburban area: Until then, each geographical network (north, west, east, etc.) had been independent of the others. As a result of the appointment, the SNCF soon came up with a proposal to link two of its other

Paris termini (Gare d'Orsay and Invalides), which were only a few hundred meters apart, and thus create another regional line (line C) crossing Paris from east to west along the left bank of the Seine.

Thanks to these four lines, most inhabitants of the Paris suburbs now have high-speed access to the urban Metro network and the city of Paris itself at several points, and the Réseau Express Régional (RER) in its present form has brought sweeping changes to the conditions of transport between the suburbs and the centre of the capital as well as between the suburbs themselves, knitting the whole urban area into a single unit.

Over the 25 years that followed, the development of the simple and coherent design he had devised and won support for continued, and Christian Gerondeau had the rare privilege of witnessing its implementation by the two major enterprises— RATP and SNCF—which continue to share the responsibility for almost all of the region's public transport.

However, Christian Gerondeau was also responsible for setting up the financial structure that would make it possible to build the RER and would also provide other cities in France with the resources to set up the public transport systems— metros, tram lines, and so forth—which they had hitherto lacked.

It was not enough to plan the boldest reform of the Paris transport system since the building of the Metro at the beginning of this century. The reform had to be accepted by the two companies concerned, and the necessary financial resources had to be made available.

F.4 A LONG-AWAITED COOPERATION

The first of these two constraints was no easy task. The two great national companies that shared responsibility for rail transport in the Paris region had a long history of noncooperation. The Metro was, after all, originally designed by the City of Paris in the teeth of opposition from the railway companies and the State, which (even at that early date) would have preferred to link the various terminus serving the capital. The Paris city councillors feared—not without reason—that the government project would accelerate the flight of the inner city population towards neighbouring areas, a phenomenon already apparent in London. The dispute, which was finally won by the City of Paris on the occasion of the Great Exhibition of 1900, led to a 30-year delay in building the Paris urban Metro whose technical characteristics— narrower tunnels, trains travelling on the right-hand track—were specially devised to make it unusable by the rail companies, which would thus not be tempted to try and take it over.

By 1969, little had changed. There was practically no contact between the two companies, which explains why they had never been able to put together a project to share their regional lines. The determination and authority of the State, coupled with the good understanding eventually established in 1972 between the RATP and SNCF, finally brought the project to completion.

F.5 AN UNPARALLELED FINANCIAL STRUCTURE

Another problem, however, was finding the financial resources necessary to carry out such a vast undertaking. The cost of operating public transport in the Paris region was already imposing a considerable burden on national and local finances. Traditionally, then as now, the user was expected to pay only a small proportion (around one third) of the cost of public transport, with the difference being made up by the State and local authorities. Under the circumstances, it was difficult to find financing to cover the necessary level of investment.

At that time, too, any increase, however moderate, in the cost of a Metro ticket would trigger massive mobilisation by the main unions and protest demonstrations on a scale that made any substantial increase in ticket prices unthinkable.

So new sources of funding had to be found, and it was Christian Gerondeau who introduced the innovative system of public transport funding known in France as the "Versement Transport" (Transport Contribution). The system is based on the concept that 80% of the working population in the Paris region central area using transport to reach their place of work rely on the public transport network and thus their employers benefit, indirectly but undeniably, from a system that gives them access to a vast pool of workers.

There was therefore a certain justification in employers, who benefit indirectly from spending on public transport, contributing to its financing. For lack of a better solution, and despite his own reservations in principle about the earmarking of financing, this was the solution put forward by Christian Gerondeau and adopted by the French Parliament in July 1971, in a law that has no counterpart anywhere else in the world. It hardly needs saying that members of Parliament for the Paris region voted heavily against the measure, but representatives of the rest of the country were massively in favour, seeing in it a means of reducing their share of the financing for a system that benefited the capital alone, since there was no government funding for provincial public transport networks.

Based on payrolls, the Transport Contribution rapidly generated substantial resources that not only relieved the financial burden on the State, but also over the next years made it possible to embark on the investment programme needed to create the Paris region's "regional express network," the RER.

F.6 PUBLIC TRANSPORT IN THE PROVINCES

The impact of the Transport Contribution was not to be confined solely to the Paris region, however. Elected representatives in the provinces were not slow to grasp the advantages of such a source of financing for their own public transport networks. The very next year, they voted the extension of the measure to the main provincial cities, and subsequently to all of them, thereby providing the French public transport systems everywhere with an exceptional source of financing.

Although it may have been responsible for certain excesses, and certainly needs to be kept within reasonable limits, it is without question the Transport Contribution that has enabled French cities, one after another, to set up their own public transport networks, which are now among the most efficient in Europe: Metros in Lille, Lyon, Marseilles, Toulouse; tram lines in Strasbourg, Nantes, Grenoble, Rouen, St-Etienne, and soon in Bordeaux, Montpellier, Orléans, Nice, and so forth. It has also enabled provincial cities, whatever their size, to establish quality bus services.

All in all, between the ages of 31 and 34, Christian Gerondeau combined his earlier thinking with his position on a team working to a reforming prime minister to bring about profound changes in the French transport landscape. He conceived and saw implemented one of the best regional rail transport networks in the world and introduced a unique financial structure that would enable all the major cities in France to set up their own public transport systems, even as he orchestrated the decisive impetus for a network of urban motorways in every sizeable French city and helps increasing threefold the intercity motorways building pace.

It has to be quoted that, even at the time, his activity was not confined to the world of transport: He was simultaneously working on questions of a totally different nature; for instance, the abattoirs at La Villette, a disastrous operation that he brought to a halt despite opposition from many quarters, paving the way for the subsequent creation of what has become one of the major attractions in the Paris region.

F.7 ROAD SAFETY

In 1972, however, there was a major question in the transport portfolio that was yet to be addressed to.

In his three years as assistant to Prime Minister Jacques Chaban-Delmas, Christian Gerondeau had witnessed government impotence in the face of the escalating number of road accidents in France. Each year saw the death toll rise inexorably by another thousand. Responsibility for the fight against road deaths was split between at least a dozen different agencies, none of which really had the resources or the power to be effective. The almost universal feeling at the time was a sense of impotence in the face of the scourge.

To remedy this disastrous situation, Christian Gerondeau proposed that for the first time in France, a single person should be appointed to coordinate the action of all the agencies concerned, reporting directly to the prime minister in order to carry the necessary authority. Convinced of the need to put an end to the annual massacre, Jacques Chaban-Delmas adopted the proposal and convinced the President of the Republic, Georges Pompidou, of the necessity. In fact, this proved to be his final reform: On the 27th of June 1972, Christian Gerondeau was appointed Interministerial Delegate to the Prime Minister on Road Safety by the Council of Ministers: On the 3rd of July, Jacques Chaban-Delmas resigned as prime minister.

F.8 AN UNPRECEDENTED MEDIA CAMPAIGN

At one stroke, given the responsibility for a task involving thousands of human lives and even more unspeakable suffering, Christian Gerondeau's role was changed. From adviser to the prime minister, destined by the nature of the post to remain in the shadows and having never once appeared before a microphone or camera, he found himself catapulted in the media spotlight. For the first time, a face was associated with the struggle against a scourge that concerned everyone in France. The media coverage instantly devoted to "Mr. Road Safety" was more than intense throughout the nine years he occupied the post.

This exceptional coverage was almost certainly due to the fact that, in addition to his powers of expression and persuasion, Christian Gerondeau came to his job with a clear idea of what needed to be done in an area of concern to the entire population. If road accident figures were to be brought down, the behaviour of road users needed to change in three crucial respects.

Speeds had to be reduced, drinking and driving curbed, and the use of seat belts established as rapidly as possible. In fact, as far as the behaviour of road-users is concerned, these three basic rules are still the keystone of any road safety policy in the developed world.

Never before, however, had the rules been formulated with such clarity, and the simple fact of their enunciation, backed up by the clearly expressed determination that the authorities were really meaning it was enough in the very first year to slow the upward trend in road accidents. From that moment, the French death toll, which had reached the historic and intolerable height of 17,000 in the year before Christian Gerondeau's appointment, began to fall and never again reached such a horrific total.

F.9 TWO KEY DECISIONS

Psychological impact alone, however, could not produce lasting effects. If the behaviour of French road users was to be changed definitively, the State would have to not merely advise but actually lay down regulations to be followed in the three target areas. During the second half of 1972 and the first half of 1973, Christian Gerondeau concentrated on the psychological preparations for the next decisive step. What was needed was to create a climate that would not only prepare public opinion to accept the necessary measures, but also, and more importantly, ensure that the political authorities responsible would take the steps that were needed. A year's intense efforts bore fruit on June 1973, when the prime minister of the day, Pierre Messmer, announced the introduction of speed limits on the entire French road network with the exception of the motorways, along with the compulsory wearing of seat belts outside urban areas.

The first measure was long overdue, and was already well established in many European countries, not to mention dating back almost 50 years in the case of North America. Nonetheless, it required infinite diplomacy for the measure to be introduced in France, including the steps necessary to present opposition groups to mobilise rapidly enough to block the move as they had succeeded in doing on many occasions in the past. The second measure, on the other hand, was a first of its kind in Europe.

To get these decisions through, Christian Gerondeau relied above all on the results of opinion polls, which showed that, contrary to what might have been thought on listening only to the vocal minority, public opinion was in fact in favour of vigorous action by the authorities.

F.10 A PRECEDENT FOR EUROPE

One of the most remarkable examples of this use of public opinion polls occurred on the subject of seat belts when, to general astonishment, France became the first country in Europe to make their use compulsory.

French drivers and passengers were no more likely than any of their counterparts in Europe to use the seat belts with which their vehicles were, increasingly, fitted. In towns, the rate of seat belt use was virtually nil, and on the open roads it was scarcely higher. One could have been forgiven for thinking it would take years to improve the situation before even beginning to envisage compulsory measures, which at the time were on no one's agenda.

Public opinion polls, however, revealed a very different situation, thanks to the juxtaposition of three key questions posed at the beginning of 1973.

The first related to the perceived efficiency of seat belts: Over 80% of French people expressed themselves convinced of their efficiency. Most of the work in this area was thus already done.

The second concerned the actual use of seat-belts: 50% of those questioned claimed to use seat belts, whereas roadside counts showed an average of only 15% use.

The third question, however, was by far the most interesting: "If the authorities decided to make the wearing of seat-belts compulsory, would you agree?" To the great surprise of Christian Gerondeau, 80% of those questioned replied in the *affirmative*. The results seemed so improbable that a second research institute was commissioned to carry out another poll. The results of the second poll were exactly the same.

Clearly, therefore, the people of France expected their government to act. It was on the strength of these polls and similar surveys on the question of speed limits, that Christian Gerondeau was able, in June 1973, to convince the prime minister of the day to take simultaneously the two major decisions, which were to change the face of road safety, not only in France but gradually throughout the whole of Europe.

This far on in time, it is difficult to imagine the impact of the two measures. For three months, it was the prevailing topic of conversation in France.

The simultaneity of the two decisions also had an unlooked-for but happy consequence. While the first (i.e., the introduction of overall speed limits on the entire road network excluding the motorways) aroused lively reactions with opponents expressing violent hostility, the second (compulsory use of seat belts) aroused no opposition whatsoever. The silent majority was actually in favour, and the vociferous minority opposed to speed limits found itself unable, in all decency, to reject the second measure and so was obliged to swallow the whole. Another factor was that such a measure had never been canvassed, and so there had been no opportunity for opposition to take shape. Here we see the extent of the difference between French institutions, which leave such decisions exclusively in the hands of government, and those of other countries where parliament is responsible and where it has sometimes required 20 years of passionate debate to arrive at the same result.

But the ball was now rolling in Europe. Just a few months before France took its decisions, Christian Gerondeau had been appointed Chairman of the Road Safety Committee of the European Conference of Ministers of Transport (ECMT). On the strength of the decision taken by the French government, which provoked much astonishment as coming from a country infamous for the undisciplined behaviour of its drivers and the hitherto disastrous consequence in terms of road safety, he was ideally placed in July 1973, to engineer the adoption by the European Transport Ministries meeting in the Hague of a resolution recommending that all European countries should move as soon as possible to make the wearing of seat belts compulsory within their territory.

The recommendation had wide-ranging repercussions and gave a kick-start to what would otherwise have been a lengthy process, since no European country at that time had envisaged such a measure. Backed by the example of France, one after another, the other European countries followed suit, thereby saving the lives of thousands of drivers and passengers.

F.11 MAKING GOOD USE OF THE 1973 ARAB OIL EMBARGO

As predicted, the months following the dual measure of June 1973 showed a sharp decrease in the number of accidents on French roads. Another event, however, following three months later, had disastrous consequences elsewhere but proved a godsend for road safety. October 1973 saw the outbreak of the Yom Kippur war, followed by the Arab embargo on oil exports.

Faced with possible petrol shortages, Western European countries reacted en masse, some by restricting traffic or even banning it on certain days, some by imposing lower speed limits, and others by a combination of the two approaches.

Most European countries decided to set the maximum speed limit at 80 km/h on ordinary roads, and 100 km/h on motorways. Christian Gerondeau and a number of others suggested adopting higher limits for France, which would be less effective in the short term but could be maintained once the crisis was over, which the limits of 80 and 100 km/h clearly never could. Limits of 90 km/h for normal roads and 120 km/h on motorways were accordingly imposed. As predicted, unlike other countries, France was able to maintain almost entirely these limits once the oil crisis was over. More than 20 years later, 90 km/h is still the rule on ordinary roads; after a brief period at 140 km/h, the legal speed limit on motorways was finally established at 130 km/h in 1974.

The oil crisis combined with the decisions already taken in Summer 1973 were to make possible a situation that would otherwise have been unthinkable: the introduction of a permanent motorway speed limit in a country whose whole tradition was profoundly opposed to such a concept, and the introduction on country roads of a lower speed limit than in many other countries in Europe, in a country with one of the lowest population densities in Europe and the longest road distances to cover.

To say that the introduction of the new speed limits in December 1973 provoked little reaction would be an exaggeration: it provoked none whatsoever, so great had been the general fear of a total traffic ban or of much lower speed limits in line with other countries.

In terms of road safety, the reduction in the accident rate received a sharp boost. Despite traffic levels globally stable compared with the previous year, the number of accidents fell sharply: from the June 1972 level of 17,300 deaths, the statistics fell to 15,636 in 1973 and 13,357 in 1974.

In two years, the reduction had reached 22%. Had the previous trend in accident figures been continued, 1974 could have reached the grim total of over 20,000 deaths!

Later on, on Christian Gerondeau's proposal, ECMT adopted recommendations about harmonising speed limits all over Europe, which were, with the exception of Germany, quite properly followed.

F.12 DRINKING AND DRIVING

In the year 1978, another major step forward was taken in the battle against road accidents in France. Taking advantage of a newly elected National Assembly, with no immediate electoral concerns to hold it back, Christian Gerondeau engineered the adoption of one of the most modern bodies of legislation in Europe concerning drinking and driving: its most notable innovations were the replacement of the enormously time-consuming blood test by a "breathalyser" test, and the empowerment of police forces to stop drivers without suspicion of an offence in order to check their blood alcohol levels. Almost 20 years later, some European countries have still to adopt these essential measures. Once again, the psychological impact was tremendous, as was the effect on road accident figures, at least in the months following introduction of the legislation.

In 1980, to combat staggering accident figures, he finally succeeded in reforming motorcycle licence regulations, an achievement that was marked by a protest demonstration of 10,000 motorcyclists marching through Paris, demanding his resignation.

In parallel with his responsibilities in the field of road safety, in 1974, Christian Gerondeau was given responsibility for the Civil Defence Directorate of the Ministry of the Interior. In this post, which carried the rank of Prefect, he was brought to grips with the major disasters that afflicted the country: oil slicks in Brittany, forest fires in the South of France (he made sweeping changes to the way these were fought), volcanic eruptions in overseas territories, and so forth. On his move to this post, he set up the National School for Firemen, a project that had been mooted for over half a century but had never as yet seen the light of day.

At the end of 1981, after 9 years in post, Christian Gerondeau stepped down from his responsibilities as national head of road safety, leaving an accident rate reduced to half of what it was on his taking up his functions.

Prior to this, in 1980, he summarised the lessons of his experience in a work entitled *Pointless Death*, which is even now a work of reference. Curiously, it was not in France that the book bore its greatest fruits. In 1992, at an International Congress in the Netherlands, Christian Gerondeau learned that his book had been translated into Russian 12 years earlier, 50,000 copies had been printed and distributed, and for 10 years it had served as the basis for road safety policy in the ex-U.S.S.R. and certain neighbouring countries, including Bulgaria, where he was later to see its effects for himself.

In mid 1982, Christian Gerondeau also gave up his post as Director of Civil Defence in order to focus his career for a few years on quite different activities, leaving the world of transport behind.

F.13 THE FIELD OF ENERGY

For the first 18 months, he was head of planning at Charbonnages de France, the French Coal Board, a position which led him to see that the future for energy would be quite different from what almost everyone at that time believed. The price of crude oil, which had already risen from $3 to $13 a barrel at the time of the first oil crisis, had just rocketed from $13 to $35 as a result of the second, and almost everyone was sure it would soon rise to $60. In 1983, in a work entitled *Energy For Sale*, which presented a wide-ranging review of the whole field of energy at national and global levels, Christian Gerondeau argued that the world was heading towards lower prices for all forms of energy, and that the decades to come would be marked by an excess of supply over demand. New energy resources were being discovered all the time while demand had begun to fall sharply thanks to the considerable progress that had been made in energy conservation.

On this occasion Christian Gerondeau spoke out against the scale, which he considered disproportionate, of the French nuclear energy programme, which was based on an assumption of unvarying growth in electricity demand. Fifteen years after the book was published, it is striking to note how events have indeed developed as predicted, and how past trends have not continued their inexorable path. There is, indeed, a striking parallel between this book and his earlier work on transport. They have in common an unwillingness to be bound by the prevailing current of opinion, and adherence to an objective and rigorous analysis of the facts. As Christian Gerondeau likes to say, he does no more than apply Descartes' first principle: "never accept as true anything I do not, myself, know to be so." Descartes also wrote: "Concordance of opinions is no proof for, when a truth is somewhat difficult to discover, it is more likely that a single man shall have found it than a whole people" . . .

It need scarcely be said that Christian Gerondeau's book on energy attracted great hostility.

Having drawn up his conclusions in the form of an indictment of the policy currently followed by the French authorities, Christian Gerondeau left the energy sector after 18 months to spend over three years as a director of a major international hotel chain.

F.14 BACK TO ROAD SAFETY

His next move was to a major French public sector financial institution—the Caisse des Dépôts et Consignations—to develop the potential of a subsidiary responsible for the promotion of tourism, a move that gradually led him back into the transport sector.

The Caisse des Dépôts et Consignations had for a long time been directing a part of its activities towards local authority investment in infrastructure and was therefore involved through it in road safety matters. With the staunch support of the Director General of the period, Christian Gerondeau worked with local authority representative bodies to set up an Association for the Development of Road Safety Techniques. It was in this context that he suggested to the government, and won approval for, the creation of a committee of experts which I had the honour to chair, and which was responsible for producing a White Paper to relaunch French policy in the field after several years of stagnation.

Published in 1989, the White Paper, which included a considerable contribution from Christian Gerondeau, for many years formed the basis for French policy in the field, and was once again responsible for reducing the accident rate.

Echoes of the White Paper reached Brussels, and the European Commission asked Christian Gerondeau to draw up a similar document at Community level with the aid of a number of experts of different nationalities. The working group set up at the end of 1989 officially reported its findings in January 1991, in a document with title "For an European Road Safety Policy," known as the "Gerondeau report," which was translated into all the languages of the Community as it then stood.

The report, which became the standard of reference not just in Brussels but in many European Community countries and beyond, had far-reaching repercussions. One of its effects was rapidly to induce the many countries that had stuck up to then to a 60-km/h speed limit in built-up areas to reduce the limit to 50 km/h, each time achieving a definitive reduction of the order of 20% in the number of road deaths in the concerned areas.

In the aftermath of the report, it was the turn of the World Bank to ask Christian Gerondeau to head another international working group, this time to assess the road safety situation in the six former "People's Republics" of Central Europe: Hungary, Poland, the Czech Republic, Slovakia, Bulgaria, and Romania.

Once again, the group's work culminated in the publication of "Gerondeau reports," certain of which were not followed up due to local political upheavals, but others of which were immediately applied with spectacular results. One case in point was Hungary, where road deaths fell by 21% between 1992 and 1993 for the same volume of traffic!

The working group's conclusions were followed up in September 1994 by a vast seminar in Budapest organised by the World Bank and the European Union, with Christian Gerondeau as "substantive co-ordinator." An unprecedented 14 Transport or Interior Ministers from 14 Eastern or Central European countries attended in person, and the World Bank report on the proceedings of the seminar is now considered as a seminal document that many countries concerned are now applying, some more rapidly than others.

At the same time, in the absence of a European Road Safety Agency as recommended by the 1991 report, Christian Gerondeau instigated the creation in 1993 of the European Road Safety Federation, based in Brussels, and of which he is currently the General Secretary. The Federation is playing an increasingly important role in road safety, in both Western and Central Europe.

Yet Christian Gerondeau's work over recent years has not been confined solely, nor even primarily, to the international arena, but has concentrated also on France itself.

His three-year chairmanship of the prestigious Caisse Nationale des Monuments Historiques (1988 to 1991), during which time he put forward major proposals for the embellishment of the Château de Versailles, the great French cathedrals, or the Châteaux of the Loire, can be no more than mentioned here, though his recommendations are gradually producing effects at a pace reflecting a time scale that is measured in centuries. Since then, Christian Gerondeau has been Deputy Chairman of the Théâtre Baroque de France.

F.15 A NEW GENERATION OF ROADS

Back in the field of transport, Christian Gerondeau was entrusted by the French government in Autumn 1991 with the delicate task of chairing an Interministerial Safety Committee as part of the project to complete the A86 motorway. The task of the committee was to establish the technical specifications for future underground motorways for the Paris region, based on low-gauge tunnels and known as "Métroroutes."

In fact, far more was involved. The very existence of this basic infrastructure vital to the future of urban transport was at stake, under serious threat from the contradictory demands of the safety services and of the technical services responsible for establishing the characteristics of the structure. The Channel Tunnel has highlighted the disastrous consequences that could result from such a situation. In the case of the A86, what was needed was to retain the compact, economical features that made the "Métroroutes" so original, and yet provide the safety services with the guarantees they had every right to demand. This was what Christian Gerondeau succeeded in doing, thanks to his twofold authority as a former Delegate on Road Safety and head of national Civil Defence. One of his proposals was that each of the two levels of the future tunnels should be transformed into an emergency access tunnel in the event of a serious accident on the other level. As a result, unanimity was reached without adding significantly to the initial costs of the project and yet guaranteeing optimum safety levels. The way was thus opened for a new generation of urban transport systems.

More recently, Christian Gerondeau has also been measuring the true cost of traffic congestion in the Ile de France region and has shown it to be much lower than was thought. He is currently pressing in France for increases in the capacity of urban motorways through the modification of current standards, as well as examining new ways of financing the road network and maybe succeeding in changing transport unit measures.

Frequently invited outside his country and acting as an international expert, he can often express his views, recommending for example the abandonment of the planned Swiss tunnels through the Alps or proposing the creation of an underground motorways network in London.

In France, he continues to work for the cause of road safety and was a prime mover behind the recent reduction in the permissible alcohol level for drivers to 0.5 grams per blood litre.

F.16 TWO MILESTONE BOOKS

Following his appointment in 1992 as chairman of France's Union Routière (Road Federation), he has written two books that offer a new vision of the world of transport. The first, concentrating on France, was published at the end of 1993, and the second, which deals with transport in Europe, was published at the beginning of 1996 and is now enlarged with a translation in English.

Christian Gerondeau is often out of step with the prevailing ideas of the time. His approach remains the same. He sticks to the facts and feels in no way bound by current thinking. As he says in his book on transport in France, he does not *a priori* trust experts who, while they may be right, are also frequently wrong.

The important thing is that Christian Gerondeau never varies in his methods: He checks everything for himself. Naturally, that brings with it a very burden of personal work—in-depth studies, sorting through innumerable documents in both French and foreign languages. It is such unremitting effort that has brought Christian Gerondeau in-depth knowledge of such diverse fields as road safety, transport planning and network operation, structure design, transport economy, air pollution, freight transport, air transport, not to mention energy, historic monuments, civil defence, hotel financing, and so forth. And it is this, too, that has built in him the strength of conviction that has frequently enabled him to get results that many would have considered unattainable. For, although he has been—and still is—in charge of high-rank managerial duties, he never stopped to be at the same time a technician, an *ingénieur* who studies himself the technical aspects of the matters he deals with, which very often allows him to oppose the prevailing views on indisputable technical grounds, and then to succeed in having the right decision being taken.

This kind of approach is, of course, possible only because he had the good fortune to acquire a background of scientific and economic training wide-ranging enough for him to be able to grasp such a vast range of subjects, in the manner of the "honest man" of the classical period. And possible, too, only because he has the gift of a creative imagination that is his main driving force.

The path that Christian Gerondeau has trodden is constantly marked by innovative projects and reforms of great value. He has helped change daily life for millions of French people through the road and public transport networks he has designed or authorized. Due to his lucidity and courage and the strength of his conviction in the face of often hostile public opinion, he has been instrumental in saving tens of thousands of lives in France and other countries and in the avoidance of an even greater number of injuries. At the beginning of 1997, he was asked by the French government to compare the British, U.S., and French policies in the field of unemployment, the most painful problem in continental Europe.

This is a well-filled career, especially useful to society, and we can only hope that Christian Gerondeau will continue his work with the same intelligence and energy.

▼ ▼ ▼

ADVICE TO THE READER

The pace of life today leaves us with little free time.

Transport in Europe is designed to take this into account. As a first approach, the reader can simply read the Introduction and Chapter 13 (the conclusion), which outline, in about 20 pages, the main arguments developed in the book. Subsequently, the reader should move to the figures and commentaries given at the end of the book.

Then, according to the reader's particular areas of interest, the final stage would be to turn to one or another of the other 12 chapters of the book, as and when time is available. They are listed at the beginning of the book and can to a great extent be read independently one from the other.

···

INTRODUCTION

Le premier précepte était de ne jamais recevoir aucune chose pour vraie que je ne la connusse évidemment pour telle.

The first precept was to accept nothing as true which I did not clearly recognize to be so.

René Descartes,
Discourse on Method

SOME COMMONLY HELD IDEAS

Since the beginning of time, human activity has been dependent upon communication, either through the exchange of ideas or through the movement of people and merchandise.

Transport plays as vital a role today as it did in the past, both in our daily lives and in the workings of our economy. In many ways it is the most important economic activity in developed countries. It could be imagined that this has led to all aspects of the subject being meticulously studied and widely known. Yet, curiously, this is not the case and although transport provides an inexhaustible subject of conversation for our contemporaries, there is perhaps no other domain where people have so many mistaken ideas.

In Europe, it is as if we automatically accept ideas on the subject that almost no one has ever thought of questioning:

- It is possible to relieve road traffic by developing the other means of transport.
- The road network works badly.
- Roads create traffic, and it is useless to build new ones.
- Congestion can only get worse and the road network will come to a complete standstill.
- City centres will be overrun by cars.
- Europeans are irrational when it comes to their cars.
- Air pollution is getting constantly worse and the air in our towns will soon be unbreathable.
- Road traffic is a major contributor to the greenhouse effect.
- Established oil reserves are diminishing and there will soon be a shortage.
- Road transport does not pay its true cost.
- If rail transport is in difficulty, it is due to unfair competition.
- International traffic causes problems at border crossings.
- Rail and river transport carry out a large part of freight transport in Europe.
- Combined transport is the answer of the future.
- Heavy goods vehicles are responsible for traffic jams.
- It is still essential to build new underground lines in European towns and cities.
- It is impossible to build new road infrastructures in densely populated areas.
- Road accidents are inevitable.
- Transport policy is influenced by a powerful "road lobby."
- Europe has a coherent transport policy.

However, all these ideas, and many others, are disproved by an objective analysis of the facts and can by refuted point by point.

It Is Possible To Relieve Road Traffic by Developing the Other Means of Transport

The idea of relieving road traffic by developing the other means of transport comes naturally to the mind. This would indeed be a good idea if it were possible, but the numerous attempts at easing road traffic by creating high-speed railways, undergrounds, tramways, specialised railways, combined transport systems, waterways, and so forth have *all* failed. For the great majority of transport that takes place on the European continent, there is no alternative to individual transport. Where an alternative does exist, the attractiveness of the car, the road, and road transport is too high. Their success, the result of the free choice of hundreds of millions of people, is such that experience has constantly shown that it is not possible to *balance* demand to any significant extent between individual and public transport, however tempting the idea may be. This can be explained quite logically for a number of reasons. Markets are to a great extent independent and the scales are very different. For example, rail freight wagons travel distances of 14 (fourteen) billion kilometres in Western Europe each year whereas the figure for all road vehicles is 3,000 (three thousand) billion, which obviously excludes the possibility of relieving road traffic in any significant way by increasing rail freight. In fact, except by resorting to coercion, only the road can relieve the road (see Chapter 4).

The Road Network Works Badly

Incredibly, nobody really knows how the road transport system works, and this despite the fact that it accounts for over 90% of the continent's needs. Nobody knows what percentage of journeys meet with problems of congestion, or, on the contrary, the number that take place with no particular problems. In other words, nobody can really answer the question "*How does it work?*," and everyone imagines that traffic jams are the dominant phenomenon. In fact, overall, the road transport system works well, contrary to what is heard most of the time. The problem is that congestion is conspicuous when free flow is not. The average home-to-work journey by car, despite the fact that it takes place during rush hours, is *19 minutes* in Western Europe, the same, in fact, as in North America. Moreover, this journey time is not increasing, whereas distances travelled continue to do so, meaning that average speeds for journeys are increasing. Ninety percent of the Western Europeans concerned confirm that they do not usually encounter much congestion on their way to work. Congestion does exist, but it is limited in time and space and the great majority of road journeys take place without encountering traffic jams, as witnessed by the wide development in industry of *just-in-time* practices. This is especially true for motorways and explains why road investments are among the most cost-effective for the community (see Chapter 4).

Roads Create Traffic, and It Is Useless To Build New Ones

Things are not that simple. Western Europe currently counts nearly one vehicle for every two inhabitants, including children and the elderly. At the present time, apart from those who work at home or who walk to work, nearly 80% of working West Europeans commute every day by car, and so this percentage cannot increase much more, even if the average journey distance can still increase. No one can drive two cars at the same time. In the majority of West European countries, the population is relatively stable and the increase in traffic is now estimated in most countries at about 2 to 3% per year on average, if not less, for both cars and heavy goods vehicles. The phenomenon is therefore perfectly sustainable as major increases in traffic are behind us, not to come. The first effect of the creation of new roads, especially those with high capacity, is that part of existing traffic is absorbed, thereby relieving the existing road network. The kilometrage of traffic per car only differs slightly in all the countries of West Europe, whatever policies are followed in terms of infrastructures. On the other hand, on the local level, everyone knows that in dense urban areas, a new road may be rapidly working near to its capacity, allowing locally more traffic to flow. But that is just a proof of its usefulness, which translates in a high level of economic and fiscal return, as well as in the opening of new opportunities to the local or regional inhabitants. Whatever the circumstances, the traffic situation is always better after the creation of new roads than it was previously. Congestion is to mobility what poverty is to wealth. It is not because there are poor people you have to fight prosperity. It is just the opposite (see Chapters 4 and 11).

Congestion Can Only Get Worse, and the Road Network Will Come to a Complete Standstill

Considering the prospects of moderate increases in traffic and changing trends in land use and ways of life, congestion may decrease in the future rather than increase if the road network is granted a minimum level of investment (in fact, very moderate when compared with the receipts it generates), and if sound operating policies are introduced. Many promising factors are at work: the demand for journeys is being transferred to the outskirts of towns; it is more evenly spaced out during the day; it is concentrated on major routes. Everything will depend on the policies adopted by the different countries and local governments. Things will get worse only if road construction is systematically opposed. Also, taking into account the prospects of improvement to road network management through intelligent transport systems and the potential offered by introducing tolls and parking fees in the areas where demand is high, it becomes clear that congestion is usually not inevitable, except in certain locations at certain times. In spite of some local problems, the road transport system is almost always more efficient for the user than its competitors, whether it be for passenger or freight transport (see Chapter 4).

City Centres Will Be Overrun by Cars

Contrary to popular opinion, road traffic has stabilised or fallen over the last decade in almost all the town centres in Europe, due primarily to changes in urban structures, improvements in road infrastructures, and in policies regarding road use and parking. It is now widely recognised that a better balance must be found in town centres between the different types of transport and the different road users: pedestrians, two-wheeled vehicles, road vehicles, and public transport, especially through traffic moderation policies and, when possible, by diverting through traffic. Public transport has a major role to play, especially in large cities. However, within this balance, an appropriate place must also be reserved for the car in order to avoid economic decline and population drain from the historic centres, which give their character to so many European towns. That means that sufficient access and parking facilities must be available, where possible under ground so as to free the surface areas. Such policies are followed by a growing number of European cities. Generally speaking, traffic conditions in most central areas have stopped deteriorating and are even sometimes improving. Problems linked to growing needs are now increasingly to be found elsewhere, because new demand is now mainly related to journeys on the outskirts of towns (see Chapter 12).

Europeans Are Irrational When It Comes to Their Cars

The attitude of Europeans and their companies with respect to cars and road transport is perfectly rational and is no different from the behaviour of inhabitants of other parts of the world. If they choose them freely, it is because they find that their use has significant, perfectly measurable advantages. The use of the car makes journey times far shorter. As mentioned above, Europeans who use the car to commute to work have an average journey time of 19 minutes. When, exceptionally, they use public transport, this journey time increases to 49 minutes. Their choice is therefore rational as the car enables them to save one hour of transport time per day for identical destination, thus greatly improving their quality of life. The same is true for other types of journeys. Similarly, the use of the truck offers numerous advantages to companies. If it is an advantage to both individuals and companies, it is also more often than not an advantage for the community, especially since the development of road transport gives rise to other positive effects outside the domain of transport (see Chapters 3 and 11).

Air Pollution Is Getting Constantly Worse, and the Air in Our Towns Will Soon Be Unbreathable

After an absence of over a hundred years, lichens, plants that are extremely sensitive to acid pollution, have reappeared in the centre of Paris after having vanished in the 19th century. Examples of such phenomena are to be found almost everywhere in Western Europe. London smog in winter is no more than a memory. Due to efforts in all sectors (industry, heating, traffic), the air is generally much purer today in most European cities than it has been for a century, and overwhelming progress has been made in the last few decades for the majority of products. Moreover, for the others, new improvements in air quality are certain since modern vehicles pollute less and less, whereas traffic volume now varies very little in dense urban areas, and because progress is also continuing at a fast pace for the other pollutant sectors (industries, heating, power stations, etc.). There is no reason why technical progress should not give results in this field as in the others. Thanks to efforts on all sides, outdoor air pollution is now extremely limited and no longer a major health problem in most European cities, and will soon largely be a thing of the past in developed countries, unlike other parts of the world (see Chapter 10).

Road Traffic Is a Major Contributor to the Greenhouse Effect

It is impossible to effectively limit worldwide production of carbon dioxide (CO_2) by limiting road traffic, because the latter is only a minor source of the product in the world. All forecasts predict that worldwide production of CO_2 will inevitably increase by 50% by the year 2010, due essentially to economic growth and the resulting rise in coal consumption in China, India, and developing countries in general, whereas the possible influence of actions taken concerning road traffic in Europe is less than 1%. In other words, it is not by acting on European road traffic that it can be hoped to obtain significant results on the planetary scale. It must be added that the precise effects of carbon gas emissions on climatic balance are the subject of great debate among scientists at the present time (see Chapter 10).

Established Oil Reserves Are Diminishing, and There Will Soon Be a Shortage

In 1960, proven oil reserves were calculated at 45 billion tons, equal to 32 years of consumption at the extraction rate at that time. In 1994, the reserves were calculated at 135 billion tons, equal to 42 years of consumption at the current rate of extraction, and this despite the quantities consumed since 1960. In fact, the threat of shortage is continually receding as oil companies improve techniques and increase exploration. Of course, one day, far from now, this will no longer be the case, and new tension cannot be dismissed for the future. But when the natural oil reserves are exhausted, it will be possible to create fuel from many other sources: first, natural gas; then, coal and oil shale. Later on, products of agricultural origins can be used, not to mention maybe in the very long term the electric vehicles that are now beginning to be introduced (see Chapter 10).

Road Transport Does Not Pay Its True Cost

Overall, road users pay the governments of the different European countries almost three times what they cost to them: 167 billion ECUs[1] compared to 57 in 1995, leaving a surplus of 110 billion ECUs. Admittedly, some "external" costs attributable

---

[1]European currency unit, soon to become the EURO. One ECU is worth 1,1 U.S. dollar according to February 1996 exchange rates.

to vehicle use—in particular, road accidents, pollution, and contribution to the greenhouse effect—must be added to the direct financial costs. However, most of the cost of road accidents is borne by users through the insurance premiums they pay, and as far as pollution and the contribution to the greenhouse effect is concerned, it is impossible to reasonably suggest that their cost amounts to anything remotely near the surplus mentioned above. Nor must it be forgotten that heavy goods vehicles provide considerable "external advantages" to national and regional development and the workings of the economy, for which they are an essential means of support. Claims that road transport does not pay its "true cost" are even more surprising as they are often made by rail companies, which on average meet in Western Europe only less than half their costs (see Chapters 3 and 10).

If Rail Transport Is in Difficulty, It Is Due to Unfair Competition

If the market for rail transport is often in regression, this is not because of unfair competition. It is primarily because, except for a few well-defined niche markets, it no longer fulfils the needs of the modern economy in the specific context of Europe, and that most of its market has disappeared due to competition from cars, buses, and aeroplanes for transport of people, and from trucks for freight transport. It is also linked to poor or appalling management. The result is that, at present, nearly all of Europe's railways are subsidised in proportions that would be unthinkable for any other activity and that can only be explained by the fact that almost all of them are nationalised, whereas other modes of transport need to balance their books or undergo heavy draining of their finances through taxation. On the whole, if unfair competition exists, it is to the detriment of air and road transport. The only exception is to be found in the United Kingdom (see Chapter 6).

International Traffic Poses Problems at Border Crossings

When two towns or two regions are separated by a border, the amount of merchandise or people moving between them is reduced by a factor of 5 to 10, compared with what would be the case if they were located in the same country. This is the "border effect." Munich has more inhabitants than Marseilles and is the same distance away from Paris. Yet there is an average per day of 25 planes with 250 seats each and 10 trains with 350 seats each between Paris and Marseilles, and only 10 planes with 125 seats each and practically no trains between Paris and Munich. The same results are shown by comparing traffic between Frankfurt-Hamburg and Frankfurt–Milan, Barcelona–Valencia and Barcelona–Marseilles, and so forth. This comparison is valid for all means of transport. The result is that, with one exception, traffic across borders is far lower than each country's internal traffic. There is, therefore, no prospect of saturation of international movement at the borders. After completion of the major sea crossings currently underway, there will be practically no more international "missing links" requiring heavy investment in Europe from an economic standpoint. Traffic forecasts that maintain the contrary are merely fanciful, as shown by the blatantly disastrous example of the Channel Tunnel. The real problems are within each individual country, and particularly in their densely populated zones. In terms of transport, Europe, contrary to the United States, is not a continent but an archipelago, and will, for the most part, remain as such (see Chapter 6).

Rail and River Transport Carry Out a Large Part of Surface Freight Transport in Europe

Surprising as it may be, the relative importance of the different forms of freight transport has no relation whatsoever to the figures given in official statistics. This is explained by the use of units of measure—*tonne kilometres*—which are meaningless. In order to make a valid comparison between the different means of freight transport in terms of their role in the economy, it is necessary, as for any other sector of activity, to study their turnover, expressed in monetary units (ECUs, marks, francs, pounds, etc.). For comparison in terms of their physical impact on congestion of the networks, it is necessary to look at the distances travelled, which are measured in vehicle kilometres. With very few exceptions, neither turnover nor distances travelled have any connection with tonne kilometres. Expressed in tonne kilometres, the railway is shown to represent 18% of European freight transport, although in reality its economic share expressed in turnover is 2 to 3%, and its physical share, expressed in kilometres travelled, is less than 1% of road traffic, all vehicles taken together. Transport policies based on tonne kilometres are consequently meaningless. These are the last vestiges in the Western world of "Gosplan" type units. In fact, road transport accounts for nearly all freight transport in Western Europe, even more than in North America, this being notably due to the "border effect," which deprives railway of most of its natural market, which is long-distance and thus international (see Chapters 3 and 6).

Combined Transport Is the Answer of the Future

Pick-up points and destinations of freight transported by truck are widely scattered and the average distances travelled are very short on the European continent. "Combined transport" techniques, which put road trailers or road containers on wagons, using the railway for part of the journey, can therefore only be used in very few cases. Taken overall, combined transport relieves road traffic to an insignificant extent—an average of 1‰ in Europe—at the same time as being in heavy deficit. Even if more, large amounts of money were spent, the result would remain marginal.

As for the creation of specialised railways capable of transporting entire trucks, this does not stand up to economic analysis. For transport of both freight and people, Europeans have overwhelmingly opted for simple, unimodal systems, and not complex, intermodal systems, implying the use of successive modes of transport and interchanges or transshipments that are penalising and costly for short-distance travel (see Chapters 3 and 6).

Heavy Goods Vehicles Are Responsible for Traffic Jams

With few exceptions, traffic jams in Europe mainly take place in two types of circumstances: in urban areas during rush hours, and outside urban areas at weekends or in holiday peak periods. In these two circumstances, there are relatively few heavy goods vehicles on the road, as they generally travel outside urban areas and during the working week. Except for very rare cases of chronic inadequacy of motorway capacity outside towns, it is therefore impossible to hold them responsible for traffic jams that mainly take place when they are not present. Wanting to do away with traffic jams by controlling the movements of heavy goods vehicles is therefore in most cases simply unrealistic (see Chapter 3).

It Is Still Essential To Build New Underground Lines in European Towns and Cities

In almost all of Europe's towns, the overall demand for transport is stable in the centres, or even decreasing, and it is in the suburbs (and even more so in outer suburban areas) that new needs arise, which can only be satisfied by the car or other road vehicles, considering the low population density of the areas to be served. Even in the most densely populated region of Europe—Paris and its suburbs—the use of public transport is stagnating or decreasing and almost all new journeys are carried out by car. The construction of new railway lines for public transport, usually extremely costly, is in no way a universal panacea, although it is justified in certain cases when there is catching up to do. Everything depends on the circumstances. The most pressing needs and the most cost-effective projects for the community usually concern road routes located in suburban and outer suburban areas where demand is increasing, and that can be used to transport both people (by car or other types of road vehicle) and goods (see Chapter 12).

It Is Impossible To Create New Road Infrastructures in Densely Populated Areas

The 21st century will see the birth of an entirely new type of road infrastructure: reduced-gauge underground motorways, or "metroroutes." Made possible by the invention of machines capable of boring large-diameter tunnels, and by the fact that these new constructions will be reserved for vehicles of about 2 metres high, which is the majority of vehicles on the road, these new infrastructures are especially suited to densely populated areas and will be as important an innovation in urban transport as was the underground railway at the end of the 19th century. Construction of the first metroroute is beginning in France, in the Paris region. In urban areas, it is not the heavy goods vehicles, which are a small minority of traffic, that should be put underground, but the cars and other light vehicles which make up most of the traffic (see Chapter 5).

Road Accidents Are Inevitable

The situation concerning road accidents, unlike that of air pollution, remains extremely serious and deeply shocking. Means devoted annually to road safety are, overall, tragically out of scale with the actual situation, which counts about 45,000 killed and 1,500,000 injured each year in Western Europe. Whereas over 60 billion ECUs are spent annually by road users through insurance companies to try and repair the damage caused by accidents, the amounts set aside for the prevention of accidents come nowhere near that figure. The situation varies deeply from country to country. There is no doubt that a more voluntarist policy would allow many countries to greatly reduce the number of victims. In addition to other necessary actions, a significant increase in appropriate road investment is of great importance, because well-conceived road network improvement is one of the most effective solutions in the long term for reducing the number and seriousness of accidents (see Chapter 1).

Transport Policy Is Inspired by a Powerful "Road Lobby"

Contrary to what might be thought, there is no road lobby worthy of the name. Road activities, by their very nature, include a number of professions: car manufacturers, equipment manufacturers, garage owners, road builders, the oil industry, transport companies, and so forth. These different professions have very little contact between them, either on a national or a European level, and have not yet managed to become an organised group. The International Road Federation (IRF) does not even have a full-time permanent representative in Brussels. In transport matters, the real lobby in Europe is that of rail and public transports, which devote high-level human resources and large budgets to the promotion of their cause, in the face of competitors who have left them with almost a monopoly for thought and action (see Chapter 13).

Europe Has a Coherent Transport Policy

The European Union, which groups 15 of the 17 countries in Western Europe, has a surprising transport policy. In most areas, it is liberal and perfectly justified. For instance, since 1st April 1997, the skies of all European Union countries have been open to free competition from all airlines, and global national subsidies are forbidden. Similarly, road freight traffic will be open to competition from all the continent's transport companies as of 1998, and no one is considering subsidies. But, as soon as it is a question of rail transport, there is a completely different approach. Massive subsidies are encouraged, whereas there are endless plans to increase taxes on road transport in order to favour a hypothetical transfer of traffic towards the railways. The policy is shown in the extreme in the area of coach transport. In half of the European Union countries on the eve of the year 2000, it is still practically forbidden to create coach lines, in order to protect the railways.

INTRODUCTION TO THE FOLLOWING CHAPTERS

These are some of the themes covered in this book, many of which may seem surprising as appearances can be deceptive. Yet they appear to be difficult to refute, as the pages that follow will try to show.

In the world of transport probably even more than in others, reasoning is too often based not on facts but on generally accepted ideas, which are unfortunately sometimes backed up by unreliable "experts" reports. The result is that even the most official organisations, the Organization for Economic Cooperation and Development (OECD), the European Conference of Ministers of Transport (ECMT) and the European Union itself are misled and often come to mistaken conclusions. There can be no point in discussing the conclusions if there is no prior agreement as to an objective analysis of the facts.

Before starting to describe the vast panorama of transport in Europe from its different angles of economy, urban policy, town and country planning, its impact on lifestyles, and competition among modes of transport, it is a prerequisite to deal with its consequences in a domain that is of another and primordial nature, as it affects human life. Despite improvements made, road accidents remain one of the scandals of our modern society, and deserve far more attention than is usually given them, as they lead to mourning, suffering, tears, and blood. They were dealt with in Chapter 1.

For their part, the description of the other faces of transport in Europe begins in Chapter 2.

CHAPTER 1

▼▼▼

ROAD ACCIDENTS: DRAMATIC INCOHERENCE

1.1 INTRODUCTION

With their trail of death, pain, and disability, road accidents are one of the scourges of modern society to which the only possible attitude can be one of revolt, but also action. Road accidents involving bodily harm are not a statistical issue; it must never be forgotten that each of them is a tragedy involving men, women, and children, and that their horror is often beyond description.

Admittedly, progress has been made in Western Europe over the last 20 years. From 1972 to 1996, according to official statistics the number of deaths per year fell from close to 80,000 to quite below 50,000, whereas traffic volume doubled over the same period, meaning that for an equivalent distance travelled, the risk was divided by more than three, and even more in some countries.

It is, of course, impossible to hope one day to eliminate all accidents, as travelling by road, like most human activities, has by nature an element of danger attached to it. But road accidents are on a downward trend and the prospect of further reducing the number of victims by half within the next 20 years is not unattainable.

Nonetheless, despite the progress that has been made, the level of road hazards remains dramatically high compared to what it could and should be. Every 10 minutes, one Western European still dies on the road, making about 140 deaths per day, without arousing much in the way of indignation. What would people say if every day of the year an aeroplane crashed with one hundred and forty people on board?

The figures are chilling. Since the signature of the Treaty of Rome, two million deaths have occurred on the roads of Western Europe! To this dramatic number of deaths must also be added the estimated one and a half million people injured each year, many of whom will suffer from tragic after-effects for the rest of their lives. In the 15 to 30 age group, road accidents constitute the primary cause of death in many countries.

If the number of accidents remains the same as it is today, one out of every three children born in Western Europe in 1995 will be injured in a road accident at some time during his or her life! To these countless direct victims must be added an even larger number of indirect victims: inconsolable parents, spouses, children, and friends, all of whose lives are so shattered or changed that many never recover. Who does not know a family that has been struck by misfortune in this way, perhaps even one's own?

Despite the progress made over the past 20 years, compared with other scourges of modern times, road accidents are one of the most serious and distressing problems of health and civilisation of our times and our society should not be satisfied until it has set in motion everything possible to reduce their number and seriousness. Yet, despite the past efforts, to which in all fairness tribute must be paid, the overall problem is far from being resolved, as the range of different situations shows.

Results are extremely different from one European Union country to another, depending on the initial situation and the policies implemented in the fields of human behaviour, infrastructures, vehicles, and emergency services. On the basis of the change in death rates between 1972 and 1992, the countries can, for example, be divided into three large groups. The first includes countries that progressed very rapidly and achieved impressive reductions in accident rates: fatal accidents were divided by 2.62 in Western Germany, 2.46 in the Netherlands and 2.08 in Denmark. The second group includes countries that have made definite progress, but at a slower pace: 1.84 in the United Kingdom and Luxembourg, 1.76 in Belgium, 1.67 in France, 1.42 in Italy, and 1.23 in Ireland. The third group consists of three countries where the number of accidents increased until 1992 due to rapid growth in private car purchases during the period in question: Greece (+92% deaths), Spain (+70%) and Portugal (+15%).

Although these changes are extremely diverse, they do leave room for hope. After the rapid progress recorded in most European countries in the 1970s, and until the mid 1980s, the number of road victims did then level off due to the rapid growth in traffic that accompanied economic expansion from 1985 to 1990. But since that date, new progress has been made in road safety, which is not only due to the economic slowdown. Good news comes from different countries, as witnessed by the evolution in the number of deaths, which is the only valid indicator for international comparisons as the injured are not counted in the same way in the different countries. Between 1980 and 1992, in Western Germany, the number of deaths in urban areas fell by 60%, primarily as a result of vast traffic-calming measures, aimed at inducing drivers to unconsciously drive more slowly, a concept born in the Netherlands where it is now widespread. In the United Kingdom, where the situation was already very satisfactory, the number of deaths decreased even further: 4,753 in 1991, 3,819 in 1993, and even fewer in 1994 and 1995 (3,665 deaths).

Study of statistics for countries that have not had good results up until now also leaves room for hope. For example, thanks to remarkable information campaigns and harsher penalties, the number of road deaths decreased in Spain from 8,836 in 1991 to 6,350 in 1993, a reduction of 28% in two years, and the trend continued in 1994! France also improved its results, registering a significant decrease in the number of accidents, due especially to a reduction in the legal limit regarding alcohol and driving and the threat of losing a point on the driving license if seat belts were not fastened. Other countries, where accidents were accepted in the past with resignation, have also made progress.

But the situation still remains very uneven. Certain countries have adopted policies that deserve praise. Others have not yet done so. But none should be satisfied with the results obtained. The death rate in 1992 was 1.1 per hundred million kilometres travelled in Great Britain, 1.3 in the Netherlands, 1.7 in Western Germany, 2.3 in France, 2.8 in Belgium, 6.2 in Spain, 7.7 in Greece, and an even higher number in Portugal. Different geographic and economic circumstances alone cannot explain such divergences since in countries where all else is similar, the accident rate sometimes varies by a factor of two. Road safety policies remain far too unequal.

This is tragic not only from a human standpoint; it also takes a heavy toll on the economy, because the annual cost of road accidents has been estimated at 70 billion ECUs in 1991 in the countries of the European Union, representing more than the gross national product of a country such as Portugal [1]! For those who may doubt this, it can be added that the turnover figures for car accident insurance in Western Europe are approximately 65 billion ECUs per year, which does not cover all the costs incurred by road accidents for the Community.

The situation is no less tragic in the countries of Eastern and Central Europe. Although vehicle fleets and traffic volumes are much smaller in these countries than in Western Europe, road hazards are no lower compared with population, considering the much higher frequency and seriousness of accidents. In 1992, there was a total of 15,600 deaths in the six former Central European satellite states (Poland, Hungary, The Czech Republic, Slovakia, Romania, and Bulgaria) and more than 40,000 in the countries of the former USSR! As these countries will probably experience a rapid increase in traffic due to growth in their economies, there is a great danger that the number of road accidents will follow the same trend if vigorous and appropriate policies are not implemented.

Fortunately, both Western and Eastern European countries have undertaken various measures that have been proved effective, and it is interesting to examine the main ones. At least eleven types of action have been undertaken with success in different countries, concerning mainly driver behaviour, road infrastructures, vehicles, and road safety financing policy.

1.2 ELEVEN MAJOR FIELDS OF ACTION

1.2.1 The Fight Against Drunk Driving

Many studies have shown that a very high proportion of drivers who were responsible for fatal accidents in Europe were under the influence of alcohol. Behaviour regarding drinking and driving does, of course, vary from one country to another depending on lifestyles and the effectiveness with which information policy and controls are implemented. Although there is no comparable data available between countries and existing figures are often underestimated, it is probable that the proportion of fatal accidents that can be attributed to drunk driving is somewhere between 10 and 30%, depending on the country! Unfortunately, further evidence of this can be found by simply reading the newspapers, which give details of the tragedies that take place every day and every weekend due to drivers exceeding the authorised level of alcohol in the blood. This level varies in West European countries from 0.2 to 0.8 grams of alcohol per litre of blood, the 0.8 gram per litre limit still being the most commonly used. Yet, this level is undeniably much too high, as it increases the risks of provoking an accident by a factor of 10, compared to driving with no alcohol at all. It should be added that this factor increases to 35 for those who have 1.2 grams per litre of blood and to 80 for those who take the wheel with 2 grams of alcohol per litre of blood—and yet this concentration is often exceeded by irresponsible drivers who are just potential killers!

The highly significant increase in risk brought about by the presence of alcohol in the blood justifies the standpoint of those who advocate that the legal limit should be lowered at least from 0.8 to 0.5 grams of alcohol per litre of blood. Five West European countries have already adopted this standard and polls show, for instance, that 75% of Germans would agree to it in their country. The rate of approval was the same in France, and in September 1995, this country was the first among the four most populated West European countries to adopt the 0.5 g/l level.

A level of 0.5 grams of alcohol per litre, which "only" doubles the risk when compared to driving with no alcohol at all, in fact corresponds to a quantity of alcoholic beverages much higher than generally thought, and its adoption by all West European countries that still maintain the 0.8 gram per litre limit is therefore to be hoped for as rapidly as possible. Even though there is no proof of a cause and effect relationship, it is nonetheless interesting to note that the introduction of the 0.5 grams per litre level in France was followed, for 10 consecutive months, by a significant drop in the number of accidents compared with the previous year, leading to a reduction of 6% in the number of deaths.

In Australia, the reduction from 0.8 to 0.5 grams per litre resulted in a general decrease in drunk driving, including the most serious cases (i.e., above 1.5 grams per litre). This is a very important observation. Those, as the German government, who oppose a reduction in the authorised level of alcohol in the blood sometimes argue that a high proportion of serious accidents attributable to alcohol are caused by drivers with a concentration of alcohol in the blood well above that of 1 gram per litre, and that such drivers would not be influenced by a decrease in the authorised level, since it is already lower than what they would generally consume. This argument has proven to be untrue, as at least part of the drivers in question change their behaviour when the authorised level is lowered; in fact, they reduce their consumption in such a way that, for example, those who used to drive with 1.6 grams per litre drive with only 1.3, and the risks increase so quickly with the concentration of alcohol in the blood that the decrease in the number of accidents due to this apparently minor modification in behaviour can be considerable.

But, whatever the authorised limit, it must be complied with as strictly as possible in order for the behaviour of a large proportion of drinking drivers to change permanently. For a long time, it was believed that such a result was unattainable, but experience has shown this to be untrue and that considerable progress was possible. This was the case for France in 1978, when new legislation was introduced authorising the police and the gendarmerie, under certain conditions, to make random checks on drivers' alcohol levels whether a driving offence had been committed or not. The announcement of this policy created a considerable stir, and the possibility of having to breathe into a breathalyser became the number one topic of conversation among the French. The radio, television, and press dealt incessantly with the matter, and every driver was convinced that within a very short time she would inevitably be the object of numerous spot checks. Many people stopped drinking too much before taking the wheel, taking to heart the road safety motto of the time—*Drink or drive: you must decide*. The results were spectacular: in the second half of 1978, almost 800 lives were spared compared to the year before. But also, alas, compared to the year after.

As is often the case, the resources devoted to enforcement had been far lower than those needed. The number of spot check operations averaged about 100 per month for the entire country. It is needless to say that drivers were quick to realise that the probability of being checked was extremely low, not to say negligible, and therefore, early in 1979, accidents resumed their previous level.

At the time, the conclusion drawn from this experience was that this type of measure could only have a short-term effect. However, this conclusion was wrong, as shown by several examples partly inspired by the French experience. As is often the case with road safety issues, the best examples are to be found in Australia.

In 1982, the State of New South Wales introduced random checks on drivers, but at a far higher rate than in France in 1978, as they represented one check per year for every three driving licence holders. The number of drivers tested amounted to one million people per year for only three million licence holders! The results were immediate and identical in pattern to those of France; the total number of deaths fell by close to 20%. However, the difference was that the Australian results lasted. In other words, this experience proved that it was possible to drastically change driver behaviour with respect to drinking and driving as long as motorists really expected to be checked. It showed, above all, that the best and only real means of ensuring this was to actually conduct a sufficient number of checks, since the public cannot be deceived for very long by mere advertising campaigns, however necessary these may be.

It is possible to act effectively against drunk driving because, contrary to popular thinking, the great majority of accidents attributable to alcohol are not due to chronic alcoholics, who are sick people, but to drivers who are normally sober but drink alcohol to excess in exceptional circumstances, such as a Saturday night dance, a party, or a wedding. This is actually a very encouraging observation that explains the importance of the results that can be obtained if these "ordinary" drivers can be induced to change their behaviour and thus fully dissociate drinking and driving.

It is interesting to note that the surveillance level in Australia, increased since then to one annual check for every two registered drivers, means that no "high-risk driver" can escape the spot checks for very long. The police concentrate their activities on the days and times—particularly evenings and nights, especially at weekends—when high-risk drivers tend to drive, so that the latter are almost sure to be intercepted several times a year.

It should also be mentioned that some East European countries—where the authorised level of alcohol in the blood is still zero grams per litre—appear to have achieved excellent results due to the high frequency of tests, and that Scandinavian countries are exemplary in terms of the number of checks and the severity of their sanctions.

In the light of these different experiences, it can safely be maintained that methods that are crowned with success elsewhere would also be successful in other European countries as long as two conditions are met. The first concerns the number of spot checks actually made, which today varies considerably from one country to another. Much progress has been made in a country like France since 1978, since there are currently more than 6 million random alcohol tests carried out per year. But this is still far from the required level which, if the Australian experience is to serve as an example, should be at least 10 million per year, as there are approximately 32 million registered drivers in France.

In the other European countries, alcohol tests are generally much less frequent, especially since some countries do not yet have legislation authorising the police to conduct random checks independently of a traffic offence, and to legally use breathalysers to measure the driver's level of alcohol, a method that is far more practical than blood tests. Yet any effective policy on the subject must dispose of these two possibilities.

The second condition for a successful policy is major advertising campaigning with an optimal level of information provided to the public. This presupposes that the appropriate means should be available for road safety information, which is not always the case—as can be seen, for example, in France, where budgets for this type of campaign are much too low. The importance of campaigning is shown by the United Kingdom, which obtained excellent results in its battle against drunk driving through very violent campaigns organised by the popular press against those responsible for drunk driving accidents, which resulted in a drastic change in mentalities and behaviour.

1.2.2 Speed-Calming

The lowering of speed limits largely explains the safety improvement made in the last two decades in Western Europe, as the influence of speed on the number and severity of accidents is actually much higher than generally imagined. Studies carried out in many countries come to a unanimous and very simple conclusion: The frequency of accidents increases as the square of average vehicle speed, and the number of deaths similarly increases to the power of four. In other words, if average vehicle speed increases by 5%, which is imperceptible to the user, the number of accidents will increase by 10% and the number of deaths by 20%. On the contrary, if average speed decreases by only 10%, the number of deaths will be reduced by more than a third! This explains that the simple act of reducing average speeds by 5 km/h would save 11,000 lives and 180,000 injuries in Western Europe every year! The time it takes to travel a distance of 10 km would then increase by 1.2 minutes if the initial speed was 50 km/h, and by 11 seconds if it was 130 km/h [2]. Many journeys are shorter than 10 km...

This holds true for both urban and country areas and explains results that may appear surprising. In 1991, out of the twelve countries then comprising the European Union, five had general urban speed limits of 60 km/h, and seven of 50 km/h. As if by coincidence, the five countries belonging to the first category had the worst results in terms of road safety. Following the recommendations of a European Commission expert group's report at the time—the so-called Gerondeau report [1]—the five countries rapidly lowered their urban speed limit to 50 km/h, even though no obligation was imposed by the Community, showing that it is possible to act simply by conviction in such a domain. The results were spectacular in all five countries concerned, and were comparable to what had happened in Denmark several years before: the number of deaths registered in urban areas fell by about 20%.

Yet the changes in average speeds that accompanied the new regulations remained imperceptible to the majority of road users. In France, speeds were reduced by 2 to 3 km/h. But, as expected, this apparently minimal reduction resulted in a sharp drop in the number of urban road deaths. This apparent paradox can be explained by the fact that the principal effect of a measure of this nature is not so much to lower the speed of the majority of vehicles, as to narrow the range of speeds actually practised. In other words, those who drove at 50 km/h obviously did not significantly change their behaviour, but many of those who drove at 80 km/h no longer drove faster than 70 km/h, the latter category of users obviously being responsible for the most serious accidents.

The situation is the same for intercity roads or motorways. In France, when the speed limit was introduced for interurban motorways, on 1st December 1973, the number of fatal accidents fell *on the same day* from 3.6 to 1.5 deaths per 100 million km travelled, bringing about an instant reduction of close to 60%, which was never challenged. In this way, lower speeds more than halved the frequency of fatal accidents. Since then, due largely to technical progress on vehicles, better infrastructures, and behaviour, this rate has fallen to about 0.5. These unquestionable results, plus those obtained elsewhere, explain why the successive governments of almost all European countries have never seriously considered abolishing speed limits. However, the question is still sometimes raised by one or another of them, and there remains one European country that has not yet introduced any overall speed limits on its motorways.

Incomplete Harmonisation

On a European level, great progress has been made in the last 20 years or so in harmonising maximum authorised speed limits. Fairly recently, the maximum speed limit in urban areas was set at 50 km/h (or 30 mph) in all West European countries, with possibilities of derogating for higher or lower speed limits. This is why in most European cities there are more and more areas where maximum speed limits are 30 km/h. There is even at least one large city—Graz, in Austria—which has chosen 30 km/h as the general speed limit, and where only certain roads can be used at 50 km/h.

Some countries have taken this philosophy even further by increasing the number of areas (*woonerfs* in Dutch, which could be called "cocoon zones") where the car is just tolerated and where it is authorised to drive only at speeds of 10 or 15 km/h, in order to give other users of the roads almost complete safety. It is not surprising that wherever they are implemented, such practices lead to significant decreases in urban area accidents. It should also be noted in this context that some European vehicles are now being marketed with standard equipment enabling the driver to limit the maximum speed to 30 km/h as and when required.

In the countryside, the harmonisation of speed limits for ordinary roads has been made in the 80 to 100 km/h range, with a majority at around 90 km/h, which is a good compromise in most countries. Various experiences have shown that in terms of accident reduction, there was a considerable difference in effectiveness between the 100 km/h and the 90 km/h level.

On motorways, except for certain parts of the German network where, moreover, accident rates are not published, speed is limited throughout Europe. The legal speed limit generally ranges from 80 to 110 km/h on urban motorways, and from 110 to 130 km/h on interurban motorways, giving a relatively satisfactory homogeneity in conformity with the recommendations given in the 1970s by the European Conference of Ministers of Transport (ECMT), which has played a major role in the field of road safety. The existence of the German exception is, nonetheless, a major deficiency in the overall system, as it induces car manufacturers to design their vehicles for high-speed performance.

However, making legislation on speed limits is not sufficient; drivers must also obey them. Of course, absolute compliance is an illusory goal, but this should not lead to false conclusions: the fact that a regulation is not obeyed by 100% of drivers does not mean that it is pointless. If this were the case, no law would ever be justified! As in any other area, everything must be done to ensure the optimal enforcement of speed limits because, even if they are not completely respected, their usefulness is undeniable.

Various converging methods can be used to this end. Some of them concern road network planning, particularly by applying traffic calming techniques that unconsciously lead drivers to drive more slowly, especially in urban areas. One of road safety's major steps in recent years has been the development of a greater awareness of the influence that road network characteristics can have on driver behaviour, which can be called its "incitativity" to good—or bad—driving. Similarly, road signs and road markings reminding the driver of speed limits should be very frequent, as is the case in most countries that have achieved good road safety results, whereas they are still the exception or even almost nonexistent in many other countries, where drivers too often have the feeling of being "trapped" when they are caught speeding.

Likewise, and as long as they are judiciously implemented, more modern ways of checking speed limits can contribute decisively to obtaining the desired results. The use of automatic equipment to record offences is far more efficient than traditional manual methods, but it is still quite rare in Europe. Automatic equipment can register 30 offences during the same time a police officer will only report one! The technical means therefore exist to ensure a sufficient number of checks, on the roads with the highest traffic flows, to make speeding practically disappear. It is now merely a question of will and, if necessary, of the required legislative changes.

"Cruise control," an automatic speed setting in the car, also plays a role in the United States where almost all vehicles are equipped with this kind of regulator, which allows each driver to choose and maintain her preferred speed, thus substantially changing motorway driving conditions when traffic is light enough to use them safely. By making driving more relaxing and restful, cruise control makes speed a relative idea, and has the added, but not negligible, advantage of eliminating the need to keep a permanent watch on the speedometer. It also avoids any risk of involuntarily breaking the speed limit and solves the disastrous contradiction that most cars on the European market are designed to be driven at speeds much higher than the maximum authorised speed limits in force practically everywhere on the continent.

1.2.3 Vehicle Occupant Protection

Car manufacturers have made enormous progress in passive safety (i.e., the protection of occupants in the case of a collision). Today's vehicles are capable of withstanding collisions with most fixed objects at speeds exceeding 50 km/h without any serious injury to the occupants. But, to obtain such results, the occupants must not be transformed into projectiles. To counter this, two complementary means of protecting drivers and passengers exist: the seat belt and the airbag.

Seat belt use has become compulsory in Europe progressively over the past 20 years, France being the first country to adopt such a measure in 1973, with the European Conference of Ministers of Transport (ECMT) recommending it immediately afterwards. At present, national legislation, backed by a European directive, not only makes seat belts compulsory vehicle equipment, but also requires front seat passengers and, with growing frequency, rear seat passengers, to wear them. But it must be noted that even though the law is the same from one end of the continent to the other, the degree to which it is respected is variable, to say the least. In some countries—for example, Germany, Great Britain, Scandinavia—it is very high, with over 90% of front seat passengers and nearly as many rear seat passengers wearing seat belts. In these civic-minded countries, the simple threat of a fine is enough to obtain the desired result as soon as the law is enacted. In some others, located in southern regions of the continent, the situation is just the opposite. In these countries, despite the existence of laws, use of the seat belt remains the exception and it is doubtful whether it will one day be possible to change the situation, so different are the mentalities from those of Northern Europe!

Between these two extreme situations, there are many countries where compliance with seat belt regulations is neither non-existent nor systematic. In France, seat belts are almost always worn on major motorways (96% in 1994), slightly less on country roads (93%), and still less in urban areas (75%), with large variations between regions, more than twice as many vehicle occupants wearing seat belts in the country's northern towns than in southern ones, with their Mediterranean character. In Switzerland, despite legislation making seat belts compulsory, in 1993 they were worn by 63% of vehicle occupants in German-speaking towns, by 39% in French-speaking ones, and by 20% in Italian speaking ones! However, it should be added that the situation has improved somewhat in France since a new sanction was introduced in 1994: one point is removed from the driver's licence for not wearing a seat belt. Spain has also had encouraging results: in 1992, the seat belt was worn by 89% of vehicle occupants on motorways, by 74% in towns and cities, and by 71% on intercity roads.

Use of the seat belt must become as widespread as possible because, contrary to what may be expected, when 80% of drivers wear their seat belts, the problem is not solved in the same proportion at all. On the contrary, it may be only half-solved, or not even that. Drivers who comply with the law on principle and thus wear their seat belt are those who take the least risks. On the contrary, those who infringe the rules are involved in the greatest number of accidents. An Australian study recently revealed that a seemingly insignificant increase in the rate of use of seat belts from 91% to 93% reduced the number of road accident deaths by 10%: the last points won are the most important. Reinforcing police checks is an essential element in this area, too, and should be considered a fundamental priority by police forces. It is all the more important because seat belts have become increasingly effective instruments of protection. Good examples of this are the addition of pyrotechnic systems, or "pretensors," which abruptly retract the seat belt when a collision takes place to prevent the driver from starting a forward movement, or progressive rupture systems designed to cushion the impact of a collision.

In addition, the effectiveness of the seat belt will be further reinforced with another piece of equipment destined to become more and more widespread: the airbag. These devices inflate instantly in the event of an accident and protect the vehicle occupants by filling the space between them and the dashboard. Airbags are now practically standard fittings in all new car models sold in the United States, both for drivers and for front seat passengers.

With their smaller size, airbags are becoming more and more common in Europe, which is all the more reassuring that it is now impossible to imagine, as was thought for a long time, that 100% of drivers will ever fasten their seat belts, particularly due to differences in national or local temperaments. The ideal protection is the simultaneous use of a seat belt and an airbag, but if this cannot be enforced, the latter will at least give minimal protection to those who refuse or forget to wear their seat belt, but without protecting them from ejection, one of the major causes of very serious and fatal accidents. This is one of the factors that combine to make airbags far less efficient than seat belts.

Car and truck manufacturers are also working to make their vehicles less dangerous for other road users in the event of an accident. Much remains to be done in this field regarding heavy trucks. It must finally be said that manufacturers' efforts are not limited to "passive" protection, but have always sought to develop "active" safety aimed at avoiding accidents insofar as possible: Cars that keep well to the road, lights, brakes, and so forth are all areas in which constant progress is made.

However, there is still one area in need of further research: the influence of vehicle characteristics on the driver. All Europeans who have had the opportunity of driving in the United States have noticed a substantial change in their behaviour due to the characteristics of the vehicles they drove: the different level of silence, automatic transmission, suspensions, and so forth that led them to drive in a different way than in Europe. In other words, a driver's behaviour on the road is influenced by the vehicle that he drives, but in ways that are still not understood. As is the case with the road network, the vehicle's "incitativity" to adopt a more, or less, dangerous manner of driving is a reality. Should car manufacturers and research institutes decide to study this phenomenon, which has not been the case to date, the results could be very interesting in the years to come, as until now technical progress has always been perceived as something that does not influence driver behaviour, which is far from being true.

It can also be assumed that all the research undertaken by manufacturers in developing "intelligent vehicles" will, one day, have positive results in terms of respecting proper distances between vehicles, speed limits, detecting drowsiness at the wheel, and so forth.

1.2.4 Daytime Use of Headlights

Among other measures beginning to appear in Europe, one which should be mentioned is the use of dipped headlights in broad daylight. This measure is already in general use, as a result of legislation, in Scandinavia: Sweden, Finland, Norway, and Denmark. It has recently been introduced in Hungary and Poland, at least outside towns and cities, and also in Austria, since 1st July 1996, on an experimental basis for two years. The measure is not limited to Europe as, since 1990, all new vehicles sold in Canada must be equipped with a simple mechanism that automatically turns on appropriate lights whenever the car is started. European tourists visiting Canada, a country in which the majority of the population lives at the same latitude as central France or Switzerland, cannot help but be surprised to see that most vehicles now drive with their headlights on, even in midsummer and in broad daylight. Yet this may be one of the most viable road safety measures in terms of cost-effectiveness. For a very limited cost, the impact on accidents may be very significant. According to certain studies, the reduction in accidents involving several vehicles could in fact vary from 5 to 45%, depending on the latitude of the country in question [3] (Figure 50). If this is so, the measure should be applied without hesitation to the whole continent, as no other one could be so cost-efficient. The issue calls for an in-depth study to be made as quickly as possible in order to weigh its advantages and disadvantages, and this has now been commissioned by the European Commission to the SWOV National Dutch Road Safety Institute.

1.2.5 Road Safety Investments

For a long time, the possibilities of improving road safety by acting on infrastructures were underestimated, due to a mistaken approach to the problem of road accidents. Often, too much time was spent on trying to find the apparent "causes" of accidents instead of devoting it to the "remedies," which are obviously far more important.

Faced with a phenomenon such as an accident, the immediate reaction is to try to find the causes, or those responsible for it. But actually, in the field of road safety, the remedies often do not correspond to the apparent causes. When analysed individually, each accident is almost always found to be due to human error, and appears to indicate that the vehicle or the road network had no, or a very limited, "responsibility" in producing the accident and in its consequences. It is therefore assumed that the road network has very little influence on changing accident levels. But this, alas, frequent assumption can easily be disproved.

Analysis of accidents that take place on traditional, well-equipped roads in good condition rarely reveals that the infrastructure was responsible. Nevertheless, when such roads are replaced by a motorway, the rate of fatal accidents is immediately divided by four or five, even though it is still the same drivers (with the same faults) and the same vehicles that are continuing to drive. In this case, it is obviously a change in the road infrastructure itself that achieved a significant reduction in the number of accidents, even though everything seemed previously to indicate that they were due to errors in road-user behaviour. In other words, the most effective remedy does not correspond in the least to the perceived causes of the accidents.

The same holds true in urban areas. Districts that have remodelled their road networks to include "traffic-calming" techniques have registered a stunning drop in the number of accidents, even though the inhabitants and the vehicles remained, of course, the same. In countries that have gone farthest in fighting against road accidents, such as the Netherlands, it is considered that improvements in the road network should now contribute up to 50% in future gains in safety.

This means that well-managed investments in road networks should be a fundamental aspect of any coherent road safety policy. These investments can be divided into two categories. Investments coming under the first category are specifically aimed at improving road safety; investments in the second category are initially motivated by economic or planning considerations, but can also have very positive repercussions regarding road accidents.

The first category covers, for example, investments made for elimination of accident black spots, for restructuring cross-roads, for equipping the network (appropriate markings, crash barriers) or adding non-skid coatings, together with any other measures that, particularly in urban areas, are aimed at traffic calming in order to incite drivers to drive more carefully (narrower roadways, coloured road surfaces, twist-and -turn traffic slowers, etc.). Unfortunately, funding for these different measures is too often insufficient compared with needs, although some are not very costly to implement. However, they do require very elaborate savoir faire, which means that specialists must be available with the proper training. Some of them are "investigators," whose task is to analyse accidents to study the circumstances and determine the possible remedies. The others are "auditors," whose task is to analyse road projects or existing networks, even in the absence of any accident, in order to identify potentially dangerous or missing structures and equipment, and to propose solutions before accidents take place. Training these investigators and auditors is obviously a priority for all communities concerned.

The second category covers investments for the construction of motorways and expressways, which, as already underlined, have an inherent high safety factor and which, through their development, have made a striking contribution to improvements in road safety in Western Europe in the past years. Considering that the total number of deaths registered on European motorways amounted to 4,300 in 1992, it can be estimated that over 13,000 lives were saved that same year due to their existence! This point is essential. Those who oppose the construction of roads of this nature, both in country areas and in cities, are an obstacle to the reduction in the number of accidents and their victims, and are taking on a very heavy responsibility. Improvements in road safety are one of the essential justifications for road investments because if roads are well-designed, they can significantly and definitively reduce the number and seriousness of accidents.

This is one of the main reasons why the creation of urban and suburban motorways and expressways, which are far safer than traditional roads, must be planned well in advance and the corresponding areas of land reserved to this effect.

In the following pages it will be shown that it is not possible, without artificial and unrealistic constraints, to transfer road traffic to other modes of transport. Attractive as it may seem, the idea that is often put forward, which consists in favouring other modes of transport in the name of road safety, transferring road traffic to them and thus contributing to the reduction in the number of road accidents, is quite simply contradicted by the facts. It is not by investing in other forms of transport that road safety will be improved, but by investing appropriately in the road network. Any other policy would be reprehensible, because it could only lead to a waste of public resources and to the perpetuation of accidents, with their trail of victims and casualties, that could have been avoided.

In this context, it is interesting to note that calculations of cost-effectiveness made to justify the implementation of road works take into account a value given to each human life saved. This value can be calculated in different ways, certain of which are based on economic theories, because each death deprives the community on average of a quantifiable unit of production. In practice, this approach has its limits, particularly in periods of economic difficulty and high unemployment. The value of a human life used to calculate economic cost-effectiveness is therefore a fairly arbitrary figure, which explains why there is such a wide variation from one country to another. It currently ranges from 0.12 million ECUs in the Netherlands to 0.6 in France and 1.2 in the United Kingdom, although the three countries have very similar standards of living. Some studies give human life even higher values, which can be seen as very positive in that the only logical answer to this approach must be to increase the resources devoted to all aspects of the fight against accidents.

This is particularly true in Great Britain where the amount that users would be willing to pay to avoid the risk of accidents is taken into account and has led to the evaluation of the total cost of road accidents being multiplied by 3 compared with the previous methods used.

No harmonisation exists on a European level regarding the value to be given to a human life, but then there is no agreement either concerning the techniques to be used to make road infrastructure safer! Surprising as it may seem, there is currently no European (or sometimes even national) working reference document containing all the rules to be respected in order to reach an optimal level of safety on streets and roads from the infrastructure side.

The current situation can only be detrimental to safety. Some countries, towns, or regions have implemented consistent and effective road network planning policies long ago, on their own initiative, and have reaped the benefits. But many others have not done so to the same extent, and accidents have not decreased at the same rate, and many deaths that could have been avoided continue to occur. Common sense dictates that this situation, which concerns the field where the highest number of accidents occur and where safety procedures applied successfully in other places are unknown, must come to an end.

It is urgent to make up for lost time by preparing technical reference documents summing up all existing knowledge on road safety on a European level. The first step has been taken in 1996, on the initiative of the Brussels Commission under the aegis of the European Road Safety Federation, with the publishing of a first technical safety guide for interurban roads [4]. Each country or each community will then be responsible for selecting and putting into practice the points that it considers are best adapted to its own particular situation.

1.2.6 Technical Inspection of Roads

It is to be hoped that the authorities responsible for road networks will go still further and decide to make the regular inspection of roads by independent institutions compulsory, thus ensuring that rules and safety practices are systematically respected throughout their towns, regions, or countries.

In all fields where safety problems may arise, procedures exist to ensure that everything is done to limit the number of accidents and their consequences. This objective is reached in two stages. The first consists in drawing up an official document defining the rules to be observed and specifying the technical procedures to be adopted. In the second stage, inspections are carried out by an independent authority to ensure that the terms of the official document are respected. These procedures are adopted, for example, for establishments frequented by the public (stores, restaurants, hotels, sports areas, etc.), which are subject to very strict rules regarding fire hazards or emergency exits, and are inspected by independent technical authorities and safety commissions. There are many other examples: high-rise buildings, ships, aeroplanes, food products, medication, and so forth are all subject to regular controls, as are road vehicles, of course.

Surprising as it may seem, the only field, in many countries, where no procedures of this nature exist is precisely the one in which the number of accidents is incomparably higher than all the others combined. Too often, those responsible for road networks—the State, region, or local authority—are able to organise the road network as they wish. For instance, the same type of cross-roads will often be dealt with differently depending on the authority responsible for it, sometimes even within the same country: roundabouts, directional islands, markings, traffic lights, and so forth. Traffic signals and equipment—or their absence—will be different according to national or local customs. Yet these are fundamental elements of road safety.

This situation is completely illogical and quite appalling. It is contradictory to oblige vehicle owners to undergo periodic technical vehicle inspections and to keep their vehicles in proper repair, and yet not systematically adopt the same procedures for road networks. Certain countries or communities more or less do this, but they remain the exception. If such measures were adopted everywhere, they would have an extremely positive effect on safety, which would then be granted the priority that it deserves in road budget allocations. As far as accidents are concerned, it is difficult to imagine an elected official or a civil servant refusing to remedy the deficiencies of the road network for which he is responsible, once the deficiencies have been pointed out and if the solutions are financially accessible.

Elected officials and civil servants are used to such procedures in all other areas of their responsibility (for example, when they are in charge of establishments frequented by the public) and it can be assumed that if such procedures were adopted, this would lead in the short term to the generalisation of techniques that have proven to be efficient in terms of road safety (especially traffic calming, which spectacularly reduces accidents).

Compulsory technical road inspection thus constitutes a priority. Proceeding in such a way would end the anarchy that often reigns in the area of road signs, where there is also great progress to be made, as is often evident to the road user trying to find his way. According to some studies conducted on behalf of the International Road Federation, deficiencies in road signs may be responsible for increasing journeys in cities by 4% and the number of accidents by 5 to 8%.

When it comes to road signs, and to road planning and equipment in general, it is important to note the great differences existing from one country to another, as any European driver who crosses a border has noticed. Despite the existence of international conventions, which standardise world-wide safety signs and make them, with the French metric system, the only internationally recognised language, signs are used in very different ways in different countries. An urban crossing, a cross-roads, or a turn will all be dealt with differently to such an extent that, as the internal borders of Europe disappear, the driver is often only aware of having crossed the border because of the different road signs' look! Sometimes the inconsistencies go even further. There is no European harmonisation of the colours used for motorway signs. In some countries, blue motorway signs indicate towns along the motorway and green ones indicate towns farther away. In other countries, it is virtually the opposite. Variations are even greater along ordinary roads, where, according to a recent study by the International Road Federation, no two countries among the seventeen that make up Western Europe have the same rules for road signs use.

But that is not the worst. In certain fields, differences affect essential safety factors. In most European countries, a solid white line in the middle of the road signifies that it is absolutely prohibited to cross it, whereas in others it can be crossed and two parallel solid white lines are required to indicate the prohibition!

Finally, it is impossible not to mention the fact that not everyone drives on the same side of the road in all European countries, since, in two of them—the United Kingdom and Ireland—drivers drive on the left, and not on the right as in all the other countries. Nevertheless, it is impossible to change this situation, if only because many motorway exchanges are not reversible, so that it would be unthinkable from a practical point of view to adapt the British and Irish networks to driving on the right, not to mention the millions of vehicles that drive along them.

These observations should not, however, lead to the assumption that nothing can be done to improve the current situation and to bring together, whenever possible, the different countries' and local communities' treatment of road signs and equipment. It is through the exchange of experiences and knowledge sharing, rather than through European legislation, that results will be achieved the most rapidly, without necessarily aiming for the impossible objective of complete uniformity throughout the continent.

1.2.7 Driver Training and Driving Licences

New drivers are inexperienced and often young and impetuous, and are therefore involved in many more serious accidents than experienced drivers. Several means of action are possible to try to reduce this "overrisk."

The first concerns the conditions under which new drivers drive their first thousands of kilometres. In continental Europe, the new driver traditionally has the right to drive alone as soon as she obtains a licence; that is, after an average of about 20 hours of driving lessons, which can obviously only give very limited driving experience.

This practice is completely different in Great Britain, where candidates for the driver's licence initially receive a temporary permit authorising them to drive as long as they are accompanied by an experienced driver, generally one of their parents. The first thousands of kilometres covered by the learner driver are thus subject to the vigilant scrutiny of an attentive person who will obviously take great care to avoid an accident, if only for the sake of his own safety and that of his vehicle. The results obtained by this method would appear to be satisfactory as British insurance companies have not observed any particular overrisk during this learning phase and do not modify their rates for clients who use their vehicles in this manner.

The results of the British system have led France to introduce "accompanied driving," which authorises young people to drive from the age of 16 as long as they are accompanied by an experienced driver and they have passed an initial training period in a driving school. Belgium adopted similar measures in 1994, even though it is still too early to categorically maintain their beneficial effect on safety. Other measures can also be considered to improve new driver safety. Measures in force in Germany are aimed at granting probationary licences for the first two or three years, which are the most dangerous.

This probational status could have a certain number of special provisions attached to it. For instance, any serious offence during the period under consideration could cancel the licence and oblige the new driver to take his driving test again. New drivers could also be subject to certain rules which would be stricter than for experienced drivers.

The most important of these could concern alcohol, known to be responsible for tragic Saturday night accidents that put so many families into mourning. As in Australia, or, in different ways, in most American states, it could be decided that, during the three years after the licence is delivered, it would be strictly prohibited to drive after consuming any quantity of alcohol whatsoever, the authorised legal limit being fixed at zero. Apart from the obvious benefits in terms of safety, such a measure would also gain widespread public support in many countries: 72% of French people agree with this measure, and even a majority of young people (60%) have a favourable opinion [5].

This is one of the most important new pieces of road safety legislation to introduce in Europe in the years to come. It is long-awaited by all parents, and a pressing call must be launched to politicians in all the different countries so that one of them will finally have the courage to take the first step. Experience shows that once this is done, the other European countries will follow one after the other, thus saving thousands of lives every year.

The use of a combination of these different measures would make it possible to hope, if not to completely eradicate, at least to greatly diminish the overrisk for which new drivers are both the primary instigators and the primary victims. The general idea is that it should no longer be possible, as is still the case in many countries, to go straight from the state of non-driver to the state of fully independent driver, but on the contrary to plan a transition period between the two.

1.2.8 The Education of Children

Children's road safety education is doubly important. It can avoid some of the accidents to which, unfortunately, many children are victims, either on the way to or from school or in other circumstances. But it is also necessary to forge the mentality of future adults and prepare them for their future responsibilities as drivers and road users.

For this reason, road safety is taught at school, to varying degrees, in all the countries of Europe. But the regularity with which this instruction is given and its quality, even its true existence, are extremely variable not only from one country to another but from one establishment (or even one classroom) to another within the same country, or even the same region. In fact, the quality of road safety instruction depends on two factors. The first resides in the degree of priority it is granted by those in charge of defining and following up the implementation of the programmes. But the result also depends on the individual motivation of each teacher concerned, which is very variable. More often than not, road safety education is better at the primary school or pre-school—playgroup—level when only one teacher is in charge of the pupils. When the child reaches secondary school, with different teachers responsible for different subjects, road safety often becomes an orphan in that each teacher considers it outside his particular field. One way of at least partially remedying this situation may consist, as is the case in France, in introducing national examinations awarding specific certificates necessary to drive motorised two-wheelers such as mopeds.

Of course, the parents' role is essential throughout childhood, together, if possible, with specialised television programmes for the young. Driving schools then take over the responsibility, which implies that appropriate educational programmes must be defined on a national or regional basis and that their respect by the establishments concerned must be controlled, so that in this way, from early childhood until learning to drive, road safety is as much as possible part of a continuing, consistent teaching programme.

1.2.9 Information Campaigns

Road safety education for schoolchildren and those preparing to take their driving licence is of utmost importance, but the task cannot be limited to this. Adult road users should be informed about the hazards they face and how to minimise them. This is one of the main aims of the information campaigns that all countries devote to road safety, with varying means and frequency levels.

These campaigns have a dual objective. First of all, they must continually remind road users of hazards. It is a well-known fact that accidents happen when people believe themselves to be safe and, on the contrary, hazards are minimised when the perception of danger is more present. Road accidents do not escape the rule, and the hazards must be emphasised continually in any possible way; otherwise, the number of victims will have a tendency to increase.

Information campaigns have another goal: to teach or remind users of the rules to obey and the attitudes to adopt. Of course, such campaigns alone cannot usually change people's behaviour immediately. But if they are well-managed, they can at least change opinions and create an atmosphere which is favourable to the establishment and control of safety rules.

Numerous approaches can and are used to set the tone of such publicity campaigns, including reasoning, humour, sentiment, civic responsibility, and so forth. But experts are in the midst of a great debate as to the appropriateness of using images and sounds reconstructing the reality of road accidents; that is, all of their utter horror. Some countries have been using this method for a long time and do not hesitate to show victims and injured people covered with blood, or parents or children screaming with pain or despair on television in scenes that unfortunately correspond all too well to reality, but which our societies most often hide to the point where road accidents become something abstract, something that, as the saying goes, "only happens to other people." A large number of experts believe the use of overly realistic images should be banned because they are so unbearable that the target audience would react by rejecting them and wanting to hide from them. Other experts disagree, and consider that, on the contrary, it is necessary in order to make people understand the seriousness of irresponsible behaviour and to help change mentalities and attitudes, to show what road accidents are really like and how profoundly shocking they are in an age that calls itself civilised.

The debate is not yet over, and will probably go on for a long time. One recent additional piece of information must be added. While the use of realism was until recently limited to a few English-speaking countries (the United Kingdom, Australia, etc.), Spain followed suit in 1992, in the face of a constant growth in accident figures, by running a series of television advertisements of almost unbearable realism. The impact of these campaigns, helped by a very substantial budget that meant that they were broadcast frequently, was quite exceptional. They reached a recognition rate of practically 100%, since anyone who had seen one of the television runnings, if only once, was unable to forget it. Contrary to what might have been expected, and similar to the experience of the State of Victoria in Australia, the advertisements were approved by over 90% of the public and protests were extremely limited. Finally, and above all, a decrease of about 20% in the number of road accidents was registered during the same period. Although cause and effect relationships should be drawn with extreme caution in road safety matters, it would seem very likely that, as the decrease took place at the same time, a major part of this reduction was due to this very realistic campaign.

The Spanish experience gives road safety campaign directors much to think about, given that, besides the technical aspects of the issue, it is impossible to remain silent about the fact that the use of such unusual means of communication in a greatly sterilised world calls for an undeniable dose of courage.

1.2.10 The Three Golden Rules

The experts may be in disagreement as to the best tone to use in road safety advertisements, but not as to their content. Admittedly, there are hundreds of rules that road users should obey, which could lead to fears that information should be scattered in many different directions. In fact, this is not the case because among all the many recommendations to be made regarding behaviour, there are three, and only three, that overwhelmingly predominate in preventing road accidents and reducing their consequences. These concern staying sober at the wheel, complying with speed limits, and wearing safety devices (seat belts for drivers and passengers, special fastenings for children, helmets for users of two-wheeled vehicles). If these three simple rules, the three golden rules of road safety in terms of road users' behaviour, were systematically respected everywhere, the tragic number of fatal accidents would decrease by more than half on the roads of Europe.

These three basic rules should constitute the permanent basis of information campaigns in all countries, which does not, of course, exclude the possibility of sometimes dealing with other more specific issues. Most European countries proceed in this manner, broadcasting advertising messages to varying degrees on the radio and especially on television. Some also broadcast informative television programmes on the subject from time to time. Many are supported by the local press. Whatever the case, investments made in public information campaigns, if well-managed, are one of the most effective and necessary means of reducing accidents, and thus deserve to be granted the resources that correspond to what is at stake, which is, unfortunately, not always the case.

It must finally be added that, besides paid broadcasting of "institutional" messages, the news gives government and administrative leaders many opportunities to appear on television, on the radio, or in the press, which, if properly exploited, can develop and maintain a favourable climate towards the road safety cause and help to continually remind the public of the fundamental rules of road safety. But it is not enough to inform—the rules must also be enforced.

Monitoring Behaviour and Follow-up of Offences

The role of the police, the gendarmerie, and the legal system in preventing accidents is obviously fundamental. Without their involvement, it would be useless to hope that the different rules and regulations capable of improving road safety could be enforced, and it is therefore essential that they dispose of the necessary resources, which is far from being the general rule.

The countries of Europe can be divided into two large groups on the subject. Some have a specialised road police force or gendarmerie under national command, whose only activity is almost always road-related and therefore essentially devoted to road safety. This is the case for all of the Central and East European countries, which inherited a well-structured, often motivated road police force from the old regime. In Western Europe, this type of organisation is much rarer, but it exists in Spain, with its Guardia Civil de Trafico, in Greece, and in Denmark.

The situation is different in other countries, which either have no national police force or gendarmerie (with police missions therefore depending on local or regional government) or do have a national police force with no special national road police, but only specialised units dependent on local command, which is quite different. It is clear that from a road safety standpoint, the existence of a national structure solely missioned to police roads is a very significant asset.

Whatever the structure of police forces, their effectiveness in the fight against road accidents also depends on their available resources. In this respect, completely new perspectives have been opened in recent years with the appearance of automatic equipment for registering and measuring road offences. Each of the three above-mentioned golden rules of road safety can benefit from this in different ways. Speed limit surveillance can be carried out with photographic radar equipment mounted either in a fixed location or onto stationary or moving police vehicles. The "return" on this equipment is such that the problem when photographs are taken by thousands is not with recording the offences, but ensuring their follow-up. In practice, large-scale use of automatic speeding offence recording equipment is therefore only possible if the processing of such offences is also entirely automatic, which can require legislative reform in some countries. It must be added that the amount of money obtained through fines is such that the cost of the necessary computer equipment is covered within a few months and that considerable volumes of money are collected subsequently and can perhaps be used profitably for further road safety actions. In the Netherlands, a national goal was edicted in the framework of a strategic plan regarding the average maximum speed levels and a maximum percentage of offenders.

The problem of drunk driving is different in that drivers must be physically stopped in order to test their alcohol level. But unlike speeding, this is less of a mass offence. When random checks are carried out, the proportion of offenders is generally quite low—a daily average of about 1 to 2%—so that what is most important is to perform enough spot checks for them to be dissuasive, particularly at night when the proportion of drivers under the influence of alcohol is much higher. Amongst other things, this assumes that all police officers or gendarmes are equipped with automatic equipment to analyse the air exhaled and are authorised to check drivers at any time. As mentioned above, not all West European countries have legislation to this effect yet, and spot checks are often too rare to have a deterrent effect.

As far as wearing seat belts and helmets is concerned, behaviour varies so much from one country to another that the police forces' tasks in each country are also entirely different. In some countries, the rules are automatically obeyed by almost every car user and so control is not a police priority, even if a careful watch must still be kept to avoid any possible worsening of the situation. In other countries, the situation seems almost desperate due to national and local mentalities being collectively against this type of regulation. In still other countries, the situation is somewhere between the two extremes. It is obviously in this last category that the influence of police checks is most important, since the rate of compliance with the legislation—and therefore its influence on accidents—depends directly on the intensity of their action and on information campaigns.

In all cases, indicators must be established to allow permanent tracking of the degree of compliance with the three golden rules of road safety and thereby guide the police forces' actions in order to optimise the effective use of their resources. While public attention is much more focused on murders or other crimes—which must, of course, be fought against—there is no area in which the police or the gendarmerie can save as many lives and avoid as many tragedies as in that of road safety.

1.2.11 Road Safety Financing Policy and the Insurance System

Road safety policy, like health and other similar areas, has two principal means of action at its disposal. In the face of a phenomenon that creates losses, not production, it is possible to act either through prevention, by limiting the number and seriousness of accidents, or through compensation, by minimising as far as possible the consequences of accidents that have occurred and making amends to their victims.

Whether for health or safety matters, it is difficult to find the right balance between the means to be devoted to prevention and those to be used for compensation. In certain cases, hazards are badly estimated, leading to excessive spending on prevention (for instance, to satisfy unduly demanding regulations). But in the case of road accidents, it is quite obviously the opposite: in road safety, the means devoted to preventing accidents are too often derisory compared with the seriousness of the problem, whereas, when accidents happen, the compensation and indemnities paid to victims and their legal successors represent overall sums that are almost impossible to imagine.

The total amount of accident insurance premiums paid by car and other road vehicle owners represents about 65 billion ECUs per year in Western Europe, or close to 200 million ECUs for each of the 365 days of the year, which, when insurance management costs are taken away, corresponds in the main part to the cost of material repairs, hospital costs, and indemnities paid to accident victims. In other words, every hour of every year, more than 7 million ECUs are devoted to trying to repair the consequences of road accidents! It goes without saying that in comparison, the sums dedicated to preventing accidents are more often than not derisory. For example, those allocated annually to road safety information campaigns generally represent in each country a few million ECUs (or the equivalent of only a few hours spending through the insurance system), and those devoted to specific road safety work on the national network amount at best to the equivalent of a few days'.

Yet, every year, hundreds, even thousands, of accidents take place with a unit cost exceeding one million ECUs due to the money that must be paid to victims who are disabled for life. Overall, in most countries, the disproportion between the means devoted to preventing road accidents and those used to try and repair their effects is astounding. Cases are known where children with a 100% disability have been granted indemnities of ten million ECUs or more in order to maintain teams of five or six people, enabling them simply to survive in awful conditions as can be imagined. But, at the same time, there is not enough money for information campaigns, for equipping the road network, or for paying police forces, which could save thousands of accidents. *What kind of absurd world do we live in?*

This dramatic incoherence is explained by the fact that the financial mechanisms involved in preventing accidents on the one hand, and repairing the damages on the other, are entirely distinct, and that at present there is almost no communication between the two. Accident prevention measures (user information, police checks, road network planning and works, etc.) are mostly the responsibility of public authorities and must be financed by national budgets or by local communities, both, as is well known to all, being subject to numerous other constraints. Costs of compensation are part of a completely different process. They result from the cost of expenses of repairing or replacing vehicles, hospital fees, or legal decisions, and they are financed by the insurance system, which adjusts its rates according to the level of compensation to be paid, but which itself takes practically no part in prevention. No insurance company, taken alone, could voluntarily devote a significant percentage of its resources to actions that would be detrimental to its financial equilibrium and that would benefit its competitors as much as itself. This is the source of the incoherence outlined above.

Some countries have nonetheless been roused by this situation, which is all the more shocking in that it is not just economic losses, but a very great number of human sufferings and lives that are at stake. Whilst not being exhaustive, it is however interesting to consider certain experiences that have been successfully implemented.

Finland and Switzerland

For about 40 years, Finland has added a "traffic safety fee" to its compulsory insurance premiums (civil or "third-party" liability). This fee yields approximately

25 million Finnish marks (5 million ECUs) per year, which for this country with nearly 5 million inhabitants represents 1.4% of the total compulsory insurance premiums. The product of this fee is paid to a statutory public organisation for which it is the main source of funding. The organisation includes representatives from large state-approved associations and the state and is mainly dedicated to road user information together with numerous other road safety promotion activities.

Switzerland also has a similar fee, albeit at a lower rate (0.75% of the amount of compulsory insurance premiums).

The Province of Quebec, Canada

An important reform implemented in 1977 in Quebec indirectly resulted in a massive involvement of the insurance system in accident prevention. This reform entrusted a single state-owned company, the *Régie de l'Assurance Automobile du Québec*, or RAAQ (Quebec State Automobile Insurance Company), with the task of providing drivers with compulsory insurance.

Under this reform, the state transferred many of its activities to the RAAQ, including organising driver training programmes and undertaking massive accident prevention campaigns. With considerable resources at its disposal, the RAAQ, which is now called the *Société d'Assurances Automobiles du Québec*, or SAAQ (Quebec Automobile Insurance Company), has managed in just a few years to profoundly change the mentalities and behaviour of road users in Quebec, thereby reducing accidents dramatically.

Whereas Quebec was once notorious for its drivers' lack of discipline and its extremely high accident rates, improvements have been considerable. In 1987, following vigorous information campaigns, the rate of use of seat belts rose to 86%, a record for all of North America. The death rate fell to 3.1 deaths per 10,000 vehicles, so that Quebec is now in a respectable place in international rankings instead of being at the bottom of the list. In 1988, the number of deaths was 22% lower than the 1985 level.

The State of Victoria, Australia

Inspired by Quebec's experience, the State of Victoria, whose capital is Melbourne, went even further and is now the most advanced example of the involvement of an insurance system in road accident prevention.

As in Quebec, there is only one institution in charge of compulsory insurance, the Transport Accident Commission (TAC), which has been entrusted not only with compensating accident victims, but also with participating in accident prevention. To this end, the TAC devoted, for the first time in 1990, 3% of the premiums it received to prevention, in not one but two different ways.

The first, relatively traditional, means concerned the financing for massive information campaigns with two main targets: the battle against drunk driving and the compliance with speed limits. Although the sums represented a very small fraction of premiums received, they were so high in absolute terms that they enabled a real blitz on public opinion. On a European scale, they would have corresponded to about one billion ECUs, whereas the road safety budget for the Transport General Directorate (DG VII) of the Brussels Commission amounted to 5 million ECUs in 1995 . . .

The second way of using the funds raised for prevention through insurance premiums is far more innovative: the TAC financed the purchase by the police forces of essential equipment necessary to enforce the traffic regulations, which were the object of simultaneous television campaigns. The equipment consisted of automatic cameras for detecting speeding offences or crossings against red lights, together with special vehicles (Booze buses) and specific material for alcohol level checks. The various equipment, which the police could not have purchased with its budget allocations, considerably increased police force productivity. At the same time, in order to face the growing number of offences registered, their processing was fully automated, to such an extent that it now takes an average of one minute to process an offence and offenders receive their notice to pay at their home address 48 hours after the offence is committed!

These combined actions—information campaigns plus a substantial increase in controls and their follow-up—brought about spectacular, almost unbelievable results. Serious speeding offences have practically disappeared, and the proportion of drunk drivers has dropped very significantly. As far as accidents are concerned, the results were even more remarkable: between the end of 1989 and 1991, the number of deaths fell from 777 to 500, or a decrease of 35%. Such success prompted the TAC to progressively increase the rate taken from insurance premiums to be dedicated to accident prevention from 3 to 8% and, in mid 1993 annual deaths fell to less than 400, representing a reduction of 50%. *In three years, the number of victims had been halved.* Even if this exceptional reduction cannot be entirely attributed for sure to the insurance system's involvement in accident prevention, it is agreed that it undeniably played a very important role.

The TAC's "return on investment" was also exceptional. The 3% devoted to prevention represented 15 million Australian dollars during 1990/1991, whereas the indemnities paid to holders of insurance policies decreased by 100 million dollars due to the reduction in the number and seriousness of accidents. It should also be noted that gains for the Community were estimated at a total of 300 million dollars for the same year; that is, three times more. As a result, the TAC had considerable financial reserves at its disposal and was able to launch its accident prevention initiatives in a third direction. It is now financing road work aimed at eliminating hundreds of "black spots."

The State of Victoria thus presents what is doubtless a unique example in the world: Rather than devoting insurance premiums entirely to trying to compensate victims of accidents, part—actually, quite a small part—is used for accident prevention, not only in the traditional fields of road-user education and training but also in favour of other aspects of a consistent prevention policy, concerning in particular equipment of police forces and improvements to the road network [6].

In fact, this way of treating the problem has advantages for all those concerned:

- All road users, who benefit from the lessening of risks;
- The entire community, which benefits from a reduction in the social, human, and economic costs of this obviously tragic phenomenon;
- Motorists, whose insurance premiums decrease due to the decline in accidents, which is higher than the additional cost corresponding to participating in prevention initiatives;
- The insurance companies, which gain by the dramatic fall in the amounts to be paid out to their policy holders and therefore bring in considerable profits in the short term.

It must be noted that, although the two examples above (Quebec and Victoria) refer to countries that have entrusted compulsory insurance to a single state company, this is by no means a necessity for the financial participation of the insurance system in accident prevention, as is seen in the case of Finland, which has maintained the traditional, competitive road insurance system used by most industrialised countries whilst creating a special road safety fund to participate in accident prevention. It can also be possible to imagine that all or part of fines linked to driving offences be appropriated to such a fund.

The World Bank, sometimes called the Globe's Finance Ministry and renowned for its concern to ensure that the principles of financial orthodoxy are respected, has just given its approval (following a detailed study) to this means of financing road safety, which it systematically recommends to countries that consult it, as it considers that its validity is undeniable. The OECD has adopted the same position.

France

Another country has just embarked on this path, on a still very minor scale, and it is too early to say if it will be effective. On the initiative of the French government, the organisations representing insurance companies reached an agreement with the former in October 1994, under the terms of which they agreed to devote 0.50% of civil liability compulsory premiums received to the road accident prevention schemes (or 0.25% of total premiums if noncompulsory insurance is taken into account). This percentage may seem derisory, and is, in fact. But the sums collected by motor insurance are so considerable that even this low percentage will nonetheless correspond to an annual appropriation of 180 million francs (30 million ECUs), an unprecedented figure for the major European countries.

The Government and the insurance companies' representative organisations will decide by mutual agreement how the money is to be used. This will be a first step in the right direction, if it is actually taken (which is not yet certain). But even if this is the case, it will still be nowhere near the level of what should be done in France as in the rest of Europe. The disproportion between the money devoted to compensating for accidents and the money available for preventing them remains scandalous in our modern-day societies, and the first European country to have the good sense and the courage to really innovate in this area on a proper scale is yet to be found.

1.3 EUROPEAN COOPERATION

Surprising as it may seem, the European Union had hardly been involved in road safety until recently.

Admittedly, it promulgated common standards for vehicles so that a car or truck produced in one country of the Union could be sold in the others. But the primary reason for the replacement of national standards by Community standards, which is now completed, was not a search for better road safety but the necessary elimination of obstacles to industrial trade.

Admittedly, the European Parliament has studied the problem of road accidents on five occasions since 1980, and asked the Council of Ministers and the Commission each time to take a more active role in this field. It is true that research programmes on cars and road traffic have been launched by the European Union (in particular the Drive and Prometheus programmes), but for them road safety remains just one objective among others.

In all fairness, the Commission has done as much as it can to encourage the European Council of Ministers to adopt several directives to be respected by Member States. But the results are extremely meagre in that only five directives have been adopted outside the domain of vehicle construction standards. Yet this is one of the worst problems that European countries have to face.

How can this seeming powerlessness be explained in an field that is so important and so vital, in the true sense of the term, for all European countries and their citizens? At least two reasons can shed some light on the matter. The first is institutional in nature. Does the European Community, now the European Union, have the right to become involved in road safety? The Treaty of Rome was not entirely clear on the subject. It mentioned safety problems, but only in a chapter dealing with the transport of goods, so that two interpretations were possible and the choice was never clearly made between them. The majority of countries considered that the

Treaty of Rome laid down a sufficient legal basis to justify, in a matter as essential as this, that community directives be drawn up and imposed on the Member States. But, on the most sensitive subjects there had always been a blocking minority—two "large" countries and one "small" one—that thought differently and opposed the measures.

In an attempt to end this situation, the Treaty of Maastricht explicitly specified road safety as one of the European Union's areas of competency (Article 75). But this does not mean that the debate is over, because the same Treaty of Maastricht contains another article that introduces the principle of "subsidiarity", which stipulates that anything that can be treated at a national state level should not be treated at the Union level. This article has led therefore once again to a minority of countries requesting that road safety be dealt with by each country individually and that, except in exceptional cases, the Union should not issue directives to the Member States on this matter. It is obviously not possible to predict today the manner in which European practices will evolve, as the majority of the States are, on the contrary, very eager for supranational intervention in the field of road safety to help them to better implement in their countries policies capable of reducing the number and seriousness of accidents.

Nonetheless, the legislative aspect is not the only one. Although they are essential, the measures that can be taken through compulsory Community directives are very few. They could, for example, deal with the maximum authorised limit of alcohol in the bloodstream or the maximum speed limits according to the type of road network. But it is impossible to imagine that there will one day be precise, constraining European directives on cross-roads design, school road safety programmes, information campaigns, organisation of controls, the level of sanctions, or organising emergency aid for the injured! Obviously, and quite rightly so, these subjects and many others will remain the domain of the different countries or even their local communities.

However, this does not mean that there is no room for European action in each of the areas mentioned above. The initiatives will not be aimed at imposing directives on Member States, but should take the form of grouping together and exchanging national savoir faire so that the experts from different countries can select the best procedures for each issue, each country, or each local community, then freely take inspiration from them. In practice, it is by publishing technical guides, developing more or less detailed recommendations, and by professional organising of exchanges that common knowledge in the field will be able to progress and that Europe will best contribute to reducing road accidents, the most advanced countries offering their experience to those with less and all having something to gain.

The United States has been using these procedures for a long time. Long before the federal government became involved in road and road traffic matters, the officials of the different American states created a number of specialised technical associations for road planning, road signs, police force action, the highway code, organising emergency services, and so forth. It is thanks to the existence of all these associations that the motorist who crosses the United States from east to west or from north to south does not have the impression of changing countries when he crosses the borders from one state to another. Nonetheless, most regulations, including the highway code itself, are not the domain of the federal government, but of each individual state. They all have technical guides at their disposal, developed by their foremost experts, and have naturally followed 99% of their recommendations.

There is no reason why things should not follow the same pattern in Europe, but the situation still remains very different, as any tourist who leaves her own country can easily see. For instance, for over 50 years the British have systematically equipped major crossroads with roundabouts, which have proved to be remarkably effective in reducing, and often even eliminating, serious accidents. Yet, with only a few exceptions, this practice did not cross the Channel until the 1980s. When it was adopted on the continent, it showed itself to be just as effective as in its country of origin, and is now widespread in France, with Germany, Switzerland, Belgium and other countries now also adopting it. Simply because such basic information was not shared, thousands of European motorists died "for nothing" for decades! Unfortunately, examples of this nature abound, whether it be for other aspects of road network planning, the implementation of traffic-calming techniques, driver training, information campaigns, police force action, sanctions policy, and so forth. But, however surprising it may seem, until recently nothing was really organised or systematically undertaken to pool the different countries' technical knowledge on the European level except in the course of bilateral meetings, seminars, or conferences, which despite their usefulness were unequal and rarely truly professional and of "recommendations" by the European Conference of Minister of Transport (ECMT), which were sometimes highly efficient but remained limited in scope.

Things are beginning to change, especially following the above-mentioned report assigned to an expert committee by the Brussels Commission in 1990 and published in February 1991 [1]. For the first time, this report revealed that the traditional working methods of the Community, which consist in drafting directives to be issued to Member Countries, were very limited as far as road safety is concerned, and that, without abandoning them, it was also necessary to find ways to pool national experiences on a voluntary exchange basis. Following this report, failing the creation of a European Road Safety Agency (which would, moreover, have been amply justified), different actions were led by the Commission's DG VII. The latter first established a "high-level group," bringing together for the first time all the member countries' national government road safety directors. In 1994, it then created four technical work groups within this organisation, dedicated respectively to inter-city road safety, the fight against drunk driving, road safety for children, and car advertising. It used the support of the European Road Safety Federation (ERSF), an institution that was created recently on the initiative of the European automobile clubs, with the International Tourism Alliance (AIT), the International Automobile Federation (FIA), the International Road Prevention (PRI), the International Road Union (IRU) (which represents road transport companies), the International Road Federation (IRF), and the Association of European Automobile Constructors (ACEA) as founding members.

This federation—together with another recently created institution for transport safety, the European Transport Safety Council (ETSC)—pleaded its cause in 1994 before the European Parliament for an increase in road safety credits, which had remained derisory until then as they did not exceed about 1 million ECUs per year, compared with the cost of road accidents for European communities, which exceeded 70 billion! The call was heard, and credits increased thanks to the support of the European Parliament Commission on Transport and Tourism, in agreement with the General Directorate concerned. Admittedly, approximately 5 million ECUs in 1995 and a little more in 1996 is still far too low a sum in relation to what is at stake, but it can be hoped that the process will continue and, above all, be amplified.

Another important European road safety event took place in 1994. Following a common mission in 1992 and 1993 in the six former communist satellite countries of Eastern Europe (Hungary, Poland, The Czech Republic, Slovakia, Rumania, and Bulgaria), the World Bank and the Brussels Commission organised a one-week seminar in Budapest in 1994, which brought together representatives from 14 countries of Central and Eastern Europe and which was attended by 15 Ministers of the Interior or Ministers of Transport in person. The seminar resulted in the publication of a synthesis document reviewing the techniques that are currently available to fight against road accidents, and this can now be considered a reference document that is also pertinent to western countries [7]. It particularly revealed that the gap between laxist road safety policies and voluntarist, effective ones could amount to 400,000 deaths in Central and Eastern Europe in the coming 20 years!

The choice of Hungary as host for the seminar was explained by the remarkable results obtained in that country. A consistent policy was introduced, leading to a decrease in road accidents in its territory of over 20%. The quality of this seminar and the high participation rate revealed just how seriously the situation was taken by the officials from Central and Eastern European countries, aware that the numbers of cars will undoubtedly increase in their countries and also how high their expectations were regarding Western Europe, which paid heavily to begin to learn to fight the scourge of road accidents.

1.4 HOPE AND FRUSTRATION

Much still needs to be done. The issue of road safety gives rise to feelings of both hope and frustration: Hope because progress has been made and almost everywhere in Western Europe the number of road accident victims is on the decline despite an increase in traffic. Frustration because, despite progress already made, it is clear that it would be possible to do so much better still, as it is clear there are large differences between countries regarding the way road safety is dealt with [8].

Sweden may be showing the way. In 1995, it adopted a wholly new approach, mobilizing the entire society—government, schools, companies, associations, and other institutions—to fight road accidents, with the idealized national target of eliminating them entirely. In 1996, the number of roadway fatalities decreased to 550, the lowest level since 1950. However, Sweden is still an exception in this approach. Too often, our societies remain passive concerning road accidents, which they accept as inevitable. There is still so much left to do to be equal to the challenge and combat the scandal of one of the most dramatic problems facing present-day civilisation.

Why is there so much indifference in the face of so much blood? Why is there so little interest on the part of the public, the media, and sometimes decision-makers themselves, whereas other causes mobilise support so easily, whether it be the protection of plants or animals or improvements to air quality, and many others, which are obviously not nearly as pressing a public health problem? Why this absurdity of spending colossal sums of money in trying to repair the consequences of accidents instead of using a fraction of the sum to avoid them? Why, when so many remedies are known, are they not systematically and immediately applied in all countries, even when they are approved by the majority of the public?

We must face reality. For too many, road deaths are of no, or little, interest. Too often, road accidents are still viewed as inevitable and do not elicit the appropriate reactions. In this area, unlike all the others, deaths and injuries are too often accepted by today's societies. Why, in spite of the hundred thousand deaths and three million injured per year on the roads of Europe, has the World Health Organisation itself just closed its European office in charge of accidents, whereas at the same time it continues to increase the resources it devotes to the fight against pollution? As Haroun Tazieff so rightly states in his book *Lignes de Vie* (*Life Lines*):

> *The road is like everything that is human. It is the best possible thing when it enables essential communication between men and nations, and it is the worst possible thing because it is the one place in the world where, apart from wars and political abominations, the greatest number of individuals are killed and massacred. Its role in massacre must be minimised, and its role in communication increased.*

Decision-makers at every level must be aware of one thing: that they hold in their hands the most precious of goods, human life. If they really want to, in most countries they can avoid tens, hundreds, or thousands of deaths. There is probably no other area in which it is possible to save so many lives with so little will and money. Until they do everything in their powers to do so, they will be guilty and answerable to their fellow citizens, as are today's societies that so passively accept, with so few exceptions, the death and suffering of so many of their members.

For it is important to realise that even when he provokes an accident, a road user is above all a victim. Of course, he may be partly responsible. But, contrary to widespread public opinion, his responsibility is secondary to that of the public authorities who set the rules of the game and whose intervention can be seen at all levels. They are in charge of school education, driver training, most information campaigns, the content of the highway code, police controls, and sanctions. They are also responsible for road network planning and equipment and standards for vehicles. In fact, despite appearances, road users' behaviour largely depends on the actions undertaken by the authorities, as is shown by many examples of extremely rapid improvements in results obtained due to the implementation of effective policies.

The road user must in fact, to a great extent, be protected from himself. For, even if he makes a serious mistake, who would dare to say that it is punishable by the death penalty, or even worse, for him or for others?

References

[1] "For a European Road Safety Policy" (GERONDEAU Report), European Commission, Brussels, 1991.

[2] "Reducing the victims's number due to high and inadequate speed," European Transport Safety Council (ETSC), Brussels, 1995.

[3] Koornstra, M., "Annotated Review of Recent Day Running Lights (DRL); Results since 1991," SWOV Institute, Den Hagen, The Netherlands, 1995.

[4] Intersafe, "Technical Guide on Road Safety for Interurban Roads," European Road Safety Federation, Brussels, 1996.

[5] Union Routière de France & SOFRES & survey, Paris, 1993–1996.

[6] Gerondeau, C., *Road Safety in Australia*, Union Routière de France, Paris, 1992.

[7] "Road Safety for Central and Eastern Europe," *A Policy Seminar in Budapest World Bank*, Washington, DC, 1995.

[8] "European Drivers and Traffic Safety" (SARTRE Report), Presses de l'École Nationales des Ponts et Chaussées, Paris 1994.

CHAPTER 2
▼▼▼

THE FOUR COMPETITORS: A LONG HISTORY

2.1 THE FOUR TRANSPORT SUPPORTS

Four supports are used for most movements of people and goods, in Europe as elsewhere: water, rail, air, and road.

2.1.1 Water

The sea on the one hand, and rivers and streams on the other, have long played a fundamental role in transporting people and, even more so, merchandise. It is not by accident that almost all the large cities of Europe were founded either by the sea or along the banks of the great waterways.

From antiquity, vessels regularly crossed the Mediterranean, leading to the creation of the Greek and Roman empires. Everyone is aware of the importance of the development of a new type of boat in the Renaissance era, which made possible not only the discovery of new continents but also the rise of Northern Europe. Sea and waterways still play an essential role today in the transport of goods between Europe and the rest of the world, and they handle part of the traffic between European countries.

Beginning in the 17th century, natural waterways were added to by a network of canals linking the different basins of many rivers, and waterways were the principal means of inland transport for heavy goods in many countries until the mid 19th century.

2.1.2 Rail

The development of the steam engine by the Englishman Watt in 1769, followed by the invention of the railway, heralded the beginning of the Industrial Age in the western world.

The second half of the 19th century and the beginning of the 20th century saw the undisputed dominance of the railway. As of about 1830, at the expense of an industrial and financial achievement that still inspires admiration, hundreds of thousands of kilometres of railway lines were constructed throughout Europe in the space of a few decades, and tens of thousands of stations were built. The effort was unfortunately carried too far, since at the end of the 19th century and the beginning of the 20th century many countries created very costly secondary lines that were rapidly doomed due to insufficient traffic. But on the whole, the railway was a revolution. By drastically changing transport conditions as never before, it offered people and goods unprecedented mobility.

At the end of the 19th and the beginning of the 20th century, many European cities built electric trams to replace horse-drawn omnibuses. Certain cities, very few in number due to the heavy investments involved, constructed underground networks that proved to be remarkable means of mass transport to complement suburban railways.

But the invention of the internal combustion engine at the end of the 19th and the beginning of the 20th century allowed the almost simultaneous appearance of two means of transport that have completely changed the lives of our contemporaries, our geography, and the workings of our economies.

2.1.3 Air

The first aeroplane, invented by the Wright brothers, took to the air in 1903 in the United States; flights took place in Europe from 1906. Blériot crossed the English Channel in 1909 and progress then followed on progress at stunning speed. However, as far as civil aviation was concerned, it was only in the second half of the 20th century, following the invention of the jet engine and the turbopropulsor, that air transport began to really contribute to the satisfaction of the needs of modern economies and bring overwhelming changes in the conditions of medium- and long-distance exchanges.

2.1.4 Road

The motor car had preceded the aeroplane by only a few years, as the major technical innovations followed one another from 1880: The first car with a four-stroke engine was developed by the German Benz; the first pneumatic tyre by the Scotsman Dunlop in 1887; the removable tyre by the French Michelin Brothers in 1891; the diesel engine by Diesel in 1897; then the gearbox, the starter, and so forth, all of which inventions are still used in the vehicles of today. The first trucks appeared around 1900.

Cars and trucks came into general use much faster than the aeroplane. The first car races were held in France in 1894 and the Automobile Club of France was created in 1895, making it the oldest such club in the world. The passion for this new means of transport was exceptional from the start—especially in France, which alone numbered 300 cars in 1895, 3,000 in 1900, and over 100,000 in 1914!

It is therefore not surprising that between the two World Wars, cars and lorries occupied an important place in the European transport scene. However, in this case, too, it was not until the second half of the century that road transport acquired the status it holds today.

It was actually a question of rebirth after a very long absence. Everyone is aware of the role played by the road network that criss-crossed the Roman Empire and helped to maintain "Pax Romana" for several centuries. But the Middle Ages saw the disintegration of this network and, consequently, the development of insular local communities.

Road transport experienced a first revival in several European countries during the 17th, 18th, and first half of 19th centuries, but remained a tributary to the very limited means of transport available at the time: travel on foot, by horse, diligence and stagecoach for people or heavy carts for goods, so that the arrival of the railway relegated it to a secondary rank for more than a century.

Things changed completely with the arrival of the car and the truck. They revolutionised the world of transport with their flexibility, their speed, and their ability to transport from door to door and everywhere. As of the beginning of the 20th century, roads became the subject of renewed interest, as witnessed in most European countries by an effort to improve the network. But, apart from an initial expansion in Germany and Italy during the 1930s, it was not until the second half of the century that a specific structure adapted to motorised vehicles began to develop throughout Western Europe, with motorways and expressways, that would enable the extremely rapid development of the transport system that now meets most of the needs of Europeans and their economies.

It must be added that the road is used not only by cars and trucks, but also by two-wheeled motor vehicles and public transport by bus or coach. Finally, the list of means of transport would not be complete without mentioning two means that also use the road network but that, unlike the others, do not require a motor.

Walking, first of all, still represents a large percentage of peoples' movements, even if it is limited by its nature to short distances; and secondly, the bicycle, which represents an extension of walking, in that it enables the cyclist to travel three to four times faster without fatigue, if the terrain and weather are favourable.

2.2 THE PRESENT SITUATION

2.2.1 A Lightning Explosion

Never has there been such diversity in means of transport, and so it is therefore hardly surprising that Western Europeans' habits with respect to transport have changed in an unprecedented way during the half century since the end of the Second World War. Not very long ago, walking predominated, the bicycle occupied a modest place, and motorised transport was the exception. Everything has changed in the span of 50 years, as evidenced by the number of kilometres travelled each year by West Europeans in or on motorised vehicles (cars, motorcycles, public transport, aeroplanes, trains, etc.).Whereas in 1950 this figure was about 500 billion, it reached 2,000 billion in 1970 and 4,400 billion in 1992, according to statistics from the European Conference of Transport Ministers and aviation companies. Motorised transport has risen in four decades from a little over 1,300 km per year per inhabitant to about 11,500; that is, from an average of 4 km per day to more than 30!

However, this progression has not affected all means of motorised transport to the same extent; it particularly concerned road transport, especially by car. In 1993, distances covered by car accounted for 3,500 billion passenger kilometres, or 80% of the total motorised kilometres recorded in Western Europe, whereas those by bus accounted for 375 billion passenger kilometres (9% of the total); by rail transport for 275 billion passenger kilometres (6%); and by air for 235 billion passenger kilometres (5%), a level that was achieved due to the remarkable progress made in air travel over the last two decades, which is still continuing at a very fast pace.

As we will see below, road transport surpasses its competitors to an even greater extent with respect to freight.

2.2.2 The First Economic Activity

Overall, from an economic point of view, transport represents a considerable part of the activity of Western European countries, as is the case in all developed countries. Curiously, its importance is not visible in the official statistics. Those published by Eurostat, for example, indicate [1] that transport accounts for approximately 5% of gross domestic product (GDP) and 5.6% of jobs in the European Union. But this is a very narrow definition that includes only transport companies in the strict sense of the term, excluding numerous other sectors linked to the transport system, such as the automobile industry, its suppliers, garages, the road construction industry, the oil industry, and many others.

To appreciate the true importance of the "transport function" within the European economy, another method must be used. It is necessary to measure the amount of money that individuals and companies spend to meet their needs in this sector, whether it be for transport of people or of merchandise. The calculations available for certain countries then give a very different picture of the importance of transport within the economy.

For instance, in France, expenditure linked to the road—acquisition and running costs of vehicles, salaries, public sector spending, and so forth—totalled 1,054 billion francs in 1993, after adjustments for double counting, or 14.5% of GDP [2]. By adding the turnover figures of railways (between 40 and 50 billion francs), that of internal air transport (about 15 billion francs), and that of urban transport (almost 20 billion), it appears that the total amount spent on internal transport is of the order of 1,150 billion francs, or approximately 16% of GDP. If international transport is taken into account, the percentage exceeds 17%. According to certain experts, it may even approach or exceed 20% if the sectors grouped under the term "logistics" are added to the basic transport activities. This estimate is confirmed by the fact that in 1994, French households devoted 16.4% of their budgets to transport, as opposed to 17.7% in 1980.

The same system of calculation would without a doubt produce very similar results if applied to other Western European countries, due to the great similarities in their respective economies. American statistics on transport indicate that in 1994, transport accounted for 16.9% of the gross national product (GNP) [3], a figure which is practically identical to that of France, and also that of Canada, which amounts to 16% [4]. These percentages vary very little from one year to the next.

For lack of precise documents, it is therefore possible to adopt the same percentages and estimate that in Western Europe, with its 380 million inhabitants and its 17 different countries, transport currently has a volume of activity close to 1,000 billion ECUs, of which around 900 are for road transport, out of a GDP amounting to approximately 6,000 billion. With respect to employment, estimates converge at fixing the number of jobs linked to transport at around 12%, or an estimate of about 18 million jobs for the western part of the Continent.

These figures are therefore very different from those given in official documents. But, as it will be shown in numerous cases throughout this book, in the transport sector the most relevant statistics are rarely cited and those that are published often give a picture that is very far from reality.

It remains to be seen why this lightning expansion in transport has taken place, and especially why the car on the one hand, and road transport of goods on the other, have come to occupy such important roles (on the understanding that this book deals mainly with Western Europe and not Central and Eastern Europe countries, although everything seems to indicate that the latter will experience, at different intervals of time, a similar pattern of change).

References

[1] "Europe in Figures," Eurostat, European Communities Publishing office, Luxembourg, 1995.
[2] "Les comptes des transports 1993," INSEE-OEST, Paris, 1994.
[3] "Transportation in America 1995," ENO Transportation Foundation, Lansdowne, VA, 1995.
[4] Royal Commission on Passengers' Transport, Final Report, Ottawa, 1992.

CHAPTER 3
▼▼▼

FREIGHT TRANSPORT: KILOGRAMS OF FEATHERS AND KILOGRAMS OF LEAD

3.1 MEANINGLESS UNITS OF MEASURE

Treating the subject of freight transport in Europe poses a curious and unexpected problem: Official statistics give a picture that has nothing to do with reality.

To measure the different means of freight transport and compare them, the only units used by all institutions that deal with the subject in Europe are "tonne kilometres", obtained by multiplying the number of tonnes transported by the distance travelled. The problem is that when it comes to comparing means of transport that are not the same in terms of transport modes used and types of product transported, the tonne kilometre is meaningless in both economic and physical terms. To be of economic significance, it should be in relation with the value of the service rendered, which means, in most cases, the invoice to the client. To be of physical significance, it should have some meaning regarding the occupancy of the transport networks.

3.1.1 The Absence of Economic Significance

There can be hardly any doubt that tonne kilometres have no economic meaning. The cost of forwarding a load of 25 tonnes by one heavy truck over a distance of

1,000 km can obviously not be compared with forwarding 1,000 loads of 250 kilos using 1,000 light trucks over a distance of 100 km. And yet, in tonne kilometres they are equal, although invoicing to the client may vary from 1 to 50 or more.

This applies all the more so when a shipment of a 30-kilo package by aeroplane over a distance of 2,000 km, to be invoiced 100 ECUs, is compared to the shipment of a tonne of ore over a distance of 60 km by barge, which will cost one ECU. Yet, in this case too, they are equal in terms of tonne kilometres.

To quote the French National Institute of Statistics and Economic Studies (*Institut National des Statistiques et Études Économiques*, or INSEE): "For 50 Francs (about eight ECUs), it is possible to import one ton of crude oil from Mexico by boat or three kilos of strawberries by plane. In other words, the economic value of the tonne kilometre varies, in this case, from 1 to 333" [1].

It is therefore obvious that reference to the tonne kilometre gives no indication of what really counts in economic terms; that is, the value of services rendered to the community. These can only be evaluated in monetary units, and it is therefore necessary to consider the amounts paid for the different means of transport by companies and citizens to satisfy their freight transport needs in order to appreciate their respective roles in the economy. These amounts can either be paid to a third party or spent internally for those owning their own vehicles. However, these amounts, which can be called the "sales," "revenues," or "turnover" of the different means of transport, and which bear no relation overall to the weight of the freight transported, are generally not shown in any European official statistics.

What would people say if the tonne was used in the chemical industry to compare the production of Chanel N° 5 with the production of motor oil? What would people say if the tonne was also used in the textile industry to compare the women's lingerie sector and that of carpet manufacturing? Such practice would seem ridiculous, and in each of these two fields, units of weight were abandoned decades ago. The different activities are compared by their turnover figures, as in every other sector except transport where, by using the tonne kilometre, they continue to compare chalk and cheese, as the saying goes. It is hardly surprising in such conditions that available statistics give an idea of the respective importance of the different means of transport that bears no relation to their economic weight.

Excluding transport of petrol by pipeline, the official statistics indicate for 1993, according to the European Conference of Ministers of Transport (ECMT), which is the authority on the subject, the split in freight transport between the three principal means of transport that share the West European market (17 countries) [2] shown in Table 3.1.

If the figures in Table 3.1 are to be believed, three-quarters of freight transport in Europe takes place by road, and the railway and the waterways share the remaining quarter. Air transport is not even mentioned because, in tonne kilometres, it is obviously insignificant.

Table 3.1
Freight Transport Modal Split in Western Europe
According to Tonne Kilomètres

Means of Transport	Tonne Kilometres (billions)
Rail	215 (17%)
Road (heavy trucks)	983 (75%)
Waterways	100 (8%)
Total	1,298 (100%)

On the other hand, no overall statistics are published on the turnover of the different means of freight transport; that is, their true role within the continent's economy. It must be pointed out that such fundamental data is equally absent from most national statistics, and it would therefore be difficult for the European Conference of Ministers of Transport or for the statistics departments of the European Union to calculate figures on a European level. But it is nonetheless possible to evaluate the turnover figures without great risk of error by using the experience of the countries where such data is known.

This is the case in France, where the share of the different means of freight transport were as shown in Table 3.2 in 1993, according to whether they are expressed in tonne kilometres or in Francs.

Table 3.2
Freight Transport Modal Split in France According to Tonne Kilomètres and Turnover

Means of Transport	Tonne Kilometres (billions)	Turnover (billions of francs)
Rail	43.6 (22.4%)	15.3 (4.5%) *
Road (heavy and light trucks)	144.9 (74.5%)	326 (95.3%) **
Waterways	6 (3.1%)	0.7 (0.2%)

Source: French National Institute of Statistics and Economic Studies (INSEE)—Transport Accounts 1993 & International Union of Railways (UIC).
*Including private fleets.
**Broken down as follows: 137 billion for transport by heavy truck by specialised companies (for another party), 65 by heavy truck for own account, and 124 for transport by light truck.

In other words, the economic weight of the three means of land transport has no relation whatsoever with the results given using tonne kilometres. Railways do not account for 22.4% of freight transport in France, but 4.5%, and road transport accounts for 95.3%, not 74.5%!

This is due to the fact that the revenue obtained by transporting one ton for a distance of 1 km using the road is, on average, 2.2 francs, whereas it is 0.35 francs by rail (or six times less) and 0.12 francs by waterway (or 18 times less). This is not at all surprising. Road transport deals with all kinds of products, often in small quantities and over very short distances, whereas railways and, to an even greater extent, waterways have a predilection to transport heavy products, in large quantities over long distances. It is logical that the economic value of a tonne kilometre should be, on average, very different in the three cases.

The situation in France is no different from that of other countries, as can be seen for example by a study of the U.S. statistics for year 1990 shown in Table 3.3.

Table 3.3
Freight Transport Modal Split in the United States According to Ton Miles and Turnover

Means of Transport	Ton Miles (billions)	Turnover (billions of $)
Railway	1,033 (41.2%)	27.4 (8.8%)
Roads	1,127 (44.9%)	272.4 (88.6%)
Waterways	340 (13.5%)	2.7 (0.9%)
Air	10 (0.4%)	5.4 (1.7%)

Source: National Transportation Statistics, U.S. Department of Transportation, 1992 Annual Report

The general orientation of these figures is no different from those of France: in the United States, the value of a ton mile by road is, on average, nine times that of a ton-mile by rail, and thirty times that of a ton mile by waterway. It is particularly interesting to note, *a contrario*, that the value of a ton mile by air is, as could be expected, the highest of all, on average 2.5 times higher than that of a ton mile by road.

In Italy, the Turin Conference for Transports (CONFETRA) calculated that the amount spent on freight transport was 1,300 billion lire in 1991 for the railway and 161,200 billion for the road, or 0.8% and 99.2%, respectively. That same year, the European Conference of Ministers of Transport indicated that freight transport in Italy amounted to 21.9 billion tonne kilometres for the railway and 182.8 for the road, or 10.7% and 89.3%, respectively.

The French, Italian and U.S. statistics therefore show very similar patterns due to the fact that on both sides of the Atlantic road transport is the leading mode, and that within this sector there is a large spread in costs depending on the nature of the transport (quantity, distance, etc.). On the other hand, the tariffs for transport by rail and waterway are, by nature, more or less aligned with those for long-distance, large-quantity road transport, for which the tonne kilometre prices are the lowest.

Using the French and American figures and data available for each means of transport, it is possible to reconstruct the true economic picture of freight transport in Western Europe, given by their turnover, which is approximately that given in

Table 3.4, excluding transport by pipeline. Of course, only gathering the real data for each country would reveal the exact values, but the general lines can be guaranteed. They are far removed from the figures obtained using "tonne kilometres."

Table 3.4
The True Freight Transport Modal Split in Western Europe

Means of Transport	Turnover
Railways	9 billion ECUs (2.5%)
Road (heavy and light trucks)	350 billion ECUs (96.6%)
Waterways	2 billion ECUs (0.6%)
Air transport	1 billion ECUs (0.3%)
Total	362 billion ECUs (100%)

In other words, there is no sharing of freight transport in Europe among the different means of transport, as official statistics try to show, but a near monopoly of one of them—road transport—with the others only playing a very limited role! If proof is needed, a perfect example was the French strike that paralysed the railways at the end of 1995 with no particular repercussions on industry, a striking display of the near monopoly of road transport. The situation had been very different in 1996 and 1997, when truck drivers blocked the roads in France and Spain. The issue is not to find out whether "all-road" is acceptable or not, but to take note that in practice it already exists, that it is irreversible, and draw conclusions from this. Road transport makes the European economy work and this one relies on road transport even more than the American economy! Such an observation is bound to be a surprise to many, because it is contrary to what is stated by official bodies dealing with the subject and by the media, which have no choice but to be their echo.

3.1.2 The Absence of Physical Significance

The above revelation is all the more surprising because the situation gets even worse if one takes into consideration not the economic aspect of the issue, but the physical side of freight transport. For, if tonne kilometres make no economic sense when comparing the different modes of transport, they make no physical sense, either. Even if the economic aspect is essential, it is not the only one to consider. The physical presence of each mode is also important because it is an indicator of network occupancy, which commands what dimensions the infrastructure should have. One simple question needs to be answered in order to measure the physical impact of transport: Should volume or weight be taken into account?

Asking the question almost gives the answer. It is obviously volume that is the proper criterion and not weight. An empty heavy truck takes up as much space as one transporting 25 tons. Weight has nothing to do with the matter. It must be added that, as far as the volume is concerned, it is not the transported product that should be taken into account but the transporting vehicle. In other words, to account for the physical aspect of transport, calculations should be made in "vehicle kilometres." But vehicle kilometres have, more often than not, nothing in common with tonne kilometres. In certain cases, a few vehicles transport many tonnes and in others the opposite is true. The space taken up by a heavy truck transporting 25 tonnes can obviously not be compared with that of a hundred light trucks transporting 250 kilograms each.

It will come as no surprise that the use of vehicle kilometres, the only units of measure that are capable of properly taking into account the physical aspect of transport, also gives results that cannot be compared with those obtained using tonne kilometres. Only a few figures are necessary to demonstrate this point and they almost speak for themselves.

According to the OECD [3], all types of road vehicles with more than two wheels travelled approximately 2,950 billion kilometres in 1993 on the roads of Western Europe, split as follows: private cars, 2,500 billion (85%); light goods vehicles with a capacity of less than 3.5 tonnes, 295 billion (10%); heavy goods vehicles, 155 billion (5%). When considering questions of road network congestion, all the categories of vehicles using the network must be considered, as there is currently no road system reserved only for heavy goods vehicles in Europe. This is an important point to stress. The aim of many official policies in Europe is to alleviate road traffic—all of it—by acting on truck traffic. That is why it is justified to put side by side the figures relating to rail freight wagons traffic with those regarding the *whole* of road traffic and not only the truck traffic, which would be inappropriate.

According to the International Union of Railways (UIC), rail freight wagons covered 14 billion km on all Western European railways in 1993 [4], or *210 times fewer kilometres* than those travelled by all road vehicles on road networks [5]. Of course, the vehicles in question are not all the same. On the road, a coefficient of two to one is often given to heavy goods vehicles compared with private cars and light trucks, even if in most cases this is not necessarily justified as it is not the length of the vehicles that is most important, but the distance that separates them. As far as rail wagons are concerned, they are equivalent in Europe to heavy trucks because they transport, on average—empty travel included—about the same load weight (13 to 14 tonnes).

The conclusion is therefore clear: The figures for road traffic and rail freight traffic have nothing in common. Generally speaking, rail freight traffic hardly alleviates road traffic at all. Given that a rail wagon is equivalent to a heavy truck, and that a heavy truck equals two "private car units," the rail freight traffic does not represent 1% of total European road traffic. Even if rail freight traffic doubled—a theoretical case, as it is constantly decreasing in most European countries—the overall impact would be negligible.

This conclusion is all the more valid for combined transport, which makes up only a fraction of rail freight traffic, although it is often presented as a panacea to alleviate road traffic—even though the figures speak for themselves. The companies belonging to the International Union of Combined Rail-Road Transport Companies dispatched 1,300,000 containers or trailers in 1993, for an average distance of 830 km. They therefore relieved road traffic of about one billion "heavy truck kilometres." Even taking into account companies that do not belong to this union, it shows that combined transport did not on average relieve European road traffic by more than one-thousandth! All the efforts that can be made at great and worthless cost to promote it will have no perceptible influence on road traffic.

The same approach holds for waterways. It can be accepted that very compact materials usually transported by waterway could in general be transported by heavy trucks loaded with at least 20 tonnes each. The total waterway traffic in Western Europe, equivalent to about 100 billion tonne kilometres, thus equals 5 billion heavy truck kilometres, or, using the same units of measure (one heavy truck = 2 private car units), 0.3% of total European road traffic.

Of course, these figures are averages. On some routes, the physical share of the railway or the waterway can be higher, and specific studies are necessary. But, as will be shown in some later examples, the major railway or waterway routes usually coincide with the busiest corridors in terms of road traffic, such that the railway or the waterway can almost always only take a very small burden off the road. The lower Rhine Valley, where the great majority of European river traffic is concentrated, is a remarkable—and unique—exception.

The Kilo of Feathers and the Kilo of Lead Syndrome

Surprising as it may seem, this conclusion is logical. A train or barge loaded with a thousand tons of ore looks impressive and everyone automatically thinks as they watch it go by that it is fortunate that such loads are not transported by road. In fact, a thousand tons of ore is equal to the load of forty heavy trucks loaded with 25 tonnes each. European motorways count tens of thousands of vehicles per day: 40 trucks more or 40 less will go unnoticed. Except in a few places, the complete elimination of rail or river freight transport would have no marked effect on road traffic!

It must be said that instinct is particularly deceptive, because it makes people think that waterways and railways greatly alleviate road traffic because they allow heavy *and* cumbersome products to be transported. But heavy products are *not* cumbersome! It is obviously light products that are cumbersome, and they are transported almost exclusively by road. It is the old story of the kilo of feathers and the kilo of lead. *By nature, waterways and railways, contrary to what people are almost inevitably inclined to think, transport heavy products, which are therefore not cumbersome, and can thus hardly alleviate road traffic.* As surprising as this may seem, transport policy in Europe is a victim of the kilo of feathers and kilo of lead syndrome. The author himself was long a victim of it in the past and has never met anyone, even among transport specialists, who is not or has never been its victim.

3.1.3 The Consequences of Using Meaningless Units of Measure

The physical approach thus corroborates and accentuates the economic approach. Railways and waterways now play only a marginal role in freight transport in Europe. Their respective weights are 2.5% and 0.6% from the economic point of view, and even less from the point of view of their average physical presence in the transport networks. This is obviously far removed from the official statistics which, due to the use of tonne kilometres, attribute the railway a weight of 17% and the waterway 8% in Western Europe, leaving governments and international authorities with the idea that there is still hope of "balancing" traffic among the different means of transport to alleviate roads.

It is thus on the basis of meaningless statistics that practically all European governments and international authorities are led to make decisions that have heavy consequences in terms of granting of credits or of taxation. In fact, the delusion that it is possible to relieve the road network by developing the other means of transport is, in 1996, at the root of nearly all European transport policies.

For instance, the Ministers of Transport from the 33 countries participating in the European Conference of Ministers of Transport held in Budapest in May 1996 approved the following points [6]:

- The considerable development in road transport to the detriment of other means of transport must be denounced.
- the development of road transport alone will inevitably lead to an impasse.
- The risks of the transport system coming to a complete standstill are such that political decisions are needed rapidly to control traffic.
- More emphasis must be given to transport by rail, waterway, and combined transport . . . by allocating substantial investments to them.
- Taxes must be introduced for those using infrastructures, particularly roads, in order to create fair competitive conditions.

This summit meeting did nothing more, in fact, than repeat the official European doctrine, which simply ignores the true facts as road transport already has a near monopoly. This is a fact and there is nothing that can be done about it, and there is no hope that the hypothetical development of other means of transport can relieve road traffic in any significant way at all, however much money is spent on this or whatever taxes are introduced.

The same doctrine guided the European Commission in March 1996 when it proposed that the amount of the tax disc (Eurovignette) required by heavy goods vehicles in several European countries should be considerably increased "to encourage transfers to rail transport."

Once again, it inspires the British White Paper "Transport: the Way Forward" [5], which proposes the objective of "reducing the transport of goods by road, by encouraging the use of railways and waterways."

Many more examples of this could be given. But the consequences of this illusory doctrine, which is almost universally accepted throughout Europe, are not limited to the taxation of road transport. They also apply to decisions on investments.

It is in this context that the German government launched a vast and very costly programme allocating in 1992, for the first time, more investment in favour of the railways than the roads, aimed at developing freight transport by rail by increasing its activity by half, to increase its share from 17 to 25% in an attempt to relieve road traffic. But these percentages refer to tonne kilometres, such that even if the objective were met, it is not difficult to predict its real impact on road traffic: it would be practically nil. This would have been obvious with the use of pertinent units of measure—vehicle kilometres—which would have shown that the true position of railway freight transport had become marginal in Germany as in the rest of Europe, and that there was no hope that this could be otherwise because journeys made by rail freight wagons are roughly equivalent to 1% of total road traffic and, if they increased by half, their effect on the road would still be imperceptible. Rail wagons covered 4.5 billion kilometres in Germany in 1993, whereas road traffic officially totalled 560 billion kilometres, of which 494 billion was by cars and light commercial vehicles, and 55 billion was by heavy trucks and trailers. It is very unlikely that the decisions made, concerning tens of billions of marks, would have been the same if these figures had been brought face to face. Allocating more money to the means of transport that represents so small a part of the traffic than to the one that is bearing nearly all the traffic is just senseless. Nevertheless, in this country as in others, the idea of increasing taxes on heavy goods vehicles to reduce road traffic endlessly keeps reappearing. In May 1996, the German Minister of Transport recommended raising the annual motorway fee (Eurovignette) for heavy goods vehicles from 2,450 to 5,000 marks as of the year 2000 "*in order to favour a transfer from the road towards the rail and the waterways.*"

In France, the breakdown of distances travelled by the different categories of vehicles was the following in 1993: 360 billion km travelled by private cars, 75 by light trucks, 23 by heavy trucks, and . . . 2.5 by rail freight wagons. For the United Kingdom, the figures are 352 billion km by private cars, 39 by light vans, and less than one by rail freight wagons.

Give me good statistics and I will give you a good policy, one might be tempted to say. The use of tonne kilometres should be systematically banned because it is deceptive and gives a false view of the situation. If, for example, the tonne kilometre is used as a reference, road transport appears to consume far more energy than rail transport. But if turnover is used as it should be (as it is the only figure that properly measures the service rendered), this is not at all the case, and it no longer supports the statement that the road is less "environment-friendly" from this point of view.

More specifically, in France, road transport consumes 14.5 billion tons of petroleum products and rail transport consumes the equivalent of 0.8 billion tons. If the consumptions are compared to the tonne kilometres provided by both means of transport, which are, respectively, 144.9 billion for road transport and 43.6 for rail, it shows that road transport requires 100 grams of petrol per tonne kilometre, while rail transport requires 18 grams (i.e., 5.5 times less).

But if the consumption, as it should be, is compared not to meaningless tonne kilometres but to turnover (i.e., the value of the service rendered to the community), the result is quite different. As has been seen, road transport turnover in France totals 326 billion francs and that of rail transport totals 15.3, which shows that the former consumes 44 grams of petrol per turnover Franc and the latter the equivalent of 48.4!

The Last of the Gosplan-Type Units

The treatment of freight transport statistics is actually quite simple. When dealing with economic weight, monetary units must be used. When studying the congestion of transport networks, vehicle kilometres should be used. Generally speaking, the Americans use these methods, although not exclusively. In both cases, the use of tonne kilometres is simply absurd. Tonne kilometres are the last remaining "Gosplan"-type units employed by the Western world. The results of the use of this type of unit on which the Soviet world based its accounting are known to all. When "Perestroika" broke down economic borders, the facts had to be faced: production counted in tonnes was considerable but, in market value, it represented almost nothing. Tonne kilometres, Gosplan units *par excellence*, lead Western European countries towards costly and erroneous decisions in the same way.

Finally, it must be added that in order to compare different types of freight transport, only the two units mentioned above can be used. There is, of course, an instinctive inclination to look for another unit of measure that could cover all transport operations, replacing the current tonne kilometre. But to do this is to fall victim of the belief that a transport operation is simply a matter of transporting an object from one place to another. In fact, many other parameters are involved: transport time, the physical constraints of the transported product, delivery requirements, logistics, and so forth. There is no more in common between the transport of a small box of fruit in a refrigerated heavy truck with a delivery time of a few hours and that of a bulk load of coal by barge with a delivery time of several weeks, than between the manufacture of a silk tie and an ingot of steel. And no one would think of looking for any common denominator other than their monetary value to compare silk ties and ingots of steel . . .

Tonne kilometres should therefore be given up completely. Admittedly, it could be argued that they remain valid for comparing similar transport processes: for example, the transport of ores over long distances. But if this method is used, it is impossible to avoid the fact that one day people will add or compare the figures obtained with others that concern transport processes with completely different characteristics and economic value. How is it possible to explain that it is mistaken and nonsensical to add or compare quantities that are expressed in what appear to be the same units, but are in fact not at all the same, as they have nothing in common but the name?

Tonne kilometres—and ton miles—must be systematically discarded and should no longer be used in any meaningful statistics (see Appendix A).

3.2 THE CAUSES FOR ROAD TRANSPORT SUCCESS

3.2.1 A Recent Change

Allowing for exceptions, the road now has a near monopoly in Europe for the transport of freight. This was not always the case.

Between the two World Wars, the railway still played a predominant role. Less than 40 years ago, the statistics indicated that—at least in tonne kilometres, the only available units—it was responsible for most freight transport in post-war Europe. According to the statistics of the European Conference of Ministers of Transport, rail freight traffic amounted to approximately 200 billion tonne kilometres in 1960. It rose to 248 in 1970, decreased to 238 in 1980, to 230 in 1992, and to 204 in 1993; this last year being characterised by a sharp drop due to the recession. It must be pointed out that the "border effect," which will be described in Chapter 6, deprives the railways in Europe of most of their market, which is that of long-distance transport. The total change over 33 years, expressed in tonne kilometres, was therefore practically nil.

And this result was only attained at the price of considerable subsidies, exceeding on average 50% of costs, or 100% of client invoicing, which would be unthinkable in any other sector of economic activity. In the absence of subsidies, rail transport of freight would have practically disappeared. Railway freight turnover was indeed halved in most Western European countries between 1980 and 1993 due to a decrease in the average unit revenue.

Road traffic, on the other hand, has continued its lightning growth: 160 billion tonne kilometres in 1960, 410 in 1970, 640 in 1980, 953 in 1992, and almost the same figure in 1993 despite the recession.

In 33 years, road freight transport in tonne kilometres was multiplied by nearly six, and over the past 20 years its average growth rate has been 3.7% per year, or one percentage point above the annual economic growth rate. In addition, tonne kilometres are known to reflect reality very badly.

For each European, an average of 25 tonnes are now transported per year by road over a distance of 100 km and it should be recalled that the road tonne kilometre is on average nine times higher in economic value than the rail tonne kilometre. And yet, contrary to what is often said, road traffic has not received any significant subsidies in comparison with its turnover during this period.

How did road transport come to occupy such an overwhelming position so quickly after more than a century of domination of the railroad and, to a lesser extent, the waterway? The answer hinges on both supply and demand.

3.2.2 Changes in Supply

The supply of freight transport has undergone a veritable revolution due to considerable progress in road transport vehicles and the creation of the motorway network, which now criss-crosses practically all of Europe.

Four or five decades ago, heavy trucks were quite different from the vehicles that travel on our roads and motorways today. Without going back so far, progress has been considerable. The "modern" heavy truck in 1971 had a load potential of 18 tonnes, compared with 25 tonnes (+38%) for its successor in 1992, and even more in some countries. At the same time, the vehicles' engine power has made such progress that for a given journey (in France, Paris-Lyon by road), experiences have shown that the average speed has increased by 40% between these two dates, all else being equal, due to improvements in engine acceleration that help the vehicle to merge more easily into moving traffic.

On motorways, average speed has increased by 21% while consumption has decreased by 32%. The "performance coefficient," integrating all these elements, has consequently multiplied by 2.5 in 21 years! It is therefore not surprising that the cost price of road transport has constantly decreased, despite increasing fuel taxes that have generally been higher than rises in the cost of living.

While cost prices have decreased, reliability, on the other hand, has constantly been improved. The frequency of flat tyres, breakdowns, and accidents, which were once the rule, has dropped sharply, and this trend can only be pursued with continuing technical progress, whether it be for tyres or the vehicles themselves.

New developments in the road network have also played an essential role. National and local roads, with their countless town and village crossings have been added to by an extraordinary web of motorways and expressways that enable vehicles to get from almost every point in West Europe to another in conditions of speed and reliability that nobody would have dared to imagine only 30 years ago. Less than 24 hours are needed to get from Spain to the Netherlands, from Denmark to Italy, or from Germany to Portugal, and, contrary to what might be thought, usually with no incertitude as to travelling and arrival times.

3.2.3 Changes in Demand

It is not only supply that has been transformed. Demand, affected by the new possibilities offered, has also undergone a veritable revolution both in its geography and in its content.

No industrial manager of any importance would have considered, just a short time ago, establishing a factory anywhere but along a railway line. Since the railway provided most freight transport, managers would have been rapidly doomed had they done otherwise.

Times have changed. Since the truck is now the dominant, almost exclusive, means of transport for the majority of activities, businesses are usually practically free to choose their location, whether it be for units of production, processing, or distribution. The road and the truck have therefore proved to be remarkable tools for regional development since they avoid the concentration of activities at a limited number of points along railway lines or waterways. Of course, such units located away from railways or waterways can then use only the road, at the very least to carry freight to the station or the port but, most often, for all their transport movements up to their final destination. The geography of transport demand has therefore been subject to overwhelming change.

Its content has changed just as much. By nature, modes of heavy transport— railways or waterways—are suitable for shipments of large masses for which delivery dates are not too tight, since these two means of transport have specific restrictions: the intrinsic slowness of the waterway, and the manoeuvres and shunting operations for the railway. Road transport has none of these restrictions. Quantities can be adapted to needs and can vary from a few kilos to several tons per vehicle, and can be unlimited by multiplying the number of heavy trucks. Capable of transporting kilos of feathers, heavy trucks can as easily carry kilos of lead. Journey times are reduced to a strict minimum since road transport can go from the point of departure to the point of arrival without unloading and reloading. This is the same as the fundamental advantage of the car for transporting people : the ability to transport from door to door.

Industrialists and the other clients of the road freight transport companies have taken advantage of the new possibilities offered to them, which has resulted not only in changes to their transport means but also in the introduction of new procedures in manufacturing and product delivery. These processes, which have developed rapidly only in the last 10 years, are known as *just-in-time* practices.

This term covers the fact that an industry, a business, or any other activity reduces its stock of spare parts or products to a very low level, on the understanding that suppliers are able to respond to orders in an extremely short time, which generally does not exceed one or two days and can even be limited to a few hours. Of course, suppliers who accept this part must in turn be organised to be able to manufacture or obtain the ordered products on very short notice and deliver them on time.

In fact, it is the whole process of manufacture and delivery that is revolutionised, thanks on the one hand to computers and on the other to road transport, with information highways becoming allies in this case to the transport highways. For example, a supermarket can fix a lead time of six hours between placing an order for the products it needs and their delivery, the orders being transmitted automatically as and when the shelves need to be replenished, with this being monitored in real time by sales analysis. In another example, a car manufacturer can do away with his stock of spare parts almost entirely, thanks to an undertaking from subcontractors to deliver them to him at the same short notice. In fact, the whole of Europe has become one gigantic factory due to road transport, to which its dimensions are perfectly fitted. Regarding freight, these dimensions are most of the time too short to require air transport, as well as rail transport.

If such procedures have become so popular so quickly in all sectors of industry and distribution, giving birth to a phenomenal development of logistics techniques (invoicing, computer processing, labelling, packaging, product finishing, etc.), it is obvious that they provide considerable savings for those who use them. Reducing or eliminating stock, which can often be extremely voluminous, not only leads to a decrease in the corresponding financial costs but also saves money on handling, reduces space occupied, and avoids loss and damage inherent to all stocking.

It has sometimes been suggested that the just-in-time system increases road transport volume by multiplying "stock on wheels." In fact, this is not easy to prove. Sooner or later, the products in question would have had to be transported from the supplier's factory to their final destination. The fact that the transport takes place at the last minute changes nothing. It has even been noted that in many cases, the just-in-time system has encouraged suppliers to relocate as close as possible to their clients in order to respond to their demands better, thus decreasing the kilometres to be covered. Admittedly, this practice may also lead to the decrease in certain unit load volumes, but statistics available in France do not show a decrease in the average heavy truck load in recent years.

In any case, if this practice has become so popular in such a short time, it is because it serves the interests of producers and consumers and, hence, of the community as a whole, through the decrease in cost prices that it entails. To say, as is sometimes heard, that the firms that use these techniques are acting in an antieconomic manner and are poorly managed is rather surprising, as it would mean that a few external "experts" are better qualified to know what is to be done than the tens of thousands of company managers who actually have the responsibility.

It must be added that, curiously, the increase in such methods makes industrial conflict more and more difficult. Strikes can now have very serious repercussions, not only on the company concerned, but also on its suppliers and its clients, and being aware of the seriousness of the consequences is therefore a great stimulus to the search for negotiated solutions.

3.2.4 Fierce Competition

Finally, there is another reason for the past, current, and future success of road transport. Road transport is not made up in each country of a single company with a monopoly, but rather of thousands or tens of thousands of entrepreneurs faced with fierce competition and obliged to be extremely competitive as they cannot depend on any subsidies whatsoever. Although this is not the principal cause of road transport's success, which is primarily due to its inherent characteristics, it is obvious that the very structure of this sector of activity has contributed to its success, opposite monopolies that did not have the same stimulus.

Fierce competition contributes to road transport efficiency, but it also has its negative side. It can tempt some companies to infringe upon regulations, such as the maximum duration of the working day or week, speed limits, maximum loads, and so forth. Such cases obviously have very serious consequences, especially as far as road safety is concerned. In response, the European Union, the national governments, and also a large number of transport companies are introducing a growing number of policies to combat this kind of behaviour. From now on, European heavy goods vehicles must not only be equipped with instruments (chronotachygraphs) that record all the driving parameters to check *a posteriori* whether regulations have been respected, but also with automatic speed-limiting instruments, making it physically impossible to exceed the authorised maximum limit.

In France, after almost two years of negotiations, a wide-reaching "progress pact" was concluded at the beginning of 1995, between the government, transport companies, and the trade unions. It stipulates that sanctions will be considerably heavier, including the possibility of imprisonment, both for company owners who tamper with chronotachygraphs or speed limiters, as well as more generally for customers who, by their orders, impose such constraints on the heavy truck drivers that they force them to break the rules. At the same time, training and reorientation of drivers has been substantially reinforced. The rules on driving times, on the time needed for other work, and on rest time have also been modified, bringing the maximum work time down to 240 hours per month in the first phase, with the aim of 200 hours in 1999, subject to European harmonisation. Finally, access to the road freight transport profession has been made more difficult.

This collective move should lead to a progressive and marked improvement in safety. Even if enforcement of such rules is obviously difficult, it is to be hoped that they will be adopted by the European countries that have not yet done so in order that those who set themselves restrictions of this nature do not have to face unfair competition from those who do not attach the same importance to safety. For this policy does, of course, have the effect of increasing costs that cannot, at least in the short term, be entirely compensated for by productivity gains that continue anyway year after year. It must be said, however, that all the corresponding possibilities have not yet been exploited in Western Europe. For example, the increase in the maximum authorised weight from 40 to 44 tonnes in countries that currently authorise only the former weight, would result in productivity gains of 10% for the vehicles concerned and 5% for heavy goods vehicles overall, and would probably favour road safety by decreasing the number of vehicles necessary to satisfy transport needs.

Whatever the case may be, road transport is one of the most dynamic sectors of the European economy. It enables it to function and makes a very large contribution to the quality of life of our fellow citizens. Road transport companies were initially composed only of very small units, but in recent years certain much larger entities have emerged that are conscious of their responsibilities, are in the forefront of technical progress, and will be major players in the continent's economy, with their word to say in the decades to come.

But the success of road transport often arouses criticism that requires analysis.

3.3 FREIGHT ROAD TRANSPORT EXTERNALITIES

3.3.1 Do Heavy Goods Vehicles Pay Their True Cost?

One largely held opinion is that road freight transport does not pay its "true cost," first of all because it is said to cost public authorities more than the taxes that it pays them and, secondly, that it does not pay the "external costs" that can be attributed to it, linked to congestion of the road network, emission of pollutants, and the accidents in which it is involved.

The hypothesis that heavy goods vehicles do not pay their true cost is one of the bases of European transport policy and that of the majority of countries in the European Union. As will be seen later, it is particularly one of the justifications for the considerable financial aid granted to railways, which are considered to be victims of "unfair" competition from road freight transport. The fact that the latter does not have to pay the total costs that it generates is cited as one of the primary causes of the supposed imbalance and inefficiencies of the European transport system.

So, do heavy goods vehicles pay their true cost? To answer this question, it is important to distinguish between a strictly financial approach and one that takes into consideration not only the financial aspect but also the "externalities" of transport.

It must also be pointed out that a number of definitions exist for the concept of externalities. For some, it only includes the effects on the community brought on by vehicle traffic: noise, accidents, pollution, and so forth. According to this most frequently used definition, "externalities" are almost always negative. For others, not only vehicles must be taken into consideration, but also the transport system as a whole, made up of the road network and the vehicles that drive on it. In addition to the negative externalities, other eminently positive ones then also exist : an increase in available space, improved regional planning and development, better quality of life, increased economic efficiency, and so forth. Finally, it is also interesting to wonder whether the transfers of financial resources between transport networks and the community, in the form of taxes (for the road) or subsidies (for the railways), are not in fact "externalities," even if by tradition economists do not see them as such.

3.3.2 The Financial Aspect

The financial aspect appears to be the easiest to define. It is "just" a matter of comparing the amounts paid by road transport to public authorities and the amounts they cost them in financial terms. In fact, the issue is not quite so simple. In terms of public finance receipts, should all the taxes paid by road transport be considered, or only part of them? On another hand, how, in terms of public spending, should the costs of construction, upkeep, and management of road networks be split between freight transport vehicles and private cars?

It is not easy to answer these questions. However, a number of studies have progressively helped to define the issue. The French authorities have come to the conclusion that at the present time, taking into account the taxes that exist in this country, the level of costs borne by heavy goods vehicles is very close to the amount spent by public authorities in their favour [1]. For all of Western Europe, it can be estimated that about 20 billion ECUs are paid annually for different taxes by heavy goods vehicles, and that an approximately equal sum is spent by the public authorities in their favour. In any case, if there is a difference in these figures, it must be very small compared with the turnover of road freight transport, which, as we have seen, amounts to about 350 billion ECUs for Western Europe, of which about 250 apply to heavy goods vehicles as such and 100 to light trucks.

A recent report on the external effects of transport, prepared at the request of the International Union of Railways (UIC) [7], considers, on the basis of restrictive hypotheses, that heavy goods vehicles cover up to 82.6% of their infrastructure costs, whereas the same coefficient amounts to only 43.1% for rail freight. This is why the debate is rarely about the strictly financial aspects of the question, but rather about the other externalities of road transport.

The Other Externalities

Some of these are negative and essentially concern three issues: unsafe conditions on roads, contribution to road network congestion, and negative effects on the environment. Others are positive.

3.3.3 Negative Externalities

The negative externalities of road transport have been the subject of numerous studies, often financed by railway companies or by ecological organisations. It is therefore not surprising that many of these studies attribute very high values to the negative consequences of road transport. However, an objective examination does not lead to such clear-cut conclusions.

Insecurity on Roads

The overall annual cost of insecurity on roads, for all categories of vehicles, was estimated until recently at 70 billion ECUs for Western Europe according to the Brussels Commission reports [8], and heavy goods vehicles are involved in about one accident with casualties out of 18, and one fatal accident out of seven, based on French statistics. As the largest part of costs that are chargeable to them are paid through their insurance premiums, the externalities that are not covered and that can be attributed to them on these grounds would appear not to be able to exceed a maximum of 3 or 4 billion ECUs.

Congestion

Contrary to popular thinking, heavy goods vehicles are neither the principal cause of congestion nor their primary victims. With some rare exceptions, heavy traffic occurs in two types of precise circumstances in Europe: on the outskirts or within large urban centres during rush hours, or at weekends and during holiday periods outside the urban areas. In both these cases, heavy goods vehicles are very rare, even absent, because they travel essentially during the week and outside rush hours and travel more than 90% of their distances outside urban zones, making the idea of fighting road congestion by trying to decrease heavy goods vehicles traffic all the more surprising. But generally accepted ideas have such weight that the great majority of European public opinion is convinced that heavy goods vehicles are largely responsible for traffic jams, which are in fact due above all to cars. This is probably a psychological result of the difference in the mass of the vehicles concerned, as heavy trucks make motorists feel uneasy or in danger, particularly when the size of infrastructures is not properly adapted. Even on interurban motorways, heavy goods vehicles account for an average of less than 20% of traffic, and rarely more than 30%. On urban motorways, the percentages are obviously far lower, particularly during rush hours.

In addition, experts in externalities, whose opinions differ on many points, generally agree that congestion of road networks should not be taken into account among the traffic externalities, as it is actually the road network users themselves who put up with most of the consequences. Many studies, such as the one undertaken by the International Union of Railways cited above, have usually adopted this manner of thinking, and have eliminated congestion from the list of road externalities even if a recent "Green Paper" of the European Union does not take this stand [9]. Anyway, this debate mainly concerns cars, not goods vehicles.

Pollution

Air pollution phenomena will be covered in Chapter 10. Overall, and contrary to commonly held opinions, we will see that pollution is rapidly decreasing for most products and even, for certain amongst them, in the course of disappearing completely, and that surprising progress has been made or is underway. It will also show that their impact on public health is minimal and without comparison to a phenomenon such as road accidents, which is, on the other hand, quite tragic but too often accepted by public opinion.

In addition, air pollution is found mainly in urban areas, whereas, as we have seen, heavy trucks travel mostly in the country areas. This tendency is in fact increasing. In Great Britain, from 1983 to 1993, heavy goods vehicle traffic increased by 67% on motorways, by 38% in rural areas and by 0% in urban areas. For all these reasons, the external costs attributable to air pollution caused by heavy goods vehicles can objectively be only very low.

The Greenhouse Effect

As we shall see later, the problem is different as far as the production of carbon dioxide gas (CO_2) is concerned in that the attribution of a "cost" cannot be made on an objective basis of valuation, because the possible impact of this gas on climactic variations is itself unknown. It is therefore a matter of conventions. It can nonetheless be noted that on a world level, heavy goods vehicle traffic is responsible for about 32% of the carbon gas emissions attributable to road traffic [3] and that the latter, according to the Environmental Protection Agency (EPA) in Washington, itself represents approximately 7% of the world-wide production of greenhouse effect gases of human origin. Taking into account the fact that European heavy goods vehicles represent only 10% of world traffic of heavy goods vehicles, it is then shown that their contribution to the world-wide production of greenhouse effect gases of human origin is about 0.3%. If it is accepted that they should be heavily taxed because of this, this should also logically be the case for many other activities that are responsible to a far greater extent for such emissions, which would lead, for instance, to increasing the price of electricity produced in traditional power stations, which are by far the largest emitters of CO_2 in developed countries, to prohibitive levels.

Noise

Another externality of road transport that must be mentioned is noise pollution, as its existence and disadvantages cannot be denied. But, as in other areas, estimates of the corresponding cost to the community vary very widely. French studies have evaluated it at 0.14% of the gross domestic product and the rate of 0.20% is often accepted on an international level [9]. If it is accepted that one-third of this can be attributed to heavy goods vehicles, the corresponding amounts would equal approximately 4 billion ECUs per year for the whole of Western Europe.

A Limited Cost Overrun

All these negative externalities should be compared with the overall turnover figure for heavy road transport, which has been seen to amount to about 250 billion ECUs. In other words, the external costs of road transport are in fact quite limited compared with turnover and do not exceed about 10 billion ECUs, or 4% of the total. Moreover, they should decrease in the future.

However, it must be stated that not everyone shares this point of view. The study conducted on behalf of the International Union of Railways quoted above [7] assessed the external costs of road freight transport at 55 billion ECUs, broken down as follows: accidents, 21 billion; noise, 12 billion; air pollution, 12 billion; influence on the climate, 10 billion; and concluded that in order to restore fair competition between the different means of transport, fuel prices would need to be increased by 0.9 ECU per litre, which meant more than doubling them on average!

Such estimates merit discussion, to say the least. The World Bank, in its report *Sustainable Transport* [10], estimates that, in developing countries, it would be justifiable to add to the cost price of petroleum products (approximately $1 per gallon), another dollar per gallon for infrastructure costs, as well as a third for environmental externalities, on the understanding that the latter are incomparably higher in developing countries than in developed countries. In all, the World Bank recommended that the price be $3 per gallon, which is 0.63 ECUs per litre and quite less than the average current price in Western Europe.

One last point is worth mentioning. If fair competition is to be restored among the different means of transport, the same rules should apply to all. Yet, on average,

European railways are subsidised by governments for amounts that exceed 100% of revenues from their traffic. These subsidies are undeniably "negative externalities" for the community. Contrary to road transport companies, whose negative external costs represent a few percentage points of their turnover, railways therefore create negative externalities exceeding, on average, 100% of theirs.

3.3.4 Positive Externalities

But there are not only negative sides to the question of externalities of transport. Although experts disagree as to the very definition of what is to be accounted for under the term "externalities," it is undeniable that some of them are positive. In order to define them, the European Conference of Ministers of Transport (ECMT) held a Round Table in 1992 [11], which started by noting that, whereas there were numerous studies conducted to study negative externalities of road transport, studies on positive externalities were practically non-existent.

The summary report on the proceedings of the Round Table drew the following remarks:

> *To date, attention has been focused on the negative externalities of road transport, especially for freight. In doing so, no mention is made of their advantages for the community. And yet such transport has accompanied, and even created structural transformations of our economies by facilitating exchange. Road transport is an integral part of the progress in our way of life. The "transport" function is fundamental to the organization of markets: it is a dynamic function in terms of the international division of labour and the intensification of competition on the markets. External advantages are created in this way for economic agents other than those who directly pay the price of services, and then circulate throughout the economic system. For certain experts taking part in this round table, the advantages of transport outweigh their costs, whatever high costs are inherent to the system of transport, especially road transport.*

Next, the Round Table reached the following conclusions:

> *With respect to road transport, many positive effects can be noted, as follows:*
>
> - *A better quality of service resulting from the fact that it is possible to obtain a number of services within a short time; it should also be noted that road transport is flexible in adapting itself to the needs of the economy;*
> - *Innovation resulting from continued technological progress, enabling the development of new products and uniformity of supply across the*

country; Gains in productivity on the part of road freight transport companies, which have a positive effects on others by reducing costs: for example, logistics organization results from the reduction in transport companies' costs;

- *An economy in macroeconomic costs: transport favours the extension of markets; these factors are at the origin of productivity gains, which circulate throughout the economy in such a way that it becomes more productive as a whole;*
- *An effect on financing when road transport companies make a financial surplus, which comes from the use of roads;*
- *An effect on employment, since road freight transport remains a job-creating sector, unlike many others;*
- *A contribution to town and country planning because road transport can reach practically any point in the territory and can thus contribute to a more harmonious distribution of activities by limiting excessive concentrations.*

The final conclusion of the round table was that "it is important not to forget the advantages under the influence of a cursory analysis that stops at negative externalities."

Thus, as common sense dictates, road transport does not only have negative externalities but also many positive ones, which everything seems to indicate as being much more important. Admittedly, there are almost no studies on the subject in Europe, but some have been made in the United States on the consequences of the deregulation of freight transport, which has marked recent years, as in Europe [12].

From 1981 to 1988 the cost of the ton mile decreased by 20% in the United States, whereas it had previously been increasing. The result was that the Americans made savings of 40 billion dollars in road transport costs in 1988 compared with 1981.

Moreover the ratio of capital immobilised in stocks in relation to the turnover of American companies decreased from 28% in 1981 to 17% in 1993, representing a gain of nearly 40%.

The link between the volume of stocks and the periods of recession in the cycles of economic activity was also completely changed. During the 1990–1991 recession, instead of increasing, for the first time the volume of stocks fell month after month because the companies could react immediately.

The traditional link between the volume of stocks and the level of interest rates was also broken. In 1993, the lowest level of stocks was registered at the same time as the lowest interest rates, which is completely opposed to the generally accepted economic theory in this respect.

Overall, the annual gains to the American economy from all the various progress resulting from the deregulation of freight transport are estimated to have been over

100 billion dollars in 1994 compared with the previous situation, due both to the reduction in transport costs and the decrease in stock levels.

It should be added that in the United States, the modern industry of "time sensitive delivery"—express transport and just-in-time transport—which appeared progressively following the deregulation of air transport in 1977 and that of road transport in 1980, represents an activity amounting to 60 billion dollars, whereas they did not exist previously!

Similar evolutions occurred in Western Europe. A recent study conducted in France gave clear results [13]. Before 1986, the prices of road transport followed the same trend as the prices of its inputs; Since the 1986 deregulation, the two curves have been sharply diverging, the input prices climbing from index 100 to 135, and the road transport prices going *down* from index 100 to 95. The debate on externalities is far from over, but it has serious repercussions.

If it is accepted that the negative externalities of road transport are very high and that the positive ones are not taken into account, the obvious deduction is that it is justified to make road transport pay high taxes in one form or another, which would result in its prices being raised. It is this doctrine that is at the root of current European policy on this subject and that motivated both the decision to raise road fuel taxes in certain countries and the decision adopted at the European level to create a special tax disc (Eurovignette) for heavy goods vehicles in countries without toll motorways. This doctrine also justifies the granting of considerable subsidies to railway companies to favour their freight transport activities.

The European Union Council of Transport Ministers, held on 15–16 December 1994, thus stipulated that "the Community and individual states should ensure that infrastructure costs and external costs be paid, insofar as possible, by the users of transport infrastructures, under conditions of fair competition, through road taxes, for example." One cannot but agree with the beginning of this statement of principle, but the last words are puzzling. Quite obviously, if unfair competition exists, it stems from the means of transport that covers less than half its costs and not from the one that, if its positive effects are taken into account, most probably pays back its total cost, if not more.

The surprising notion that is often upheld in Europe is that road freight transport is "too cheap." As this is often presented as a reproach, it makes this sector of activity strangely different from the others in that, in general, everyone is delighted when prices decrease due to gains in productivity and to the efforts of firms for the general good of the community. The prosperity of Western countries relies for a large part on its moderate transport costs. Maybe the time has come to investigate more closely some of the current ideas on this subject.

References

[1] "Les comptes des transports en France en 1993," INSEE-OEST, Paris, 1994.
[2] "Transport Evolution 1970–1993," *European Conference of Ministers of Transport (ECMT)*, Paris, 1995.

[3] "Motor Vehicles Pollution—A strategy for reduction by year 2010," OCDE, Paris, 1995.
[4] "International Railway Statistics 1993," *Union Internationale des chemins de fer (U.I.C.)*, Paris, 1994.
[5] "Transport : The Way Forward." *HMSO*, London, 1996.
[6] Press release, 80th meeting of the Council of Ministers, ECMT, Paris, 1996.
[7] "External Effects of Transport," *IWW, INFRAS, Union Internationale des chemins de fer (UIC)*, Paris, 1994.
[8] "For a European Road Safety Policy" (Gerondeau Report), European Commission, Brussels, 1991.
[9] "Towards fair and efficient pricing in transport," *A green paper by the European Commission*, Brussels, 1995.
[10] "Sustainable transport," *the World Bank*, Washington, 1996.
[11] "The advantages of the transport modes," Round Table No. 93, *European Conference of Ministers of Transport (ECMT)*, Paris, 1994.
[12] Delaney, Robert V., "SINCLAIR WEEKS was right," *Transportation Quarterly*, ENO FOUNDATION, Lansdowne, VA, Spring issue, 1995.
[13] Souley, H., "L'effet de la dérégulation du transport routier de marchandises de 1986 sur les prix et sur les flux," *DEA de l'Ecole Nationale des Ponts et Chaussées*, Paris, 1996.

CHAPTER 4

▼▼▼

THE ROAD NETWORK: ONLY THE ROAD CAN RELIEVE THE ROAD

4.1 RADICALLY CHANGED NETWORKS

The development of motorways has completely transformed the European road network in the past four decades. Before the Second World War, there were only the few thousand kilometres of *autobahn* in Germany and *autostrada* in Italy, and practically nothing anywhere else.

But things have totally changed since then as Western Europe now counts approximately 40,000 km of motorway each used by an average of 35,000 vehicles daily, with an annual traffic that therefore amounts to about 500 billion vehicle kilometres, out of a total of approximately 3,000 billion for all of the continent's road networks.

The complete change introduced by motorways in relation to traditional road networks must be stressed. An ordinary two-lane road is considered to be saturated at about 10,000 vehicles per day in country areas, whereas, as we will see, the capacity of a motorway can reach more than 10 times more. As for average trip speeds, they are frequently multiplied by two, and far more still in urban areas.

The density of the motorway network is at about the same level from one West European country to another, with an average of about 130 km per million inhabitants within a range of 110 to 170. Exceptions to the rule are some Mediterranean countries, where the development in the numbers of cars on the road took place later than elsewhere, and Great Britain, which, with only 54 km of motorway per million inhabitants, distinguishes itself significantly from other countries with a similar level of development by being behind them in this respect.

Motorways therefore play an essential role in quantitative terms, but they have also transformed the qualitative side of road transport in Europe. Trips of several hundred or even several thousand kilometres are now possible, both for people and for freight, with swiftness, reliability, and safety conditions that were previously unknown.

At the same time, the ordinary road network has also been considerably extended and transformed. Narrow, badly surfaced streets and roads, or even dirt tracks, have given way to smooth, modern roads. In many countries of Europe, it is almost impossible to find a farm, however isolated, that does not have a surfaced road leading to it. In addition, the road network is now more and more often equipped with safety equipment that did not exist in the past (guard-rails, road signs, markings, lightings, etc.) even if it has not yet moved to the next stage, which will be the "intelligent" road (which will be covered in Chapter 11).

At the present time, in addition to its 40,000 km of motorway, Europe has close to three million kilometres of roads and streets that almost entirely criss-cross its territory.

Despite its current level of development, road traffic continues to progress in Western Europe, at a now moderate average rate of 2 to 3% per year for private cars, the same as for heavy goods vehicles. It should, however, be noted that whereas the increase in traffic of cars is generally quite regular and withstands fluctuations in the economy, this is not the case for trucks, which are more sensitive to such fluctuations, and which, on the contrary, accentuates them.

Approximately 70% of the kilometres travelled are for intercity trips, whereas traffic in urban areas amounts to about 30%, although the distinction between urban and rural areas is not clear-cut due to the geographical spreading of housing and economic activities and to variations in definitions of suburban and urban areas from one country to another.

The increase in traffic is not distributed in an equal way geographically. It tends to be more marked on the major routes—motorways or expressways—than in the rest of the network, as the former attract medium- and long-distance traffic, which increases more rapidly than local traffic. In both country and urban areas, the tendency is towards concentration along a relatively limited number of large, high-capacity roads that drain off the traffic, and this is obviously a favourable factor in solving traffic problems, which are then focused on them.

4.2 THE TRUE SCOPE OF CONGESTION

4.2.1 A Surprising Lack of Knowledge

But before studying the remedies to traffic problems, it is necessary to have a definite opinion about them. Is the situation serious or not? In other words, how does the road transport system work? How congested is the road network?

Many think that congestion is the major problem, and that it can only get worse with time. This is what could be read in the White Paper defining the official position of Brussels on transport, published in December 1992: "*We are heading towards an intolerable situation which will lead to the cardiac arrest of the transport system (. . .) Things cannot go on like this.*" Such an approach leads many decision-makers to conclude that it is better to invest in means of transport other than the road, which they think will lead to an impasse.

It is, consequently, important to know how bad present-day congestion actually is, and this leads to a very simple question. Every day, there are approximately 400 million car movements in Europe, together with probably more than 50 million freight transport vehicle trips. How many of them are faced with problems of congestion, and how many are not (i.e., the trip is made from start to finish without any particular trouble)?

The answer to this question is obviously fundamental because it alone can provide a true image of the way the road transport system works. Yet, fundamental as it may be, the answer is unknown. In no country of Europe is anyone capable of answering it. It has never been the real subject of studies, so that it is impossible to know the actual situation and free reign is given to preconceived ideas holding that congestion is a very widespread, even dominant, phenomenon. Surprising as it may seem, no one has the slightest idea of the way the transport system really works even though it is responsible for over 90% of the Continent's needs and represents close to 15% of its gross domestic product (GDP). No one can answer the following elementary question: "What is the percentage of trips that are hindered by traffic jams and what is the percentage that are not"?

4.2.2 A Sea of Free-Flowing Traffic

For its part, the Union Routière de France (French Road Federation) has tried to tackle this issue, and the results obtained were surprising [1] Studies carried out on its demand, which simply corroborated the results of many other national or local sources, confirmed that Europeans who travel to work daily by car (that is, four-fifths of those who use a motorised form of transport) take an average of 19 minutes to get to work (see Figure 6). No more than 10% of them spend more than 30 minutes getting to work, which hardly suggests a high level of overall congestion in the road network, since most of these trips take place during rush hours.

To confirm this, the Union Routière de France asked the same people if they usually encountered many traffic jams on their way to work. Ninety percent of them answered in the negative; only 10% replied in the affirmative, which is consistent with the low commuting times cited above. In other words, even during rush hours, the immense majority of car trips are unhindered by serious problems of congestion. Among those who commute to work daily by car, 96% of Germans, 93% of French, 89% of Dutch, 88% of Italians and 81% of the British declare that they do not normally experience much congestion on their usual route. Even if this assessment is by definition qualitative and if the answers are less positive in the United Kingdom where there are less motorways, the results are nonetheless quite impressive!

The same is even more true outside rush hours, when congestion is often of an exceptional nature. Finally, had the same questions been asked of truck users, who circulate much more frequently outside rush hours and in the country rather than in urban areas, the results would have given an even more positive view of the situation.

In order to do away with the incertitude, French toll motorway companies, which currently operate only intercity motorways, are building up a "traffic indicator," aimed at identifying the percentage of trips made by cars or heavy goods vehicles on their roads without meeting with problems of congestion. The indicator's first evaluations have estimated it at approximately 98% on weekdays. And yet some of these motorways are used by an average of about 50,000 vehicles per day.

In Great Britain, the average motorway speed for cars is 70 mph (113 km/h), which is precisely the authorised speed limit. Whereas British motorways are among the most used in Europe, only 4% of car traffic drives at less than 50 mph (80 km/h) [2]!

The same holds true for continental Europe. For example, a Swedish truck and coach manufacturer with a factory located in the west of France is presently supplied parts that are sent from Scandinavia by truck. These take no more than 32 hours to make the trip, with a possible variation of no more than one and a half hours, despite a ferry crossing and travelling across six of the most densely populated countries in Western Europe!

Contrary to what might be expected, the situation is not even much different for annual summer holiday travel. In answer to the question, "Did you encounter much congestion when you left for your summer holidays?" 84% of the French people interviewed in 1992 and 1996 gave a negative reply, even though this is the most difficult period of the year, during which France is also criss-crossed by massive movements between the North of Europe and the Mediterranean coast [1]. Indeed, the summer traffic jams in France are declining year after year due to improvements in the motorway network.

Even in large towns, the situation is not as different as could be imagined. In towns of more than 100,000 inhabitants, the average commuting time by car is *18* minutes in France (outside Paris), *25* in Germany, *17* in Great Britain (outside

London), and *19* in Italy [1]. In the Paris area, it does not exceed 27 minutes, about the same figure as in the London area.

4.2.3 Unrealistic Appraisal

In summary, these different studies lead to the conclusion that probably more than 90% of road trips in Europe are not subject to congestion of any importance. They shed a very different light on traffic conditions compared with the normal views. When the French are asked to estimate the proportion of their fellow citizens who are faced with heavy traffic problems during their daily commuting by car, the average reply is 49%, or seven times higher than the real figure [1]!

In such conditions, it is not surprising to see that people's views on traffic are generally pessimistic and that the prevailing idea is that which is expressed, in all good faith, by the Brussels authorities: *"Things cannot go on like this,"* whereas in fact things, generally speaking, are actually working well, if not very well, on the European roads, even if there are obviously exceptions—almost all of them in large urban areas—for which solutions must be found.

One-Way Information

If these assertions run counter to generally held ideas, it is probably partly due to the fact that drivers are systematically given only negative information about the state of road traffic. The fact that traffic is flowing freely between Dax and Mont-de-Marsan, in France; between Bari and Altamura, in Italy; between Shrewsbury and Welshpool, in Great Britain; or between Bamberg and Coburg, in Germany is not news. On the contrary, the radio informs the French public daily about all the rush-hour congestion on the *Boulevard Périphérique* around Paris or the motorways in the Paris region, the British about difficulties encountered on the M25 Motorway that skirts London, the Dutch about problems on the Randstat motorways, the Germans about what is happening on the Rhine Valley motorways, and so forth.

However, the total number of kilometres of motorway that regularly fall victim to traffic jams probably does not exceed 1,000 or 2,000 km during the working week out of the 40,000 km of European motorways, and this is often only for a few hours per day and usually in one direction only. Such is the real situation, but it is obviously not indicated in the messages motorists receive, which are focused on the exceptions and not the general situation.

If congestion were omnipresent, would our fellow citizens continue to choose the car and road transport in general? Would "just-in-time" be such a great success? In fact, the road and more precisely the motorway transport system has an enormous capacity, and congestion is relatively rare in comparison with the total number of trips in each country.

But the basic data are not available. This is one of the most glaring of the considerable shortcomings regarding transport knowledge in Europe and it must be resolved urgently by defining a certain number of indicators and measuring them regularly, as it has begun to be done in the Paris region and in some other places. How can there be valid discussions on a topic when even the most elementary data is not available? Airlines and train companies know what proportion of their planes or trains arrive on time, and know to what extent their passengers may be subject to delays. This is one of the fundamental parameters of their management. But no equivalent exists for the road in Europe.

Such indicators, when they are introduced, will reveal more or less perceptible differences between countries and parts of the same country. But overall, the traffic situation is like a free-flowing sea dotted with islands of congestion, not the opposite. Nonetheless, most of those who have studied traffic phenomena seem to have fixed all their attention on congestion; in other words, the tree and not the wood. They focused only on what was not working, forgetting the most important thing, which is that most of the road network works well most of the time.

4.2.4 Congestion Cost

Congestion Localised in Time and Space

This obviously does not mean that congestion phenomena do not exist, but that they must be viewed in their relative context.

Will they get worse, will they level off, or even decrease? The answer, which directly concerns the future efficiency of the economies of the different European countries, is mainly in their hands. It will depend, above all, on the policy each country follows on road infrastructures. Because, even if congestion is never the general rule, it is nonetheless responsible for significant losses as it affects the movements of tens of millions of citizens and millions of commercial vehicles each day.

Every day of the year, approximately 680 million trips are made by individuals by car in Western Europe, lasting an average of 20 minutes. Even if only 10% are faced with congestion, making the trip last 10 minutes longer than in free-flowing traffic, the corresponding additional time amounts to 11 million hours per day, or four billion per year, which, based on an average value of time of eight ECUs per hour, would represent about 32 billion ECUs, or 0.5% of the GDP of Europe without taking into account trucks. Obviously, these values are only given as a guideline as the real figures are unknown, but they do reveal the potential scope of the problem.

Admittedly, estimations of economic consequences due to congestion do exist in certain countries and on an international level, but they are so disparate and are based on hypotheses so different that their credibility is relative. One of the most credible is perhaps the estimate made in the Netherlands, which evaluates the cost at 3 billion guilders for 1994, or 0.6% of the GDP. It is reasonable to suggest that the overall average percentage for Western Europe is lower, due to the fact that the Netherlands is the Continent's most densely populated nation. However, the "estimates" reported by the OECD suggest the figure of 120 billion ECUs, or 2% of the GDP of Europe. But these estimates are entirely unfounded. At best, this is only an "average" of estimates given by the different member countries on completely different bases, and which vary from 0.2% to 3% of GDP, or a ratio of 1 to 15. Even within a single country—Great Britain—according to the OECD itself, they vary from 1 to 3 depending on sources [3]!

The adoption of unjustified values can have serious consequences. The above-mentioned OECD estimated scope of road congestion costs constitutes the basis of the "Green Paper" published at the end of 1995 by the Brussels Commission under the title: "Towards Fair and Efficient Pricing in Transport: Political Options to Internalise the External Costs of Transports in the European Union" [4]. This "Green Paper" states that "a recent investigation by the OECD calculates road congestion in developed countries at approximately 2% of the GDP," and deduces that road transport should be taxed more heavily. Yet, an attentive examination of this "recent investigation" reveals that it is a working document citing, with no justification, estimates from another report, the latter report referring to documents dating from about 20 years ago, in which it is impossible to find anything resembling a serious study of the subject. For that matter, the "Green Paper" itself mentions (p. 37) that a detailed OECD study carried out in 1995 evaluated the cost of congestion in France at 19 billion francs, or about 0.25% of the GDP of that country, or *eight times* less than 2%!

4.2.5 Congestion Definitions

There are three main means of evaluating congestion costs.

Reasoning in terms of a "given road network," the only nonarbitrary way to calculate additional time due to congestion, would be to compare for each trip the time that is actually necessary and the time that would have been necessary in the absence of any traffic (for instance, at 2:00 a.m.), and add together the additional time for all trips based on this reference. But is it reasonable to fix the objective of being able to drive at any time of day, including rush hours, as if it were 2:00 a.m.? The reply is obviously that it is not. If traffic was constantly at its 2:00 a.m. level, the road network would be very different.

Second, it can also be decided that there is "congestion" only below a certain traffic speed. The Americans use this principle and consider that congestion takes place on their urban motorway networks when driving speeds fall below 35 mph (56 km/h), thus leading them to estimate congestion costs of 35 billion dollars per year (0.6% of the GDP) in the United States for this network [5].

congestion only add a few seconds to the average length of trips by car, which is about 20 minutes in Western Europe. Even in large urban areas, the average extra time is very low, which is proved by the fact that the average trip times there are also not very far from 20 minutes.

In the Paris region, attention is focused on the fate of the 150,000 drivers who every morning of the working week commute from their suburb to their place of employment in the city of Paris itself and are regular victims of traffic jams, even if they nonetheless may save time compared with public transport. Most French people think that these motorists are representative of the majority of the inhabitants of the Paris region. But the Paris region has five million workers, and these 150,000 drivers therefore represent only 3% of the total figure! Close to two million other inhabitants of the region get to work by car in the suburbs in an average of about 25 minutes, but no one ever mentions them [7]! And things are obviously even better in the rest of the country, which represents 80% of the population. It can also be added that in France, only 4% of the workforce is employed more than 40 km from home as the crow flies, but that their trips account for 50% of the total kilometres travelled between the home and the workplace [8].

4.3 ROAD INVESTMENTS

Having said that, even if congestion only concerns a small fraction of all trips, it nonetheless results in negative effects that justify appropriate road investments. Numerous studies collected together by the World Bank, based particularly on a comparison of the pace of development of different countries or regions depending on the amount they invested in transport infrastructures, logically concluded that when well-chosen, they produced a far higher return on investment for the community than other public or private investments, and that, on the other hand, their insufficiency is a heavy handicap to economic expansion [9].

It is important to stress that additional travel times due to congestion are not the only factor to take into account when speaking of road investments. In many cases, they are justified for other reasons. When an ordinary road that passes through many villages is replaced by a motorway, trip times are often divided by two, if not more, even if there was no actual congestion beforehand. Such road projects can reduce or eliminate the isolation suffered by the regions in question. The same phenomenon can be felt even more in urban areas, where the creation of motorways and expressways can often divide trip times by three or four, thus significantly increasing the perimeter of influence of towns and the areas open to urban land use, improving the working of the economy and the quality of life (Fig. 9), whilst also offering significant time savings for those who use them. The construction of new road infrastructures thus results in both significant amounts of time saved and an overall positive effect on land use, even when there was previously no congestion.

Finally, when well-managed, this also leads to major gains in road safety, and this is clearly far from being the least important point.

4.3.1 Contrasting Opinions

The opinions of the population and the authorities on projects to extend or enlarge road and motorway networks vary widely from one country to another. European nations can be roughly classified into two categories, depending on whether the construction of new motorways and the reinforcement of existing motorway capacity is favourably considered or not.

The first category includes (to begin with) countries where the number of cars on the roads is still lower than elsewhere and where both the public and the authorities are eager for a motorway network to be constructed, as it is obviously lacking. Countries such as, for example, Spain, Portugal, and Greece, not to mention the Eastern European countries—including former East Germany—have good reason to put motorway construction at the head of the list of national priorities. Sweden and other Scandinavian countries have also, at least until recently, been favourable to the construction of new motorways. This may appear surprising, considering the Scandinavian's attachment to environmental protection, but it must be said that motorway builders have made considerable progress in diminishing the negative impact on the environment and making roads fit into the landscape, often very successfully. Whereas in the past no measures were taken to limit the visual impact or noise level of motorways, things have fortunately changed and modern projects, on the contrary, give them great importance, sometimes going as far as to partially or totally cover the constructions or build them underground in densely populated urban or suburban areas. This justifies the inclusion of environmental improvements among the benefits of such projects.

France is also among the countries to favour the extension of its motorway network. In 1993, this country decided to accelerate the completion of its national motorway web and is constructing more than 300 km of motorway per year; that is more than all the other West European countries combined! This will give France, in less than a decade from now, the largest network in Europe, at least in terms of its length. It must be said that the existence of a toll system provides substantial resources that self-finance most of this development without having recourse to the national budget. Roads have so many advantages for their users that, after already paying far more than their cost to the government, particularly through fuel taxes, they hardly balk at paying over again, through the tolls, the equivalent of a doubling of already high fuel prices; this in exchange for time saved and a quality service.

The existence of tolls, which from an economic standpoint were long considered nonsensical in interurban areas because they turned potential users away from the motorway and increased its operating costs, has in fact given very positive results in those countries using them, once the first few years (which usually require financial government help) are over, and on the condition that the money recovered is actually used for the benefit of the existing motorway network and its extension.

The situation is obviously very different in countries that traditionally finance their motorway networks entirely out of the national budget. Those opposed to the construction of new motorways or the development of existing ones find a sympathetic ear in the government, which is all the more happy to save money in that it usually already devotes significant sums to the transport sector, but to the benefit of the railways. Contrary to what is often thought, competition among modes of transport is not so much for capturing markets as for obtaining credits from the government.

This second category of nations, where new motorway construction has become very difficult due to a combination of opposition from a large part or the majority of public opinion plus government budgetary difficulties, consists of countries where the density of the network is already high or where it is difficult to differentiate rural motorways from urban ones. It is, paradoxically, in these countries, where traffic density is the heaviest and consequently the needs are most pressing, that resistance to road network expansion is at its highest. This particularly includes the Netherlands, Belgium, and the western part of Germany. The United Kingdom's government has gone a step further and almost completely abandoned the creation of new motorways through budget financing, its sole objective now being to enlarge existing ones.

It should in fact be noted that in the latter country, the restrictions do not only cover motorways, but also the other types of roads. During the 1995–1996 budget year, only one new road project was launched with state funding, compared to an average of 40 to 50 at the beginning of the decade.

4.3.2 New Means of Financing

The United Kingdom has, on the other hand, innovated in the field of financing for road infrastructures. Five new projects, including two for improvements to existing motorways, were entrusted to private groups in 1995 on a DBFO (design, build, finance, and operate) basis. The chosen concessionary companies will be paid year after year from public funds by "shadow tolls," calculated on a pro rata of actual traffic and based on a toll payment per vehicle, agreed in advance.

The principle of this new means of financing road infrastructures is particularly interesting in that it combines many advantages. First, it gives rise to the productivity gains that generally result from projects being handled by the private sector. It also avoids the additional costs, diversion of traffic, and important loss of economic performance that are inherent to traditional toll systems. It avoids having to meet users' and political opposition to tolls. It can work not only for creating new roads, but also for enlarging existing ones. Finally, it spares the public authorities from having to finance the works in question immediately.

Of course, the public authorities then have to pay the concessionary company during the following years via the fictitious tolls. But it is important to take into consideration that building a new road project leads to important additional tax revenues, coming on one hand from fuel taxes collected from the induced traffic, and resulting on the other hand from the fact that road infrastructures contribute to the development of economic activity and thus result in tax revenues that are all the more important in Western Europe since the tax rates levied by the public authorities are amongst the highest in the world. A recent study made on behalf of the Union Routière de France, the first of its kind, would appear to indicate that tax revenues resulting from the creation or improvement of road infrastructures may be in the region of the current real interest rates, or even higher [10]. In other words, payments to the concessionary companies may in fact be covered by the additional tax revenues collected by the public authorities, and the road infrastructure may not cost the latter anything at all. . . It should be added that the yearly payments to the private builder of the road do not necessarily need to be linked to the future volume of traffic but may be agreed upon independent of it, as is the case in Germany.

At the end of 1996, various other countries—Spain, Portugal, Finland, and Austria—were studying these new means of financing by the private sector, which could be applied not only in country areas but also in urban areas where the collection of real tolls is ruled out until the eventual implementation of electronic tolling systems. For their part, other countries have introduced annual tax discs, or vignettes, that are required to use their motorway network and provide important revenues.

4.3.3 The Enlargement of Existing Motorways

In many places, where the territory is already sufficiently covered with road links, it is no longer necessary in Europe to plan to build new motorways. Those that already exist should just be enlarged by adding new lanes.

However, even enlargement encounters great difficulties in a number of countries—Western Germany, The Netherlands, Great Britain, and others—where the impression is sometimes given that some people will oppose on principle anything that might make trips easier for cars and trucks. Indeed, the reasons given for opposing the increase in existing motorway capacity in these countries rarely withstands analysis.

Some are linked to a growing volume of air pollution that would result from such operations. Yet, as Chapter 10 will show, air pollution is on very strong downward trend and is no longer a priority issue. In addition, emissions are much lower when traffic flows freely than when it is subject to congestion. Other reasons given are technical or financial in nature. However, very often there is sufficient space to enlarge existing motorways at a reasonable cost in relation with the amount of traffic concerned. Curiously, the ease with which enlargement can be carried out technically has nothing to do with the density of the country in question. It is much easier in the Netherlands, which has the highest population density in Europe but where space for enlargement was set aside for motorways from the beginning, than it is in France, where this is rarely the case in urban areas although it is one of the least densely populated countries on the continent!

Preparing for the Future

It must be stressed at this point how absurd it is to create a new motorway in a country area or, even more so, in an urban area, and not systematically reserve sufficient right of way and plan bridges and other structures so that they can one day be made to accommodate four lanes each way, which is the generally accepted maximum limit. The Americans have quite rightly taken these steps for decades in order to preserve the future, without even mentioning the many motorways and *parkways* in the United States that have a central divider strip that is so wide that cars driving in the other direction can barely be seen. They offer their users incomparable driving comfort, which is unfortunately missing in Europe where, often for lack of imagination and audacity, motorways too often have a strictly utilitarian character, partially explaining the lack of enthusiasm they arouse. If there is one piece of advice to be given to the countries of Eastern Europe, which are only just beginning to create their motorway networks, it is this. The additional cost is minimal when the motorway is under construction compared with the considerable savings to be made on subsequent enlargement, not to speak of the fact that it may sometimes be extremely difficult at a later date. And even if it never becomes necessary, the pleasure of using a wide, spacious motorway for generations will justify the choice made. As in the United States, the standard sizing for every new surface motorway in Europe should be eight lanes (2 × 4), even if it is usually enough to create only four of them initially. It is very surprising to note that some countries in Western Europe persist in building numerous motorways with two lanes in each direction, especially in urban areas, without allowing for possibilities of enlarging them and therefore often organising future congestion, with all the disadvantages that it will bring.

4.3.4 More Flexible Standards

A few words must be said about motorway standards. Generally, the standards specify that each lane should be 3.5 or 3.6 metres wide, and that there should be a sufficiently wide continuous emergency hard shoulder on each side of the motorway. In fact, it is possible, when necessary, to make savings compared with the standards.

Those for German motorways were reduced in this way in early 1995, thus gaining two metres of total width and saving 1 billion marks for 2,600 km on new constructions and on the enlargement of existing motorways from two lanes both ways to three lanes both ways.

In urban areas, where speeds are lower, it is possible to go even further, as will be seen in the following chapter, and consider lane widths equal to or lower than three metres for lanes where heavy goods vehicles are prohibited, together with the elimination of the hard shoulder. With a little imagination, the capacity of many motorways can thus be increased, often far more easily than expected.

This has been shown in the Netherlands in 1996, where, following the example of certain towns in America, the hard shoulder of one of their most congested motorways (A28) was transformed into a normal traffic lane for six months, despite reluctance from the safety departments. The immediate effect was a substantial reduction in traffic jams, enabling many users to change the times at which they travelled. The test was such a success, with no known negative impact on safety, that it was greeted with enthusiasm and the decision was made to continue the experiment indefinitely and extend it to other motorways, particularly as there do not appear to have been any negative effects on safety. This way of doing things could very possibly be a considerable and unknown reserve of road capacity in many other places in Europe.

Other opposition to the actual enlarging of existing motorways is linked to the fear of the negative impact of this type of operation as far as noise and visual factors are concerned. However, it is usually possible for enlargement projects either not to change the impact on the immediate environment or even to improve it by installing, for example, noise protection barriers when it is a case of renovating motorways that were built at a time when few or no precautions were taken to protect the environment. It is important to realise that, contrary to what is sometimes claimed, the motorway network actually takes up a relatively small surface area. On the assumption that the land used by an average motorway has a total width of 40 metres, the 40,000 km of European motorway take up a total of 1,600 km^2, or less than 1/2000th of European territory, even if it must be recognised that areas affected by noise are far larger.

It is not even always necessary to increase the amount of land used by the motorway. For instance, ministerial departments in the Netherlands are considering a project to double the A1 motorway in the Amsterdam area by adding a superposed structure. It is not possible in mid 1997 to say whether this project will be carried through. But it is a fact that such structures can be built without increasing noise for nearby residents (by covering them with a continuous casing), and that building costs can be substantially reduced by reserving their use for light vehicles, as will be seen in the following chapter.

The potentialities of increasing capacity to a certain extent by applying "intelligent transport" techniques should also not be forgotten. Whatever the technical solution chosen, it is clear that more and more it will be by acting on the existing motorways that it will be possible to satisfy new traffic demand increases.

4.3.5 Does the Road Create Traffic?

One of the most important reasons for the reticence towards increasing existing motorway capacity is of another nature. As we have seen, it is due to the fact that a large part of the population has the impression that it is useless to construct roads or to increase their capacity because roads create traffic and the contest between growing infrastructure and growing traffic would be lost before it even started.

Even an institution as prestigious as the OECD does not hesitate to write, *"It is recognised that the construction of new roads does not really solve traffic congestion problems because it leads to very strong demand for movements by car, which quickly uses up the new added capacity"* [11]. This way of seeing things is, on the whole, mainly mistaken. Traffic volume in a country, a region, or a built-up area, depends above all on economic and demographic factors, on the geographical location of activities, on the level of car ownership, on changes in production and distribution of products and services, and on user preferences among means of transport. This explains why the volume of traffic per driver differs only slightly in all the countries of Europe, whatever policies are followed in terms of infrastructures [12].

On the other hand, an improvement in the network can have an influence on traffic demand locally, especially when congestion existed beforehand. But this simply shows that it is a useful investment, as it allows for more trips or for longer ones, for the benefits of the economy, and the inhabitants' quality of life. And in such cases, good sense shows that an increase in capacity can only result in a decrease in the prior congestion level, and cannot create it, and certainly cannot make it worse, even if at times the new road becomes congested [13]. When a flooded field is drained, the drain itself can become full and some puddles may remain. But there will obviously be less water in the field at the end of the process than at the beginning.

Potential demand cannot expand infinitely, and the number of trips per day and per person in developed countries, which corresponds to the rhythm of everyday life (work, school, shopping, visits, leisure activities, etc.) is in a way a kind of universal constant. It differs relatively little from an average of a little more than three (Figure 3). On the other hand, the average distance travelled per trip cannot increase indefinitely.

Finally, increases in capacity brought about by enlargement can be very significant. Transforming a motorway from two lanes each way to four lanes each way allows, all else being equal, daily capacity on a country motorway to rise from about 50,000 vehicles per day to about 110,000, or an increase of more than 100% as central lanes have a higher capacity than side ones. Given a supposed average growth rate in traffic of 3% per year, this simple operation can satisfy new demand for over a generation without any creation of new road links, especially since the long-term trend is to a slowing of the rate of traffic progression in a continent that now has a stable population. Increasing capacity, which has the objective of meeting needs, is not in the least bit shocking. What company owner faced with a heightened demand for his products would act differently and would not invest to meet it?

But is it possible to size the European motorway network in order to meet demand in the foreseeable future? To answer this question, it is necessary to distinguish between intercity and urban routes.

4.3.6 Intercity Motorways

For intercity motorways, the answer is almost always affirmative. Average traffic on the European motorways currently stands at about 35,000 vehicles per day, all vehicle categories included, which is very far from the levels of traffic mentioned above. Moreover, this is only an average and a very large number of European motorways—probably three quarters of them—do not currently exceed an average of 30,000 vehicles per day, so that there is no perspective of saturation for them, especially if the motorways are extended to three lanes both ways, which is to be hoped as it encourages coexistence between private cars and heavy goods vehicles whenever traffic exceeds about 30,000 vehicles per day (even if it is not absolutely necessary with regard to the road's capacity).

Only a very small part of the European intercity network already has much higher traffic figures, reaching or exceeding 50,000 vehicles per day, which is often considered to be the physical, if not psychological, limit for free flow on a 4 lane (2 × 2) motorway. Several solutions can then be considered to face foreseeable increases in demand. The first consists in increasing the capacities of the routes in question by enlarging them not only to three lanes both ways, with an average theoretical capacity of 80,000 vehicles per day, but to four lanes both ways when needed.

As a general rule, there is nothing physically against the enlargement of the majority of Europe's most heavily used intercity motorways to four lanes each way, except in a few limited points or sections. This result can be obtained either by slightly adapting the rules in force on standards for the roadway and hard shoulders or by reconstructing parts of them. The real problem is one of financing, although the traffic levels on the routes concerned are such that the economic return for the community on investments in increased capacity for heavy traffic situations is obviously very high.

An increase in the number of lanes should thus in most cases be sufficient to satisfy traffic needs for a very long time. In intercity areas, there are less than 200 km of European motorways today—mainly in the United Kingdom and in Germany—where average daily traffic exceeds 80,000 vehicles per day! In the future there will probably therefore be only a very few rare situations that may possibly require additional measures and where, as is already the case for some American routes, it would be justified to double the existing motorway on site with an additional motorway; for example, two or three lanes each way, which would "frame" the original one. Even if such cases are very rare, there is no reason to exclude such a possibility *a priori* if there are no imperative geographical obstacles. In such situations, it might be worth considering whether the additional motorway might be reserved for heavy goods vehicles, thus putting an end to problems of coexistence with private cars, or, on the contrary, reserved for private cars, thus limiting construction costs and encouraging its integration into the surrounding landscape.

In summary, outside urban areas, the solution is to adapt motorway capacity to demand, to the benefit of the regions and countries concerned, and there is no real reason not to do this.

Variable Capacity

If this is not done, traffic difficulties will appear but they will not necessarily completely block the motorways concerned. The absolute maximum capacity for a motorway is actually a great deal higher than the figures mentioned previously, which correspond to relatively free-flowing traffic conditions. If demand exceeds these levels, traffic will continue to flow, but less freely. In other words, average speed will decrease, allowing traffic to exceed by 50%, or even more, the values mentioned above (50,000, 80,000, and 110,000 vehicles per day for two lanes both ways, three lanes both ways, and four lanes both ways).

But such results can only be achieved at the price of discomfort and loss of time—and therefore money—for road users and the community, since the average speed of private vehicles will, for instance, fall from 120 to 80 km/h, or even less. It must be said that the variation in motorway capacity depending on traffic speeds explains why it is possible to tolerate, if necessary, different widths along the same motorway, with, for example, a section with two lanes both ways being inserted between two sections with three lanes both ways, without necessarily reducing the overall capacity of the motorway.

It is only above these traffic levels that temporary or long-lasting traffic jams will occur, resulting in even higher losses, even if they can be attenuated by appropriate traffic management measures limiting the extent of the stop-and-go phenomenon.

It must finally be added that, in countries where intercity motorways have a toll system, it is possible to influence traffic by financial incentives to encourage users to take less-travelled routes or to stagger their trips during the day (as in the very successful experiments conducted in France), either to induce drivers to change their time schedule or to choose an alternative route [14].

In summary, the problems of adapting capacity to needs for intercity motorway links should usually find solutions, depending on each particular case, by a combina-- tion of the enlargement of existing motorways, the possible construction of an additional motorway on site in very rare circumstances, or the creation of parallel motorways further away when this is possible, as well as appropriate traffic management measures (even in the absence of toll systems).

4.3.7 Urban Motorways

Traffic is by far the highest in urban or suburban areas. The most common reaction as far as the possibility of meeting the corresponding demands is one of scepticism. This reaction is obviously sometimes justified, particularly in the centres of very large cities, where public transport networks—underground railways, suburban trains, and so forth—have led to the creation or the maintaining of a very high density of offices, shops, and (sometimes) housing. Innumerable motorways would need to be constructed in order to make the centres of London, Paris, or other large European cities accessible to all those who wished to drive to the city centre! Traffic demand must therefore be restrained, and this can be done mainly through a control on parking spaces until a general urban toll can perhaps be implemented in the more or less distant future. In such circumstances, unless underground roads are constructed, demand must be adapted to supply and not the reverse.

But the situation is very different outside the central areas. In practice there, only the car can respond to the great majority of needs. Everything then depends on road network planning and building policies.

An Extreme Case

The United States is proof that it is possible to meet the transport needs of vast cities by depending almost entirely on the road, as is shown in the extreme example of Los Angeles. Contrary to tenacious, lasting legend, things run rather smoothly in this urban area, which already had 14.5 million inhabitants in 1990 and that depends almost exclusively on the car to satisfy its transport needs. Of those who work in Los Angeles, 88% commute to work by car, 4.5% by public transport, 4.9% on foot, while 2.7% work at home.

In this respect, Los Angeles is no different from almost all the other large American cities. It is also no different as to the average home-to-work commuting times of its inhabitants. The average is 24 minutes, which is remarkably short for a city of this size. But most surprising of all, this length of time has not varied since 1967, whereas the population has more than doubled since that date and distances between home and the workplace have not ceased to increase, currently averaging 20 km, travelled at an average speed of 51 km/h from door to door. This is the opposite of the image, which has it that Los Angeles is at a standstill during rush hours and that commuting times commonly exceed one hour or more, whereas in fact, the average traffic speed has increased significantly in the last few decades [15].

It is amazing to see how similar the clichés can be on both sides of the Atlantic! They led the California authorities to invest in two own-site public transport lines aimed at raising the percentage of public transport users from 2% (for all purposes) to 10%. The first line financed is 22 miles long and was introduced on the route from Los Angeles to Long Beach at an investment cost of $877 million and costs approximately $40 million annually to operate. Today the line is used by only 30,000 passengers per day, including 3,000 to 4,000 former motorists, so that the cost price for each car trip avoided can be calculated at . . . $103!

The Los Angeles case is interesting because it demonstrates that even large cities of well over 10 million inhabitants can have good, functional road transport systems that can cope with demand. The situation is not very different in Europe for trips taking place between two suburban areas, in which case the car holds a near monopoly. It must immediately be emphasised that this identity regarding the use of road transport on both sides of the Atlantic in no way implies similarities in urban shapes and land use, because the car is capable of serving very different types of areas, such as the suburbs of Los Angeles or Atlanta (where population density is very low) or those of Hamburg or Stockholm (where land use is strictly controlled).

Of course, no European could ever have the idea of wanting to transform the old Continent's towns into replicas of Los Angeles. But the facts must not be confused. It is not because of their transport system that most American towns do not have a historical centre similar to those of European towns. It is simply because they hardly existed one or two centuries ago.

The European Balance

In fact, large European cities function largely like their American counterparts in that they use the car and a network of roads or motorways for most of their needs, but they also have a public transport system serving town centres. The fortunate combination of these two systems of transport allows Europeans to retain a density of activity in the city centre that generally does not exist on the other side of the Atlantic.

But even in European cities, it should not be forgotten that the car is by far the dominant means of transport both in terms of numbers of trips and turnover (or economic value). In a region such as Paris, which has 11 million inhabitants, the combined annual turnover of the two large public transport companies (RATP and SNCF-Banlieue) including contributions from local communities and employers is 22 billion francs (about 3.5 billion ECUs) per year, whereas the sums that road users—private and commercial—devote to cars and to road freight transport vehicles amount to 160 billion francs, or almost eight times more [16]! The motorway networks of the Paris area in France, or the Ruhr region in Germany, are not significantly different from those of the largest American cities.

The trend will continue in the future because most, if not all, of new demand for transport in Europe, allowing for exceptions, is located in the suburbs or outer suburban areas. The American example shows that there is nothing to stop the road and motorway network having enough capacity to meet the demand, particularly since urban motorway traffic flow can be much higher than that of intercity motorways. In the Paris region, there are motorways with two lanes each way that handle more than 100,000 vehicles per day, with three lanes each way that handle more than 150,000, and with four lanes each way that handle more than 200,000. In many places, there are 30,000 vehicles per lane per day, when 20,000 vehicles is usually considered to be the standard in other major urban areas. The capacity therefore reaches about *double* the level that is considered to be normal for motorways in country areas, particularly due to a better staggering of the demand during the day and lower driving speeds.

Moreover, such road traffic flow is far higher than that of most public transport lines. Except for the central parts of very large cities with several million inhabitants, such as London or Paris, it is rare to see the public transport lines—metro, suburban trains, trams—amount to or exceed 12,000 passengers during rush hours and 60,000 per day, both directions combined. However, many urban motorways are used by more than 10,000 vehicles during rush hours and more than 100,000 per day, amounting to close to 150,000 passengers daily without counting the heavy and light trucks that are also present. It goes without saying that the theoretical capacity of the railways is higher than that of the motorways. But what counts is not theoretical capacity, but actual traffic flow. The real mass transport infrastructures of European cities are for the most part motorways and not public transport lines, as shown in Table 4.1, which demonstrates that a great part of the very heavily trafficked motorways in Western Europe is located in the Paris area. Finally, the possibility of constructing underground roads cannot be forgotten, especially in central parts of cities. These have practically no environmental disadvantages and their development, which will be examined in the following chapter, will undoubtedly mark the century to come.

4.3.8 High-Profit Investments

Whether investments are in intercity or urban motorways, it is always a case of investing to meet needs. This is all the more justified in that road investment operations are usually highly profitable, not only for users and the community but also for the authorities as, nation-wide, roads bring in far more money than they cost.

Table 4.1
Kilometrages of High Traffic Motorways in Five European Countries (Urban and Nonurban)

Average Daily Traffic	60,000 to 80,000	80,000 to 100,000	100,000 to 120,000	120,000 to 150,000	150,000 to 200,000	Above 200,000
The Netherlands	450	130	110	90	35	0
Germany	1250	400	160	50	15	5
Great Britain	380	410	140	70	6	0
Spain	245	82	92	61	47	10
France	288	175	135	50	50	55
Paris Region	128	87	68	38	50	55
Total	2613	1197	637	321	153	70

Source: National Road Traffic Surveys.

Investing in roads is one of the most essential factors in each community's preparation for the future. Dysfunctions in road networks, which are the primary system of transport of all European communities, can rapidly deteriorate if the necessary investments are not made in time to respond when needed to progression in traffic.

Such delays are all the more regrettable in that investments necessary to ensure that road networks function well are relatively minor taken in the overall context of the transport system comprising the car, the truck, and the road. As we have seen, the total amount spent on the road transport system represents about 15% of the gross domestic product of West European countries, or an approximate total of 900 billion ECUs for the continent. Yet the total expenditure devoted to road infrastructures in Western Europe did not exceed 71 billion ECUs in 1992 [17].

In other words, users cover 92% of the total amount devoted to the road transport system. In addition, the remaining 8% also includes operating expenses paid by the authorities (police forces and administrative expenses) so that road building and maintenance only account for about 5% of the entire system's cost. This is the primary reason for their high profitability. It would be illogical to allow companies and individuals to continue to acquire and maintain vehicles and yet not be prepared to pay the relatively modest sums compared with their expenses to enable them to use them correctly and ensure that the economy runs smoothly.

4.3.9 New Ways of Managing the Maintenance of the Road System

Traditionally, most or all of the road system, either intercity or urban, is directly managed by national or local authorities, organised accordingly, with their own technical departments being in charge.

Recently, however, in the wake of the privatization trend, some countries are considering transfering this task to private companies not only for specific links, but for the whole of their network, reversing a time-old method.

In Europe, Great Britain can be cited, as this country has been recently taking the lead in this direction in this field as in many others. The Highways Agency in charge of the national road network is reducing accordingly its task force from 2,400 in 1994 to 1,400, with the longer term prospect of eliminating it entirely.

On the other hand, the Highways Agency announced in mid 1996 that it was opening a tender for managing the maintenance of its road network in six zones on a total of 24, the tendering being open both to private enterprises and to local authorities. The longer term idea is to entirely privatize the activity of the Highways Agency through a concession system organized in five to eight large zones. Only a very limited central administrative body would then continue to exist. Its task would be to issue the terms of reference for the concessions and to control their enforcement. It has to be added that Great Britain, in adopting this behavior—if political changes allow it to happen—is going in a direction opposite to traditional ways of managing road maintenance in Europe and is still isolated from the old Continent. Along the same lines, the British government was planning in 1996 to create five to six private Regional Traffic Control Centres that would be charged with managing traffic all over the country.

4.4 ONLY THE ROAD CAN RELIEVE THE ROAD

One of today's most widespread and popular ideas concerning investments in transport is that it is possible to relieve the road of its traffic by transferring part of it to other types of transport. This transfer concept dominates European transport policy and that of many individual countries. At first glance, it appears to be common sense. Is it not shocking to see the national heritage of railways and waterways so badly used while roads are so crowded? Is it not common thinking that there are too many vehicles on many of our roads, and that it would obviously be better if there were fewer?

However, this "common-sense" idea, shared by 92% of French people, rests on an assumption that is contradicted by the facts (i.e., that other means of transport can be used as substitutes for road transport). Unless restrictive measures are taken, experience shows that no such transfer has ever taken place. The idea is attractive, but it does not work. The markets are different and very often of completely different magnitude. For both the transport of people and freight, for intercity travel or for urban travel, it is impossible to relieve the roads by transferring their traffic to a nonroad infrastructure. This is the conclusion that results from the examination of all known, concrete examples.

4.4.1 Intercity Travel

When the Paris-Lille *TGV* high-speed train line was first opened in May 1993, the French press insisted heavily on the fact that the new line would divert an important part of traffic from the A1 motorway linking the two cities, which are about 200 km distant. The newspaper *Le Monde* wrote on 23rd May 1993: "During rush hours, the TGV Nord line plans to take almost one-third of A1 motorists. SNCF (French National Railways) directors are counting heavily on the fact that as most of the railway line runs parallel to the motorway, drivers will be able to compare, when they see trains pass them at 300 km/h." To help obtain the desired results, a costly advertising campaign in the winter of 1993–1994 showed the French television audience tense motorists behind the wheel, supposedly stuck in traffic on the motorway, and then contrasted these images with those of TGV passengers enjoying the comfort and tranquillity of this remarkable means of transport.

A first assessment of the results can now be made and is absolutely clear: *the new TGV has had practically no impact on the traffic on the motorway that runs parallel to it.* During the first three months of 1993, before the TGV line was opened, traffic had remained practically identical to that of the same period in 1992. It was the same in the last three months of 1993, *after* the TGV line had come into service. The 1994 results followed the same pattern. To be more precise, a detailed analysis of motorway use by private cars using the motorway from start to finish showed that the amount of traffic diverted as a result of the opening had probably been about 4%. But as such trips represent only about 30% of overall motorway traffic (cars and heavy goods vehicles combined), the TGV's impact did not exceed about 1% in total, which explains why it remained imperceptible, taking into account usual monthly variations.

The fact that 96% of the motorists who used the motorway along its entire length stayed faithful to it can seem very surprising given the undeniable advantages of the TGV. But this can only be a surprise to those who imagine that trips between the Paris region and the north of France consist solely of businessmen living in the centre of Paris who take business trips to the centre of Lille, and vice versa, whereas in fact the great majority of those who use the motorway need their car at one or both ends of their trip. They are often motorists who go from the suburbs of Paris to a final destination 20 or 30 km from Lille, or even more. Moreover, many of them have to stop on the way to visit customers, friends, or family. Others need their car to transport heavy objects or packages, and so forth. For these people, the TGV has changed nothing; they still need their car.

This does not mean the SNCF has not seen its traffic increase along these routes. On the contrary, the rise in traffic following the opening of the TGV line was very significant, amounting to approximately 30%. But this was essentially due to new movements made possible by an improvement in the service offered or by changes in fares, not to motorists who had given up their cars: the two markets are different. Although the high-speed train can compete with the aeroplane on certain distances because both are forms of public transport, experience has shown that it has no notable influence on road traffic, an individual means of transport, and that it cannot relieve the road at all. France had already noticed this when its first two high-speed lines were opened, one towards the south-east, the other towards the Atlantic Ocean. Germany also had the same experience. Along the Munich-Hamburg route, the ICE increased the market share for the railway from 12.8% to 14.6%, the share for air fell from 1.8% to 1.4%, and the road's remained practically unchanged, with 84% compared to 85.4% previously [18]. Studies performed for the Highway Users Federation in the United States regarding Amtrak reached the same conclusion. It goes without saying that what holds for high-speed trains is even more true for regional ones. Even when the latter are put in service at great expense, and even when the number of passengers who use them increases, impact on road traffic remains imperceptible. The fast train that now connects Strasbourg and Mulhouse, in Alsace, has only attracted 600 motorists per day out of an average road traffic of 50,000 (i.e., around 1%). Therefore, intercity rail investments cannot be justified on the grounds of lightening road traffic.

4.4.2 Urban Transport

The situation is the same in urban areas. At the end of the 1980s, the Dutch opened a new railway line between Amsterdam and the centre of Almere, about 30 km away. The new line had the effect of putting a brake on the long-standing tendency towards a growing use of the car to the detriment of public transport, and even slightly reversed the trend. But this was only the case for travel from the centre of Almere to Amsterdam. Observations made in another part of Almere showed that the new line had no repercussions on the distribution among means of transport: the bus continued to be insufficiently competitive and the train too far away. The overall result was that the new railway line had no visible influence on road traffic between the two towns [19].

Other Dutch experiments had already given the same results. New railway lines between Zoetermeer and Schiphol and an own-site bus line near the city of Krimpen resulted in a marked increase in public transport users, but no corresponding decrease in the number of drivers along the same route was able to be proved. A simulation carried out in this country on a national level showed that even if public transport were carried to its highest imaginable level everywhere (creation of underground, train, and bus lines in all towns, the opening of stations in all villages, etc.), which is obviously an unrealisable hypothesis, road car traffic would not fall by more than 5% in the Netherlands [19].

In France, the opening of the first underground railway line in Toulouse (600,000 inhabitants) in 1993 was a considerable success from the attendance point of view. This line alone increased the number of users of the entire public transport network by 30%. But its impact on road traffic remained very limited. This is hardly surprising. Public transport had previously provided less than 20% of motorised travel in the area and the car more than 80%. The increase in public transport users therefore corresponded to 5% of the number of trips in the city and its suburbs. But only about one-fourth of this additional traffic was due to former motorists who switched to public transport. Road traffic in general declined by only about 1%, which is imperceptible in a town and its suburbs, whereas the cost of the investment in the underground railway line exceeded 3 billion francs (500 million ECUs), which, as in Los Angeles, amounts to a prohibitive cost per driver dissuaded. Many such examples can be given. The new tram line in Saint-Denis, in the northern suburbs of Paris, encouraged 3,000 car users to switch to it daily, but more than 160,000 cars continue to use the neighbouring A1 urban motorway each day.

Even in Swiss towns, where a probably unique effort has been made in favour of public transport, total car use has hardly changed in the absence of measures restricting their use. The city of Zurich inaugurated an entirely renovated public transport system in 1990, consisting particularly in a light regional rail network costing 2 billion Swiss francs (1.3 billion ECUs) and offering new connections, cross-town lines, a new central station, a tunnel under the city, an increase in the number of trains, and so forth. Following these radical changes, the number of public transport passengers rose by 20% during the first year of operation, and by 5% the following year, raising the annual number of public transport trips to 470 per inhabitant, which is probably the world record. But despite these results, there was no perceptible influence on road traffic volume in Zurich: traffic flow at entries to the city remained identical, leading the OECD to note that "*the car remained attractive, even when the quality of public transport was very high*" and to deduce, surprisingly for an organisation that as a rule is supposed to be market-oriented, that "*it was essential to limit the attractiveness of trips in private cars*" [11]!

The conclusions are the same everywhere. In the best of cases, new public transport infrastructures can generate their own new traffic, but they cannot relieve road traffic. On the other hand, in the long term, investment in public transport can encourage certain activities to become concentrated in city centres, which does not necessarily make finding a solution for transport problems easier, even if there are other reasons to justify it (see Chapter 12).

Therefore, as far as the transport of people is concerned, either for urban or long-distance travel, contrary to what everybody is inclined to think *a priori*, experience constantly shows that investments devoted to other means of transport do not take any noticeable traffic away from the road.

4.4.3 The Transport of Freight

As we have seen previously, freight transport only confirms the above patterns. Not only are the freight markets for the road, the railway, and the waterway mainly essentially different, both geographically and by the nature of the transport to be provided, but there is also a disproportion in their scale. What is the significance of the 14 billion kilometres travelled each year by rail freight trucks compared with the 3,000 billion kilometres travelled each year by all road vehicles in Western Europe?

It is obviously impossible, overall, for a development in rail freight traffic to relieve road traffic, which must be considered by adding all categories of vehicles, since both cars and trucks use the same infrastructures. With perhaps one exception, studies carried out on specific transport corridors only confirm this impossibility. The existing rail freight traffic itself rarely relieves existing motorways of more than a few hundred or barely a few thousand trucks per day, whereas the latter have traffic levels of tens of thousands of vehicles daily.

And what is true for railways is even more so for waterways as their overall tonnage transported, for the whole of the continent, is equivalent to less than half that of the railways. The traffic along the latest major waterway project in Europe— the Rhine-Main-Danube junction, which links the two largest rivers of the continent—does not exceed 6 million tonnes per year, which corresponds to a traffic of about one thousand trucks per day, for an investment very much higher than that of a motorway which is used by tens of thousands of vehicles per day. Given, as we have seen, that the value of transporting one tonne by road is, on average, about twenty times higher than by water, it can be seen why this project was unsound in economic terms and why it was seriously considered abandoning the works when they were already under way. This was not done, however, because it appeared politically delicate to leave such a major project unfinished, considering the enormous sums of money that had already been spent. Is it not true that the German Minister of Transport in office about 15 years ago said on this subject, "that it was the most absurd project since the Tower of Babel"?

It can therefore be seen that neither the railway nor the waterway can really influence road traffic volume. The European continent can only claim one possible exception to this rule, which is the lower Rhine Valley between the Ruhr and the port of Rotterdam. It must be said that this corridor is the route for most of Germany's heavy industry towards the exterior of the continent. Given the strength of this industry, it is not surprising that the density of freight flow along this route has no comparison elsewhere in Europe. The traffic to be transported is enormous, either by river, railway, or road, and on this particular route the waterway and the railway obviously fulfil a role that it would be difficult to replace.

For this reason and because it did not want to see German traffic escape to the benefit of Hamburg along the new north-south railway line recently constructed in Germany, the Netherlands decided in April 1995 to construct an east-west railway line on its territory, to be used only for freight transport between Rotterdam's Europoort and the German border. This line, named "Betuwelijn," is expected to have an annual capacity of 60 million tonnes and will cost 13 billion guilders (about

6.5 billion ECUs) for 120 km, able to be covered in one hour. Whether this new line can alleviate road traffic along parallel motorways, or at least avoid its increase, and whether the result obtained will match the considerable cost of the project, remain to be seen.

But this is a unique case in Europe. Everywhere else, the amount of traffic capable of being deviated from the road due to investment in railways or waterways is marginal with respect to the flows along Europe's great motorways, due to the entirely different scale of traffic. This applies to an even greater extent to combined transport, as its volume represents only a fraction of rail freight traffic and concerns only a few limited routes.

The border effect, a European specificity that will be described later on in Chapter 6, and which greatly reduces the rail freight market, cannot but act in the same way.

In summary, an objective examination of the facts and figures leads to a surprising conclusion. For both people and freight, with the possible exception of the lower Rhine Valley, it is impossible to alleviate road traffic in anything but a marginal way by developing other modes of transport.

Things would obviously be different if it were possible to impose the choice of means of transport on users. The countries of Eastern Europe proceeded in this manner until their liberation from communism in 1989. The railway and, to a lesser extent, the waterway, monopolised almost all traffic there, at the price of delays and considerable costs to the economy. But in this case, too, everything has changed since economic actors have free choice of their decisions. The railway, which no longer benefits from authoritarian measures, has seen its traffic collapse, while road traffic is literally exploding. It is important to remember that, actually, in any market economy, it is not the central power that decides on the distribution among modes of transport, but millions of individuals who act in their own interests, but also in those of the community, and that experience has shown that it is practically impossible to influence their choice, contrary to what most people believe in Europe.

Unless restrictive measures are imposed, which no one can seriously consider as a general rule in our market-oriented countries, the fact must be faced when new transport investment is planned that only the road can relieve the road.

References

[1] Union Routière de France & SOFRES surveys, 1993–1996, Paris.
[2] *Transport Statistics Great Britain, 1996 Edition,* The Department of Transport, HMSO, London.
[3] *Urban Travel and Sustainable Development,* OCDE, 1995, Paris.
[4] "Towards Fair and Efficient Pricing in Transport: Political Options to Internalise the External Costs of Transports in the European Union," European Commission, 1995, Brussels.
[5] *Mobility Facts,* Institute of Traffic Engineers, 1992, Washington.
[6] *Internalise the Social Costs of Transport,* OCDE, 1994, Paris.
[7] Enquête Générale de Transport 1991–1992. Préfecture de la Région Ile-de-France, 1995, Paris.
[8] Enquête Nationale de Transport 1993–1994. INSEE, 1996, Paris.

[9] *Annual World Report 1994,* World Bank, Washington.
[10] *La rentabilité fiscale des investissements routiers,* Rémy Prud'homme, Observatoire Economique des Institutions Locales (L'OEIL) Université de Paris XII, 1996 Créteil.
[11] *Managing Congestion and Road Traffic Demand,* OCDE, 1994, Paris.
[12] *World Road Statistics,* International Road Federation (IRF), 1995, Geneva.
[13] *About the SACTRA report—The danger of nihilism in road policy,* Sir Foster, 1995.
[14] LAFONT R. "Toll Modulation," *Routes/Roads* (IRF), April 1996, Geneva.
[15] *The Facts About "Gridlock" in Southern California,* Reason Foundation, 1993, Los Angeles.
[16] *Les transports de voyageurs en Ile-de-France,* Préfecture d'Ile-de-France, 1994, Paris.
[17] Dieckmann, A. *Towards More Rational Transport Policies in Europe,* Die Deutsche Bibliothek CIV, Cologne, 1995.
[18] La Vie du Rail n° 2466, Juillet 1994, Paris.
[19] *Substitution of Travel Between Car and Public Transport,* Bovy, Vanderwaard, baanders, Rijkswaterstaat, Dutch Ministry of transport, Rotterdam, 1991.

CHAPTER 5
▼▼▼

METROROUTES: THE INVENTION OF THE CENTURY

5.1 A NEW CONCEPT

In transport as in any other area, innovations sometimes occur that fundamentally change the realm of possibilities. This was the case for the railway and then, at the end of the last century, with the appearance of the underground railway (also called the subway, metro, U-Bahn . . .), which enabled large towns to free surface areas and reach or maintain considerable densities of population and activity whilst at the same time functioning properly and avoiding being stifled. Later, urban and suburban motorways opened up an unprecedented amount of land to living space and urban activity. But since the invention of the underground railway over a century ago, no major transport innovation has taken place in central areas of towns and their suburbs.

Until now. For things are now due to change with the imminent appearance of an entirely new kind of underground motorway that could be called "metroroute." The term "metroroute" is proposed for it combines the word "métro," associated with underground transport in many cities of the world, and the word "route." It summarises this kind of structure well and is easily memorised.

Metroroutes are the brainchild of two engineers[1] from the French public works company G.T.M who, like so many other people, were victims of the daily morning motorway rush-hour traffic converging on Paris and therefore imagined an entirely new type of road infrastructure in 1987. Their proposal is a combination of technical progress and an idea.

The technical progress is that which has been made over the last 10 years by tunnelling machines that can bore circular tunnels and were notably used in the construction of the Channel Tunnel.

The idea, on the other hand, is quite simple. It is based on the observation that if there are roads at surface level that permit movement of vehicles of all sizes, especially heavy goods vehicles, then road network capacity can be increased by creating new low-gauge roads reserved exclusively for private cars and light commercial vehicles, which represent a very large majority of traffic.

The combination of this technical progress and this common-sense idea enables an entirely new type of structure to be imagined. In an underground tunnel with an internal diameter of about 10 metres, it becomes possible to build not two traffic lanes, as is usually the case with road tunnels, but six lanes split between two superposed levels, dividing the costs by about three for equal capacities. A motorway can then be built in a space hardly larger than that taken up by certain underground railways. These tunnels open up an entirely new perspective for motorways in the centres of urban areas, giving birth at the end of the 20th century to an innovation as important as that of the underground railway at the end of the 19th century (Figures 14 and 15). The idea could also be transposed to aerial structures built, for example, above certain existing motorways, whose cost would be very much lower if they were reserved for light vehicles and whose noise impact on the environment could be non-existent if they were covered by a protective casing, a solution that is considered more and more frequently.

5.1.1 The New Tunnelling Machines

Building tunnels has always been a delicate operation. Admittedly, it is less difficult in rocky areas where the ground is stable once it has been bored with explosives. But most towns are located on land of sedimentary origin where this is not the case and where, until recently, it was almost impossible and always extremely costly to consider building large-diameter deep tunnels.

Tunnelling machines were first developed in their modern form in Japan and have progressed spectacularly in recent decades, not only concerning the diameter of the tubes that they are able to bore, but also their reliability, their performance,

---

[1] Mr. Jean Pehuet and Mr. François Lemperière, graduate engineers of the École Polytechnique and the Ecole Nationale des Ponts et Chaussées (Paris).

and their cost, so that a whole new sphere of opportunity now exists for the creation of tunnels in sedimentary or mixed ground.

Tunnel-boring machines are not a recent invention and tribute must be paid to the Franco-British engineer, Marc Isambard Brunel, who developed the first ones at the start of the 19th century, paving the way for the creation of the London underground network. The first important underground railway line built with this technology under the direction of the engineer Mr. Greathead, was inaugurated by the City and South London Railway Company in 1890 and was rapidly given the name "the Tube" due to the tunnel's cylindrical form, which also meant that the vehicles using the tunnel adopted the same characteristic shape. Over a century later, admiration is still inspired by this combination of the use of the era's most modern techniques, which allowed workers to progress at the rate of about 5 metres per day and the imagination, even audacity, that allowed the British Capital to build its extensive underground railway network ahead of all the others and at a relatively low cost.

But the tunnelling machines used in those times were mainly designed to bore through argillaceous soil, which offers little resistance, and the diameter of the tunnels could not exceed about four metres. It was not until the 1980s that a new generation of modern tunnelling machines equipped with shields appeared, offering three advantages: firstly, they can bore in many different types of ground; secondly, they can bore much wider tunnels, as within a few years their maximum diameter increased from 8 metres to 10, then even to 14 metres (as is the case for the Tokyo Bay underground road tunnel currently under construction); and thirdly, they are more and more powerful and reliable.

The efficiency of modern tunnelling machines was spectacularly displayed during the Channel Tunnel construction, as its two main tubes have an external diameter of nearly 8.5 metres. Although the project experienced various setbacks that delayed its opening, these did not involve delays in boring its three tunnels. After a relatively slow start due to the unprecedented nature of the project, some tunnelling machines even reached a record of more than 1,000 metres per month, and the tunnels' civil engineering works were completed on schedule, whilst remaining a minority share of the project's overall cost.

Although shield tunnelling is not the only method that exists today, it is more and more technically reliable. Some tunnel boring machines are built to function in dry terrain. Others are designed to bore in water-saturated or potentially saturated soil. Although tunnelling machines are obviously at their best in homogeneous terrain with little risk, they can also function in heterogeneous soil. There can still, of course, be unforeseen difficulties that can be quite considerable, as shown in the case of the tunnels linking Copenhagen to the rest of Denmark, or those for the North Lyons bypass in France. But their technique is now more and more mastered and they are used successfully to create new underground or railway lines under many cities, such as in Paris, London, and elsewhere.

5.1.2 Decreasing Costs

Modern tunnelling machines have another major advantage: the total cost of acquiring and operating them has significantly decreased at the rate of about 4% per year, and will continue to do so, so that the cost of the structures that can be built with this technology are often becoming competitive in dense urban areas with that of surface structures.

It is well-known that the construction costs of surface roads and motorways—when they are possible in physical and political terms—continue to spiral in urban areas. When all the costs are added together, including possible land acquisitions, temporary diversion of various existing networks (roads, water, electricity, gas, etc.) and their subsequent reconnection, building road interchanges, providing environmental protection, and even sometimes having to create anyway certain underground sections, the price of motorway projects in urban areas can be very high. The range of costs per kilometre is, admittedly, very wide. But in many large European towns, costs of 50 to 150 million ECUs per kilometre, and even more in some localities, are not rare if the zone is relatively dense or if natural obstacles exist. In the Paris region, the cost of constructing a missing section of the new circular A86 Motorway to the north, about 4 km away from the inner Paris ring road (Boulevard Peripherique) will amount, according to forecasts, to about 5 billion francs (800 million ECUs) for 6 km, even though the necessary rights of way have already been reserved for a long time. To the east of Paris, a Marne River crossing for the same motorway is scheduled to cost 2.5 billion francs (400 million ECUs) for 1.6 km, or close to 1.6 billion francs (250 million ECUs) per kilometre. And France is not an exception, as shown by the Docklands Extension in London, where the cost of the "Limehouse Link Road" amounts to £200 million per mile (160 million ECUs per kilometre), or the Basel Franco-Swiss Link, or countless other urban projects.

Such costs are justified by the economic return on these exceptional projects, which will accommodate very heavy traffic. But as time passes, the costs of projects situated in dense urban areas will climb higher and higher, and they will face increasingly difficult financial problems. On the other hand, more and more frequently, metroroutes will offer the advantage of relatively stable costs amounting to about 650 million francs, or 100 million ECUs, per kilometre, (including financial and study costs). These costs are likely to decrease with time as technical progress advances, being said the precise cost per kilometre obviously depends, among other things, on the number and type of interchanges. In addition, it will become increasingly difficult, if not impossible, to build traditional surface roads and motorways in urban central areas. Although these remain relevant in suburban areas as long as the appropriate measures are taken to protect the environment, underground structures are often the only feasible solution in the densest areas.

5.2 TECHNICAL CHARACTERISTICS

But before examining the future use of metroroutes and their possible impact on urban transport, it is necessary to describe their general characteristics more precisely.

5.2.1 A Special Commission

To define them, the French government set up an interdepartmental commission at the end of 1991, and its conclusions (see Appendix 2) were published in June 1992. The opportunity was granted through a project to complete the A86 Motorway west of Paris on a stretch of 10 km that had been on hold for 30 years. It must be said that this area of the Paris region has many wooded areas and historic monuments and, especially, the town of Versailles!

IIistorically, this project was not the first. Initially, the first metroroute was projected in 1988 under the city of Paris itself. Under the code name of LASER (liaison autoroutière souterraine express régionale), it would have been composed of a loop under the French capital, with five suburban motorway links joining it. This project would undoubtedly have allowed drivers to move around Paris, to use the expression of its promoters, as if every month were the month of August, so great was its capacity to relieve the streets, avenues, and boulevards of Paris of a large part of their traffic. Although it was without doubt the most judicious of all the projects, it was ahead of its time and, like another competing project to build a motorway under Paris, was set aside.

A second plan was to build an underground duplicate of the southern section of the inner Paris ring road, the *Boulevard Périphérique,* which is often saturated since it has only three lanes each way. Polls showed this project met with the approval of 84% of Parisians, who often suffer from congestion along this ring road, which carries one-third of the capital's traffic. Although this project, which is the responsibility of the municipality, is not abandoned, it has not yet been implemented, mainly for financial reasons. The situation is the same at present for a project called "MUSE," proposed on the initiative of the Hauts-de-Seine Department in the western suburbs of Paris and aimed at combining car and public transport levels in the same structure, and for an underground link between Roissy-Charles-de-Gaulle Airport and Paris, which is currently under study and is being promoted by the Paris Chamber of Commerce and Industry.

5.2.2 A Government Project

For this reason, the A86 project, which comes under the sole authority of the French government and presents an economic return for the community estimated at nearly 30% in 2010, will be the first such construction, given that it will be operated with a toll system, as is the nearby (but traditional design) A14 motorway, which was opened at the end of 1996. The interdepartmental commission set up to define its characteristics first outlined how the structure would function. As it will be a very long underground passage, the commission established that it should operate under constant surveillance, using the latest "intelligent road" technology developments, and recommended a speed limit of 70 km/h, which is close to the optimum as far as capacity is concerned.

5.2.3 Ten Metres in Diameter

The interdepartmental commission then reflected on the size to give to the cross-section of the structure. It first calculated the necessary road width, which could obviously be narrower than that of a traditional motorway since there would be no heavy goods vehicles and since speed limits would be lower than usual and would be continuously monitored and enforced. The calculations resulted in the recommendation of an internal width of 9.6 metres at the car driver eye-height, compatible with an internal diameter of approximately 10 metres for the structure. This allows three traffic lanes to run side by side on the two levels, due to the fact that the vehicles using them would generally have the average European car width of 1.7 metres (unlike heavy goods vehicles, which can reach 2.55 metres in width).

5.2.4 At Least Two Metres High

A 10-metre internal diameter can also allow each of the two traffic levels a ceiling height of 2.55 metres and could thus admit all vehicles up to 2 metres high, if standard traffic signs are used, or even 2.15 metres high if traffic signs are specially adapted. Furthermore, the actual internal diameter, taking into account building safety margins, will in practice probably be about 10.4 metres and not 10 metres. As for the section to be bored, it would not exceed 90m^2.

5.2.5 More Than 90% of the Traffic

If a study is made of the vehicles on French roads, which are not very different from those of the other European countries, it appears that a height of two metres can admit 96% of the vehicles in circulation (i.e., all road vehicles except coaches, caravans, heavy goods vehicles, and larger vans). Admittedly, these last types of vehicle drive more often, on average, than the others and can account for up to 15% or more of the traffic on certain routes. But during rush hours, obviously the times of day when extra capacity is more needed, the proportion of traffic they represent is nearly always less than 10% in dense urban areas.

In other words, due to a remarkable coincidence that makes this concept all the more interesting, the tunnel's width requirements produce optimised underground roads capable of admitting 90 to 95% of the vehicles in circulation in dense urban areas during rush hours! By another coincidence, the required internal section, approximately 10 metres in diameter, is the same size as traditional two-lane road tunnels of normal size. It must finally be added that a slight increase in this diameter may allow certain metroroutes to be used in the future by specially built public transport vehicles if there is sufficient, but not too heavy, traffic to warrant it. Stops could then be specially fitted into the nearside lane, cars using the other two exclusively. The structure would thus function simultaneously as a motorway and a public transport system, with the advantages of both.

Even if this is not the case, metroroutes would obviously have considerable hourly capacities. Although not fully equivalent to the capacity of motorways with three continuous lanes both ways, due to the necessity to restrict it to two lanes at interchanges, the tunnel could nonetheless accommodate 8,000 to 10,000 vehicles per hour (both directions combined). In urban areas, this may allow for up to 100,000 vehicles per day, transporting more than 130,000 people and allowing tolls to finance, if needed, a sizeable part of the investment and operating costs. It can be added that low-gauge light trucks will also be able to use these tunnels. In urban areas, the majority of freight transport is provided by such vehicles and not by heavy goods vehicles.

It must nonetheless be noted that competition from free, surface roads will almost always mean that projects of this nature cannot be entirely financed by the private sector and that mixed financing must therefore be foreseen, which will alleviate the burden on public finances but will not entirely eliminate government, or others', involvement. Three urban toll roads of traditional design have already been conceded to private or semiprivate companies in such a way in France—in Marseilles (the Prado-Carénage Tunnel), in Lyons (the northern bypass) and in Paris (A14 motorway)—with some contractually-agreed direct or indirect support from the public authorities. As far as the western section of the A86 motorway is concerned, it is the revenues from tolls on the concessionary company's already existing motorway network that will provide the major part of the necessary financing for many years to come and that have enabled the operation to be mounted and the first metroroute to be constructed.

5.2.6 Maximum Safety

The interdepartmental commission also studied the problems of ventilation and safety. The former issue is being made much easier due to technical progress, which has considerably reduced, and will continue to do so, the amount of pollutants that are emitted. The latter is being made easier by the existence of the two superposed, independent traffic levels, which allows one level to be used to reach or evacuate the other through staircases in case of an emergency. It must be noted for that matter that many fewer accidents take place in underground structures than in ones above ground, particularly due to the absence of bad weather and crossroads and to greater vigilance on the part of drivers.

Finally, the interdepartmental commission defined the characteristics of the structures linking the underground motorway with the ground level and concluded that there were no technical obstacles to the creation of metroroutes. It particularly stressed that, contrary to normal-sized underground motorways that require large cuttings, links with roads or streets on the surface would be far less expensive to construct, relatively easy to install, and be very inconspicuous as they would look rather like car-park entrances due to the height limits for vehicles. In fact, low-gauge will allow easy insertion of entry and exit points whereas for normal-sized tunnels they are often purely and simply impossible to construct in a dense urban environment. Planners instinctively want to make only heavy goods vehicles drive underground, as for the Japanese project in Tokyo, or to build mixed infrastructures as is the general rule in Europe and elsewhere. It should be added that infrastructures reserved for light vehicles can be designed with far steeper slopes than those that have to cope with heavy vehicles. In an urban context, it is far more logical to make only light vehicles travel underground, both because they are more numerous and also because the tunnels are then much easier and much cheaper to build.

5.2.7 Safety Kills Safety

Contrary to other safety commissions, such as the one for the Channel Tunnel, the commission that worked on the metroroutes carried out its investigation not only with the obsession of minimising risks for future users, but also with the aim not to impose, in the name of safety, expenses of uncertain or marginal effectiveness. The commission was fully aware of the fact that any added unjustified investment or operating cost could only have a negative influence on safety, either by jeopardising the feasibility of the construction itself or by leading to a waste of public and private capital that is so urgently needed elsewhere in projects whose impact on safety is undeniable. In fact, the approach retained has been the same as the one used by the British engineers in the 19th century who, due to the technological limits of the time, were obliged to adopt very restricted dimensions for their "Tube" tunnels. Minimising should be a constant obsession for underground works, although this lesson has obviously still not been understood by certain on the Continent at the end of the 20th century.

The French commission did everything possible to avoid this pitfall as it was fully aware that it was working not only for the A86 motorway project, but for a new generation of tunnels that are destined to multiply in Europe and elsewhere.

5.3 FULLY NEW PROSPECTS

5.3.1 Objective 2000

At the end of the investigation, the French government began procedures to declare the structure of public utility, a necessary step before work on the 10 km of the A86 motorway could begin. In spite of some strident local opposition (which was difficult to understand in view of the fact that the structure would be as discreet as an underground railway line and would only have three or four surface-level entry/exit points, which make it very environment-friendly), the public utility investigation committee, set up at the start of 1994, came to a positive conclusion in November of that same year, implicitly taking into account the fact that, if it had been a project for a railway line presenting exactly the same characteristics, there would most probably have been no, or very few, negative reactions.

The final government decision was made on 8th December 1995. It entrusted the financing and construction of the project to a promoter, the private motorway toll company Cofiroute, a good example of the dynamism of the French motorway sector. Construction is beginning in 1997 and the first section of this entirely new kind of project should open in 2003, practically a century after the first Paris underground railway line was opened, showing the creativity of a country that has often been at the leading edge of technical progress, especially in the area of transport.

5.3.2 The Third Dimension

This innovation will be able to radically change urban transport, not only in the Paris region where it will be capable of alleviating the traffic problems in the central part of the region once it is applied on a large scale, but also in other large cities in developed countries. Its similarity to the underground railway, or metro, is striking. In both cases, the third dimension is used, both to allow increased traffic flows under better conditions and to alleviate the roads at the surface of part of their traffic, to the environment's benefit. It is not a surprise it has sometimes be called "a metro for cars."

Like the underground railway, metroroutes have a dual mission. The first is to stop users from being at the mercy of traffic and give them an entirely new advantage regarding road transport in urban areas: a guarantee as to how much time a journey will take, given that journey times will be particularly short. Since access is limited, only 10 minutes will be necessary at any time of day to drive more than 10 km, whereas it now sometimes takes three to four times longer to travel the same distance in large cities. The existence, in addition to the existing network, of a network that guarantees journey times will be of great advantage to the economy of the areas in question. For instance, the benefit to companies will be that executives, whose time is of high value, will no longer lose precious time in traffic jams on these routes. The user would be able to choose between a high-speed paying network and a lesser-speed nonpaying one. But even those who chose the second option would enjoy a benefit from this new type of structure. It will consist in the fact that considerable relief will be brought to surface traffic in their area of influence, thanks to their high capacity. In fact, paradoxically, most of the time saved as a result of this type of motorway will not be by those who actually use them, but by those, including trucks, who will remain at the surface and travel better although they will not have to pay tolls.

Of course, such an achievement can be lasting only if traffic does not increase excessively, but everything suggests that this will be the case, as demand for car travel is already stabilising in city centres in Western Europe, and car traffic can be kept under control, at least in central areas, by good parking policies, not to mention the possible long-term prospect of general urban road tolls. As the president of the French Public Transport Union declared: "To win just one or two points of market share from cars, we must make colossal investments in public transport. (. . .) Let's bury the cars and give back its basic role to the urban landscape: that of being a pleasant and friendly place."

In fact, traffic studies on specific projects in the Paris region revealed that, due to the absorption capacity of the metroroutes, they will drain traffic and relieve surface traffic significantly, enabling planners to "reconquer" surface roads and streets for the benefit of pedestrians, bicycle users, and public transport. Metroroutes have an outstanding capacity compared with the capacity of traditional roads, with their cross-roads, traffic lights and so forth, which can rarely accommodate without severe problems to the environment more than 30,000 vehicles per day, and often many fewer. This observation explains the metroroute promoters' motto: "Drive better below to live better above."

5.3.3 The Great Projects of the 21st Century

In the Paris region alone, the metroroute programme officially registered in the region's development plan for the year 2015 amounts to about 100 km for the central part of the region, where five million people occupy a surface area of 500 km^2 within an area of 25 to 30 km in diameter. This could be one of the greatest public-work construction sites of the 21st century in Western Europe, although it is impossible at the present time to predict its rate of implementation, and this for an unexpected reason. It appears that the traffic situation is no longer deteriorating in the central part of the Paris region, for various reasons that will be detailed in Chapter 12, and this could make the project less urgent than previously forecasted. However, it is planned that another 2-km prototype section of métroroute, with an internal diameter of 8.40m (therefore even more restricted as it will only accommodate two traffic lanes on each level) could come into service in the short term in the scope of the MUSE project.

But many other projects can be considered in other parts of the European continent. A large number of urban underground road tunnels are already projected or under construction in many different countries such as Germany, Sweden, or the Netherlands, which have declared them to be priorities.

At a time when there is more and more concern for the preservation of the environment, the solution of building underground roads will be judged preferable in an increasing number of cases. But apparently none of these countries have considered the métroroute solution, which divides the costs by a factor of around three. For example, the city of Stockholm has just launched an exceptional underground road construction programme, but with traditional dimensions, therefore making it far more costly.

Others, such as the city of Geneva, have abandoned in the face of the high costs, having failed until now to think of the solution of a low-gauge tunnel, although it would seem to be particularly appropriate for the project of crossing the famous lake.

But the urban area that appears to offer the largest field of application of the low-gauge concept is certainly London, where the demand for transport is considerable and where, far more than in Paris, the economic activity suffers from a serious deficit in road capacity in the central part of the city. The cost of creating a traditional surface motorway network in the central part of London was estimated, in 1969, to be the equivalent of 130 million pounds per kilometre (1996 value) and would, today, be far more than that and, furthermore, would be environmentally and politically intolerable. A low-gauge underground system would be acceptable and far less expensive.

On the European continent as a whole, hundreds more kilometres of roads of this type can be projected, not to mention the other parts of the world, particularly the large cities of the developed Asian countries where demographic density and financial resources are particularly adapted to such projects. Even in North America, where the amount of space available usually makes it unnecessary to resort to underground structures, the solution cannot be excluded in selective places. Once the process gets under way and the first project of this nature is introduced, the advantages will be so evident that projects will burgeon in many places, the metroroutes usually being all the more justified the closer they are to city centres. A life-sized model built in Orléans, France, has proved the relevance of the project and surprised most visitors with the impression of space given by its design features.

Of course, as was the case with the underground railway, this type of project will only be justified in specific cases with a very high demand, considering its cost. Nevertheless, besides its use in and around large cities faced with chronic traffic problems on large sections of their surface area (which justify large underground networks), shorter metroroute tunnels can be forecasted in smaller towns at points where specific traffic problems often occur, and maybe even along very specific stretches of rural road networks.

CHAPTER 6

▼▼▼

THE RAILWAY NETWORKS: A LIMITED FUTURE

6.1 PAST AND PRESENT SITUATION

6.1.1 Past Evolution

Throughout the second half of the 19th century and until the beginning of the 20th century, the railway played a dominant (even overpowering) role in the world of transport in Europe, both for movements of people and goods. It is difficult for us to imagine its fascination for people at the time and how much it changed their way of life, making a complete break from the restrictions in movements that had existed until then.

Whereas it had always taken days, even weeks, to go from one end to the other of most European countries, journeys could suddenly be counted in hours. There was an explosion in the exchange of men and goods that was unprecedented in the history of Man and the railway carried Europe (and more generally speaking, the entire developed world) into the industrial era.

The first steam locomotive was built in England in 1804, and the first passenger line opened in 1825 between Stockton and Darlington. Shortly afterwards, between 1833 and 1835, the first passenger lines appeared in their turn on the Continent, in France, Belgium, Germany, and so forth. Everything then moved with a breathtaking swiftness that is still astounding today, so intense was the infatuation with this true technical revolution and the energy mobilised so great. Europe had 40 km of rail open to traffic in 1825, which rose to 432 in 1835, then 2,762 in 1840, 9,000 in 1845, 23,000 in 1850, 51,000 in 1860, 103,000 in 1870, and 150,000 in 1876, a half-century later. The major part of the network, serving tens of thousands of stations, was then in place.

The impact of the railway revolution was enormous. In France, for example, whereas five million journeys were made by stagecoach in 1835, the number of train passengers reached 90 million in 1870, and 400 million in 1900! For thousands of years, the very great majority of Europeans had remained sedentary, with the surroundings of their native village as their only horizon. The railway brought them into the age of mobility and trains with evocative names made their way night and day throughout the continent: Flèche d'or, Train Bleu, Rembrandt, Talgo, Rubens, Flying Scotsman, Barbarossa, Etoile du Nord, Orient Express, Frans Hals, and so forth.

At the same time, the railway took over most freight transport, and no factory imagined for one instant setting up in a location without a railway line. The railway brought together the biggest barons of industry, the best bankers, and the best engineers, and was undeniably the greatest economic and industrial project of the 19th and early 20th centuries. But the dawn of the 20th century saw the appearance of competitors that would completely change the context of transport in Europe as elsewhere: the car and the truck on the one hand and the aeroplane on the other.

In truth, the threat was still limited until the Second World War. Contrary to what happened in the United States, in Europe the car remained the luxury of a privileged minority between the two wars, since in 1939 there were only about eight million private and commercial cars on the continent. For the immense majority of the hundreds of millions of Europeans, the railway continued to be the only accessible form of intercity travel. Around 1930, the total number of train passengers for the whole of Europe most probably reached five billion per year, which is close to its current level.

As far as freight transport was concerned, trucks experienced strong growth at the same time. But they were still relatively few in number, unreliable and low-performance, and, allowing for exceptions, the absence of motorways limited their possibilities of competing with the railway, even if their presence was far from negligible.

The battle between rail and road raged during this period and often ended with the victory of the former, especially since the most brilliant and influential minds of the period continued to work for the railway companies, whereas road transport was for the most part provided by a myriad of artisans or small enterprises, almost always headed by former truck drivers—many of whom had only an elementary level of education. In some countries, policies were implemented that were voluntarily hostile to trucks and coaches, with the precise aim of favouring the railways.

Nevertheless, the depression of the 1930s and the fall in traffic put an end to the independence of the railway companies that had built and operated the networks from the beginnings. Throughout Europe, they fell into the hands of the States, either before or after Second World War, and most of them were reorganised into one national company in each country: BR (Great Britain), SNCF (France), SNCB (Belgium), RENFE (Spain), DB (Germany), FS (Italy), DSB (Denmark), CFF (Switzerland), SJ (Sweden), CP (Portugal), CIE (Ireland), NS (The Netherlands), NSB (Norway), VR (Finland), OBB (Austria), CFL (Luxembourg), CH (Greece).

6.1.2 Present Situation

The nationalisation of European railways changed the picture drastically and profoundly marked the evolution of rail transport in the second half of the 20th century by allowing it to avoid the rules of the market, with very serious consequences whose full scope is only just being realised today. At the end of the 20th century, nearly all European railways are in an extremely difficult posture.

In terms of traffic, the figures are different for passengers and freight. From 1970 to 1993, passenger traffic in the networks of the 17 Western European countries, expressed in passenger kilometres, rose slightly from 210 billion to 282 billion. But this progression, which was made in a period when the continent's economy continued a steady expansion, remained moderate, about 1.4% per year on average, and lower than the gross domestic product (GDP). Over the same period, car journeys more than doubled, increasing from 1,586 billion to 3,356 billion passenger kilometres, or 12 times more than rail traffic. As for internal European air traffic, which started from practically nothing just three decades ago, it reached 260 billion passenger kilometres in 1995 and continues its lightning growth.

As we have seen, the trend for freight was even less favourable, as traffic decreased over the same period from 254 billion tonne kilometres to 240 in 1992— and even lower in 1993—whereas road freight transport also more than doubled in the same period (from 430 billion tonne kilometres to around 950 billion). In addition, as we have seen in Chapter 3, the corresponding rail freight turnover has become marginal in comparison to that of goods road traffic.

Even so, the figures for both passengers and freight do not reveal the economic realities of the situation. Despite the fact that they are so disappointing for the railways, they were only obtained because the different European States accorded them special fundings that distorted the rules of the market and have now gone beyond the limits of what is bearable by national economies when these are faced with severe budgetary difficulties.

According to statistics published by the International Union of Railways [1], the operating losses of Western Europe's railway companies reached 11.7 billion

ECUs in 1992, representing close to 37% of their operating costs (which amounted to 32 billion ECUs). And these deficits occurred despite additional subsidies for infrastructure and operating costs, which totalled 27.6 billion ECUs for that same year!

In total, railways cost nearly 40 billion ECUs each year in the budgets of the various nations of Western Europe, whilst revenues from traffic amount to only about 30 billion. In other words, users of the railway pay, on average, less than half the true cost of the service they receive, and the national governments (i.e., the taxpayers) must make up the difference. This means that if fares were based on true economic realities, tariffs should more than double on average in most countries, which would lead to the disappearance of almost all the railways' clients. The truth is that, under present conditions, the real market for the railway has to a great extent vanished due to competition from the road and the air, and that most of its activities are maintained solely at the price of subsidies that are so high that they would be unthinkable in any other sector of the economy.

But this broad overview is not enough as situations vary from one type of activity to another, and more detailed examination of both freight and passenger traffic is necessary.

6.2 FREIGHT TRAFFIC

Freight traffic involves four different types of activities: individual wagon transport, block train transport, combined transport, and, in some extremely rare cases, complete trucks transport.

6.2.1 Individual Wagons

The shipment of freight by individual wagon was the dominant means of transport from the latter half of the 19th until the mid-20th century. Two alternatives are possible, depending on whether the consignor possesses a private branch line or not. In the first case, and this is by far the most frequent, the freight to be transported is loaded onto the wagon at the source factory. In the second case, the freight must be transported to a freight station by another means of transport before being loaded onto the wagon.

Once there are enough wagons, they are formed into trains and transferred to a marshalling yard where they are split up and reformed into other trains, depending on their destination. The same procedure takes place upon arrival: if the consignee has a private branch line, the wagon is transported to him with the aid of a special locotractor. If not, it is left in a station where the consignee must retrieve the freight shipped to her or him.

The simple description of these procedures is enough to explain why it is far more simple and economical to load goods onto a truck that will transport them to their final destination without wasting time and money in transhipments. In all the countries of Europe, transport by individual wagon, which used to handle most of rail freight and was highly labour-intensive, is now falling drastically and probably due to disappear completely because of competition from a much more practical means of transport. On most Western European rail networks, the corresponding traffic was divided by three or four, sometimes even more, between 1979 and 1990, and a great majority of those responsible for such matters consider that this trend is inevitable and that traffic by individual wagon will almost completely disappear within the next few years.

Only the German railways plan to implement, at great cost, a policy to try to go against the current of this trend. The idea is to develop rail wagons or groups of wagons that can go by their own means from the branch line to the marshalling yard. In the first phase of the programme, the wagons would be equipped with an independent diesel motor and a driver's cabin. In the second phase, they would be entirely automatic and run without drivers along rails often also used by passenger trains. Reservations can obviously be made about projects of this nature, given the many technical problems and safety hazards inherent to them, and their complexity and cost hardly seem to enable them to compete seriously with road transport.

6.2.2 Block Train Transport

Block train traffic has not experienced the same abrupt decline as individual wagon traffic, and in fact for many networks occupies a central position in terms of railway freight. In 1992, it accounted for 89% of the tonnage transported by British Railways, 63% by Deutsche Bundesbahn, 59% by SNCF, 55% by the SNCB, and so forth.

Although fewer direct expenses are involved, the majority of such transport is far less profitable than that made by individual wagon, as it concerns transport of ore, coal, grain, rubble, and so forth, all products of low unitary value that could not support high transport costs. Curiously, one of the principal markets for block train transport is that of new cars sent from manufacturers to distant markets, although it is not possible to know whether this activity is financially profitable for the railways.

The problem is different from that of individual wagons: the market for block trains is not by nature condemned to die. But it is usually in deficit when total costs are considered. It is simply a question of reaching, at least, an equilibrium between the cost price and the price at which it is possible to sell the service, which is in turn dictated by the competition from road transport. In some cases—serving iron mines, for example—rail transport by block trains may be the most economical solution. But quite often it can only be competitive because it is highly subsidised, both in terms of running the trains and financing the infrastructures used, and because users do not therefore pay the true costs.

6.2.3 Combined Transport

Combined transport is a third means of transporting freight by rail. It entails the transport by special freight wagons of either containers arriving by truck or by water (sea, river, or canal) or trailers carried by road tractor into a specialised loading station and then picked up at the station of destination by another road tractor near to the final destination point. The expression "combined transport" does not normally cover the transport of complete trucks by rail wagons, which will be examined later.

The idea of combined transport is attractive. Nonetheless, its future is much more limited than it could be hoped, as the head of SNCF rail freight explained to the French National Assembly in July 1994 [2]:

> We are obliged to invoice a tonne transported by combined transport two and a half times less than for the individual wagon. Transfer and road link costs are added to the rail transport part of combined transport: compared to a road competitor's price of 100, the amount corresponding to the rail part of our service can only be 40. The few kilometres to be travelled by road absorb between 20 and 25% of costs at each end, and 5% must be added to this for handling costs at each of the two stations. In other words, what kills combined transport is not the rail service offered at all, but the high costs of servicing by road at each end.

It is difficult to state more clearly that, except perhaps over very long distances, for which transport at each end and transhipment costs are less important, combined transport cannot compete with road transport unless it is very heavily subsidised.

It is often considered that combined transport can be justified when the distance travelled exceeds 500 km. But if a policy of true costs was adopted, the break-even point would probably be much higher. In view of the facts outlined above, it is obvious that prices invoiced by the railway companies for combined transport usually cover only a small fraction of the real costs. Nevertheless, combined transport has an excellent image on a European Union level and in many countries (both with decision-makers and public opinion), and its further development is often seen as one of the priorities, if not *the* priority, of transport policy. A recent survey among French opinion leaders has shown that 97% of them thought it would be appropriate to give combined transport a high priority, when 18% only expressed the same view regarding truck transport, which, anyway, will in fact fulfil almost all the additional transport freight needs in the coming years [3]. The reason is simple: the idea of relieving road traffic by putting containers or even trailers onto trains can be easily imagined and is therefore very attractive. Unfortunately, as we have already seen, the idea does not stand up to analysis as the markets of the two means of transport are of such different magnitude and characteristics.

A series of restrictive conditions must be met before a combined transport line can exist. First among them is the existence of sufficiently large amounts of potential long-distance traffic to allow complete trains to be formed, together with the fact that flow in traffic must be balanced at at least 80% to avoid empty return trips. This would reduce to a few dozen the number of possible lines in Europe, because the great majority of freight transport takes place over particularly short distances, due notably to the "border effect" (which will be described below). What is more, companies that use this type of transport need to have specific equipment, with a higher tare than conventional road vehicles and therefore providing mediocre performance. If they are not present at the arrival point, they then have to find an intermediary to pick up the container or trailer and take it to its final destination. The maintenance of equipment and the follow-up of its movements are also specific to this form of transport.

In short, everything is more complicated, by nature, than using road transport from start to finish, which explains the current low development rate of combined transport and why it has almost no effect on road traffic in Europe. Along the most frequently used routes, combined transport registers a traffic of one or two hundred "boxes" per day and therefore takes one or two hundred trucks off the road. But most large European motorways have a traffic approaching or even widely exceeding 50,000 vehicles per day, all categories included. . . .

Combined transport only benefits from its current enthusiasm because the financial and physical data are not truly known. In fact, it is only in some very specific cases—major traffic routes, very long distances, transport of containers arriving by ship, and so forth—that it may be economically viable. And this is not even certain in the specific case of the European continent. There is therefore no justifiable reason to subsidise it as, contrary to appearances, it cannot significantly alleviate road traffic.

6.2.4 Transport by Rail of Complete Trucks

The possibility of transporting complete trucks by rail is also one of the ideas that most appeals to public opinion. As the French railway company (SCNE) inaccurately declared during a recent public relations campaign: "*Putting trucks on trains makes good sense.*" Unfortunately, this "good sense" comes up against many obstacles, some of which are economic. Others are strictly physical because the characteristics of existing railways do not normally allow for freight wagons loaded with trucks: they would not fit under the bridges and tunnels of most European railway networks!

In 1994, the German railways abandoned the four internal routes of this sort that they operated, as traffic continued to decrease from year to year, and have maintained only some international links.

The projects for the construction of new "rail motorways" specially reserved for complete truck traffic does not stand up to analysis due to the considerable

Great Britain have a combined population of 120 million inhabitants, or 20 times more. In other words, without even considering inevitable extra costs, the project is the equivalent, for the Swiss, of boring 30 Channel Tunnels. . .

If the project is carried through, there will be two possibilities. The first consists in establishing tariffs to try to cover the construction and operating costs. But the result of this is obvious: The prices would then be so high that no vehicle would use the new infrastructures, which would have been constructed for nothing. In addition, all the trucks journeying between Germany and Italy would continue, as they mainly do at present, to pass through Austria, and to a lesser extent, through France. The second possibility consists in establishing tariffs that do not take into account construction costs in any way. But the English Channel is a good example that (for this type of structure, which requires special rail shuttles) operating costs alone are very high. It is therefore certain that even operating costs would not be covered by tolls due to the low number of potential users, and that this would also require subsidies. It is difficult, to say the least, to understand the logic behind a policy that would deliberately attempt to attract traffic into Switzerland, and result in the Swiss taxpayers not only having to pay the initial investment in the tunnels but also subsidise their running costs.

The Swiss decision is all the more incomprehensible in that Switzerland's major route—the Zurich-Berne-Geneva motorway—runs from east to west and not from north to south. It has a daily traffic of about 50,000 vehicles on a motorway with two lanes each way, which is obviously not wide enough for comfortable driving conditions and, therefore, urgently deserves enlargement. On the other hand, the number of trucks likely to cross Switzerland between Germany and Italy is about 1,000 per day. The influence on the total traffic volume in Switzerland resulting from the twin tunnels project would therefore be negligible.

However strange this may seem, it was mainly to fight against the greenhouse effect that many Swiss citizens decided to vote in favour of this project which, if it comes into effect, would reduce vehicle traffic in their country by less than one to two per thousand, in return for colossal investments and running costs.

But, it is uncertain whether this project will be implemented. It is so difficult to finance that a new referendum is planned in mid 1997 or 1998 to obtain the population's approval for the massive tax increases necessary to pay for it. It would perhaps be safe to bet that the project will be rejected, because even the rich Swiss Confederation has to do its arithmetic and it has a reputation for doing that rather well. As goes an old saying, the first step in the construction of a tunnel is to try to find a means to avoid building a tunnel!

A Deserving Policy

Austria has adopted a different policy that is interesting to study. Due to its geographical situation, and to a lesser extent the Swiss ban on high-tonnage heavy goods vehicles, a very large share of road traffic between Germany and Italy passes through Austria, mostly via the Brenner Pass motorway, which is easier than the other Alpine crossings and has an average of about 3,000 heavy goods vehicles per day. The figure is modest compared with the traffic along many other national routes, but it is normal that the local population deeply resents it in this mountain site.

In order to limit in the short term the effects of this traffic that adds little to the local economy, Austria introduced an original "ecopoint" system. Every vehicle is assigned a certain number of ecopoints according to the volume of nitrogen oxide that it emits. The more the vehicle pollutes, the more points it gets and vice versa. Next, each country is allocated an annual quota of ecopoints, which must not be exceeded. Thanks to this system, the total volume of pollution emitted by traffic crossing Austria can be controlled, this being the final objective. In 1993, during preliminary negotiations concerning its entry into the European Union, Austria fought for acceptance of the ecopoint system as well as the objective to progressively reduce annual authorised quotas by 60% by the year 2003. After a long and hard struggle, the country finally won the battle.

We have now entered into a "virtuous circle." At the start of 1995, most of the authorised ecopoints were used. To meet the requirements of the planned reduction in ecopoints and possible increases in traffic, transporters therefore cross Austria with their most recent vehicles, which give constantly improved performance in terms of pollution but also noise. It will be particularly interesting to see how the race between technical progress and the legislation will evolve. Modern vehicle specifications have undergone such great reductions in emission levels that it is possible that the traffic will in fact be able to increase substantially whilst still respecting the annual quota of ecopoints. If this should be the case, it will be undeniable proof of the continuing improvement in vehicle emissions, even though it will not have any real influence on the quality of the air breathed by the local populations, which is already excellent, as we will see in a later chapter on pollution. This already happened in 1994 and 1995, when there was a significant increase in the traffic on the Brenner motorway to the detriment of the routes through Switzerland and France, which led the Austrian government to consider doubling the toll on the Brenner Tunnel, although this move met with the opposition of the Brussels European authorities.

In addition, trans-Austrian motorways are very far from being saturated due to trucks as, contrary to what might be imagined, the main traffic consists not of trucks, but private cars, which are seven times more numerous. But cars, like coaches and unlike trucks, are welcome in Austria because they are an essential part of the economy of the Tyrol, a region that is one of Europe's most popular tourist destinations.

Despite there being no problem of motorway capacity, there is in this country too a project for the construction of a trans-Alpine rail link. Constructed under the Brenner Mountains, there would be a "base tunnel" 54 km long. Its total cost is estimated at more than 15 billion ECUs, or even more if the entire link to be constructed between Italy and Germany is taken into account, with the cost to be shared among the three countries concerned. As a result, it is highly doubtful it could be constructed in the forseeable future.

An Unjustified Fear

Finally, France is also concerned by Alpine traffic in its own set of particular conditions. The two major routes that cross the Alps via the Mont Blanc and Fréjus Tunnels have very low traffic flows considering the capacities of the motorways leading to them and of the tunnels themselves. An average of 5,300 vehicles use the Mont Blanc Tunnel daily, including 2,500 heavy goods vehicles; and 3,500 vehicles use the Fréjus Tunnel, including 2,000 heavy goods vehicles. By comparison, it is interesting to note that the St. Gothard Tunnel, located exclusively within Switzerland, already has an average daily traffic of 16,000 vehicles! In other words, contrary to widespread opinion and the findings of various studies, there is no prospect of the two Franco-Italian road tunnels being saturated before the middle of the 21st century. This perspective is even more remote in that the considerable progress made regarding emissions of pollutants by heavy vehicles fundamentally changes the basis of the problem by removing the former forecast limits, which were mainly connected with difficulties in ventilating long tunnels [6]. And it must also be added that a third road tunnel is projected beneath the Mercantour Mountains between Turin and Nice, which would increase the capacity for Alpine crossing still further.

Nevertheless, France also has a project to construct a new railway to cross the Alps. The project is for two consecutive tunnels, 18 and 54 km in length, respectively, and is aimed at two objectives: firstly, a high-speed passenger train service between Lyons and Turin, and secondly, trains for transporting trucks. As a combination of a high-speed line and a "rail motorway," its cost would obviously be very high, amounting to a minimum of about 70 billion francs (11 billion ECUs).

If this project were to come into being, what would its potential traffic be? Transferring trucks onto trains would inevitably imply costly and penalising manoeuvres. In addition, it is estimated that construction work would take about 15 years. By that time, the existing road tunnels will be largely amortised and their tolls could be much lower than they are now, perhaps even completely eliminated. If the projected rail motorway is to be used at all, trucks would have to be prohibited from using the existing tunnels and the motorways that lead to them. France, however, is not in the same situation as Austria, which is crossed in the majority by traffic that does not concern it, or only to a small extent. Two-thirds of the traffic that crosses the Alps between France and Italy has France as its origin or destination. France has many motorways that handle much higher levels of heavy goods traffic than Alpine motorways. What could be the justification for banning heavy goods vehicles from these Alpine motorways alone, when they are among the least used in the country? If it is also taken into account that passenger traffic between Lyons and Turin is extremely low due to the border effect, this project also becomes even more astonishing, to say the least.

The true solution to the disadvantages currently suffered by those neighbouring the Alpine tunnel access motorways does not lie in the illusory, extremely costly, and very belated rail projects, but in constant improvement to heavy goods vehicles specifications on the one hand and to existing motorways on the other, so that their impact on the environment will be increasingly reduced, with protective structures being built in certain places, if necessary.

In summary, the traffic between Italy and the rest of Europe is split among a number of routes and in no way justifies, even accounting for prospective growth, the implementation of any such pharaonic projects that would undoubtedly be very costly to taxpayers and to their possible users. Is it really necessary to financially move Italy several hundreds of kilometres from the European continent (i.e., to create the equivalent of the English Channel in the heart of the Alps)?

6.2.7 A Difficult Future

All things considered and allowing for exceptions, the future of freight transport by rail in Europe, whether in the form of individual wagons, block train, combined transport, or *a fortiori* rail motorways, appears to be in jeopardy.

It calls for considerable sums to be taken out of the budgets of the different countries and the main argument used to support it does not stand up to analysis because, except maybe for the very special case of the Lower Rhine Valley, the facts show that the railway cannot truly relieve road traffic.

A False Monopoly

It is sometimes argued that it would be unhealthy to depend on an "all-truck" policy and that to avoid a monopoly, road transport cannot be the sole or overwhelming option that responds to the European continent's freight transport needs, as competition is necessary. This is very strange reasoning since, if it were true, this would presuppose that there is no competition within the road transport sector. Yet competition is in fact at its fiercest in this very area, one of the closest to the world of Adam Smith with the existence of tens of thousands of trucking companies of all sizes, naturally spread throughout each country, whereas on the contrary, the rail transport companies have a monopoly on their network in most countries.

What would the reaction have been if it had been suggested when the first transatlantic air transport was developed that it was essential to maintain steamships so that air transport would have some kind of competition? It is common knowledge that despite the disappearance of steamships, competition is particularly fierce among airlines.

Therefore, it is not a serious problem if there is no competition among different means of transport as long as competition exists within the sector that is best adapted to the market. Actually, the very use of the term "monopoly" is unfounded. According to the dictionary, a monopoly exists "when a firm or a category of firms is shielded from free competition." This is obviously not the case for road transport and it would be better to speak in terms of "exclusivity" rather than "monopoly." However, whatever views are held, road freight transport already has a near exclusivity in Western Europe in practice, as we have seen in the previous chapter on freight transport.

6.2.8 The American Railroads

The fact that there is a prosperous industry for freight transport by rail in the United States may make the above conclusions somewhat surprising. But there are three major differences in this respect between Western Europe and the United States.

The first fundamental difference is the absence in America of the border effect, which considerably decreases the potential long-distance traffic in Europe. The border effect cuts out the railways' major natural market in the field of freight, which is long-distance transport, or international transport in the case of Europe.

The second difference is partly linked to the first. Distances that must be travelled are much longer on the other side of the Atlantic Ocean. The average distance over which freight is transported by rail is 194 km in Europe against 1,200 in the United States, or six times more, which is obviously a factor that plays heavily there in the favour of trains.

Moreover, American rail networks are used almost exclusively by freight trains, passenger traffic having practically disappeared, except for the suburbs of some large cities and the rare intercity routes run by the public company Amtrak. Consequently, maintenance of the rails is very cheap as they are only used by trains that are less demanding in terms of speed, and even less for comfort.

Human productivity is incomparably higher in America than in Europe. In 1992, the total staff for all the American railway companies amounted to 206,000 employees for a traffic of 1,650 billion tonne kilometres. If it is assumed that the "freight" activity occupies a third of European network staff, approximately 350,000 employees work in Western Europe for a traffic of about 220 billion tonne kilometres.

In the first case, each employee handles eight million tonne kilometres; in the second, 13 times less. Anyone who has travelled around the United States has encountered their immense trains of 60 freight wagons or more, often drawn by three, four, or five diesel locomotives, with only two railwaymen on board. This explains why rail companies are very profitable in the United States despite the lack of subsidies and the continual reduction in tariffs [7], whereas in Europe the sales price, almost always dictated by road transport competition, usually covers less than half of the cost price, with which it has usually lost any relation whatsoever.

6.3 PASSENGER TRAFFIC

The situation of the railways is very gloomy in Europe with respect to freight, but is less so for passengers as some sectors of activity in this market have an undeniable future.

Passenger traffic, as for freight, is composed of very different types of markets that can be divided into four categories:

- High-speed lines;
- Other major intercity lines;
- Regional or inter-regional lines;
- Suburban transport lines for large towns.

Each of these categories deserves separate examination as they must be situated in the general context of the passenger transport market, which is characterised by the fact that a very large majority of the population now has access to a car, either as a driver or a passenger, and that air travel is becoming increasingly efficient and popular for medium and long distances.

Faced with dual competition from the car and the aeroplane, intercity train lines are facing difficult times in most European countries. Admittedly, overall traffic has hardly varied in the past 20 years in many countries, but this result has only been achieved, allowing for exceptions, at the price of increasingly large subsidies, heavy investments, and passengers paying low rates (the elderly, the young, worker's special rates, etc.). Its future would be completely dark if considerable technical progress had not been made, which has enabled the creation of high-speed lines and improvements in performance of the trains using existing ones.

At the beginning of 1997, four European countries have new high-speed lines in operation: France, Germany, Spain, and Italy.

6.3.1 High-Speed Lines in France

France has the longest and most substantial experience in this area in Europe. Of course, Japan opened the first high-speed train line, or Shinkansen, in 1964 between Tokyo and Osaka—even though it did not exceed 200 km/h at the time—and the traffic of 300 trains with 1,200 seats per day is incredibly high, far beyond that of Europe. Different studies have clearly shown that without its high-speed train lines, Japan's economic development would not have been as successful as it was.

The SNCF took the idea and perfected it, then developed rolling stock and infrastructure of increasingly higher quality and performance. The French TGV presently holds the world speed record of 511 km/h and is the only train in the world that is reaching or exceeding 300 km/h in commercial use. The SNCF is also responsible for the idea that the same equipment could use new high-speed lines and run along the existing network, which would be modernised if necessary. This is an essential point because it means that new lines are not merely used to link one city to another but also to serve entire regions, as the same trains can use the new rails and conventional rails in the same journey. Exchange between Paris and Lyons, for instance, only represents a part of the traffic along the new line linking the two cities.

This was the basis for the design and construction of the three main new lines in operation today in France: one between Paris and south-eastern France, the second between Paris and the Atlantic Coast, and the third between Paris and northern France.

The first, which links Paris with Lyons, has a new 391-km section and is used by trains that now reach speeds up to 270 km/h; the first section of the line was opened in 1981 and the second in 1983.

The second new line has a common section out of Paris, which then divides to serve Tours and Le Mans, respectively. It is 280 km long in total, was opened in 1989–90, and is used by trains that reach maximum speeds of 300 km/h.

The major part of the third new line was opened in 1993, and it has a common section from Paris to the outskirts of Lille, where it is divided into two lines, one westward towards the Channel Tunnel near Calais and the other eastward towards the Belgian border. The lines built in France are thus the beginnings of a T-shaped network whose western branch has been serving London via the Channel Tunnel since 1994 and whose eastern branch will serve Brussels, and will later be extended towards Rotterdam and Amsterdam on the one hand, and towards Liège and Cologne on the other, forming a remarkable network within one of the world's richest and most densely populated regions (Fig. 32). In total, the corresponding lines total 330 km in French territory and are used by even swifter trains that reach 320 km/h in commercial use.

High-speed traffic on the south-eastern and Atlantic networks each count about 20 million passengers per year and the northern network about 5 million domestic passengers, so that the trains that use these lines account alone for more than 40% of the passenger kilometres on the SNCF's long-distance lines. As for the Paris-London link, the SNCF, after announcing a higher figure, now hopes that traffic will one day amount to 10 or even 15 million passengers per year, which could be considered rather optimistic as the number of passengers did not exceed 3 million in 1995, which was the first operational full year and about 5 million in the second year.

Traffic levels on the south-eastern line have given a sufficient financial return to enable the SNCF to state that it was financed without special aid. On the other hand, the Atlantic line received from the French government a subsidy of 30% of its investment costs. The northern line's revenues are very far from being sufficient to cover the investment and operating costs. Infrastructure costs alone have reached 18.5 billion francs (3 billion ECUs) for the 330-km network, including 16% for environmental protection measures.

Overall, the investments granted in favour of high-speed lines are responsible for a large part of the French railway company's catastrophic level of debt, which was only possible because of the national government's guarantee.

In a little over a decade, France has managed to breathe new life into its long-distance rail passenger network and has stabilised its traffic overall, and is, up to now, gradually being imitated by other European countries.

The French experiment is particularly rich in lessons, not only from a technical standpoint, as was witnessed recently by the choice of the TGV rolling stock for South Korea's first high-speed line, but also as a demonstration of how high-speed trains can position themselves within the transport market. Their niche market has been clearly shown as being mainly for journeys in a time range of one to two-and-a-half hours from station to station.

A Very Precise Niche

The car remains a serious competitor for journeys of less than one hour by high-speed train (i.e., about 250 km) because of its ability to transport door to door. Of course, for those journeys that both start and end in the vicinity of TGV stations, the train has an undeniable time advantage. But the advantage disappears if, as is often the case, the point of departure and the destination are not in this situation. Someone living in the suburbs of Paris heading for a destination 15 km away from Lille, which is 220 km from Paris, saves no time with the TGV. This explains why the Paris-Lille link, although it has achieved an increase of approximately 30% in passenger traffic, has, as we have already seen, had no perceptible influence on A1 motorway traffic between the two cities, even though the motorway is exactly parallel to the railway.

On the other hand, above a certain journey time, the aeroplane becomes the high-speed train's competitor. French experience has shown that the aeroplane is not competitive when TGV journey times from station to station were about two hours long. The TGV has thus resulted in a great reduction in air traffic between Paris and Lyons, Paris and Rennes, and Paris and Nantes, all being two-hour train journeys. But this is not the case for the Paris-Bordeaux line, which has had a three-hour TGV link since 1990. Air Inter, the national airline at that time, has retained 80% of its traffic along this route, a much higher figure than expected.

The French experience confirms that the TGV's domain of excellence reaches its limit at journeys lasting about two and a half hours. This is further confirmed by several other examples. The London-Brussels link via the Channel Tunnel was opened in 1994, but was a commercial failure as the journey time was 3 hours 15 minutes. Whereas the train's capacity is 794 seats, the average number of passengers was about 200 in 1995.

On most routes, a very clearly defined threshold point exists therefore for high-fare customers, which corresponds to journey times of about two and a half hours. The reason is simple. Below this limit, it is possible to do a return trip on the same day whilst having enough time to work at the destination. When travel distances are lower than 1,000 km, or even moderately higher, the flight time is approximately one hour, which makes the door-to-door journey time by plane less than or equal to three hours. Businessmen and businesswomen on every continent have become accustomed to returning home in the evening. Even for longer stays, this category of travellers, which is the large majority of the TGV's upper income clientele, is not prepared to lose four or more hours per one-way trip given that it often takes at least one hour to get to and from stations at both ends.

It is therefore competition from airlines that explains why this two and a half hour threshold point is so well-defined. The undeniable advantages of a high-speed train—comfort, regularity, departure from and arrival in the city centre for those whose points of departure or destinations are not in the suburbs—are limited to this time factor. The limit can, however, be somewhat lengthened in the case of a line linking two towns that have particularly difficult access to their airports due to their size. This is the case for the Paris-London line, which despite a journey time of three hours by fast train is still a competitive option for those travelling from one city centre to the other in comparison with air transport. This is also the case for the Tokyo-Osaka line, but it has not stopped the Japanese railways from introducing trains that go at 270 km/h, reducing the journey time to two and a half hours, precisely to allow businessmen to return home the same day.

Except for cases of this nature, experience shows that the aeroplane is only marginally affected by competition from high-speed trains once train journey times approach or exceed three hours. On the other hand, it is not difficult to predict success for the London-Brussels link, once the new line currently under construction in Belgium reduces journey times between the two cities to 2 hours 40 minutes in 1998, and to forecast that victory will be definitive once the new British line becomes operational at the start of the next century, assuming all goes as planned, reducing travel times to just over two hours. By the same time, the Paris to London line will take two and a half hours, ensuring the supremacy of the railway along this line for the large majority of its customers.

This point is very important. It shows that for high-fare passengers, the high-speed train is the aeroplane's competitor and not the car's, which has its own market. It also shows that this means of transport is particularly well-adapted to Europe's dimensions since this type of train is most appropriate for maximum distances of about 500 to 600 km and that longer distances are rare within any single European country.

But it also reveals the limits of this remarkable means of transport. It is unrealistic to imagine that passengers paying high fares will use the train for journeys exceeding about two and a half hours. Of course, there are customers who are prepared to accept longer journey times, but these are customers with limited financial means for whom the value of time is not an important factor, many of whom benefit from reduced rates, frequent in many countries for historical reasons and that must then be compensated by the state.

The French railways have observed that the value of time, reflected in the prices users are willing to pay, was six times higher for first-class business passengers than for those travelling for personal reasons in second class [8]. But even these customers paying lower rates are in fact on the decline due to increasing competition from airlines, which also offer reduced rates although they are not subsidised.

Finally, the border effect must be taken into account. As we have seen, whenever a border must be crossed, traffic is divided by five to ten, or even more. Despite official forecasts [9], it would be utopian to imagine that rail traffic of any significance could take place between Paris and Berlin, Paris and Milan, or Paris and Madrid. What customer would be willing to pay anything but a ridiculously reduced-rate price to spend six hours in a "high speed" train from Paris to Berlin, four hours from Paris to Milan, or eight hours from Paris to Madrid when all these journeys can be made in one or two hours by aeroplane?

It must be said that a tradition seems to have been established in Europe whereby rail traffic forecasts are systematically unrealistic. The difference usually goes unnoticed because the taxpayers make up for the shortfall. But this is not the case when infrastructures are financed by private capital. For example, the ORLY-VAL link between Paris and Orly airport registered traffic of 1.3 million passengers per year against forecasts of 4 million (i.e., a ratio of one to three). ORLYVAL is the first metropolitan railway in the world without a driver, but also practically without passengers, which resulted in the total loss of the capital and bank loans. It was the same story for the Channel Tunnel, which registered a traffic of 3 million passengers the first year, compared to the official estimates of 15 million (i.e., a ratio of one to five). These are not isolated cases.

In the Paris region, the TGV high-speed train station in Massy was supposed to handle 1.7 million passengers, but in fact counts 400,000. The TGV high speed train station at Roissy airport was supposed to handle 2.5 million, but counts only 700,000. As for the new line from Paris to Lille, its traffic has been half the estimated figures. In reality, traffic can grow by 30% when a new infrastructure is created, but not by 200% or more. And yet this is nothing compared to the forecasts made for international rail links. Whereas at present the rail traffic between Lyon and Turin is practically non-existent, the official simulations [9] show traffic figures of about 6 million passengers per year in 2010. One third of these would be diverted from the road, whose total current traffic is less than one million people. Another third would come from air transport, whereas the only air link that could be concerned is the Paris-Milan flight, whose traffic is also less than one million passengers per year, and which is, what is more, outside the high-speed train's domain of relevance as the journey time will still be four hours once the latter is introduced.

If such a rail link is actually brought into service, the ratio between the forecasts and the results would probably be about one to ten, and the same is more or less true for the other European "major projects" that the governments and the European Commission in Brussels periodically bring up as priorities . . .

It should, however, be said that budgetary difficulties in all the European states make their implementation less and less probable. Regular calls are made for private financing to take over from public financing, as if this were a miraculous solution, but they are obviously not answered, as a change in the means of financing a project cannot make it profitable when it is so far removed from any economic or financial justification.

The surrealistic character of the forecasts, for both national and international routes, can only be explained by the fact that the European railway companies have had no counterbalancing power opposite them, for reasons that will be detailed in Chapter 13 of this book.

Thus, the conclusion reached after examination of the realities of the transport market is that, with the exception of the London-Paris-Cologne-Amsterdam "golden star," the high-speed train market is exclusively national in nature due to the distances that separate the major European capitals, a factor that must be added to the border effect. Contrary to what may be imagined, and also to unrealistic official forecasts that assume that the train can take over a large part of road and rail traffic on the long-distance international links, the spending required to link the different national rail high-speed networks and eliminate Europe's "missing links" is economically unjustified due to the extremely low level of foreseeable traffic.

This quite obviously does not mean, *a contrario*, that all national projects are justified, as the cost of a high-speed train new line is extremely high. In an attempt to recover part of its investment on the 220-km Paris-Lille line, the SNCF is forced to price first-class return tickets at 800 francs (120 ECUs). TGV trains are cheaper to acquire than aeroplanes, but the ground infrastructure is considerably more costly, whereas the air is free.

After 13 years of operations, the French TGV is rich in lessons. User statistics show that the intercity passenger train is not necessarily condemned to die in Europe as in the United States. There is a market for it within a well-defined journey time. It can then play an eminently positive role in the economic life of European countries, whose dimensions are particularly suited to this type of transport.

But there is another, financial, side to the coin. The construction of new high-speed lines appears to be extremely expensive, even if the accounts of most European railway companies are so impenetrable that it is difficult to extract the cost even of existing lines.

Admittedly, the financial return for the railway company is not the only consideration, and the economic return for the community (which may be higher, as is the case for other transport investments) must also be taken into account. But the cost of constructing new railway lines today is such that, in a country like France and even according to calculations made by the SNCF, no project is economically or *a fortiori* financially justifiable beyond the three lines mentioned above, and additional costs needed today to integrate structures within the environment make the situation even worse.

Nevertheless, enthusiasm for high-speed trains is so high that France has embarked upon an extension programme going beyond the three new existing lines. Within the scope of a national long-term development plan, which allows for the construction of nearly 5,000 km of new lines, two supplementary sections were first opened in 1993, bringing the total of new high-speed lines in service to 1,214 km. The first bypasses Paris to the east, creating a direct link between Lille and Lyons in three hours, stopping at the Roissy-Charles de Gaulle Airport and Disneyland Paris on the way. However, this line's traffic is very low because traffic between French regions is fairly limited, in view of the economic and demographic dominance of the Paris region. The second line, 150 km in length, bypasses Lyons, with a station at Lyon-Satolas Airport and is the initial section of a link between Paris and Marseilles and Montpellier, both located on the Mediterranean Coast.

An Empty Station

Special mention should be made of the brand new station constructed in Lyons-Satolas Airport in the name of fashionable "intermodality." Although it cost over 650 million francs (100 million ECUs), it is ignored by users (less than 100 travellers use the station daily and practically none of them to connect to an aeroplane) and probably always will be. This is not in the least surprising as the new line that passes through the station runs from Paris to Marseilles with almost no stops along the way, and it is difficult to see why any air passenger would land in Lyons to get to either of the two cities, which each have their own airports. It remains to be seen if the Roissy-Charles de Gaulle Station near Paris, which allows inhabitants of northern and south-eastern France to take the TGV to get to the airport, will rise to the expectations of its developers and justify the amount of money spent on it, which is highly improbable as the actual traffic levels are far lower than forecast.

Two Additional Lines

In September 1993, the French government also decided to launch two other new railway projects. The first is an extension of the above-mentioned Lyons line to the

Mediterranean, to complete the Paris-Marseilles and Paris-Montpellier links. The second is the construction of an entirely new railway line between Paris and Strasbourg. Nevertheless, according to the SNCF, the derisory economic return on the latter line would not justify its construction. This would be in the region of 2% for an investment cost of at least 30 billion francs (nearly 5 billion ECUs). For such capital, it would be possible not only to offer the flight free of charge to all the passengers who fly at present between Paris and Strasbourg, but also to make each of them a present of at least five times the cost of their ticket!

Some people openly recommended that the project should be abandoned despite the international commitments undertaken with Germany to build a Paris-Strasbourg-Berlin line, which would lead (as we have seen to) a six-hour journey on the "high-speed" trains. Nevertheless, at the end of 1996, the French government confirmed that the project will be implemented anyway, with work beginning in 1998, although no time schedule was announced regarding the precise staggering of the work.

Other aspects of the French national development plan concerning high-speed railways are of more or less similar nature, not to mention the international lines towards Italy and Spain for which foreseeable traffic is so low that it could be simply handled by a few aeroplanes or coaches each day. As the President of the Spanish railway company declared in 1991 [10]: *"There is not enough traffic between Barcelona and the French border to justify a high-speed train. The journeys that do take place are between Madrid, Saragossa, and Barcelona."* In all likelihood, "tilting" trains, which will be described below, will finally emerge as the only appropriate solution on many sections, moreover capable of giving the French railway industry a new market. This is the path that it is following in 1997 by designing tilting equipment, which will be capable of travelling at 350 km/h on new lines and over 200 km/h on traditional lines, and which will be available as a prototype in 1998.

6.3.2 High-Speed Lines in Germany

Germany was the second European country to enter the world of the high-speed railway. Its first new lines running a new type of fast train, christened ICE (Inter City Express), opened in 1991. German policy on the issue is quite different from that of France. To date, only 426 km of new lines have been brought into service, running from north to south: one is 327 km long and runs from Hanover to Würzburg; the other is 99 km long, between Mannheim and Stuttgart. The current maximum authorised speed limit on these lines is 250 km/h. But these two new lines are supplemented by a network of about 1,000 km of conventional track that has been upgraded to accommodate ICE trains at 200 km/h. In other words, contrary to the situation in France, there is no particular breaking off point in service for the user between the new lines and the conventional upgraded ones since the differences in speed are slight.

The new German lines have another characteristic: their cost is three times higher per kilometre than that of the new French lines constructed to date. It was said that the price per kilometre was about the same—40 million—except that in one case it was in deutschmarks and in the other in French francs! One of the reasons for this surprising disparity is that one-third of the new German lines are underground, not only due to the local environmental lobbies, particularly powerful in Germany, but also for a technical reason. Unlike the French tracks, the German ones built until now are used not only by passenger trains, but also by freight trains running at 160 km/h, meaning that the slope cannot exceed 1.25%, compared with 3% for the French lines, which can be more easily adapted to relief, thereby requiring less civil engineering works.

In the future, the Germans intend to continue to combine sections of new lines and sections of old ones upgraded for traffic at 200 km/h and thereby reach a network of about 2,000 km by the year 2000, which the ICE will use at 200 km/h or more.

Among the "major works" projects approved in principle by European heads of government in 1994 were a high-speed connection between Berlin and the French border via Frankfurt and Strasbourg and another between Berlin and the Italian border via Munich. In addition, a new 250 km/h line is projected between Stuttgart and Munich. The federal government would finance all these works in full, as part of the reform of the German railways, which we will analyse below. But, as in France, budgetary restrictions led to decisions in 1996 to reduce the programme for the creation of new lines to the profit of improvements to existing lines and to encourage the development of tilting rolling stock. Nevertheless, the German government has given his green light to a new line between Cologne and Francfort and another between Berlin and Hanover. It announced it will do the same for another one linking Munich and Nuremberg, despite its planned extremely high cost of 16 billion deutschmarks.

Overall, with Germany's high population density (twice that of France), and the relatively low average distances travelled, high-speed trains seem particularly well-adapted to the country's geographic context given that the passenger is not asked to pay the cost of infrastructures, but the taxpayer. Users of the ICE travel an average distance of 310 km, which corresponds to well below two hours of travel time.

As in France, the introduction of high-speed trains in Germany has increased rail traffic by around 25%, but without decreasing motorway traffic. As we have seen, on the Hamburg-Munich line, the railway's share of the market rose from 12.8% to 14.6% with the ICE, air transport declined from 1.8% to 1.4%, and the motorway remained practically unchanged: 84% against 85.4%. [11].

Technically, ICE trains are very different from French TGVs. The train's architecture is different: conventional carriages in the first case and articulated ones in the second. The axle load is also different: 20 tonnes for the ICE, and 17 for the

TGV, such that the latter could run in Germany, but the current ICE cannot run in France nor in any other country that has adopted the same standards. The ICE is considerably more luxurious than the TGV, with television screens even incorporated into some seat backs, so that its cost price per seat is, logically, more than one-third higher than that of the TGV.

Lastly, there is the Hamburg-Berlin "Transrapid" project. This system has no wheels and does not ride on steel rails, but is suspended above its concrete rails by way of controlled electromagnetic action; it is laterally guided by other electromagnets and accelerates and brakes with its linear motor. After years of research and spending estimated at more than a billion ECUs, this train now appears to be operational and capable of running in excellent conditions in terms of comfort at more than 400 km/h. The German government has made the decision to launch, at a cost of about 9 billion deutschmarks, a first 282-km line between Hamburg and Berlin, which would then be only 53 minutes away from each other. However, this project has given rise to much protest because it will be impossible to link it with the existing rail system, because it is too costly and because in its current form the project would require the construction of raised infrastructures built on highly unattractive, 5m-high concrete posts. Traffic estimates, which count on more than 10 million passengers per year, have also been strongly challenged, so much so that one of the companies that promoted the project withdrew from it in the spring of 1996. It must be said that the history of rail traffic forecasts in general can only encourage scepticism. If the initial schedule is nonetheless respected, the Transrapid could make its first appearance in commercial service in 2005. However, at the beginning of 1997, more and more voices were demanding the termination of this project on the grounds that it constitutes a waste of money, and its future was less than guaranteed.

6.3.3 High-Speed Lines in Spain

Spain was the third European country to introduce a new high-speed rail system. It is 471 km long and links Madrid with Seville, whereas traffic between Madrid and Barcelona would have been higher. The Universal Exposition of 1992, among other factors, tipped the scales in favour of the Andalusian city.

Its infrastructures cost nearly 3 billion ECUs, much higher than initially expected. Unlike the rest of the Spanish rail network, the new line has the standard European gauge, meaning that most of its stock is restricted to the new tracks. Construction of the line was decided in 1986 and it was opened in April 1992. Amidst fierce competition, French TGV rolling stock was chosen, with some modifications in design and technical characteristics.

Thanks to a top speed of 300 km/h, a direct journey between Madrid and Seville now takes 2 hours 15 minutes, compared with 5 hours 36 minutes previously, and this has logically taken 75% of Iberia Airline's traffic on this route. About three million passengers use the train each year, which obviously has little in common with the first two French lines that transport 20 million passengers each per year. Consequently, as is the case in France for the Paris-Strasbourg project, the true unit cost price per passenger does not begin to compare with that of the aeroplane, current revenues covering only operating costs and not even touching the investment costs, which relativizes assertions according to which this line is "profitable."

The next new high-speed line planned in Spain will link Madrid and Barcelona, the country's two major economic centres. Work was due to begin in 1995, but at the beginning of 1997, all the financing is far from being established. It has to be added that the distance between Madrid and Barcelona is noticeably greater than that between Madrid and Seville, which will force Spanish engineers to use all their imagination and skill to keep journey time between the two towns below the two and a half hour limit; otherwise, full-fare users will prefer the aeroplane.

Spain has also started major works to modernise the rail arc between Madrid-Valencia-Barcelona, so that it can be used by trains travelling at 200 km/h.

As for the link with France, the principle of which is regularly restated by the two governments, its potential traffic could only be derisory with regard to its cost.

6.3.4 High-Speed Lines in Italy

The fourth country to enter onto the high-speed stage is Italy, even though it was actually the first country in Europe to decide to adopt this solution. In 1992, after 22 years of construction, the "Direttissima Line," linking Rome with Florence, was opened in its full length. This new line is designed to support speeds of 250 km/h on 238 km of its length, with some sections capable of being used at 300 km/h. It is intended to be the first section of a vast T-shaped network, with the vertical stem going from Naples to Milan and the horizontal bar from Turin to Venice. A total of 1,000 km of additional lines are planned, with 300 km of viaducts and tunnels, at a currently estimated total cost of 20 billion ECUs. It is impossible to foresee the pace at which the programme will be achieved as although it was due to be completed in 2002, it has come up against much serious local opposition. Nonetheless, in mid-1996, it was announced that financing to the sum of 10,000 billion lire (5 billion ECUs) is being set up, including 4,000 for financing 71 km of new lines—of which 93% is in tunnels—between Bologna and Florence, which would bring the journey time down from 55 to 35 minutes . . . A perfect demonstration, in Italy as elsewhere, of the strength of conviction of the railway sector. Nevertheless, at the beginning of 1997 work is only going on on the Rome-Naples link, for which prices are constantly increasing, and a two-year delay in excess of the planned schedule has already been announced.

In terms of rolling stock, a feature of the Italian railways is particularly interesting. In fact, they have adopted two different types of train. The first, the ETR 500, which can reach speeds of 300 km/h and is starting to be introduced into regular service on an experimental basis, has conventional high-speed train characteristics. The second, the ETR 450, which have been in use for several years, have the characteristic of being "tilting" (i.e., equipped with a system that automatically inclines the carriage to counteract centrifugal force in bends, enabling it to turn round at speeds 30 to 50 km/h higher than conventional trains without any discomfort to passengers).

Of course, this type of equipment is not shown to its greatest advantage on the new lines with their wide bends, but on the old lines where they can save important amounts of time compared with traditional trains. The tilting equipment transforms conventional lines into "semihigh-speed" lines, with a very limited cost for the modification when compared to the construction costs of entirely new tracks, with the additional advantage of allowing trains to serve intermediate stations on the line. It is therefore not surprising to see that this type of equipment, which is also produced elsewhere, is gaining ground in many European countries—Switzerland, Spain, Germany, Sweden, and Finland. The United States and Canada have also adopted the idea in principle, after abandoning (with maybe one exception) the idea of constructing costly new lines. This would appear to be a particularly wise compromise for networks that cannot or do not wish to spend considerable sums of money for the construction of new lines where the traffic does not justify it. The future of the railway in Europe depends largely on tilting.

6.3.5 High-Speed Lines in Other European Countries

Three other countries of Western Europe will soon become members of the high-speed rail club using new infrastructures. Great Britain, Belgium, and the Netherlands have projects that extend the network created in northern France.

Great Britain has decided to build a new line between the Channel Tunnel exit and London. Whereas Margaret Thatcher's governments had always said that the line should be created without public money, the fact is that such a project would never be financially profitable for a private investor alone. The British government has abandoned the former position and announced that it would now be willing to contribute financially to the construction, perhaps covering half its cost. In 1994, it launched an international invitation to tender, and named the winner in February 1996. It is a group made up of the well-known company Virgin, which also owns an airline, the intercity coach company "National Express," and the American group Bechtel. The cost of the project is estimated at 3 billion GBP (3.7 billion ECUs) and will be subsidised to the sum of 1.4 billion GBP, with the appointed group also receiving important property holdings, all on a 999 year concession. On the other hand, it will bear all the risks of the operation, which will therefore cost the taxpayers far less than the corresponding rail links in France and Belgium. Virgin has fixed itself the objective of doubling Eurostar's traffic in 18 months.

The new line will be 109 km long and will arrive at Saint Pancras' Station in London. It will be particularly expensive to construct as it partly crosses the county of Kent, which is one of England's most beautiful regions and where great precautions will have to be taken to protect the environment. If all goes well, work can begin in 1997 and end in 2002, making a saving of half an hour between the British capital and the continent and eliminating the restrictions on the "Eurostar" trains, which presently have to use a time-worn line often saturated with suburban trains.

As far as Belgium is concerned, work is well underway on its section of the new line linking Brussels with the French border. The line will be 80 km long and has been held back some time due to local protest, but should come into service fully in 1998, instead of in 1996 as initially planned. As we have seen above, the line should be extended on the one hand towards the Netherlands and on the other towards Liège and Cologne. At the end of 1996, the Belgian and Dutch governments reached an agreement regarding the route of the future high-speed link between their countries and its financing, with the aim of opening it in 2005.

There seems to be no doubt that in the medium term this part of Europe, one of the most densely populated in the world, will have an exceptional high-speed railway network linking its large cities, with remarkable comfort and speed. Journey times will then be shortened to 1 hour 40 minutes between Amsterdam and Brussels, 1 hour 20 minutes between Paris and Brussels, 2 hours 10 minutes between London and Brussels, 2 hours 30 minutes between Paris and London, 1 hour 40 minutes between Brussels and Cologne, 3 hours 10 minutes between Paris and Cologne, 3 hours 15 minutes between Paris and Amsterdam, and so forth. At the cost of extremely heavy investment, which will never be anything like recovered from the users, the countries in question will possess an unequalled communication system, which can be viewed in two contrasting ways. In financial terms, the operation is clearly not justified. The governments of all the countries concerned, or, rather, their taxpayers, have assumed a huge part of the infrastructure costs, inevitably to the detriment of other calls on public finance, not to mention the money lost by stock-holders and bankers on the Channel Tunnel. On the other hand, in terms of the quality of transport between major cities or viewed as a symbol of European unity, the view is, on the contrary, undoubtedly positive and will favour exchanges among neighbouring countries as long as travellers are not asked to pay the true cost of their journeys. But are financial imperatives not imposed on everyone in future? As the World Bank rightly says, sometimes making us wish that it would come and give its advice to Old Europe, "the concept of economic efficiency is not synonymous with technical efficiency. A technically superior infrastructure is only economically superior if the additional revenues which result from its technical superiority exceed the additional costs brought about by its construction and operation [12]."

6.3.6 The Outlook for High-Speed Lines

Seven European countries have taken steps towards creating high-speed railway lines; that is, those capable of accommodating speeds of 250 km/h or more. In mid

1995, 1,214 km of new railways were operating in France, 471 in Spain, 426 in Germany, and 238 in Italy, or a total of 2,350 km. If the projects currently in the planning stages are all carried through, this figure would be more than doubled in the decade to come.

But all European States are currently facing financial difficulties, all the more restricting as they have undertaken, in compliance with the Treaty of Maastricht, to reduce their budget deficits with a view to the adoption of a single European currency. For this reason, it is more than doubtful whether all the projects will be implemented. They may be scaled down considerably or even stopped altogether. It is likely that attractive intermediate solutions, such as the progressive improvement of existing rails and their possible use by high-speed tilting trains, will receive more and more attention, as is already the case in a growing number of countries. It must be added that on a world-wide basis, realistic prospects for creating high-speed lines are extremely limited, and for a long time will concern only a very small number of countries since those with the highest potential traffic do not generally have the means to finance such infrastructures. In the United States, there is only one project being seriously considered. It is in Florida, which is in a very special situation in that it is one of the leading tourist destinations in the world and a destination in which a high-speed railway line could be considered as an additional attraction linking the great amusements parks near Orlando and the city of Miami. It should be added that the fact that Florida is flat would obviously be particularly favourable to such a project.

The international competition launched in this respect was won by the Franco-British group GEC-ALSHOM, with the proposal based on equipment close to the French TGV. The state of Florida committed itself to granting an annual operating subsidy for the project to the amount of 70 million dollars per year. But it is not sure such an amount would be sufficient. At the beginning of 1997, it is too early to know whether in these conditions the organisation of the operation's financing will be able to be finally concluded.

In the rest of the world, it is impossible not to mention the incredible potential market for high-speed railway lines in China. With its 1,400 billion inhabitants, this will obviously in the long term be a domain of predilection for high-speed and high-capacity railways.

6.3.7 Other Long-Distance Lines

New lines are only a small part of the European railway networks that will always be mainly based on the conventional lines inherited from the past, which can in turn be divided into two categories.

The first are the lines that have enough traffic to justify them being maintained. Some of them are in the continuation of new high-speed lines and can be used by their rolling stock. In France, nearly 6,000 km of railway are used by TGV equipment, whereas new lines represent only 1,214 km. This explains why TGV-type trains account for 40% of total SNCF long-distance traffic. In Germany, ICE trains also transport a large part of long-distance DBAG passenger traffic.

There are other long-distance lines that are not linked to high-speed lines but that have traffic levels that justify their existence.

There are, however, more and more lines where traffic is continually decreasing or very small and the average number of passengers per train can be counted in dozens, not hundreds. It goes without saying that in such cases costs are much higher than revenues, sometimes by a factor of three or even far more. This is why many countries are asking serious questions as to the future viability of these little-used train lines.

6.3.8 Coaches and Trains

The notion of public service is often put forward to justify keeping train lines with low traffic, but this is a misuse of the idea. Admittedly, it is in the general interest to make a public transport system available between communities of a certain size, to be used by those who do not have access to a car. But the train is not the only answer to this need, nor is it often the best. The potential of coaches is unrecognised in many Western European countries since national railway companies have always successfully opposed the creation of coach lines that could compete with them. Examples nonetheless exist proving, as in the case of North America, that medium- and long-distance intercity coach lines using the road, and particularly the motorway network, can meet the need for public service and also have the advantage of being inexpensive for passengers and profitable for the companies that run them— if necessary, with the help of public subsidies, which are extremely limited in size when compared with the cost of maintaining railway lines. One of these lines exists in France, between Marseilles and Nice, operating to everybody's satisfaction and costing nothing to the public authorities.

Contrary to many other European countries, intercity coach lines were authorised in Italy on a large scale. The peninsula now possesses about 6,000 long-distance intercity coach lines operated by 1,300 firms. They criss-cross the country and not only serve small towns but also link all the large cities: Rome, Naples, Milan, Turin, Florence, Padua, Bologna, Verona, and so forth in an exceptionally dense network, usually via the motorways. The liberalisation of coach transport, helped by sizable subsidies, resulted in a real explosion in the corresponding traffic. Italian bus and coach traffic nearly tripled from 1970 to 1992, climbing from 32 billion passenger kilometres to 88 billion (+175%), whereas in the rest of Western Europe it grew by only 25%, or seven times less! In other words, the creation of coach lines gave birth to new mobility, to the advantage of both the Italian people and their economy, without, for that matter, numbers of passengers on long-distance train lines particularly suffering. It is mainly a new market that appeared. The same is true in Great Britain. The deregulation of coach traffic was among the first decisions made by Margaret Thatcher. It is not surprising that in 1997, two British coach companies are among the most powerful in Europe and rapidly expanding into other European countries.

Coaches meet the needs of passengers for whom travel time matters little but who attach great importance to paying as little as possible. These are young people or people with low incomes and so forth. The coach is by nature a social means of transport. In Canada, a return ticket between Montreal and Quebec—250 kilometres—costs only $52 Canadian (30 ECUs)! In Great Britain, coach users pay two to three times less than for the train.

But the rules on free circulation and free competition that are stipulated in European treaties seem to be ignored by many countries, and by Brussels, with respect to coaches. Many Europeans do not even imagine that regular intercity coach lines could exist in place of the usual rail connections. A recent Swiss poll carried out for the International Road Union showed that, *a priori*, two-thirds of the Swiss were not in favour of transferring the existing railway routes onto the road. But it should be added that when the same people were informed that such a measure could greatly reduce the railway deficit and therefore taxes, the majority of replies became affirmative. An equivalent study carried out in France provided neighbouring results [13].

At the end of 1996, the European Commission decided to launch a study to know the actual situation in the different member states in the field of coach and bus transport. . . .

6.3.9 Regional and Inter-Regional Lines

There is no precise definition of regional lines. They come somewhere between long-distance lines, with an area of activity that begins at about 150 km, and suburban lines, whose length rarely exceeds 30 or 40 km. Regional lines are subject to competition from the car, and for this reason (but allowing for exceptions) their traffic has fallen drastically over the past few decades and is nearly always incapable of covering the costs necessary to keep them in service.

More and more frequently, the financial responsibility for these networks is transferred from state to regional and local government, so that the latter can use their knowledge to take the most appropriate decisions by weighing the cost of subsidies and the benefits for their constituents. As is the case with long-distance lines, the choice must be made between maintaining existing lines, which often means further investment to make the necessary improvements or permanent subsidies, or abandoning the railway in favour of the more flexible and less expensive solution of coaches. But it must be added that an informed decision can only be taken if the railways accounts are clear and truthful, and this is generally not the case.

6.3.10 Suburban Networks

Finally, there is a fourth category of passenger traffic that uses the railway network each day to link the major European towns with their respective suburbs.

As will be explained later in Chapter 12, these networks play an essential role in the proper functioning of many large urban centres, particularly as they allow large numbers of workers to reach their place of employment and other places of activity, which would obviously be impossible if they all had to commute by car. It is these railway networks that allow the largest European urban areas to maintain a high density of employment, business, and, sometimes, inhabitants in the town centres. The merits of suburban trains are undeniable and this justifies the fact that they should be improved as and when possible, even if the number of users is often in decline in Europe due to a movement of jobs away from the centre, as is the case for the Paris region where the number of suburban railway passengers decreased from 567 million in 1991 to 535 in 1994, and further again in 1995 and 1996, without this questioning their essential contribution to the life of the city.

References

[1] Dieckmann, A. *Towards More Rational Transport Policies in Europe*, Die Deutsche Bibliothek CIV, Cologne, 1995.

[2] Commission d'enquête sur la S.N.C.F.-première séance, Assemblée Nationale, Paris, 9 février 1994.

[3] Union Routière de France BVA Survey, July 1996, Paris.

[4] *Echanges franco-allemands: effet frontière important*. Notes de synthèse OEST Ministry of Equipment, Nov. 1993, Paris.

[5] *Les Pyrénées bloquent encore 90% des échanges*, Notes de synthèse OEST Ministry of Equipment, Jan. 1995, Paris.

[6] *La diminution des émissions polluantes des véhicules routiers et ses conséquences bénéfiques pour les tunnels*, Michel Marec, Revue Générale des Routes et Aérodromes, April 1996, Paris.

[7] Delancy, Robert V., "Sinclair Weeks Was Right," *Transportation Quarterly*, ENO Foundation, Lansdowne, Virginia, Spring 1995.

[8] Transport 2010, Commissariat Général du plan, 1992, Paris.

[9] *Trafic et Rentabilité de réseau Ouest-Européen de trains à grande vitesse*, INTRAPLAN-INRETS, München-Paris, 1993.

[10] La Vie du Rail n° 2286, March 1991, Paris.

[11] La Vie du Rail n° 2466, July 1994, Paris.

[12] *Sustainable Transport*, The World Bank, 1996, Washington.

[13] Union Routière de France, SOFRES Survey, 1995, Paris.

CHAPTER 7
▼▼▼

THE MAJOR RAILWAY
REFORMS: THE BRITISH AND
THE OTHERS

The former chapter overview has shown that there is no doubt that the railway is in Europe still pertinent for passengers in two fields: that of each country's internal medium-distance, heavy traffic routes and that of suburban and possibly regional trains needed to keep large urban zones functioning properly. But two of the train's other traditional markets, freight transport and other intercity or regional passenger lines, only survive with substantial help from public treasury, due to competition from air and road transport. There has been an overwhelming change in the span of a few decades without us really realising it.

This explains why all European countries now find themselves confronted with one of the most difficult problems ever. Faced with stagnant or declining traffic, the number of staff employed by the national railway companies no longer matches needs and the traditional railway workers statutes, usually exceptionally favourable, add to the difficulty. Operating deficits have reached levels that are no longer tolerable for national budgets. There have been various different reactions to this situation.

7.1 EUROPEAN UNION POLICY

European Union policy on railways was the object of a directive adopted in 1991 by the Council of Transport Ministers, marking an important stage in the history of the European railways (Directive 91/440). This directive rests on a certain number of considerations or assumptions, which can be summarised as follows:

- The railways currently occupy an important position in European transport and constitute a vital element of the transport sector in the European Community, both for passengers and freight.
- The position of the railway is in decline despite the many advantages offered by this means of transport, and this is neither normal nor desirable.
- One of the causes of this decline is that road transport does not pay its true cost and that the railways suffer from unfair competition, particularly in terms of freight transport.
- Insufficient investment in all means of transport in the 1970s also contributed to the difficulties of the European railway networks.
- One of the missions of the railway is to relieve the road network, which risks becoming paralysed due to growing congestion.
- Another cause of the railways' difficulties comes from their management, which is monopolistic and technocratic and therefore poorly adapted to a market economy.
- Past trends must be reversed: the success of a common transport policy will depend in great part on the success of the railways.
- It should be possible to make railways a profitable, efficient activity, adapted to the market.

These initial considerations or assumptions resulted in a certain number of decisions external to the railway sector, such as those that aim to raise the cost of freight transport by road through the creation of specific taxes.

In terms of the railways, Directive 91/440—which does not cover urban, suburban, and regional railway networks—sets the basis for what could be a real revolution, the main points being as follows:

- The management of railway companies must follow the principles that apply to commercial businesses and must be independent of national governments; the objective is in particular to balance their budgets.
- If the States impose public service constraints, they should compensate the railways for the corresponding costs; the companies should be responsible for their decisions on internal organisation: supplies, marketing and pricing of services, decisions on personnel, formation of international joint ventures, and so forth.
- Their accounting systems must separate infrastructure management from operations management; these two activities may or may not be entrusted to different public or private entities. The chief aim of this separation would be to allow network usage fees to be calculated for the trains running on the networks.

- International railway company groups carrying out international combined transport of freight are guaranteed access to national networks.
- The States should write off all or part of the existing public railway company debts.
- The States should take the necessary measures to develop national railway infrastructure, taking into account the overall needs of the Community as and when necessary.

Of course, this directive inspires much comment, given that it is mostly based on false assumptions. Before analysing it, it is particularly interesting to view how certain major European networks stand six years after this directive was published, as some have gone much further than the directive requires whereas others have not yet really begun to implement it.

7.2 GERMAN RAILWAYS

German railways deserve mention first, since they are the continent's largest and have achieved an important reform, due in part to the reunification of the two Germanys.

West German railways (DB or Deutsche Bundesbahn) had long been a major preoccupation of successive German administrations, due to their heavy financial burden on the federal budget. Overall, traffic changed little from year to year, whether in terms of passengers (38-billion passenger kilometres in 1970, 40 in 1980, 42 in 1985, and 45 in 1991) or freight (70-billion tonne kilometres in 1970, 64 in 1980, 63 in 1985, and 63 again in 1991). But with a staff of 240,000 in 1991, the financial burden on the federal government continued to grow to such an extent that 16 attempts were made in the past 30 years to rectify the situation, all fruitless [1].

East German railways (DR, or Deutsche Reichsbahn) were in an even worse situation, given that for a traffic of only 10-billion passenger kilometres and 18-billion tonne kilometres they had no fewer than 260,000 employees at the time of reunification.

With more than 500,000 railway employees in total, the situation could obviously not continue. Forecasts made in 1992 showed that due to the upgrading of the East German network, if nothing were done, DM 420 billion would be needed over 10 years, and annual losses would reach DM 40 billion (21 billion ECUs) in the year 2000.

Even rich Germany could not reasonably face such a prospect without any reaction, and a reform of the system was considered essential. In fact, along with telecommunications, this was one of the largest reform projects Germany had undertaken since the war and even required a modification of the Constitution.

The primary objective of this reform was not to make the railway profitable at any price but to give it future prospects and increase its share of the transport market, especially in order to relieve road traffic. This reflects one of the basic ideas of the Community policy described above. As far as freight transport is concerned, the aim was more precisely to increase the train's share from 17% to 25% of tonne kilometres shipped within Germany. In other words, the reform is based on the assumption that the train carries a large part of the country's freight transport and that an increase in this share is essential to the country's economic well-being and to relieve the roads.

In fact, the first part of this assumption is false due to its use of meaningless units of measure, which in turn implies that the second part is also false (see Chapter 3). As in the rest of Europe, the train's true share of freight transport is actually very low. Expressed as turnover, it represents approximately 4% (DM 6.4 billion in 1994, compared with about 150 billion for the road). Expressed in kilometres travelled, it represents, as we have seen previously, the equivalent of less than 1% of German road traffic, with 4.5 billion kilometres travelled by rail freight wagons in 1993, compared with 560 billion kilometres travelled by all road vehicles (heavy and light goods vehicles, cars, etc.). This means that if the objective set by the German government is reached, at the price of colossal subsidies, the overall relief to road traffic after 10 years will be far less than 1% in relation to its present level, whereas road traffic is currently increasing at an average of about 2% per year. It would be difficult to find a clearer example of how harmful it can be to rely on meaningless statistical units, which mislead even governments and induce them to take inappropriate decisions.

Given this primary objective, and the secondary one to reduce the financial burden on the federal government in the long term, the reform carried out in Germany has the following key components [1]:

- The federal government is to wipe off the company's debts in full (i.e., DM 66 billion).
- It is to abandon fictitious accounting assets of DM 77 billion.
- It is to assume responsibility for a 10-year infrastructure investment programme worth DM 110 billion, based on the principle that the state also finances road infrastructures (though no mention is made of the fact that road users pay much more through taxes than they cost the public authorities).
- It will take over all retirement commitments begun as of 31st December 1991, such that the company will pay the equivalent to what would be paid in industry.
- It transfers financial responsibility for regional passenger services to the Länder and grants them as compensation a subsidy reaching DM 9 billion in 1996 and 12 billion (nearly 6 billion ECUs) in 1998, on the understanding that the Länder will have the option, if they so wish, of replacing railway services with coach lines.

- It will assume responsibility for the negative financial incidence of operating the former East German network.
- It grants the former East Germany Länder a specific subsidy of DM 33 billion.

The two railway companies, DB and DR, were merged and changed status: they became a limited liability company under common law, the DBAG, created on 1st January 1994. This entity deals with both the federal government and the Länder for regional transport. One of the aims of the transformation is to change mentalities and procedures in the railways to make them adopt those of private sector companies and to balance their accounts in future. For example, if the DBAG does not receive adequate subsidies for loss-making routes, it will be legally bound to cease their operation. In addition, newly recruited personnel no longer have civil servant status, but adhere to a common-law collective agreement. In the near future, however, priority has been given to a drastic reduction in the work force, which has already fallen from more than 500,000 in 1990 to 306,000 on 1st January 1995, and should be at 220,000 on 31st December 1997. This major reduction will require early retirement schemes and voluntary leaving incentives, as well as an almost complete freeze on recruitment. Until 1995, most staff reductions concerned former East German railway employees who, through a quirk of history, had private status. But future reductions will also affect the personnel of the former DB and maybe require layoffs.

The DBAG is, of course, applying the European directive of 1991 on internal organisation. As of 1st July 1994, a new tariff working out was introduced, taking into account the separation between infrastructure and operating accounts. In two to three years, four distinct companies are due to be created within a holding company and will be responsible, respectively for infrastructure, long-distance passenger lines, regional transport, and freight.

In the longer term, it is planned to dissolve the holding company, with each of the four entities becoming independent of the others (i.e., there would no longer be a capital link between the three operating companies and the one in charge of infrastructure). Privatisation is not out of the question at a later date. It may affect regional lines before then, as responsibility for them was transferred to the Länder as of 1st January 1996, with corresponding operating subsidies, and the latter are now entirely free to take any decisions they think fit.

As of 1994, the DBAG was divided into different departments, which are in fact operational units:

- Long-distance passenger transport;
- Regional passenger transport;
- Passenger stations;
- Freight transport;
- Infrastructure;

- Traction;
- Maintenance workshops.

One of the major difficulties faced by management was the lack of a reliable accounting system. In 1994, the new president of the Germany railways declared before an investigation commission of the French National Assembly [1]:

It really makes you wonder what the federal state has done in the last few years, when you think that a company with a turnover of DM 25 billion (14 Billion ECUs), which costs the taxpayer about as much in subsidies, has no serious accounting system. But I know why this accounting system was not created in the past: it would then have been possible to see where the taxpayers' money went and I think certain people did not wish this to be the case.

It should be added that there is nothing uniquely German about this situation and that until recently, most European railways were managed more like government departments than like private sector companies.

Germany has now achieved most of this reform, which entailed a change in its Constitution, the passing of five structural laws and 140 regulations with the aim of upgrading all the networks and rolling stock in both the East and the West. The reform has two aspects. It involves substantial expenditure on the part of the federal government, including truly massive investment that reached DM 15 billion in 1994, entirely financed by public funds, and followed by others of huge magnitude during the following years. The second aspect involves making a drastic reduction in staff in order to limit salary expenses, a large part of the network's expenditure. As of 1994, the DBAG was able to announce an initial profit of DM 89 million, against a deficit of 15 billion in 1993, after the federal government wrote off its entire debt and also assumed responsibility for all the above-mentioned expenses, in particular all infrastructure investments.

Taxes on road fuel were particularly increased by 0.16 DM (0.08 ECU) per litre in 1994 with the aim of partially financing the railways, in the name of an illusory balancing between means of transport.

Will the railways cost the German taxpayer less in the long term than the amounts that were forecast prior to the reform? It is not certain, but whatever the answer, analysis of the reform clearly demonstrates that the solution adopted is extremely costly and cannot be considered as an option by other, less rich, countries, as the overall cost of the reform is estimated at a minimum of DM 150 billion, in the hope that the public burden will at last be reduced. Above all, it is questionable if not dangerous in that it transfers huge costs to the federal state (roughly DM 40 billion a year), thus enabling the railway company to present accounts showing profits that do not reflect the true picture, and is therefore a brake on the real reduction in costs for the national community. Mainly dictated by unrealistic if not ideological considerations, the reform is almost the exact opposite of the policy adopted by Great Britain.

7.3 BRITISH RAILWAYS

If Germany's railway reform can be called an unprecedented upheaval, the term revolution is not too strong to describe the reform taking place in Great Britain, where achievements almost defy description.

Like all other European networks, British Rail found itself faced with a steady erosion of its market and this led in particular to an almost complete disappearance of its freight activity. Although the burden of the railway on taxpayers was much lower in Britain than in the other European countries, British Rail reacted by creating 27 "profit centres" within the company in recent years, through internal reorganisation without precedent in any other European network, particularly involving the introduction of a serious analytical accounting system, separating total expenditure (infrastructure and operations) among the different activities and thus revealing the true costs, line by line.

But the British government went even further than the railway company itself by announcing in 1992 that its objective was to fully privatise the railways with the aim to improve their operations and to control and reduce their characteristic deficit insofar as possible and desirable.

The privatisation did not give birth to a few large commercial entities, but to about 90 distinct companies! Only one, Railtrack, is in charge of infrastructure, but no less than 25 companies are responsible for passengers, many of which operate only one line, three are responsible for freight, three for rolling stock, fifteen for maintenance and rail replacement, and so forth. These last ones compete with their sister companies and even other private-sector companies, each logically aiming to earn and maximise profits. The operating companies have been privatised by way of concessions for given lengths of time when the others have just been sold, sometimes providing the government with sizable amounts of money.

The operating concession time lengths were either short (seven years) or long (15 years, for example) when it was necessary for the bidder to heavily invest in rolling stock. The bid was awarded to those either proposing the highest amount of money to the government or, more often, to those requesting the smallest subsidy from the government for a level of service specified in terms and conditions of the concessioning contract. The final objective of the reform is to minimise public spending by introducing competition at all levels, as experience in other sectors has shown that productivity gains of about 20% to 30% are possible in the short term in the case of privatisation, on the understanding that to meet the objective particularly implied a change in the railway workers' contracts to bring them in line with private law.

The British decisions concerning the railways can only be fully understood if they are put in the context of the vast privatisation programme undertaken in the United Kingdom over the last 10 years, in most cases successfully. In the transport sector alone, the London bus lines were privatised by tender, with surprising results. Between 1985 and 1993, the kilometres travelled by vehicles (i.e., the supply) increased by 24%, operating costs fell from £650 million to £500 million, and the quality of service improved distinctly, as the percentage of improper service fell drastically from 17% to 1.5%. As the number of customers remained stable, the cost to the government (i.e., the taxpayers), fell from £400 million per year to . . . £58 million without a significant increase in tariffs [2]!

In this context, it is easy to understand that the railway "privatisation" process was carried through to completion. At the beginning of 1997, it was certain that even if a Labour government is elected, the situation will not be reversed, especially since some of the privatised companies will have been bought by the railway employees themselves.

A complex set of mechanisms have been devised to enable the system to work. It is not a simple matter. Each company operating one or more lines has to deal firstly with the government concerning its rights and duties under the franchise, secondly with one or more rolling stock supply companies, and thirdly with Railtrack—to which a license fee is paid for use of infrastructures for which it now has the overall responsibility.

As for Railtrack, it works on the one hand with line operators, or franchisees, which may possibly mean several companies for a single route in the future, and which will be its source of revenue, and on the other hand with companies dealing with rail maintenance, renewal, and construction, which are selected by invitations to tender. In turn, rolling stock supply companies also use invitations to tender to select their suppliers and fleet maintenance companies.

This process, which is very similar to what exists in other sectors of economic activity but entirely new in the European railway sector, has been crowned with success despite the numerous prophecies on both sides of the Channel announcing its failure. As from April 1994, British Rail ceased to be an integrated company and Railtrack was created to assume responsibility for infrastructure. There was a harsh strike by pointsmen in 1994, but it ended without the principles of the privatisation being questioned. In November 1994, the British government announced its decision to privatise Railtrack as of 1995 or 1996, underlining the fact that the company possessed assets estimated at several billion pounds and that their objective was that Railtrack, which controls the 11,500 km of rail and the 2,500 stations that make up the British network, should earn profits of 5% on this capital, increasing to 8% in a few years. Even before its privatisation, Railtrack announced a 10-year, £10 billion investment programme for renovation, electrification, and so forth.

Railtrack, which registered profits before tax of £272 million for the 1995–1996 financial year was successfully privatised on 1st May 1996, with the operation bringing in a revenue of £1.7 billion (2.1 billion ECUs) for the British Treasury. In November 1996, it was able to announce a 76% increase in its profits for the April–September period.

But this privatisation was only the final stage of a process begun in August 1995 with an initial privatisation: the Red Star messenger service was purchased by some of its executives for the symbolic price of £1, with British Rail taking care of redundancy payments to 700 employees. A new, much more significant sale took place in November 1995: the entire rolling stock was sold to three companies specially created for the occasion, one by British Rail executives.

The concessioning of the 25 passenger lines or groups of passenger lines was pursued at the same time, with the aim that over 50% of passenger traffic will be managed by private companies by the end of the first half of 1996. The largest of such lines or groups of lines had 4,000 employees, which gives an idea of how important this break-up will be.

By mid 1995, nearly 40 groups or companies had expressed an interest in running the foremost three networks (SouthWest Trains, turnover: £280 million; LTS Rail: £60 million; Great Western: £160 million). Of course, the process was met with protest on principle from railway employees and their unions, but their opposition was not very strong in a country already used to privatisations.

On 19th December 1995, the 930-km regional and suburban rail network South West Trains were awarded to the largest British coach company (Stagecoach), with the new owner receiving a sliding scale annual subsidy. On 20 December, the Great Western and LTS networks were bought out by their employees with the support of several banks and even a coach company. Throughout 1996, sales continued, both positive and negative, with offers from buyers from all over the world. For instance, an important French private company—the "Générale des Eaux" group—became the concessionary of one of the leading suburban networks in London. The corresponding concession agreement is a good example of what can be obtained through privatisation. Whereas the network concerned—the South Central Network—showed an annual deficit of £90 million, the concessionary company will only receive £70 million the first year, and £30 million after seven years, whilst agreeing to respect terms of reference that particularly specify an improvement in service quality and a control on ticket prices during peak hours. The concessionary company must therefore make substantial increases in productivity and improvements to the quality of service, to the benefit of users, whilst the burden on the British Treasury will be divided by three! The same private French company won a second tendering in August 1996, and thus operate a fifth of the British passenger railways, a paradox as it is coming from a country stubbornly opposing up to now almost any change regarding its own nationalised railways. In proceeding this way, the British authorities consider that they are giving the railways a real chance for the future by allowing them to become as competitive as possible under the best possible conditions. In fact, the British government did no more than come into line, under special conditions, with the world trend towards privatisation, or to be more exact, concession of railways. One of the bases of this change is to adjust staff numbers to needs, by offering the surplus personnel high severance pay, in the region of one or two years' salary, which, as experience has shown, is repaid almost instantaneously by the savings made. By acting this way, the new owners of the British networks are successfully reducing their staff by up to 20% in one year, in a country where the level of unemployment is the lowest of the European Union. It is not England that has adopted an original position, contrary to what is thought in continental Europe. In this field as in many others, it is continental Europe that is not on the same wavelength as world evolution.

This does not mean that in future the railways will no longer weight on the British budget at all. The future will tell. The principle of subsidies to certain franchisees has been maintained in order to keep some loss-making lines in operation. But the government has two clear objectives: firstly to minimise spending and increase efficiency by introducing competition at all levels; and secondly to make transparent decisions, which implies that it must be possible to calculate case by case what it costs to keep each line in service so that informed choices can be made as to whether a line should be maintained or closed and replaced by a road service. In fact, passenger rail routes will be divided into three categories. Quite a number, will be profitable without subsidies (e.g., leading lines such as the London-Edinburgh), others can be maintained by granting "reasonable" subsidies (especially in the suburbs), and still others will be abandoned and replaced by coach lines providing equivalent or similar services given that there is complete freedom in Great Britain in this area since the arrival of Margaret Thatcher and that a vast network of coach lines is already in operation without subsidies.

As for the three companies responsible for freight transport, they were purchased as a block in March 1996 for £225 million (270 million ECUs) by the American railway company Wisconsin Central Transportation, which grouped them into a single entity. Contrary to certain passenger lines, the contract excludes the granting of subsidies in the future, since the idea of public service is considered meaningless when applied to freight, given that road transport services are available throughout the country. Of course, it will be up to the new company to gain maximum benefit from the major commercial advantage provided by the new Channel Tunnel, especially for combined transport, if the market justifies it.

On the whole, the British government intends to reduce its total contribution of £2 billion in 1993 to £740 million in 1996–97 and far less later on, and local authorities will, of course, be free to contribute financially to the operation of certain lines if they wish to keep them in operation.

7.4 TWO OPPOSITE POLICIES

The end goal of the British approach is exactly the opposite to Germany's, which can be explained by two specific points. The British primary objective is to drastically limit the railway's financial burden on the State or even entirely eliminate it, which is not necessarily out of reach—not to seek an illusory "balancing" among the modes of transport. This reform also comes from the fact that British Rail had a modern accounting system that is still lacking in most railway companies on the continent. This accounting system provides information on the exact grand cost of each service and therefore enables a comparison to be made between subsidies and services rendered, allowing costs to be broken down network by network and line by line and the calculation of the corresponding cost to the community.

This perhaps explains why the overall cost of the railways to the taxpayer, although it was one of the lowest in Europe with £2 billion in 1993 (2.5 billion ECUs) compared with about 50 billion francs in France (i.e., 8 billion ECUs), (some official estimates even put the latter figure at 70 billion francs [3]) and 30 billion deutschmarks (15 billion ECUs) in Germany, was considered intolerable, whereas it is accepted elsewhere.

The second major difference between German and British policies is due to the fact that the clear objective of the British was to immediately privatise the entire railway system, thereby producing very many small companies, on the understanding that there is nothing to stop the idea of grouping them into a few larger entities at a later date, if needed. It can be seen to a certain extent as a return to the historical roots to optimise the railway's chances, the idea being to introduce as much competition as possible without distorting the rules of the market with massive subsidies, either for investment or operations. In this domain probably more than in any other, Great Britain deserves the nickname it is sometimes given today: the "Laboratory of Europe."

In Germany, however, privatisation remains a distant and somewhat hypothetical objective. If it should ever happen, it would give birth to only four large commercial entities, perhaps with the exception of the regional networks. In summary, Great Britain is in the process of dramatically reducing the cost of the railway to its treasury (i.e., the taxpayer), whereas it will not really occur in Germany in the decade to come. According to official estimates, the railways will cost the astounding sum of DM 350 billion to the German budget in the next 10 years, taking into account the investment programme planned, subsidies to the Länder for regional passenger services, and voluntary leaving pay for staff. Only much later, after this phase of stabilisation and restructuring, may the cost to the federal government decrease somewhat.

Another fundamental difference is the way the investments are financed. In Germany, where the primary objective is to develop the railway's share of the market, with the illusory aim of relieving roads, the railway company has a *right* to state-financed investments regardless of traffic revenues, both for infrastructure and rolling stock. For example, on 1st December 1994, the DBAG placed an order with the German railway industry for 420 locomotives and 339 regional transport trains for approximately DM 4 billion, with a supplementary option for 500 locomotives and

200 regional transport trains to a total value of DM 3.5 billion. It was quite rightly called the contract of the century! Likewise, massive investment is under way or is planned for infrastructures, including constructing the new lines mentioned previously and the renovation of existing lines.

The British approach is quite the opposite. They consider that the railways have no automatic right to investment and that any investment made should, as in any other activity, depend on revenues, which could include a certain level of subsidies where this appears to be justified. It is the profits from the sale of their services that should allow Railtrack and the rolling stock supply companies to invest, whereas state subsidies will be granted only to keep lines running when public service requirements justify this.

In other words, the German policy is based on the assumption that the railways should benefit from specific aid, which in fact means that they escape from the laws of the market on the grounds of a set traffic objective, whereas under the British policy, the railways should follow the rules of the market all the more and, especially, finance their investments themselves because their greatest competitor—the road— more than covers its costs due to the different taxes it pays. Although both countries have followed the 1991 Brussels Directive, it would be difficult to imagine two more fundamentally contrasting policies. Just as their foundations are different, so will their consequences be the government's contribution being brought down to a very low level in Great Britain and continuing to approach 1% of the GPD in Germany (i.e., one-third of the 3% of public debt allowed under the Treaty of Maastricht criteria), for results that are out of all proportion to the costs.

But Germany and Great Britain have not been the only countries to implement railway reforms. While railways in some countries have not changed at all, other nations have already begun to act.

7.5 SWEDEN

This is the case, for example, in Sweden where the railway was split into two entities in 1988, one in charge of infrastructure under the responsibility of the state, and the other of running the network with the status of a company (Statens Jarnvagar or SJ). This reform has had the advantage of bringing about transparency since the experts were no longer in one and the same body, which had previously concealed the truth about operations and costs. The State then consented to a massive increase in infrastructure investment, considered necessary because of accumulated delays in upgrading the system, in this country where very specific climatic conditions often make the railway a desirable option during part of the year.

Certain regional or freight lines were opened to competition that led to SJ losing its operating monopoly and resulted in costs often falling by about 20%.

Most important, the national railway management changed completely. Most of the executive directors were dismissed, and others with private sector experience were recruited. From 1988 to 1994, the number of maintenance workshops decreased from 35 to 13; marshalling yards from 35 to 6; and personnel dropped by almost half, from 29,000 to 15,000.

At the same time, the State invested heavily in network renovation. After five years, traffic volumes are identical or higher, with the same number of passengers and more freight. But the deficit of the SJ has been practically cut in half, falling from 850 million kroner to 440, due in large part to staff reductions. The Swedish railways are now the leaders in Europe in terms of traffic per employee, at least when counted in tonne kilometres. SJ has become a modern, dynamic company with a new logo, renovated stations and trains, and so forth. Tilting trains have been purchased, offering far better performance to passengers. Along the major Stockholm-Gothenburg route, journey times dropped from about four hours to three and should decrease still further, for about one-twentieth of the cost of building a new high-speed line that would have reduced the journey time to two hours. In other words, for 5% of the cost, 50% of the results were achieved. The Swedish government has thus been able to set three financial goals for the company in the years to come: a 7% return on investment after taxes, a shareholders' equity ratio of 35%, and self-financing of all new trains and stations, all without any subsidies. This objective was attained in 1994. A new reform adopted on 5th May 1994, and effective from 1st January, 1995, opened the network to full competition [1]. Nevertheless, the cost to the government remains very high, and it is in charge of the infrastructure. In fact, the reform resulted in an overall *increase* of the cost to the Swedish budget. In 1996, the total spending of public money for the railways amounted to approximately 13 billion crowns (1,5 billion ECUs) for a country of 8 million inhabitants! As in Germany, a tricky process gave the impression that railways were becoming "profitable," when, in fact, the taxpayers had to pay more and more.

7.6 THE NETHERLANDS

The Netherlands has also implemented a railway reform in the last few years. The railways play a special role in this very densely populated small-size country where the distinction between "long-distance" and suburban or regional lines is often difficult to make.

The underlying idea of the reform is to organise the national railway company into four units designed to become profit centres, concerned respectively with infrastructure, property, freight, and passenger transport (this last activity being the most important). Each of these four units is composed of a certain number of subsidiaries and departments. A new specific entity was also created to allocate rail capacity and fix timetables between the passenger transport unit and the freight unit, on the understanding that operators will not be required to pay fees for the existing infrastructure until the year 2000. However, it is planned that they should pay for the tracks that have not yet been constructed, which will particularly concern the high-speed tracks. It would nonetheless be surprising to see such an objective actually reached.

The "passenger" unit, which is by far the most important one, will be divided into four geographic networks in order to help implementation of the new entity's principles: decentralisation, responsibility at lower levels of the hierarchy, and priority to the customer.

The company's new freedom is wide-reaching because, as in other countries, the railways have been authorised to participate in invitations to tender for the selection of the second national telecommunications supplier. All things considered, the aim is to undertake a complete cultural transformation over a period of five to seven years, after which subsidies should practically disappear.

Personnel will be adjusted according to needs and the company plans to cut 4,800 jobs (18%), with a certain number of compulsory layoffs. The Dutch railways are no different in this respect from the railways described previously in that all have made considerable reductions in staff following the loss of part of their market.

7.7 BELGIUM

The four networks above mentioned have undertaken bold, even revolutionary reform in one case, but many others are not so advanced. Belgium commissioned an international consulting company to carry out an audit and the results, published in November 1994, were, to paraphrase the Minister of Transport, a "bombshell." Whereas the company's debts amounted to 100 billion Belgian francs (2,5 billion ECUs) at the end of 1994, the audit revealed that despite subsidies covering 20% of investment costs for new lines, this debt would increase to 528 billion francs (13,6 billion ECUs) in 2005 if the programme to construct high-speed lines to the Netherlands and Germany continued as planned, and that the net deficit of the SNCB would then reach 47 billion Belgian francs per year (1,2 billion ECUs).

In this context, the Belgian government decided to temporarily halt construction of the new high-speed lines towards Germany and the Netherlands, without abandoning the plan outright, to have time for reflection, although work would continue on the new high-speed line under construction between Brussels and the French border towards France and England, which (according to the railway employee unions) would not achieve profitability of more than 2%, if not less.

At the end of 1995, it was planned that the rest of the network would be divided into four categories of lines (A, B, C, D), with only the former two being kept up to current standards; the latter two being given minimum maintenance in order to operate at reduced speeds.

In July 1996, the Belgian Cabinet adopted a massive investment plan, inspired by the true European tradition of the railways' "right" to subsidies. It amounts to

370 billion Belgian francs (10 billion ECUs) for the period 1996–2005, including 116 billion (3 billion ECUs) for the completion of the high-speed lines.

7.8 FRANCE

In mid 1996, the French railways have not yet undertaken any reform programme of note. Their situation at the end of the 20th century can only be understood in its historical context.

In the 19th century, as everywhere else in Europe, France was covered with a very dense rail network, constructed by the most important entrepreneurs and financiers of the period. But, as elsewhere, the end of the century saw the birth of the car, closely followed by the truck, which were greeted with such enthusiasm in France that many inventions followed and France had the largest number of cars in the world at the start of the 20th century

The first world road convention took place in Paris in 1908 and the Minister of Public Works at the time, Mr. Barthou, was able to declare, without surprising the audience in the least: "There is no excessive pride in stating that this convention had to be held in the first country to bear witness to the phenomenal expansion of the car industry and which also possesses an incomparable road network."

Road vehicles saved France from defeat upon two occasions during World War I. In the first case, Parisian taxis carried reinforcements to the front, resulting in the first victory of the Marne. In the second case, a steady stream of trucks carried reinforcements night and day over a period of several months to Verdun by the road that came to be known as the "Sacred Way," in fact the first actual "motorway" in the world.

It is true that the total number of army vehicles had increased from 250 in 1914 to 90,000 in 1918. The option to use trucks was chosen during the first months of the war and the organisation of convoys reached perfection, enabling the transport of whole divisions, which disorganised the German lines.

Field Marshall E. Ludendorff, commander-in-chief of the German Imperial Army declared after the war: "France's victory in 1918 was the victory of French trucks over German railways."

The lesson was quickly forgotten on the French side, but not by the Germans, and the victory in 1940 was to some extent the victory of the German trucks over the French railways. If General de Gaulle had not been an officer in the cavalry, there can be no great doubt that he would have pleaded the cause of trucks as he did that of armored vehicles.

After the First World War, France remained the foremost European producer of road vehicles (cars and trucks) until 1929, due to the unhindered development of the market, which reached the figures of 170,000 cars and 52,000 trucks in that year.

But at the same time, the railways began to experience great financial difficulties, which led them to ask for and obtain special concessions from successive governments: firstly the creation of a "common fund" to cover their debts, and then the implementation of a policy restricting the use of cars and trucks through the adoption of increasingly drastic measures.

Fuel taxes were increased very sharply and trucks became subject to taxes on weight and size that were 27 times higher per tonne kilometre than those paid by the railway, such that the truck market dropped precipitously. It declined from 52,000 sales in 1929 to 28,000 in 1933, whereas, despite the depression, production continued to rise in the other European countries.

But as the financial situation of the railways was in the meantime continually worsening, a new set of measures was implemented in 1934 aimed practically at *prohibiting* the use of trucks and coaches by affecting both their technical characteristics and the conditions of their purchase and use.

The authorised width of trucks was decreased from 2.50m to 2.35m, the length to 10m, and the maximum load to 15 tonnes from a previous figure of 22 tonnes, which also rendered the vehicles unexportable. Similarly, a decree issued in April 1934 prohibited companies from purchasing trucks except to replace existing vehicles! All roads links along rail routes were eliminated and an exorbitant licence fee was created for road transport, designed to compensate the railway deficit [4].

In summary, transport by truck became practically impossible, except for a few local routes that were part of an authoritarian "co-ordination" plan, which also applied to coach passengers: on the few lines that were maintained, the authorities sometimes imposed stops simply so that they would not be more rapid than the trains [5]!

The results of such a policy were predictable. Truck sales fell to 18,000 in 1935, one-third of the sales in 1928, whereas exactly the opposite happened in Germany, where they increased from 14,000 in 1929 to 40,000 in 1934, and in Great Britain, where they amounted to 91,500 vehicles in the same year. The French truck industry was therefore virtually annihilated and horse-drawn vehicles were seen to reappear, as *they* were not affected by the quotas!

The absence of modern trucks to transport troops and equipment undoubtedly played a large role in the French debacle in the face of the German forces in 1940.

Nevertheless, contrary to the hopes of those who campaigned for these constraining measures, they did not change the financial situation of the railways at all, and this led certain perceptive specialists to state in 1936, "we should not have confused the problem of transport with that of the railway deficit" [4].

The railway debt continued to worsen and led to the nationalisation of the entire railway system in 1938, amalgamated within the Société Nationale des Chemins de Fer (SNCF) and the state took on the considerable debt that had accumulated over 10 years.

Nonetheless, there was some isolated protest against the policies followed, defending the road in its battle with the railway. An article published in the French journal *La Vie de l'Automobile* in 1932 [6] summarises the road defender's arguments very well, as the following excerpts show:

> *The railway has gone bankrupt. It will be vain to try to hide the whole truth from the public and, if our 'leaders' really have the general interest at heart, they must try to resolve this serious problem without weakness and without biased judgement. The upper echelons of railway management would have us believe that these are only temporary difficulties, due to the world-wide depression. That is an illusion. (. . .)*
>
> *We have always signed away the future by counting on continuing and unlimited increase in rail traffic. The time has come to end this system. There can be no excuse for our continuing to ignore the considerable progress which has been made in road locomotion within the last few years. At present, car and truck transport has become a part of our lives. It is already the leader among our different means of transport because the value of the services it renders far exceeds the total revenues of our railways. (. . .)*
>
> *As for the 'public service' argument, it does not stand up to analysis. Is not the true goal of 'public service' to serve fellow citizens? And if a citizen prefers to serve himself, what right do we have to stop him? Is it treasonous not to use the railway? (. . .)*
>
> *Why should we force freight to lose time and complicate it with a double transhipment while the truck is perfectly capable, all by itself, of directly and swiftly transporting freight between any two points in the country even if they are 1,000 kilometres away from each other? (. . .)*
>
> *Even though one train has a much greater capacity than one road vehicle, it is nonetheless true that the maximum traffic of a rail line is less than that of a road for the simple reason that trains can hardly follow each other at intervals of less than five minutes (several kilometres) whereas coaches and trucks only need the space of a few seconds (a few dozen metres). Although a truck load is 50 or 100 times less than for a train, the road still has the advantage. And its superiority is flagrant in the case of an 'autoroute', i.e., a road reserved exclusively for car traffic. (. . .)*
>
> *It is sheer utopianism to believe that our country can continue for much longer to endure a system of transport that drains it of 8 billion Francs each year (. . .).*

With hindsight, it is hard to believe that these words were written about two-thirds of a century ago. The arguments made were nevertheless entirely unsuccessful in a country where, with its long tradition of Colbertism, power was—and still is—concentrated in the hands of a small élite of talented individuals who gave no chance to those who contradicted them.

Over 60 years later, the French situation is surprisingly similar to its state between the two World Wars, even if nobody questions today the fact that suburban networks are essential and the pertinence of using the existing high-speed lines.

It is interesting to note that one of the measures taken in 1934 is still in force today. Astonishing though it may seem on the eve of the 21st century, it is still forbidden—with rare exceptions—to create intercity coach lines in France. It is possible to take a coach from Paris to Lisbon or London, but not to Alençon, Lyons, or Strasbourg, or from one provincial town to another! And yet there are obviously potential customers for this flexible and inexpensive means of transport.

Like almost all the other European railway networks, the SNCF is currently in dire financial straits. Its debt, which was only possible because it is guaranteed by the state, is approaching the sum of 200 billion francs (30 billion ECUs). According to statistics published to the International Railway Union, income from users reached 40 billion francs in 1993, of which 24.7 billion came from passenger traffic and 15.2 billion from freight traffic [7].

Expenditure rose to approximately 90 billion francs in the same year and the State paid most of the difference, both through budget allocations under different headings and by guaranteeing the increase of the company's debt, which as everybody knows, will in the end have to be borne by the State (i.e., the taxpayers).

Most surprising of all, a series of ingenious accounting expedients showed the official "deficit" to be only 8 billion francs in the same year, concealing the scope of the problem from the French population. It is also hard to believe that the company continued to be authorised to invest more than 20 billion francs (3 billion ECUs) per year over the past 10 years, partly for the high-speed lines, even when it was quite obvious that it had no chance whatsoever of being profitable.

At the end of 1995, the debate finally became public in the context of a general plan to reduce public spending, which is now considered to be a national priority, and during discussions on the contract that was to fix the rules between the State and the SNCF for the five years to come.

As it stood in December 1995, the plan included the following points:

- The transfer of local lines to all or part of the regions with corresponding financing, in order for them to be able to select the best way of servicing the areas concerned, either by maintaining the railway or by opening coach services;
- A reduction in future recruitment;
- A reduction in the volume of annually authorised investment;
- A request for increased management efforts in the company;
- A plan for the State to take on the debt progressively, partly by lump sum payments and partly linked to actual sales performance.

But the announcement of this general plan, and particularly the re-examination of the special retirement status of railway employees (who can retire in France with full pension at the age of 55, or 50 for train crews!) and a general reform of the national public health system, led to a general strike in the railway and Paris underground services, which forced the government to withdraw its project.

The outbreak and scope of the movement surprised only those who knew little about the issue and who then began asking themselves a certain number of questions.

What can explain the radical nature of this movement, one of the most marked social conflicts in France's history? Was it because the railway employees were too attached to their special status or the unions too conservative in their refusal to give up any rights they had acquired? Was it because the SNCF was too rigid in its management or that the government was at fault or inadequate in its handling of the situation? All these issues certainly played a role. But there is another reason that not yet been mentioned.

In France, as elsewhere, railway employees have a real passion for the job that they have chosen to exercise. The railway is almost a religion for them. Whatever may be heard to the contrary, it would be wrong to think that the great majority of railway employees do not do their job with devotion and conscientiousness. Yet, despite their attachment to their trade and the sense of responsibility that most of them have, the French railway employees are obliged to face the results of their company: stagnation or reduction in traffic and, above all, an apparently unlimited increase in the burden on the public treasury. Even though everything possible has been done over the decades to hide the truth, the true figures, which amount to tens of billions of francs per year, have now become, more or less, public knowledge.

It is this contrast between the efforts made and the results registered that was in large part responsible for the strike at the end of 1995. The French railway employees feel that they are not appreciated, even though they consider they have done their best and do not feel that they are to blame. In this context, it is natural for them to revolt against what they feel is a profound injustice and try to find those responsible for it.

Some are accusing the government of not doing its duty. However, as far as the French government is concerned, it has not ceased to devote considerable sums of money to the railway in the past years. The president of the SNCF in post in 1995 bitterly noted that, between 1984 and 1993, investments had amounted to 150 billion francs (23 billion ECUs) for the main network, of which a little more than half was for the TGVs, and that between these two dates the corresponding traffic had still fallen by 7%, whereas road traffic increased by 30% and air transport by nearly 100%. With the exception of the Paris suburbs, the situation is worse for all other passenger traffic and for freight. As we have seen, the turnover of railway freight is approximately 15 billion francs whereas freight road transport's volume of activity, all vehicles combined, is 320 billion francs per year.

In fact, the primary cause of the unrest within the French railway is to be found in its appalling management, as well as in a worker statute dating back to the times when the railways had no competition. The headquarters in Paris now count no less than 11,000 people; train drivers are actually driving trains, on average, 11 hours per week. As in any badly managed company, the employees are, of course, not content.

The great railway and underground strike that marked the end of 1995 in France was rich in other lessons. It clearly revealed precisely where the railway was still necessary and where it has ceased to be vital. For the first time, contrary to what might have been thought and what was often said, the paralysis of the railways did not paralyse France.

A representative opinion poll [8] dealing with the first two weeks of the strike revealed that 93% of the nonstriking French had not missed *a single* day of work due to the strike, the proportion reaching 97% in the provinces and 75% in the Paris region! The same poll indicated that only 1% of the French had been prevented from going to work at all by the strike, that it had made it very difficult for 9% of them and somewhat difficult for 10%, but that it had had no effect on 80% of the population.

In fact, only the Paris region was badly handicapped by the railway strike, but that was due to the fact that not only the railways but also the metro and bus went on strike. The provinces, which represent 80% of the French population, continued to work with practically no major setbacks for individuals and even more so for companies, since road transport of freight filled the gap left by rail transport.

In normal circumstances, nobody denies the convenience and efficiency of high-speed railways, but other means of transport were immediately made available to substitute them. Airlines were only too happy to make the most of the opportunity and increased the frequency of their flights and used high-capacity aeroplanes along the major TGV routes (Paris-Lyons, Paris-Nantes, Paris-Bordeaux). Likewise, temporary coach lines sprung up on these routes as well as on dozens, even hundreds, of other smaller routes, revealing the existence of a latent market, as the government did not refuse them the right to operate in such trying circumstances for the country.

All this confirmed that modern societies have an extraordinary capacity to adapt. This was evident in the Paris region. On paper, the simultaneous railway, bus, and underground strike should have entirely paralysed the French capital. Everyone is aware of the high flow of passengers who normally use the remarkable suburban railway networks, the underground, and the buses to get to Paris daily: 31% of people who work in the region use the underground or the bus each day and 11% take the train, representing a total of almost two million people.

Nevertheless, despite a complete stoppage of trains, undergrounds, and buses, absenteeism was very low and the region's inhabitants seemed to show unlimited creativity in imagining solutions for getting to work. Some took to leaving home by car at 5:00 a.m. in order to avoid heavy morning traffic as much as possible. Others rediscovered the joys of walking and hitchhiking—solidarity was reborn in Paris.

Bicycles, normally absent, reappeared everywhere in the streets of Paris, as did roller skates and skateboards. Many people refrained from returning home and slept at friends' homes or even at the office. All relatively large-sized companies organised car-pooling and cars occupied only by their driver became fewer in number. The authorities organised the introduction of private bus lines between certain suburban stations and Paris, as well as subsidized boat services on the Seine River.

All in all, the population of Paris showed remarkable endurance and acceptance in the face of the problems, to the surprise of outside observers. Of course, for many, the strike was a real ordeal, with complete changes from their normal hours, short nights, and extremely long journey times. But this particularly affected those who normally used the suburban trains, which represents only 11% of the region's workers. Those who usually took the underground or the buses often chose to walk or ride a bicycle since they had shorter distances to cover.

Finally, it must be remembered that in normal circumstances, 45% of the region's inhabitants go to work by car, 10% on foot, and 3% on two-wheeled vehicles and that these people, especially in the suburbs, were less affected, if at all, by the strike.

Within two weeks, a new equilibrium was established. Whereas at the start of the strike there were 640 km of traffic jams each morning on the motorways and major routes of the region (beating all the records), the length was decreased to 200 km after two weeks. Centre-city shops lost part of their clientèle during this Christmas shopping period, but suburban shopping centres broke all previous sales records.

Of course, such a situation could not have lasted for very long and everyone was greatly relieved when the underground and railways began running anew after three weeks of interruption. If it was doubted, the essential role of public transport for the everyday life of the Paris region had clearly been confirmed. However, in fact, it was more the underground and bus network strike that had been harmful than the railway strike.

At the beginning of 1997, the French government adopted a reform that financially separated the country's transportation infrastructure from operations by creating a new special body, the "Reseau Ferre de France," and by transferring to it a portion of the debt of the SCNF. The positive aspect of this decision is that it will allow a better understanding of the real cost of the different SCNF services and a better control of infrastructure expenses. Although this may allow the SCNF, as in Germany or Sweden, to present a balanced budget, the taxpayer will still pay huge amounts of money, but to other bodies. The real challenge lies in reducing costs in the face of limited receipts. Only the British are now achieving this goal—at least in Europe.

7.9 THE UNITED STATES

It would be interesting to end this chapter on the great railway reforms by describing the approach to railways that prevails in North America.

The liberal tradition that reigns in the United States stopped them from considering nationalisation of their railways at any point, even when they were faced with the same difficulties as in Europe coming from competition from cars, coaches, or aeroplanes for passengers and trucks for freight. Market forces, therefore, were left to do their work. They led to private companies almost completely abandoning passenger lines and focusing their activity on freight transport only, in remarkable conditions in terms of productivity since deregulation, as described in a previous chapter. At the same time, a reorganisation of the market through buyouts, mergers, take-overs, and so forth resulted in the survival of only about 10 of these companies. As in all other sectors of economic activity, personnel work forces were constantly readapted to market changes.

Europeans are often surprised that the United States has not built high-speed railways similar to those being introduced in Europe, particularly in the northeast of the country between Boston, New York, Baltimore, and Washington. But this should only surprise those who are unaware of the American mentality. Despite the historic role the railways played in conquering the West and uniting the country, the railways are considered to be an activity like any other. Of course, there is no opposition in principle to their possible development. But since the Americans have the choice of travelling by car, coach, or aeroplane, and since these means of transport generally work well and are profitable, the federal government and the different States see no reason why they should have to heavily subsidise this fourth means of transportation that would compete with the other three. The only aid given to the railway by the federal government concerns Amtrak, a publicly owned company that manages a small number of passenger lines, especially in the northeast corridor between Washington and Boston, and on six other major routes.

But the federal government only grants it very low subsidies and it is therefore not surprising that it has never seriously considered financing new, very costly rail infrastructures, but at most encourages improvements to existing lines and helps acquire tilting trains, which would run much faster than present trains and would be more comfortable for passengers. Even if this does not provide a service of the same quality as a new line, it is nonetheless an efficient solution, at a far lower cost than that required for building new infrastructures. As we have seen, the decision was made at the start of 1996 for the Washington-Boston route.

If any proof of the difference in mentalities between Europe and the United States was needed as far as the railways are concerned, the Texas high-speed train project provides an eloquent illustration. Having sought to sell their high-speed equipment in North America for a long time, some European rolling stock manufacturing companies managed to convince Texas authorities several years ago to discuss the creation of a high-speed network in that state. The network was to be in the form of a triangle linking the three cities of Dallas, Houston, and San Antonio. The Texans set the rules of the game from the start: they agreed to the creation of such a network but legislation and ethics prevented them from granting the slightest subsidy, particularly due to the fact that there are many air connections between the three cities carried out by private aviation companies. If it is also taken into account that the three cities have, like many other American cities, an immense surface area with many different centres and that they each have several airports with service to innumerable destinations, it was obvious that the rules of the game set by the Texas authorities killed the project before it ever began and that it was useless to even study it.

But the European industrialists, used to States that always pay in the end, launched into a bitter battle to be "chosen" by the Texas government. The French, with their TGV, won the struggle against their German competitors. But in fact, they only won the right to lose money. After much discussion with financial institutions and after continuing to spend substantial sums of money, they reached a conclusion in mid 1994 that had been obvious from day one: it is impossible to find private funds to finance a project that had no hope of ever being profitable.

7.10 CANADA

Canada studied the transport question through a Royal Commission on Passenger Transport, and after serious consideration adopted in 1993 a position close to that of the United States [9]:

> *The guiding principle is that, both today and in the decades to come, what Canada needs is a system financed by passengers who use it and which does not rely on subsidies, government services and centralized control. Transport should be treated like any other business activity (. . .). We believe what is needed is a system governed by the market. Instead of the public authorities supplying most of the infrastructures, we think this should go to the market and the authorities should limit themselves to the roles of arbiter and decision-maker (. . .). Passengers should pay the true costs of the transport they use and those who do not travel should not have to pay for those who do (. . .). The costs of a transport system should be visible and the public authorities should be obliged to justify their decisions (. . .). All means of transport should be placed on an equal footing (. . .).*

In line with this report, and in accordance with the world-wide trend ignored at present in continental Europe, Canada privatised its two public railway networks.

It is therefore of no surprise either that after having considered creating a new high-speed line linking Quebec, Montreal, Ottawa, and Toronto, Canada will probably acquire tilting equipment that would allow trains to run on existing tracks at higher speeds and to gradually upgrade its existing lines, which is far cheaper option than the creation of new ones.

As the newspaper *Le Devoir* stated in September 1995,

If the private sector can only finance Can. $ 6 billion for the new line, what could possibly justify taxpayer contributions of Can. $12 billion in addition with no returns? (. . .) Is there such a great need for transport between Montreal and Toronto to incite us to proceed with a project that has no hope of being profitable? (. . .) It seems obvious that the only answer to the Quebec-Toronto high-speed project is to shunt it onto a side track (. . .).

The Canadian conclusions, which could only be challenged for political motives, are obviously the opposite extreme of the European Union policy described in the beginning of this chapter and the policies of many European countries that assume that it is normal that there should be substantial, often massive, permanent subsidies for financing railways infrastructure or operations, which in fact comes to the same thing.

It is difficult to understand why the European policy for the railways is so different from the other transport policies, for instance, in the intercity passenger transport sector where there is no discussion on the fact that motorists pay far more overall in taxes than they cost, and where the rules stipulate that airlines must balance their books.

With the current exception of the British, almost all European governments unconsciously consider it normal that the railways should be treated differently from the other means of transport and other economic activities. Only the fact that the railways were nationalised throughout Europe over five decades ago and have thus completely escaped the rules of the market and more or less dictated their policy to public authorities and public opinion itself can explain what might otherwise be inexplicable.

7.11 THE JULY 1996 EUROPEAN COMMISSION WHITE PAPER

The European Commission White Paper "A strategy for revitalising Community railways," published in July 1996, is basically in line with the 1991 Directive and presents not much in the way of innovation [10].

It is based on a sound observation: Railways continue to lose their share of the market due to competition from other means of transport and mismanagement and to cost intolerably large sums of money to member states. But it relies on the same assumptions and once again maintains unambiguously that the railway is, on principle, better than all other means of transport and that it is "paradoxical" that its market share is diminishing.

Once again, the community document also reaffirms that "no one can be unaware of the worsening of road congestion," although, overall, this is untrue.

The document's guiding principle is therefore that a solution must absolutely be found to halt the decline of the railways in order to relieve road traffic, particularly for freight traffic for which new investments must be made. As we have seen, railways cannot relieve road traffic because their scope is entirely different. In this respect, the Commission still reasons in tonne-kilometres and continues to maintain that rail freight represents 16% of total freight traffic in Europe, whereas, considered from the angle that counts here (i.e. occupancy of the transport networks) freight wagon trips represent less than 1% of those of all road vehicles (see chapter 3).

This biased view of the situation leads the white paper to put forward the following two initial conclusions:

- Member states must stabilize the finances of the railway companies and erase their debts.
- It is legitimate for member states to continue to subsidize rail infrastructures "in the short term" "to compensate for the external costs that road transport does not pay," and to alleviate road traffic.

In other words, it is legitimate for states to continue to pay for infrastructures in the name of alleged unfair competition from road transport.

The White Paper does, of course, contain other recommendations, particularly with regard to:

- The separation of infrastructure accounts from operational accounts;
- The prohibition of operating subsidies other than "for motives of public utility service" (thereby actually enabling most operating subsidies to be continued);
- The extension of freedom of access to the networks to new operators;
- The opening of European "freeways" for goods transport, with easier access procedures and reduced waiting time at borders;
- The need for the railway companies to act "more like normal companies," which is obviously impossible under such circumstances.

The document's overall bias in favour of the railway prevents it from reaching the necessary conclusions. Even if some of its points are wise, it does not tackle the real problem and allow members states to continue their unjustified expenditure, which is strictly forbidden for other transport modes and in the other sectors of the economy.

The British example, which will inevitably compel recognition from the other European countries as its brilliant success gradually becomes obvious, shows the necessity of a completely different approach, based on a few key points:

- There is no reason to give the railways a special status among transport modes.
- Above all else, as more than strongly recommended by the World Bank, the "monolithic" status of the railway companies must come to an end and the

existing networks must be divided, or "unbundled," into numerous entities so that the true costs are revealed and real competition becomes possible at all levels.

- True costs must be the guiding principle, and, as a general rule, there is no valid reason for states to subsidize rail infrastructures even in the "short term." The latter must be paid for by their users.
- This objective can only be reached through a real transfer to the private sector that allows reducing costs in very high proportions.
- It will then be possible to reduce public subsidies considerably or even sometimes to put an end to them, whilst at the same time giving the guarantee of a quality public utility service that will not only be maintained but actually improved, within the framework of strict terms of reference. Contrary to what is often fallaciously stated, it should be emphasized that the privatization process in Great Britain has given rise to improvements in service quality and not the contrary, thus explaining its gradual acceptance by public opinion. When justified, subsidies should go only to the operating companies and not to the infrastructure, which hides the real cost.
- There is no reason for maintaining loss-making services in the field of freight, where the notion of public utility service is not justified.

This approach has now been adopted by most countries throughout the world with the exception of those in continental Europe. It is the only solution capable of giving the railways a real chance in the long term.

References

[1] Les transports ferroviaires et l'Europe. Rapport d'information n° 1484. Assemblée Nationale, Paris, 1994.
[2] "Deregulating in Great Britain," *Public Transport Magazine,* UITP, Nov. 1995, Bruxelles.
[3] *L'Europe, avenir du ferroviaire—Rapports officiels,* Aspe Editions, Paris, 1995.
[4] Laubard, P., "Incidence de la réglementation nouvelle des transports sur l'industrie automobile," *Journal SIA,* March–April 1936, Paris.
[5] Faroux, C., "Un grave problème: la coordination du rail et de la route," *La vie automobile,* 25 Feb. 1996, Paris.
[6] de Coninck, M., "Il faut déferrer le fer," *La vie automobile,* 10 Oct. 1932, Paris.
[7] International Railway Statistics 1993, Union Internationale des Chemins de fer, Paris 1994.
[8] Union Routière de France, SOFRES Survey, 1995, Paris.
[9] Final report. Royal Commission on passenger transport in Canada, 1992, Ottawa.
[10] Rail Transport Future, A white paper by the European Commission, Brussels, 1996.

CHAPTER 8

▼▼▼

THE GREAT SEA CROSSINGS: TITANIC CONSTRUCTION PROJECTS

By the end of the 20th century Europe will have built exceptional constructions to link two islands and a peninsula with the Continent after thousands of years of separation. One of these projects, the tunnel under English Channel, has made the headlines for years, but there has been much less said about the others although the scale of the works involved is just as great. They concern the fixed links currently under construction or planned in Denmark, and which will anchor Scandinavia to the continent.

8.1 THE CHANNEL TUNNEL

Practically everything has already been said about the Channel Tunnel, whose construction is the fulfilment of a dream that lasted nearly two centuries. The idea of digging such a tunnel between England and France was seriously considered for the first time in 1802. Many different projects were imagined throughout the 19th century. While many were completely utopian, others were quite feasible with the technology of the period and were the logical extension of the extraordinary expansion in the railway network that marked the last century.

In fact, things were not far from succeeding, as The Channel Tunnel Company was created in 1872 for the express purpose of building the tunnel and, with the approval of the English and French governments, obtained a concession in 1876, and even began boring observation galleries in 1880. In the same year, however, *The Times* launched a vigorous press campaign against the tunnel, and the Gladstone government (which had firmly supported the project until then) was obliged to give in in mid 1882, putting a stop to any new initiative to create a tunnel for the following decades. The arguments made against it had concentrated on the potential threat to national security and the need to preserve Britain's insular character.

It was not until 1957 that the idea resurfaced, resulting in a new concession in 1972 and the start of work in 1973. But, mainly for economic reasons resulting from the oil crisis of the same year, the British government again changed its mind and the first gallery-boring sites were closed in 1975, and the concession company, the Channel Tunnel Group, was compensated for the costs incurred.

The third attempt was to be successful. This time, the governments of Margaret Thatcher and François Mitterrand agreed to authorise the construction of a fixed cross-Channel link on the understanding that it should be financed entirely by private funding.

An international competition was launched in 1985 that generated four projects, each supported by groups of companies and banks. One of them, Euroroute, proposed the construction of two railway tunnels and a road structure composed of a series of large-span bridges near the two banks of the strait and an underground passage in the centre. Another, Europont, planned to build a two-lane railway tunnel combined with an entirely aerial road link via a suspension bridge supported by pylons 340m high. A third group, Transmanche Express, proposed a shared road/rail structure consisting of two tunnels of 11m in diameter that could be used by both road vehicles being driven by their drivers and by trains.

But due to difficulties in ventilating underground road structures and the potential hazards of bridges to navigation, the final choice went to the rail-only project, based on the same principles as the 1875 and 1973 attempts. However, this time the two tunnels were designed to accept not only passenger and freight trains, but also shuttles to be used to transport cars, trucks, and coaches to the other side of the Channel. This added element led to the construction of tunnels with an internal diameter of 7.5m, larger than those that would have been necessary for conventional trains.

So, there would be five different traffic categories: shuttles for trucks, shuttles for cars, shuttles for coaches, passenger trains ("Eurostar"), and freight trains.

The work began in 1986, and the civil engineering works, on the whole, went well. After a laborious start, the tunnelling machines proved to be exceptionally efficient, sometimes advancing 30m per day. The first link-up took place on 30th October 1990, and the boring was completed on schedule. On the other hand, as everyone knows, equipping the tunnels and the construction of rolling stock and their respective adaptation to the infrastructures exceeded both the time limits and the costs. It was only in December 1993 that Eurotunnel, the company responsible for the tunnel's financing and operations, could take possession of it. The tunnel was initially planned to open to traffic for the summer of 1993 but became operational only at the end of 1994, first for truck shuttles, then for Eurostar passenger trains, freight trains, car shuttles and, in 1995, coach shuttles. In fact, it was only during 1995 that the tunnel started to become fully operational.

It is neither surprising nor exceptional that there were delays for such a highly innovative construction project. But the financial consequences were even more serious because they added to the massive overspending on construction and equipment, and to the not less massive overevaluation of the revenues, with the result that by mid-1995 Eurotunnel's financial situation was desperate. The total bill—including construction, equipment, and interim interest payments—came to approximately 16 billion ECUs, compared with initial estimates of 8 billion ECUs. Even if these figures are not absolutely comparable, there can be little doubt that the shareholders have lost most of the money they invested and that the banks that lent Eurotunnel almost most all the financing necessary to carry out the project will also need to abandon much of their loans.

The two countries on either side of the Channel appear to have kept to their promises in that the structure in itself has cost them nothing until now, nor is it expected to in the future unless it becomes necessary to aid Eurotunnel financially (for instance, via their railway companies). Nevertheless, it cannot be said that the two governments have not contributed at all, since they have financed or will help finance the land-based infrastructures giving access to the Tunnel and, in particular, the high-speed railways linking the Tunnel to Lille at one end and to London at the other.

8.1.1 Truck and Car Shuttles

The first months of operations proved the concept was technically viable. As of May 1995, the Tunnel absorbed one-third of the heavy goods vehicle traffic between Calais and Dover, although this one only represents a quarter of the 12,000 trucks that travel on average every day between Great Britain and the Continent. At the start of June 1995, traffic even reached 1,375 trucks in a single day. As of mid-1995, the Tunnel was also handling 25–30% of the private car traffic between Dover and Calais, a route that handles half of the car traffic between Great Britain and the Continent, and it hopes (as is the case for trucks) to gain at least 50% of the corresponding market.

During the first half of 1996, heavy goods vehicle traffic has stabilised with 48,000 vehicles transported for the month of June alone (i.e., about 44% of the traffic between Calais and Dover, or about 13% of traffic between Great Britain and the Continent).

All things considered, the Tunnel will not make an enormous difference in the road transport of goods between Great Britain and the Continent as its tariffs are close to those of the ferries—for a maximum reduction in travel time of about one hour in normal circumstances. It should be added that the severe fire involving a freight shuttle train in November 1996 has led to the interruption of this activity for a long period, at a high cost to the company.

On the other hand, 30 million passengers cross the English Channel by ferry each year, most of them with their cars, and Eurotunnel hopes to capture a large part of this existing market and also create a specific market as often happens when new supply increases the options open to users. Eurotunnel traffic reached 178,000 cars for the month of June 1996.

It must nonetheless be added that, whether it be for trucks or cars, competition by sea remains extremely fierce, with the ongoing development all along the Channel of special port infrastructures for loading and unloading ferries, not to mention new, high-speed ships that reduce crossing times by sea between Dover and Calais to only 45 minutes (i.e., less than for the Tunnel) together with modern Hovercraft that make the journey in only 22 minutes.

But, for both trucks and cars, Eurotunnel policy is now to outmarket sea competitors by setting its fares somewhat under their cost prices in order to maximise its market share and revenues.

8.1.2 Eurostar

After an initial year traffic of 3 million passengers in 1995—instead of the forecasted 15 million—a monthly record of 438,000 Eurostar passengers was recorded in June 1996, in line with an annual forecast of 4 to 5 million passengers. No one can doubt that the Tunnel will profoundly change the flow of passengers journeying without cars between London and Paris and London and Brussels, especially when the high-speed railway line linking the Tunnel with the British capital comes into service. There can be hardly any doubt that apart from taking over a high percentage of current air traffic, the Tunnel will also create new traffic, inasmuch as many of Eurostar train fares are now set at very low levels and no longer aim at covering the real costs, (that is, including investment, which is, in any case, an unattainable objective). Some fares are so low that they do not cover operating costs, including Eurotunnel fees. At the present time, SNCF is losing 1 billion francs per year on its Eurostar activities.

The British company European Passenger Services, which handles the Eurostar links on the British side, has been under private ownership since 1st June 1996. Among its shareholders is Richard Branson, owner of the Virgin group, who has made it known that his ambition is to increase traffic from 3 million in 1995 to 30 million when the new rail link between the Tunnel and London comes into service in 2003, making the British capital a 2 hour 30 minute journey from Paris or 2 hour 10 minutes from Brussels. Even if the above-mentioned traffic objective seems out of reach, it will be particularly interesting to see what results can be obtained by private management and marketing. This will depend to a great extent on the remuneration that will be asked for—or not—by the French and Belgian national railways for their services.

Curiously, considering the five categories of traffic that will use the Tunnel, it could become saturated at certain times of the day and the year without being able to increase its revenues to any great extent due to competition from the ferries and from airlines, which force it to fix its tariffs at half the initially forecast rates.

One of the most obvious effects of the creation of the Tunnel have been indeed to exacerbate competition for cross-Channel traffic. The Tunnel itself changed its tariff policy in 1995 and 1996 by reducing its prices to such an extent that it caused serious difficulties for the cross-Channel ferry companies and the airlines on the London-Paris and London-Brussels lines. Faced with this fierce competition, the two main ferry companies entered into discussions in the spring of 1996 with a view to a merger, which was achieved at the end of the year. It must be said that competition is completely unbalanced. On the one hand, the ferry companies and airlines must balance their accounts. On the other hand, this is not the case for Eurotunnel, which is unable to pay its debts and their interests, or for the railway companies, which are subsidised at varying rates by the states concerned. In the summer of 1996, some return tickets from Paris to London were available at less than 70 ECUs . . . .

Although it is an undisputed technical success, the Channel Tunnel is thus a financial disaster. There is no doubt that if its final price had been known from the start, as well as the fares that would have to be set due to competition from ferries and air transport (which have made spectacular productivity gains), no private funding would ever have been found to carry out the project. Besides the French and British governments via the high-speed lines and their railway companies, it is finally the Eurotunnel shareholders and the banks that will have subsidised the Tunnel to allow it to compete pricewise with the other means of transport. The existence of other modes of transport leaves Eurotunnel no room for manoeuvre to raise its rates, whether for passengers, cars, or trucks. This is one of the reasons for the difference between revenues initially forecast, estimated at 1 billion ECUs for 1994, and the extremely weak results actually registered of approximately 300 million ECUs in 1995—hardly enough to cover operating costs! Forecasts for 1996 predicted an increase of 50%, which would leave an operating profit, but of no possible match to the financial costs. In these conditions, the state of near bankruptcy that was announced in September 1995, with about 10 billion ECUs of debt, was inevitable.

In summary, the Channel Tunnel came both too late and too early. It came too late because it was not constructed at a time when the railways were at their apogee a century ago—this would have placed it among the world's greatest construction projects ever. It came too early because with the significant progress now being made and to come in the field of pollutant emissions by cars and trucks, it could be possible within one or two decades to build very long road tunnels with very little or no intermediate ventilation stations, whereas this was impossible a few years ago when the hybrid type of tunnel was selected for crossing the channel.

It has to be added that, as the Tunnel is now existing and properly working, it is wise to make the best possible use of it, as it provides its passengers a remarkable level of convenience and comfort between three of the greatest European cities and civilization centers—especially between the two greatest European cities: London and Paris.

8.2 THE DANISH PROJECTS

Most Europeans probably do not know that Denmark, unlike other European countries, is not a continuous land mass. Copenhagen is located on the island of Zealand and is separated from the rest of Denmark by the Grand Belt Strait and from Sweden by the Öresund. In both cases, the distances separating the island are very large— 15 km in the first case and 17 km in the second. In both cases, up until now ferries have provided crossings for cars and trucks as well as trains, obviously causing costly delays and transhipments.

This will change in the near future. Denmark decided that two fixed links were to be constructed almost simultaneously, each for both road and rail services.

Unlike the Channel Tunnel, cars and trucks will not be forced to take shuttles and will be able to drive through freely without transhipment. With the exception of one tunnel section under the Öresund, they will mainly use gigantic bridges, whose construction is helped by the shallow depth of the Straits. Certain sections of the bridges will pass just above the water level, but there will also be a 1,624m suspension bridge over the Grand Belt, built with 254m piles with the roadway 65m above sea level—a world record—in order to allow the passage of the numerous ships that sail in these waters.

For the railways, they will use bridges for some parts of the links and tunnels under the sea (like the Channel Tunnel) for others.

Begun in 1991, the first crossing—the Grand Belt—has encountered a myriad of difficulties on its railway link tunnel due to problems in adapting the tunnelling machines and to very heterogeneous ground, found to be unfavourable for the construction work. But the problems were solved at the cost of doubling the initial estimates, and on 15th October 1994, Prince Joachim of Denmark was the first to cross, on firm ground and under the sea, the Strait that had always divided his country. The Grand Belt crossing opened to railway traffic in 1997, and is due to open to road vehicles in 1998, which will be an important moment in the country's history as for the first time most of its territory will then be a single entity. Whereas it took one and a half hours by ferry to link the island that holds the country's capital to the rest of the country, in the future it will only take 10 minutes by car and 7 minutes by train! Estimates logically predict that road traffic will double and rail traffic will triple even during the first year of operations.

From a financial standpoint, the costs for the road structures over the Grand Belt should be recovered within 13 years, thanks to tolls of about 20 ECUs per journey. The situation is different for the railway structures, which are part of a leasing agreement with the national railway company, DSB, and are therefore guaranteed by the Danish state (i.e., the taxpayer) even if, in summer 1996, discussions were reopened due to the sharp increase in the cost of the railway tunnel.

The second crossing, that of the Öresund, has an international scope as it will link Sweden with Denmark and, from there, with the entire European continent. The companies responsible for constructing the crossing were selected in 1995 and its opening is scheduled for the year 2000. It will also be a complex structure, composed of a combined traffic suspension bridge, a low bridge, and a tunnel for which, due to the difficulties encountered in the construction of the first project, submerged caissons were chosen rather than boring tubes. Traffic provisions are just as optimistic in this case because the structure will place the Swedish town of Malmö at less than half an hour from Copenhagen and 20 minutes from its airport, thus giving birth in this part of Europe to a new urban centre of two million inhabitants. Tolls for road traffic will likewise be used to cover the costs. When the two fixed structures open, it is obviously expected that the corresponding ferry links, which are currently among the most frequently used in the world, will cease their activity.

But these will probably not be the only two crossings for very long. A glance at a map of Denmark shows that there remains a third strait, the Fehmarn Belt, across which a fixed link could be built to link Copenhagen directly with Hamburg, thus avoiding the need to take a long detour by way of the Jutland Peninsula. Less urgent than the others, this third group of structures is nonetheless likely to be pursued at the beginning of the next century, even if the project is difficult and costly, which led the Deutsche Bank to withdraw from it in May 1996.

Taken together, these three projects will constitute about the same magnitude of work as the Channel Tunnel, and admiration must be felt for Denmark, with its five million inhabitants, for launching operations that will significantly alter the face of north-eastern Europe and will anchor Scandinavia to the continent.

8.3 THE STRAITS OF MESSINA

Once these construction projects are completed, there will only be one more major project to achieve to make the geographic unity of the continent almost complete: a gigantic suspension bridge, 3,300m long and 65m above the sea, will cross the

Straits of Messina to link Sicily with Italy. The first draft projects exist already in the form of a motorway with two lanes each way and a double railway, at a current cost estimate of three billion ECUs. In mid 1996, new credits have been released for studies despite opposition from the Italian Minister of the Environment.

CHAPTER 9

▼▼▼

AIR TRANSPORT: LIGHTNING GROWTH

Almost nonexistent four decades ago, internal European air transport has since experienced lightning growth. Its advance has nearly always exceeded that of the gross domestic product (GDP), meaning that in 40 years it has become the second most important means of passenger transport on the Continent in terms of turnover, coming after the car. Between 1954 and 1995, the number of seats available to passengers with the large European companies increased from 23,000 to 415,000, and many internal and regional airlines were born.

This success is no coincidence. It is the combined result of several factors. Improvements in the reliability and safety of aeroplanes and their environmental sensibility is the most important of them: Accidents have almost disappeared and aeroplanes are no longer greatly affected by the weather.

9.1 A DEMOCRATISED MEANS OF TRANSPORT

A reduction in costs is the second factor. For an international journey of 1,000 km, passengers used to have to pay an average of $400 (1995 value) in 1955 whereas it now costs $200 to travel the same distance, or even less on a charter or domestic flight. Yet living standards were multiplied by 5 on the Continent during this same period! Among the many factors that explain the decrease in air transport costs is the lower unitary fuel consumption: a modern aeroplane consumes three times less kerosene per passenger transported than the first jet aeroplanes.

Contrary to the image that still sometimes persists, the aeroplane has become a cheaper means of transport for many medium to long distances than many of its competitors when true costs are taken into account, and its use has therefore become banal. At present, more than one out of every two Western Europeans has taken an aeroplane at least once in his life—compared with 2 to 3% 25 years ago—and many fly every week or every month on business.

It is therefore not surprising that approximately 300 million intra-European air passengers were counted in 1995, of which 125 million travelled on domestic flights within a country, 115 million flew on regularly scheduled international flights and 60 million on international charter flights, particularly between Great Britain, Northern Europe, and the European Mediterranean or Atlantic destinations. These passengers travelled a total of 260 billion kilometres for an average journey of 860 km—compared with 1,200 in the United States—and generated 45 billion ECUs in turnover. In Western Europe, the aeroplane has outmatched the railway by far in economic terms, as the latter's total revenues for passenger traffic do not exceed 20 billion ECUs.

Of course, the recent recession slowed down this movement for a certain time, but its growth has started once more, as regular, international European traffic rose by 7% between 1992 and 1993, again by 9% in 1994 compared with 1993, and 8% in 1995 compared with 1994, which amounts to 25% in three years.

Although air traffic now serves all of Europe and has opened up towns and regions that would otherwise have been isolated from the economic circuit, a few air routes are particularly important because of their high traffic. Twenty-six are used by over one million passengers per year, of which seventeen are internal to one country only, and nine are international (compare Figure 29), nearly all of the latter concerning London due to Great Britain's eccentric geographical position, the presence of the Channel, and also London's role as hub for transatlantic traffic. These three factors resulted in London becoming the world's leading aeronautical platform in 1995 with 81 million passengers, ahead of New York and Chicago (77 million), with Paris handling 55 million, Frankfurt 38 million, and Amsterdam 25 million.

The predominance of domestic routes (i.e., internal to one country) among the most heavily travelled routes reveals the influence of the "border effect," which reduces movements between two towns by a significant factor when they are not located in the same country and whose influence has already been emphasised for the other means of transport.

9.2 THE NEW RULES OF THE GAME

European air transport was for a long time mainly in the hands of national companies owned by the different countries, which considered them an essential tool for prestige

Table 9.1

Air Traffic Routes With Over One Million Passengers in 1994 (Traffic in Millions of Passengers Per Year)

Domestic Flights

Paris-Nice: 2.8	London-Glasgow: 1.6	Frankfurt-Berlin: 1.5
Paris-Marseilles: 2.3	London-Edimburgh: 1.7	Frankfurt-Munich: 1.1
Paris-Toulouse: 2.2	London-Manchester: 1.2	Frankfurt-Hamburg: 1.2
Paris-Bordeaux: 1.4	London-Belfast: 1.4	Düsseldorf-Munich: 1.1
Paris-Montpellier: 1	Madrid-Barcelona: 2.1	Rome-Milan: 2.1
Paris-Strasbourg: 1.1	Barcelona-Palma: 1	

Regularly Scheduled International Flights

London-Paris: 4	London-Frankfurt: 1.5	London-Geneva: 1
London-Amsterdam: 2.2	London-Brussels: 1.2	London-Zurich: 1.1
London-Dublin: 2.6	London-Rome: 1	

International Charter Flights

Düsseldorf-Palma: 1.2

and even sovereignty and which granted them more or less complete monopolies, with international routes between two countries being divided amongst them. But for slightly more than 10 years now, the air transport world has completely changed with the introduction of new rules and with the privatisation of a growing number of national companies. This evolution, which is currently ending what had been usual practice for many decades, is largely the result of European Community transport policy based on opening the market to competition. Today, the air links between European Community countries are unrestricted. Any European airline can operate on them. In 1997, domestic routes in each country in the Community will be completely open to competition. Finally, routes will be open between European Community countries and those outside it. The Netherlands and Germany have already signed an "open skies" agreement with the United States. The United Kingdom is also following suit, as the result of a planned agreement between British Airways and American Airlines.

Different countries have reacted to this entirely new rule at different speeds, depending on their economic culture. The swiftest reaction came from the British, who were in fact largely responsible for the movement when British Airways was privatised in 1982 under the momentum of Margaret Thatcher, thus providing the main British airline with a long head start on its competitors. A drastic cost-reduction policy, a decrease in personnel, and high-pressure marketing rapidly allowed British Airways to become the most competitive European airline. It was able to reduce its fares, make a profit even during the recent recession, acquire companies in the other countries of Europe, and implement a world-wide equity participation policy. In little more than a decade, this former loss-making national company thus became in certain respects the number one airline in the world and began again to create employment.

The other European companies reacted later, more or less quickly. For example, after showing a deficit in 1993 and 1994, Lufthansa made a substantial recovery in 1995 with profits before tax of over 1.5 billion francs.

Air France has started, by forced marches, to make up for accumulated lost time. Overall, the drop in turnover has been curbed. It had fallen by more than 3 billion francs between 1990 and 1993, and then increased by nearly 2 billion francs between 1993 and 1996. Air France was losing 8 billion francs in 1993, but should hopefully balance its accounts in 1997.

As the liberalisation movement is still incomplete, it is not yet easy to identify all its consequences. Most appear to have been beneficial. Productivity gains have been significant: from 1985 to 1995, the European airline company productivity per employee increased by an average of 80%, to the benefit of users. As in all other sectors, competition has had a positive effect.

Of course, this result was not obtained without serious difficulties for the companies, and air transport is still characterised by a certain weakness in its financial results. Today, the main airlines are returning to a profit situation in the image of British Airways and Lufthansa, and others are on the way to a recovery. From 1990 to 1994, 37,000 jobs had to be cut in European air transport, representing an 11% decrease in the number of employees, but this downward trend was reversed for the first time in 1995 with an increase of 3%.

The situation is even more eloquent in the United States: between 1980 and 1985, air transport cut 10,000 jobs per year; since then it creates 20,000 per year. Today, there are one and a half times more air transport employees than in 1980. Moreover, the laws of economy back up the claim that the significant drop in the costs of air transport has enabled the creation of large numbers of jobs in other sectors of activity due to transport cost decrease.

Deregulation has other unexpected consequences. Whenever the number of air transporters increases on a given route due to newly introduced competition, the number of flights users can choose amongst also obviously increases. More frequent flights and lower prices result in more passengers, as has been seen in France where the number of passengers increased by about 25% on the lines newly opened to competition, even if this increase cannot expand indefinitely in the short term. The result is that the average number of passengers per flight is tending to decrease, forcing airlines to use smaller aeroplanes that are slightly more costly per seat offered, which has not stopped the overall result from being positive considering general gains in productivity.

This is why the average capacity of aeroplanes used by the members of the Association of European Airlines (A.E.A.), which had risen regularly for four decades from 40 seats in 1955 to 145 in 1983, has fallen since that date to 130 seats per aeroplane in 1993.

9.2.1 The American Deregulation

It is now interesting to look towards the future and try to discover what it holds in store concerning the evolution of airlines and air traffic in general.

On the first point, recent American experience is an interesting indication as it is similar to what is happening in Europe at present. On his arrival at the White House in 1976, President Carter decided to "deregulate" the air transport sector and the appropriate measures took effect in 1978. Any new or existing airline was authorised to operate on any route it wished within the United States, which had not been the case previously. During the first phase, there was a veritable explosion in both the number of airlines and the number of flights between American airports, all in the context of ferocious competition and particularly spectacular price wars. The battles were so intense that within a few years only nine large airlines remained as survivors: American, United, Delta, Northwest, US Air, Continental, TWA, America West, and Southwest. In contrast, several renowned airlines, which had seemed among the most stable of all (Pan Am, Braniff, Eastern, etc.) went bankrupt and disappeared.

This period saw the emergence of a number of new companies, but even more so, of buyouts and bankruptcies. Paradoxically, after a decade, the American skies are mainly in the hands of about the same number of companies as existed before deregulation, perhaps even fewer. Each airline tends to operate in its geographic sector of choice and has one or several hubs that serve to concentrate and split traffic and manage connecting flights.

Although deregulation has undeniably produced positive effects on the other side of the Atlantic Ocean by forcing airlines towards significant productivity gains that have led to a continual lowering of fares, it has also had a certain number of negative effects, one of which is the suppression of low profit-making, local routes— but this disadvantage could be eliminated if limited subsidies are granted.

9.2.2 Changes to Come

If the American experience is to serve to a greater or lesser degree as a precedent for Europe, which currently counts 25 international airlines within the Association of European Airlines and countless national or regional ones, it is clear that large-scale mergers, reorganisations, and alliances are to be expected in the years to come, and they will undoubtedly lead to a complete restructuring of the airline world that has existed for 50 years and that, until recently, had seemed unchangeable. Strong alliances have already been formed, such as those between British Airways and

American Airlines or Lufthansa and United Airlines. In France, Air France and Air Inter Europe announced that they will be merged in April 1997, and further alliances are to be expected.

Next to the traditional actors undergoing their revolution, new operators are making their appearance, as in the United States. They will not look at long-distance routes, because they are too expensive in investments for stopover and commercial and management costs. They will concentrate their efforts on local traffic. With reduced-cost aeroplanes, strictly minimum service, secondary airports with lower fees, a maximum of subcontracting, and so forth, these "low-cost, low-fare" companies are attacking, or will do so, high-traffic lines between Community member countries or within them. Ryan Air, Easy Jet, and Virgin EBA are examples of such companies.

European air transport will therefore be reconstructed around these two poles. On the one hand, the groups and network integrators, with a global offer regarding services and networks, competitive in quality and price terms. On the other, new, low-cost operators, with networks limited to local point-to-point services, but with absolutely unbeatable prices.

Finally, another very recent development must be mentioned in the area of freight, which is the appearance and lightning growth of express delivery services, an activity that was practically non-existent just a few years ago. They now represent a volume of activity that can be counted in tens of billions of dollars world-wide and whose main operators are well-known to all: UPS, Federal Express, DHL, TNT, and so forth.

Deliveries can be made world-wide in a few hours, opening completely new horizons and making vast changes in the operating conditions of many different activities. It should, however, be added that the fact that the European continent is relatively limited in size means that in many cases the most appropriate means of transport for such services remains the road, contrary to intercontinental links or internal links in larger continents.

9.3 AIR TRAFFIC CONTROL: A SOLVABLE PROBLEM

Air traffic will undoubtedly continue to grow, which brings up the question of whether the air traffic control system on one hand and airports on the other are capable of dealing with this, especially since the current tendency towards reducing average aeroplane size increases the number of flights. The year 1989 was a particularly difficult year for airspace problems: 17% of European flights registered delays of more than 15 minutes due to congestion in the sky or at airports.

It must be said that the European air traffic control system is archaic. Each country remains master of its airspace, such that Western Europe has no less than 52 control centres that answer to about 20 administrations of different nationalities! To stay in contact with air traffic control, pilots must, for example, switch radio frequencies 12 times between Paris and Hanover. If it is added that a large part of this space is subject to strict restrictions as it is reserved for military purposes, it is hardly surprising that the use of European airspace is very far from optimal.

But this remark is a source of optimism in itself since the possibilities for improvement are considerable. Without changing any of the principles of current air traffic control or administrative structures, much progress was accomplished between 1989 and 1993. The proportion of flights subject to delays of more than 15 minutes due to congestion in the skies or at airports decreased in Europe by more than half, falling from 17% to 7%. But since then the situation has deteriorated once more, as the level of flights subject to delays of more than 15 minutes was 15% in 1995, or almost the same as in 1989. These bad results are mainly due to an increase in traffic resulting from the movements towards liberalisation implemented since 1993.

In the longer term, it is commonly recognised that a double restructuring of the system is necessary, both in the technical and administrative fields. Air traffic control technology is essentially based on the use of radar, invented on the eve of World War II. The principle has not undergone any basic modification in decades, and places the burden of responsibility for the system, and thus flight safety, on air traffic controllers who often find themselves under extremely tense, difficult working conditions in peak periods and can only watch over a limited number of flights each, thus limiting airspace capacity accordingly.

Today it would actually be possible to follow an unlimited number of planes within a few metres accuracy by using satellite positioning equipment. Surprisingly enough, this type of system is being implemented for fleets of trucks and cars, for ships, or trains, and air transport is now lagging behind the other means of transport! When the day comes that such a system, long demanded by all those in charge in this sector, is finally operational, it is obvious that the controllers' task will be significantly easier and that airspace capacity will increase to such an extent that it will be able to meet needs far beyond present demands. The satellite positioning system developed for the American Defence Department (GPS), and often used for other purposes, may be part of the answer.

Another necessary reform would be to replace the 20 or so variedly heterogeneous national air traffic control systems used today by the introduction of a single authority and thus put an end to the system inherited from the past that no longer corresponds to present-day requirements.

Conscious of the acute problem of congestion in the European airspace, the European Commission gave its approval in March 1996 to a White Paper aimed at accompanying the liberalisation of European skies by a restructuring of responsibilities and control procedures.

In particular, this makes provision for reinforcing and extending the responsibilities of the CFMU (a central traffic control organisation, based at the Eurocontrol headquarters in Brussels) in order to view joint management between civil and military users of the European airspace in the long term. Air traffic control management is the only operational function for which the White Paper considers a centralised action, within the framework of a reinforced CFMU structure. The other operational tasks (supply of communication services, aviation, surveillance . . .) should, according to the European Commission, remain the responsibility of the member countries, although this is not the position adopted by the AEA, which advocates the option of centralisation—combining monitoring and supply of services in a single entity.

9.4 AIRPORT ENLARGEMENT

Airport congestion is the second problem raised by future growth in European air traffic. By nature, this situation only concerns a very limited number of platforms located in the Continent's major exchange hubs. Up until now, these centres have managed to meet growing demand by building new terminals, decreasing intervals between aeroplanes on landing and on takeoff, adding runways wherever possible, and distributing traffic when applicable among several platforms, as is the case in London or Paris, for example.

Although there is no guarantee that these steps will always be able to meet growing traffic demand, everything points to the fact that the margin for accommodating an increasing number of aeroplanes is still very high for most European airports if American airport performance is taken as a guideline. In addition, some airports, such as Roissy-Charles de Gaulle in Paris, have vast reserves of land that can be used to build new runways, so that no physical saturation is foreseen for them from a technical standpoint.

Although the impact of using higher capacity aeroplanes on the busiest routes should not be overestimated, it is not possible to exclude that measures be taken in the future to encourage such action in order to reduce the number of flights. Some countries are already trying to move in this direction. The increasingly vociferous reactions to noise pollution from those who live in the vicinity of airports must be considered. Fortunately, recent years have seen extensive, ongoing progress in this field. As well as fuel consumption, the noise emitted by each aeroplane has constantly decreased over the decades, so much so that the areas subject to a given high noise level are getting smaller and smaller. At London's Heathrow Airport, the surface area exposed to an average noise level exceeding 63 leq (noise exposure index) fell from 96 square kilometres in 1988 to 69 in 1991, and the number of inhabitants concerned fell from 162,000 to 109,000 (Transports Statistics in Britain, 1994, HMSO, London).

In fact, a lot depends on geographic circumstances. Some airports are situated in areas where there is no disturbance to inhabitants (for example, if they are located in nonurban areas or on land reclaimed from the sea). Others, however, are surrounded by heavily built-up areas, and in such cases it is normal to take measures to compensate the inhabitants concerned, at least by soundproofing their homes or by buying the homes closest to the runways. But on the whole, the changes taking place are positive. Pilots are requested to take altitude as quickly as possible on takeoff, so that areas with high noise pollution are increasingly confined to airport land and will no longer overflow into the surrounding residential areas. It will never be possible to completely eliminate noise made on landing, but progress is making each generation of aircraft less noisy than the preceding one, and engines are usually on a low setting in these circumstances.

Paradoxically, the problem of noise from aeroplanes is perhaps easier to limit in the long term than the noise pollution from motorways or high-speed trains. In any case, air transport has become so vital to the economies of regions and countries with airports, and the investments are so considerable, that it is now inconceivable to think of closing an airport, and the only option is to take measures restricting the number of flights, as is the case for Paris-Orly—which is limited to 250,000 flights per year—and to introduce "curfews" at night.

As for air traffic's possible impact on changes in the balance of the upper atmosphere, it must be recognised that on the basis of current knowledge in the matter, it is impossible to determine either its extent or its precise nature.

9.5 UNFAIR COMPETITION

Before closing this chapter, it would be interesting to mention the competition faced by European air transport on certain routes due to the creation of high-speed train lines. Whereas competition is minimal between individual and public transport, it can, on the other hand, be extremely fierce in some circumstances between the train and the plane.

In France, the introduction of the high-speed train line linking Paris with Lyons in two hours—as opposed to four hours previously—reduced air traffic between the two cities by 65% and stopped it from growing for a number of years. The high-speed rail link between Paris and Nantes, which also takes two hours—as opposed to three previously—reduced the number of air passengers by 45% along this route when it was brought into service. Rapid Eurostar trains on the Paris-London and London-Brussels routes via the Channel Tunnel have also already had important repercussions. For instance, air traffic between Paris and London fell from 4 million in 1994 to 3.3 million in 1995, a 20% drop. The effect of competition from Eurostar was still deeply felt in 1996 as the offer from the railways was not yet stabilised and continued to increase, whereas, on the contrary, the tariffs fell. Air traffic between Paris and Brussels was also greatly affected by competition from the train, whose journey time was reduced to two hours. In 1998, when this journey will take only 1 hour 20 minutes, air transport will occupy only a marginal place. This will also be the case to a certain extent when the Paris-London line is completely finished.

This situation would be perfectly normal if the rules of competition were respected, but the airlines concerned do not think that this is the case. The airlines must assume almost all the costs they generate. Through the payment of fees, they finance the airports they use—even including the police security forces—and the air traffic control required. In addition, they must balance their accounts, and the Brussels Commission keeps careful watch over national governments to see that they do not subsidise their national airlines, or only on a one-off basis to make them economically viable before their possible privatisation.

As we have seen, the rules of the game are entirely different for railways. The States and even the European Union finance rail infrastructure, especially new lines, and this is not only allowed but recommended. It can take on different forms, such as taking on the total cost of investments, granting subsidies, guaranteeing loans or, more generally, by the State taking over a network's entire deficits and all or part of its debt.

In fact, the states are authorised to pay the deficits of their rail networks while they are prohibited from doing so for air transport, and railways can thus sell their services at rates that have no relation whatsoever to the real costs. How can it be explained that on a route such as Paris to Brussels, the tariff proposed by the French and Belgian railways for an "economy" class return trip should by 409 French francs (65 ECUs) in 1996, whereas the true overall cost price is probably at least five to ten times higher than that due to the enormous infrastructure costs linked to building the new line between the two cities and the very low traffic levels due to the border effect? It is easy to take part of the market share, at the taxpayer's expense. This difference in treatment is incomprehensible to airline company managers, especially since experience has constantly shown that the construction of high-speed train lines does not relieve road traffic in the least and can only marginally affect the overall number of flights that criss-cross the European airspace every day.

These same managers emphasise that if the principle of true prices were applied and the cost of infrastructure were paid by users, train tickets would usually have to be sold at a much higher price than air tickets, as the latter have the advantage of much lower ground infrastructure costs than railways. They declare that, contrary to what most Europeans think, air transport is very often a much more economical solution than the railway. This is why French airlines that are members of the Federation of Air Transport (*Chambre Syndicale du Transport Aérien*) decided to consult the French Trade Practices Board (*Conseil Français de la Concurrence*) on the conditions of competition between air transport and the TGV high-speed train. As for British Airways, it considered for a time challenging the legality of the aids granted by the British government to the concessionary company for the new rail line that will link the Channel Tunnel to London.

They also point out that in terms of regional planning, reduced-capacity aircraft can reach specific locations far more easily than high-capacity trains at an incomparably lower cost, and that it is as if European political leaders and public opinion have not really integrated the fact that air transport exists. The truth is that its turnover is already a good deal higher than that of rail passenger transport (45 billion ECUs against 20) even without taking into account air freight (which is beginning to grow at a rapid pace, and whose intra-European turnover figures are approaching 1 billion ECUs for 1.2 million tonnes transported).

They find it typical that Community "Trans-European Network" transport projects hardly ever apply to anything but railways and ignore the needs that are covered much more cheaply by airlines, as if European regional development could only be carried out by the railways. In summary, they do not understand why two competitors' ways of meeting the same needs (i.e., the transport of passengers or possibly freight) should be subject to such different treatment, which is contrary to the principles that inspire other areas of Community and national policies.

CHAPTER 10
▼▼▼

ENVIRONMENTAL POLLUTION: UNRECOGNISED IMPROVEMENTS

10.1 AIR POLLUTION

The past years have witnessed considerable progress in most areas of technology. Pollution emissions in the atmosphere have been no exception to this rule. It is common knowledge that, at least in developed countries, modern factories give off far fewer harmful products into the atmosphere than before. The case is the same for domestic heating installations, now subject to strict standards. Those who still need convincing need only take a glance at an old postcard showing an aerial view of Paris, London, Berlin, or any other European city, which will inevitably show the city invaded by blackish or yellowish smoke from factory and building chimneys.

Road vehicles have been similarly affected. Pressure from the public, increased efforts on the part of vehicle manufacturers and the oil industry, and, it should be said, the increasingly exacting standards that they have been submitted to, have all led to great progress being accomplished. Most Europeans are quite aware of this fact, and they know that modern vehicles generally pollute less than their predecessors due to better technology and equipment. Factories, heating, and road vehicles undeniably pollute the atmosphere much less than they did several decades, or even a few years ago.

It is therefore all the more surprising that when questioned, most Europeans answer, against all logic, that town air is more and more polluted and this is all the more unlikely in that traffic has, on the whole, been stabilised or is even on the decline in central urban areas.

It must however be added that public opinion on this issue varies widely from one country to another, showing that information to the public on the real facts of the issue is very unequal, as, with reserves for certain Mediterranean geographical exceptions, changes in air quality have generally followed the same pattern in all Western European countries with the same causes producing the same effects.

Before explaining these diverging opinions, it is first necessary to describe, as objectively as possible, the situation regarding the quality of air as it stands at the end of the 20th century.

This is no easy task. There is an instinctive tendency to speak of *the* air pollution as if it were something that could be measured with a single indicator, which would alone be able to show whether things were improving or getting worse. Yet there is no such single indicator and there never will be and any that are invented to synthesise pollution problems, either now or in the future, can only be mainly meaningless.

There are at least eight main categories of products that are emitted or liable to being emitted into the atmosphere as a result of road traffic, and they are often independent of each other. The concentrations of some of these products can increase whereas others decrease or disappear. This is therefore the first problem, as nonspecialists cannot fully grasp the variety of so-called pollutant products because these products are, as will be shown, extremely diverse by nature from every possible standpoint. The public will inevitably speak of *the* pollution, whereas this generic term has no meaning.

What is more, the general public has a natural tendency to identify pollution with what it can see (i.e., visible smoke) and what it can smell (which can often be unpleasant). However, there is no link between what can be seen or smelled and what is dangerous. A gas such as carbon monoxide (CO) is deadly at high concentrations and kills several thousands of people every year in buildings heated by badly adjusted combustion equipment. Yet carbon monoxide is colourless and odourless. Inversely, a gas such as sulphurous anhydride emits a well-known odour of rotten eggs but is not in the least dangerous at the usual concentrations. Mention can also be made of places such as stables and pigsties where the dominant odour is quite repulsive, but nobody has ever suggested that those who work there run any kind of risk. Nevertheless, trying to convince public opinion that a road vehicle can emit unpleasant fumes or odours without its being a health hazard is clearly Mission Impossible.

A scientific approach to the issue is nonetheless perfectly feasible, as long as pollution is not considered as single entity (as this is not the case), and each of the eight main categories of products that make up pollution are examined separately and objectively. These eight categories are sulphur dioxide (SO_2); lead (Pb); carbon monoxide (CO); volatile organic compounds (VOCs), including unburned hydrocarbons such as benzene; dust and particles; nitrogen dioxide (NO_2); ozone (O3); and, finally, carbon dioxide (CO_2), which is not a direct health hazard but can pose problems of another nature.

But, before examining the situation for each of these products, their area of geographic influence must be mentioned. For some of these products, air concentration varies from metre to metre depending on the distance from the pollution source, and the geographic character is therefore "microlocal." For other products, the concentration is relatively evenly spread for a given neighbourhood or urban area, and the geographic area to taken into account is therefore "local." For still others, the correct scale is "regional." Finally, one of these products can only be considered on a "planetary" scale. This chapter will show that such differentiations are generally ignored or not mentioned, and this often leads to serious errors of interpretation.

10.1.1 Sulphur Dioxide (SO_2)

Sulphur dioxide has been the great pollutant of the industrial era since the 19th century. It is an acid gas produced by the combustion of coal or fuel containing sulphur. The gas transforms into sulphuric acid when water is present and is therefore the primary cause for acid rains. Sulphur dioxide is very dangerous to public health when high concentrations are present in the atmosphere. The combustion of coal containing sulphur was responsible for more than 4,000 deaths during a dramatic episode due to smog in London in December 1952, when SO_2 concentrations in the air reached daily values of 2,000 micrograms (thousandths of mg) per cubic metre ($\mu g/m^3$), also associated with high dust content.

Fortunately, such situations belong to the past in Western European countries. Due to strict standards imposed since then, the World Health Organisation (WHO) recommendation of an annual average of 50 $\mu g/m^3$ of SO_2, is now respected virtually everywhere. The average annual SO2 content in the air in Paris was divided by ten in one-third of a century, going from 210 $\mu g/m^3$ in 1960 to 21 in 1993, and London can claim less than 30 $\mu g/m^3$ today, compared with more than 300 in 1960.

The contribution of road traffic to total SO_2 production is quite minor everywhere, since only diesel fuel, and not petrol, contains sulphur. It is 4% on average in Western Europe. In addition, new European standards on the sulphur content of diesel fuel are currently being implemented. The maximum authorised content was about 1% 40 years ago, decreased from 0.3% to 0.2% on 1st October 1993, and has decreased further to 0.05% on 1st October 1996. If it was needed, it could reach in the future levels even closer to zero, as is the case at present in Sweden.

In summary, it is obvious that the contribution of car traffic to the production of SO_2, already very minor, is in the course of becoming marginal.

10.1.2 Lead

The situation is similar for lead. Presented a number of years ago as a danger to plant and human life, lead emitted into the atmosphere by road traffic is being drastically reduced in all European countries due to the use of unleaded petrol and to the fact that traditional "super" (premium) petrol now contains four times less lead than before.

Already, in a town such as Paris the lead content in the air in 1992 was six times lower than in 1988 and has dropped even lower since then, so that the concentrations registered are more than ten times lower than those specified by the current European standards.

Catalytic exhaust systems on all new petrol-driven cars sold in Europe from 1st January 1993, which accept only unleaded petrol, mean that the total disappearance of lead emitted by road traffic can be expected in the near future, as is already the case in the United States.

10.1.3 Carbon Monoxide (CO)

Carbon monoxide is a good illustration of the importance that must be given to the area of geographic influence of each product. Carbon monoxide's influence is "microlocal." This means that the product can be undetectable by traditional measuring equipment just a few metres from a source. Its concentration can vary from 1 to 10 in less than 100m. This finding calls for several remarks. First, speaking of carbon monoxide content levels for an entire urban area is obviously meaningless. Most of the time, the measuring equipment is placed where it can detect the highest concentrations: in the middle of cross-roads, on the edge of pavements and so forth where no one spends a great deal of time! Yet these are the results usually cited, and not those of observations carried out in places more representative of the population's living patterns, where such concentrations are a good deal lower.

Second, since carbon monoxide levels are microlocal in nature, it is meaningless to talk of overall volumes of emission for a country or a continent. This is, for that matter, an observation which applies overall. Very often, air pollution matters are considered using as a base the quantity of products emitted into the atmosphere within, for example, a country. But what counts for human health is the concentration of the product in the air that is breathed. For many products, there is absolutely no connection between the amount emitted in a region or country—or *emissions*—and the concentrations of these products in a specific place, which are called *immissions*. Taking into account what was stated above, this is obviously the case for carbon monoxide, which does not stop the authorities from studying overall emission levels of this product by country, even by continent, although this is meaningless, and practically never mentioning the only thing that is of interest from a health standpoint—that is the concentrations of the product where people actually live (and which are almost always very low).

The third remark is also of a general nature. When French specialists on the subject wished to measure the carbon monoxide concentration in the air caused by traffic, they naturally went to the most heavily used motorway in the French capital and in Europe, the *Boulevard Périphérique*. To their astonishment, they discovered that the concentration of carbon monoxide was two and a half times lower in the midst of traffic than inside the vehicle where they were carrying out the tests, and that furthermore this level increased by four whenever someone began smoking. This is a specific case illustrating a general rule: contrary to what is often thought, closed spaces are almost always more polluted than the open air, even in the midst of traffic. The best solution to improve the air quality in closed spaces is to open windows and not close them, even in towns.

Many examples could be given to illustrate this point, which is all the more important in that most of our contemporaries spend more than nine-tenths of their time inside (flats, offices, workshops, shops, restaurants, public transport, cars, etc.), whereas almost all the research, regulations, and spending on pollution concerns the air outside buildings, and not inside where the real problems are often to be found.

Our fellow citizens can be fully reassured as to carbon monoxide. Although this gas can be deadly when concentrations reach 1,000 mg/m^3 during one hour, which can only happen in a closed space, the WHO rightly recommends that this gas should not exceed an hourly average concentration of 30 mg/m^3, or 30 times less. Such a concentration is practically never reached in the open air. In areas frequented by pedestrians in Paris, the annual average is of the order of 2 to 5 mg/m^3. Some measuring equipment does temporarily register excesses in the WHO recommendations for maximum hourly rates. But, as we have seen above, the equipment is very often placed in the middle of cross-roads (i.e., in places where nobody stays for more than a minute) and so this takes all meaning away from any possible cases in excess of the recommended levels, which are designed to protect human health, not that of the measuring equipment.

The already satisfactory situation can also only improve with the spread of catalytic exhaust systems for petrol-driven cars, one of the objectives being precisely to divide carbon monoxide emissions by a factor of about 20 [1]. As is equally the case for SO_2 and lead, there are no longer any problems linked to the emission of carbon monoxide in the open air by road traffic. Problems can only arise in closed spaces—garages or tunnels—and this is one reason why such structures must have efficient ventilation systems. One of the unexpected results of increasingly strict standards imposed on modern vehicles is that the construction of very long road tunnels will be made easier in the future, since ventilators and air exhausts can be spaced further apart and they will be less costly to operate. In Lyons, the main local tunnel, which was equipped with 4,000-kw fans 25 years ago, is now refurbished with 2,100-kw fans.

10.1.4 Particles and Dust

Particles and dust, which are always present to a greater or lesser extent in the atmosphere, are of diverse origin. Some are natural (pollen, sand, etc.) while others are emitted by factories and heating systems, and still others are produced by road traffic. This last category comes primarily from diesel engines and particularly from the direct fuel injection diesel engines with which heavy goods vehicles are equipped.

Overall, the concentration of particles in the air has significantly decreased in the large European cities in recent years. In Paris, it has decreased from 110 $\mu g/m^3$ in around 1960 to 30 in 1993; that is, divided by nearly four, which particularly results in building façades becoming dirty far more slowly than before. The progress is firstly the result of efforts to clean up factories and heating systems. As a comparison, it is interesting to note that nonnatural emissions of particles into the atmosphere equal 4 kg per inhabitant per year in France and probably in the other countries of Western Europe as well, whereas they equalled 130 kg per inhabitant in Eastern Europe in 1990!

Although the situation is positive overall, road-traffic emissions are nonetheless responsible for two negative effects. First, they are largely responsible for the production of minute particles (0.1 to 0.2μ). Second, their overall emission volume increased up to 1992, due essentially to the increase in heavy goods vehicle traffic. The proportion of particles produced by traffic out of total emissions increased from 20% to 33% between 1980 and 1992. However, the quantities are now receding due to new vehicles improvement both for trucks and cars. Again, it must be emphasised that speaking of overall quantities produced is meaningless. The heavy goods vehicles responsible for most of these emissions travel outside urban areas for 90% of the time, whereas the corresponding pollution problems are urban in nature.

In addition, such emissions will continue to decrease in the future. Indirect-injection diesel engines have already undergone considerable improvements. The particle emissions of an average car decreased from 1.1 g/km in 1960 to 0.1 in 1994. Heavy goods vehicles are now also moving in this direction, whereas until recently they were relatively behind private vehicles in this respect, precisely due to the fact that they mostly drive in the countryside and rarely in urban environments where this type of problem exists. Between 1990 and 1995, the rate of particles emitted by new heavy goods vehicles decreased from 0.6 g/kWh to 0.36 and will not exceed 0.12 in the year 2000. The figure will have been divided by five in one decade. Other progress is not to be excluded, especially with regard to fuel composition, which can have an impact on the volume of particle emissions. There should therefore be a significant decrease in emissions, which will obviously only reach its full scope as and when the heavy goods vehicles on the roads today are replaced by newer, more efficient ones.

Yet how dangerous are these particles to human health, given that they are very small in size and therefore *a priori* more likely to affect the human body? It has often been said that these particles cause cancer. Actually, there is nothing sure about this. There have, of course, been studies conducted on animals (rats), which were forced to breath diesel exhaust fumes for their entire life. Some of them developed cancer, which is hardly surprising since the concentrations to which they were exposed were about *1,000 times higher* than those in the atmosphere of European cities. But the same experiments using hamsters gave no such results, suggesting that there may be a specific cancer creation mechanism in rats. The results of experiments carried out on an animal species are not necessarily transferable to another—including the human species.

The comparison of what happens in the case of tobacco, for which no one denies the hazards, is particularly enlightening. A number of categories of population exist for this product:

- Those who do not smoke and *are not* exposed to others' smoke;
- Those who do not smoke and *are* exposed to others' smoke;
- Those who smoke occasionally;
- Those who smoke an average of five to ten cigarettes per day;
- Those who smoke ten to twenty cigarettes per day, and so forth.

"Samples" of several million people can be found for each category, which has meant that reliable relationships have been established between the degree of exposure and risks (lung cancer, heart failure, etc.).

The situation is completely different for products emitted by engines, whether run on petrol or diesel fuel. It is impossible to divide the population into such distinct categories. In a given geographic zone, apart from those exposed to job-related hazards, everyone breathes more or less the same air. Of course, the concentrations of different products are not the same in towns as in the country. But it is obvious that a comparison between the health of town and country dwellers cannot reveal anything about the particular effects of the emissions in question, so numerous are the other factors that come into play: lifestyle, nutrition, occupations, living conditions, natural pollution, and so forth. Moreover, concentrations relating to outdoor air pollution are nowhere near what workers are exposed to.

This is why such comparative studies will never be conclusive. Those who declare that a hazard exists cannot provide any proof and this explains why no country has banned diesel engines, which do have the advantage of consuming less fuel. At the very most, doubts can be expressed. Fortunately, the technical progress mentioned above has been such that, within a few years, the concentration of possible cancer-causing products in the atmosphere, which was already extremely low compared with those produced by tobacco in closed places, will decrease even further.

10.1.5 Volatile Organic Compounds

Volatile organic compounds (VOCs), a somewhat esoteric term, covers a series of products, most of which are hydrocarbons such as benzene, which accounts for 3% of the VOCs emitted by engines. In the same way as other pollutants, VOC emissions are strongly decreasing at present, with initial decreases being accentuated with the spread of catalytic exhaust systems. In 1996, 40 times fewer VOCs were emitted over the same distance by a new petrol-driven vehicle than in 1970!

It is therefore not surprising that the concentrations observed in the air of European cities are also in steady decline. Concentrations of benzene, for example, vary from 40 to 100 $\mu g/m^3$ in the immediate vicinity of traffic to 3 or 4 away from traffic, with concentrations differing widely from one place to another as the product is "local." Benzene, of course is classified as a product that causes cancer. But the few cases of leukaemia due directly to this product were found in persons who absorbed concentrations of 300,000 $\mu g/m^3$ over a period of many years in the workplace, or 10 to 100,000 times more than the amounts normally found in the urban atmosphere. This means that the risks linked to benzene produced by traffic, if they exist, can only be extremely low. It should also be pointed out that most food products also contains benzene. According to the World Health Organisation, every egg contains 25 to 100 μg of benzene, meaning that the amount of benzene absorbed by eating two eggs is about the same as that absorbed by breathing the air in European cities for 24 hours. Fortunately, no proof of any danger exists for such doses.

10.1.6 Nitrogen Dioxide (NO$_2$)

Whereas the concentration of carbon monoxide, lead, dust, SO$_2$, and volatile organic compounds is declining rapidly or even disappearing in the atmosphere, particularly in towns, this is just beginning to be the case for nitrogen oxides.

This is logical. Until now, half of the nitrogen oxides produced were the product of petrol-driven vehicles and the other half of diesel vehicles. Until recently, relatively little progress had been made towards diminishing the individual emissions of each vehicle so that, until recently, the total production of nitrogen oxides emitted by traffic had tended to slightly increase overall. But this does not mean that the concentrations breathed by the city dwellers also rose. Once again, a distinction must be made between emission and immission. In Great Britain, for instance, total nitrogen oxide emissions *doubled* from 1977 to 1993 whereas average annual concentrations *decreased* in the centre of London over the same period (see Figure 41).

But things are now in the course of changing fundamentally. Catalytic exhaust systems for petrol-engine vehicles became compulsory on 1st January 1993 in all European countries, although some had already anticipated the measure previously, and the result is that unit emissions of nitrogen oxides by vehicles sold after that date were divided by about five! In other words, as and when vehicles are replaced, total emissions due to petrol-driven cars will progressively be decreased even further.

There is a myth on this subject that must be dispelled. It is sometimes said that catalytic exhausts are not very useful because they are only efficient after a journey of several kilometres (i.e., often at the moment drivers leave the vehicle). Numerous studies have shown that this was simply not true. For example, the French Transport Research Institute (INRETS), states [1] that

> . . . *in the immense majority of cases, when the vehicle is warm, but also when it is still cold, the presence of the catalytic converter results in a significant decrease in the emissions of regulated pollutants, whatever the length of the journey. The only exception is that nitrogen oxides are emitted in greater amounts during journeys of less than one kilometre when the car is still cold. But this situation is very largely compensated by the gains with respect to longer journeys.*

Within a few years, progress should make catalytic exhaust systems effective as of the first few seconds of use due to the implementation of new European standards.

The second half of current nitrogen oxide emissions, produced by diesel-engine cars and especially by heavy vehicles, can now be studied. Changes are also underway in this area. Unit nitrogen oxide emissions by new heavy goods vehicles were lowered from 18 g/kWh (Euro 1 Standards) in 1990 to 8 (Euro 2 Standards) in 1995, and further tightening of standards will lower them to 5.5 g/kWh in 2000, representing a reduction by a factor of three in 10 years. Of course, the impact of this decrease will only be felt progressively, as more and more new vehicles replace old ones.

As of 1st January 1996 or 1st January 1997, new diesel cars must be equipped with catalytic exhaust systems, and this will similarly greatly reduce nitrogen oxide emissions.

In other words, whatever the category of vehicle, considerable progress has been made or is programmed, and there will inevitably be marked reductions in unit nitrogen oxide emissions. The result should be in the form of a progressive reduction in the concentrations registered in each urban area, given that for the nitrogen oxide, which could cause health hazards—nitrogen dioxide (NO_2)—and which is essentially the result of the transformation of the nitrogen monoxide (NO) initially emitted by engines, the concentrations are not too different from one area of a town to another as this product has a relatively homogenous geographical distribution.

The first decreases in atmospheric concentrations have already been recorded in certain towns in countries that anticipated European directives for compulsory catalytic exhaust systems for petrol-driven cars. The average annual level observed in the city of Karlsruhe decreased from 70 $\mu g/m^3$ in 1989 to 54 in 1991. In the centre of Düsseldorf, the average concentration decreased from 82 $\mu g/m^3$ in 1986 to 54 in 1992 and has changed little since that date. According to the Swedish Meteorological Institute, the average NO_2 concentration has decreased by 27% in 1993 and by 35% in 1996 in Stockholm since 1988–1989 due to catalytic converters, which have been compulsory for new cars since 1998 and, consequently, are becoming more and more prevalent. In Bern, Switzerland, the decrease has been 30%.

But nitrogen dioxide concentrations, like those of other products, are not constant throughout the year and are subject to sudden variations several times a year, called pollution peaks. This happens when there is a reversal of temperatures, during which, as there is no wind, the air close to the ground is blocked by higher layers. It is then possible that the air may not be renewed, or very little, for one or several days. In such circumstances, nitrogen dioxide concentrations can, for several hours during the day, reach abnormally high levels for Western Europe, exceeding, for example, 200 $\mu g/m^3$ or (very rarely) 400. That is why the European Commission drew up a directive stating that the concentration should not exceed 200 $\mu g/m^3$ in any of the Member States for more than 2% of the time, or 175 hours per year.

Most European towns already comply with the above directive. The only exceptions are southern European cities with particular geographic circumstances, such as Milan and Athens. But, overall, things can only improve with the massive reduction in emissions that will be witnessed in the coming years.

10.1.7 Misinterpreted Directives

It is important not to mistake the meaning of the directives drawn up by the Brussels authorities. It is particularly interesting to see how they are actually drawn-up. The starting point is the World Health Organisation's studies, carried out, as is normal, by doctors. For a product with noncumulative effects such as NO_2, they try to determine, using experimental or statistical studies, the limit below which no effect can be observed in human beings. This limit is called the "lowest observed effect level." The term "effect" should not be confused with "danger" as there is usually no connection. For instance, it can be a case of irritation of the eyes, acceleration of the pulse, respiratory uneasiness, and so forth, whereas a health hazard generally only happens at concentrations far higher than the "lowest observed effect level."

Next, the WHO applies the " principle of precaution ", meaning that no effect on health, however small, can be tolerated. It therefore adopts a "precaution factor" to define the concentration levels that it *recommends* should not be exceeded. For example, it has noted that concentrations of nitrogen dioxide in many kitchens with gas cookers can frequently reach 2,000 $\mu g/m^3$ without any recorded negative effects on health. The WHO also noted that asthmatics exposed to concentrations of

560 $\mu g/m^3$ for a half-hour whilst undertaking physical exercise showed lung capacity variations of 10%, a change "within the limits of physiological variation and not necessarily harmful"[2]. However, by applying the principle of precaution, the WHO recommended on this basis that average hourly concentrations of 400 $\mu g/m^3$ and a daily average of 150 should not be exceeded.

The European directives mentioned above were developed on the basis of these recommendations and oblige Member States not to exceed concentrations that are even lower than those recommended by the WHO as they apply a further "precaution factor." As far as nitrogen dioxide is concerned, the directives specify that the concentration of 200 $\mu g/m^3$ (i.e., half the amount recommended by the WHO) should not be exceeded more than 2% of the time, or 175 hours per year. Consequently, the Member States must alert the population, according to the circumstances, as follows:

- Level 1 is set at an hourly average of 200 $\mu g/m3$—official departments must be alerted.
- Level 2 is set at 300 $\mu g/m3$—the authorities and the public must be notified.
- Level 3 is set at 400 $\mu g/m^3$—it is call the "alert level" and calls for possible countermeasures to be taken (traffic restrictions, etc.).

But in practice, this last level is very rarely reached in most cities of Western Europe, if ever, and the real alert level has became is Level 2, at which the media and the population should be informed. The result of this procedure is that Member States are asked not to exceed concentrations that, contrary to the almost unanimous belief, have *no connection* with a hazard to health and even less to life.

The above procedure calls for two remarks. The first is that only a handful of specialists are truly acquainted with it. The general public and even the authorities responsible for the matter inevitably associate the levels specified in the European directives and national legislation with the idea of danger, although there is no connection. But how can the public understand that there is no danger when they are told that the "alert" level has been exceeded? And yet many city dwellers, frightened by this alert level, will return home to find concentrations of 1,000 or 2,000 $\mu g/m^3$ in their very own kitchen and suffer no health consequences, according to the World Health Organisation itself [2].

The second remark is that there is great inconsistency between the subject of pollution and many other public health questions. As we have seen in the chapter on road accidents, they are the cause about 140 deaths and 1,000 injuries per day in Western Europe and about the same in Eastern Europe, and the general reaction to this is largely indifference except for spectacular accidents. In contrast, in most European countries there is nothing to prove for certain that there has been a single death linked to pollution of the atmosphere due to road traffic, except perhaps in the case of particularly vulnerable persons, already close to death, for whom pollution will be an aggravating factor rather than a direct cause of death, which specialists describe as the "harvesting effect" [3]. And yet, today's society seems to agree to paying considerable amounts of money without counting in order to decrease air pollution.

On the one hand, society accepts tens of thousands of deaths and injuries. On the other, it considers that "health has no price" and the slightest physiological impact will not be tolerated. This inconsistency is, to say the least, particularly serious because it leads to considerable wastages of resources and is obviously not a consistent public health policy.

This kind of thinking is not limited to Europe. It is the same in the United States. Harvard University's Center for Risk Analysis [4] carried out a study in which it reviewed more than 500 measures taken by American administrations and showed that, to save one year of human life, the Environmental Protection Agency had passed regulations costing the community an average of $7,629,000, whereas measures imposed by the National Highway Safety Administration would save one year of human life at a cost of $78,000, the Federal Aviation Administration for $23,000, the Consumer Product Safety Commission for $68,000, and the Occupational Safety and Health Administration for $88,000. In other words, to obtain the same result in health terms, today's societies agree to spend 100 times more on environment than on road safety or other areas of public health, thus being completely inconsistent and lacking in respect for public and private funds' proper use.

At the very least, it would be useful to explain to the general public what the limits in the European directives and national regulations regarding the quality of the air really mean, by informing them rather than frightening them. The general public can be completely reassured. In most European cities, despite the very strict standards of the Community directives on nitrogen dioxide concentrations, they are nonetheless respected. They were respected even before catalytic exhaust systems were introduced and, since technical progress on vehicles is continuing, they can only improve. In addition, for this product as for most of the others, the highest concentrations can be found in closed spaces, not in the open air.

10.1.8 Ozone

Unlike the products that have been examined up to this point, ozone is not directly emitted by road-vehicle engines. It appears as the result of complex chemical reactions that sometimes occur between NO_2 and volatile organic compounds (VOCs) in the presence of the sun's ultraviolet rays. These circumstances occur a few times a year in most regions of Western Europe. For a few hours, ozone concentrations in the air reach temporary peak levels over vast areas that sometimes include several countries. It is in no way a local phenomenon. However, it should be noted that average ozone concentrations are usually *lower* in towns than in the country, as curiously, another product emitted by road vehicles—nitrogen monoxide (NO)—destroys ozone in its presence! Whereas the average yearly ozone content in the Northern Hemisphere is about 50 $\mu g/m^3$ in the country, it is often half as much in large European towns (e.g., 22 $\mu g/m^3$ in Paris or London, 30 in Zurich), and even lower along major traffic routes. If ozone concentrations have permanent, adverse effects on health at any concentration, as some studies have tended to show, then it is best to live in towns to limit their consequences, preferably on the edge of a heavily used road, where many studies have shown that the average ozone concentration was at its lowest!

But the situation is not the same everywhere in Europe. Once again, certain southern European towns that have already been mentioned stand out, since the average annual ozone concentration reaches 57 $\mu g/m^3$ in Turin and 80 in Athens [5]. Nonetheless, such levels are not very different from those that exist in the countryside and are nowhere near the quantities registered in Mexico City, for example, where the annual average concentration borders on 400 $\mu g/m^3$ [6], which sometimes leads one to wonder what all the talk in Western Europe is about.

In Europe, it is thus not average concentrations that are attracting attention, but pollution peaks. A varying number of times per year, depending on the town and the weather conditions, ozone concentrations can approach or exceed levels of 200, even 250 $\mu g/m^3$. Such levels may give rise to eye irritations as well as a weakening of the respiratory system for adults or children engaged in long, intense physical exercise. Ozone may also contribute to asthma and is a risk factor for people with this condition. But peak ozone concentrations only occur a few times per year in most Western and Northern European countries and last each time for only a few hours out of the 8,760 each year, which obviously lends no credibility to the theory that ozone levels are the cause of a general increase in asthma phenomena. Unfortunately these attacks take place throughout the whole year, and not only on a few days.

The increase in cases of asthma is more likely to be due to better insulation used in modern homes, as this encourages the proliferation of acarians and the accumulation of dust and chemical substances due to lack of air renewal. Once again, closed places are more polluted than the open air. A comparative study found that more asthma attacks took place in West Germany, where the outdoor air is much purer, than in East Germany, where it is more polluted but where homes are not as well insulated.

But the most exhaustive, remarkable study on ozone and other pollutants comes from the United Kingdom [7]. Drafted for the British Ministry of Health, its conclusions are the following:

—   *As far as the initial onset of asthma is concerned, most of the available conclusions do not reveal a role played by atmospheric pollution (except the possible effects of some biological pollutants such as pollen and spores).*

— As far as the aggravation of symptoms or the onset of asthma attacks are concerned, most asthmatics are not affected by exposure to non-biological concentrations of pollutants that commonly exist in Great Britain. A small proportion of asthmatics can show significant clinical effects that may necessitate an increase in medication or medical advice.

— Factors other than air pollution play a role in the initial onset of asthma and asthma attacks and are much more important than air pollution in this respect.

— Seasonal fluctuations in asthma attacks are complex and have little relation to the cyclical variations of the principal pollutants. The peak in asthma problems at the beginning of the summer takes place after the maximum ozone level period and the peak in asthma problems at the beginning of autumn occurs after ozone concentrations have begun to decrease. Other explanations are available to explain the periodical nature of asthma and it is unlikely that exposure to air pollution is a determining factor in these regular fluctuations (. . .)

— Asthma has increased over the last thirty years in Great Britain but this is unlikely to be due to changes in air pollution.

Geographic studies have shown that breathing difficulties are higher along coastal areas (Wales and Cornwall) than in other places, notably London! The conclusions of the report on this point are the following: "Asthma distribution in England and Wales shows little relation to the regional distribution of the principal pollutants. Hospital admission and mortality rates show no clear geographic tendency and probably depend more on the characteristics of the medical care system than environmental factors."

In most countries, observations have not been carried out over a sufficiently long period to know whether ozone pollution peaks have worsened or not in the last few years. Observations made in Switzerland, which operates more than 100 observation stations (making it one of the best European monitoring systems), did not detect any clear pattern between 1981 and 1992, either for peak concentrations during the summer months where they are the most numerous or in the number of times the quantity of 120 $\mu g/m^3$ was exceeded [6].

In Great Britain, however, the results are unambiguous: the pattern over the past 20 years has moved towards a reduction of ozone concentrations (Figure 40). In the United States, where catalytic exhaust systems that reduce concentrations of both nitrogen oxides and volatile organic compounds have been widespread for some time, the Environmental Protection Agency has registered a reduction of 20% in ozone concentrations in large towns. Although the elaboration of ozone is an extremely complex matter, most experts think that a decrease in the production of NO_2 and VOC concentrations, which is now also under way in Europe, should result in a decrease in the size of ozone peaks, but it will take a long time to prove this.

In the meantime, there is a debate on whether it would be wise to restrict traffic during ozone peak periods. But experiments made in Germany in the summer of 1994, prohibiting the movement of vehicles not equipped with catalytic exhaust systems and introducing set speed limits, did not detect any positive effect on changes in ozone concentrations. On the other hand, the restrictions had a negative impact on industrial and (particularly) commercial activity, including a heavy drop in turnover for small businesses in the town centres concerned, proving how much economic activity is linked to road traffic.

An additional difficulty is that ozone pollution peak periods usually last only a few hours and they are impossible to predict with any degree of certainty at present. They also usually occur in the afternoon, when it is, of course, very difficult to take swift emergency measures to restrict or prohibit traffic.

Finally, a recent study carried out by the Swiss Federal Department of the Environment of Forests and Sites [8] showed that the ozone emitted locally represented only 20% of the ozone present in a given urban area during an ozone peak and that 80% came from other sources: 15% from "natural" ozone, 35% from emission sources all over Europe, and 30% from the ozone reserves created by emissions within an area of 500 to 1,000 km. It must be stressed again that ozone peaks are above all regional, or even national or continental, but not local. The study concluded that even if there were no human emissions in Switzerland of the substances that go to make up ozone (NO_2 and VOCs), peaks of 100 to 150 $\mu g/m^3$ would nevertheless still be observed. Similarly, in Los Angeles, estimates indicated that the permanent elimination of traffic—purely hypothetical, of course—would only reduce the ozone content by 10%, compared with what would happen if all vehicles in circulation complied with the most recent standards [6].

It will therefore be particularly interesting to see if the measures taken since 1995 in Germany to combat summer smog, following fierce debates between the federal government and the opposition-controlled Länder, will produce any effect, which would be surprising. Whenever a concentration exceeding 240 $\mu g/m^3$ is registered in three stations located at least 50 to 250 kilometres apart, and if the weather forecast for the next day is unfavourable, the authorities would ban petrol-driven vehicles that do not comply with the recent emission standards, but without introducing a special speed limit of 80 to 90 km/h on roads and motorways as the opposition-controlled Länder had wished. In any case, the conditions of implementation are such that it is highly unlikely that these restrictions will be applied very often, not to speak of the numerous planned exceptions for specialised vehicles.

The meteorological circumstances were such in 1996 that there were almost no ozone peaks over Europe, contrary to the previous years.

10.1.9 Carbon Dioxide (CO_2)

In contrast to the products described previously, the presence of carbon dioxide in the atmosphere has no potential direct influence on human health in its present concentrations in the atmosphere. It has become an object of interest for another reason. Carbon dioxide is one of the products contributing to the greenhouse effect that is warming our planet, and any change in its concentration in the Earth's atmosphere can therefore influence the climate. Nevertheless, the factors involved are particularly complex and it is essential to separate known facts from hypotheses.

The Certainties

It is known that the "natural" greenhouse effect results, above all, from the presence of water vapour in the atmosphere and that other bodies contribute to this, such as carbon dioxide (CO_2), methane (CH_4), nitrogen protoxide (N_2O), and a few others. Without the greenhouse effect, the earth's average temperature would be −18°C instead of +15, or a difference of 33 degrees, which would not allow life as it is known to exist.

It is also known with certainty that the concentrations of certain greenhouse gases in the atmosphere have substantially increased since the start of the industrial era. This is the case for carbon dioxide, whose concentration has risen by about 25%, and methane, which has doubled. But it must be added that the bodies in question are present in extremely low quantities in the earth's atmosphere as their concentration is more than *3,000 times* lower than that of water vapour.

It is also known, through analysis of ice that has accumulated for hundreds of thousands of years in Greenland and Antarctica, that the earth's climate has undergone immense variations in the past, with numerous ice ages during which the average temperature of the planet was five to seven degrees (celcius) lower than it is today. Without going back so far, a thousand years ago the temperature of the earth was, on the contrary, higher than it is today, as the Vikings found Greenland covered with vegetation, and it was lower just two or three centuries ago, as the River Seine in Paris could be crossed on foot every winter as it was always frozen, which is never the case today. For the past century, variations in the earth's temperature have been, on the contrary, extremely slight. Measurements appear to show, but with no absolute certainty, that the temperature has risen by about half a degree since the mid 19th century. It has to be added that recent years have been relatively warm.

Last among the certainties is the fact that carbon dioxide emissions will continue to increase within the next few decades. According to the most recent forecasts of the International Energy Agency, annual carbon dioxide emissions will increase by 50% between 1990 and 2010, and three-quarters of this increase will be due to developing countries such as China, East and South Asia, and so forth, and not to the developed countries. The result is that whatever efforts the developed countries may undertake, their influence on the world's future production of carbon dioxide will remain relatively modest. Forecasts show that coal consumption in China alone will rise from one billion to three billion tonnes per year and that there is nothing to be done about this because it is essential to the country's economic development and the improvement in standards of living of its inhabitants. The International Energy Agency indicates [9] that "an obvious consequence of this situation is that any international initiatives aimed at reducing carbon dioxide emissions that are not adopted by developing countries cannot have any significant effect on overall emissions, and even less on atmospheric concentrations." And, obviously, no one can stop the growth of the Chinese economy . . .

The Uncertainties

The list of certainties stops here. The effects of the increase in carbon dioxide and other greenhouse gases in the atmosphere on the Earth's climate is unknown at the present time. No proved correlation exists between the increase in the concentration in carbon dioxide in the atmosphere in the past century and the very slight increase in temperature that probably took place during the same period. Detailed analyses seem to show that the latter has been irregular and that it was more significant at the beginning of this century, when carbon dioxide content varied little, than in the third quarter of the century, when it substantially increased. Temperature variations have been much more brutal in the past, with no correlation to the variations in the previous carbon dioxide concentration.

More generally, there are great uncertainties as to the way the climatic "machinery" works, as it appears to be an extremely complex system, with very little being known about the roles of water vapour, clouds, other greenhouse gases, the ocean, and so forth, or about the way they all interact. There are so many unknowns in this field that it will probably take several decades before things become clearer.

Uncertain Models

Of course, scientists have tried to identify the influence on the climate of a future increase in the concentration of carbon dioxide in the atmosphere. Computer models have been designed and forecasted an average increase in temperature from 1.5°C to 4.5°C within a century, with possible dramatic consequences for the climate, vegetation, and even ocean levels. But such models are only valid in the limits of the hypotheses on which they are based. The results of the current models are limited by computing power and still more by the little knowledge available and thus offer no certainties. Even Nobel Prize winners confront each other on the matter, and the debates on the influence of the increase in atmospheric carbon dioxide content on the Earth's climate are bound to continue for decades more, for as long as the scientific facts have not been established in this matter. All that remains is to ardently hope that those who predict an apocalypse are wrong, because it is basically a situation for which very little can be done.

The "Piaf Theory"

Faced with the possibility of a risk, all the countries of the planet met at two exceptional world-wide summits, in Rio de Janeiro in 1992 and in Berlin in 1995, and decided to take measures to limit the world's carbon dioxide and other greenhouse gas emissions insofar as possible, applying the principle of precaution, sometimes curiously called the *Piaf Theory*, named after the French singer of the song entitled *Je ne regrette rien* ("No Regrets"). This theory holds that, in the absence of certainties, actions must be undertaken "as if" a risk existed so as not to endanger future generations.

It is within the framework of this world effort that road transport's contribution should be judged. Road vehicles are not the source of the majority of carbon dioxide of human origin. In fact they are very far from it as they account for about 14% of production of this gas. If the carbon dioxide produced by other sources (fires and deforesting) and if other greenhouse gases (methane, etc.) are taken into account, then the percentage due to traffic in world-wide greenhouse gases emissions should be halved. According to available estimates, carbon dioxide emitted by road vehicle traffic accounts for approximately 7% of the total "additional" greenhouse gases produced every year. It is clear that if it were possible to reduce by a quarter the average consumption of road vehicles throughout the planet, the corresponding decrease in world-wide production of greenhouse gas would be about 2%, which must be compared with the inevitable 50% increase predicted by the International Energy Agency over the next 20 years due to the growth of Third World economies.

The Scapegoat

In other words, the truth is that it is not possible to significantly influence the production of greenhouse gas by taking measures regarding road traffic. This is even more true for transport taking place in Europe, as it consumes only about 20% of total road fuel used world-wide: its contribution to any kind of change in human greenhouse gas production can only be symbolic.

In truth, if developed countries wish to combat world-wide carbon dioxide production, they have only one means of doing so. This would be the replacement of the traditional thermal electric power stations—which run on natural gas, oil and, especially, coal, and which produce more than one-third of the carbon dioxide emitted in developed countries—with nuclear power stations that emit no carbon dioxides at all. Only one western country has systematically implemented a policy of this nature: France. It has practically stopped using fossil fuel for electricity production and therefore not only no longer produces carbon dioxide but also allows other European countries to reduce their emissions by importing French nuclear-generated electricity. With total net emissions of 1.8 tonnes per inhabitant per year,

France therefore emits almost one-third less carbon dioxide than the average of the other European countries in proportion to their population. But, in most Western countries the idea of building nuclear power stations is excluded for the time being, not the least for economical reasons, as producing electricity from natural gas is nowadays cheaper. Attention has turned to road vehicles, which, despite their minor influence on how things could evolve, have become a scapegoat.

There is therefore a gradual effort towards reducing European average car fuel consumption to about five to six litres per hundred kilometres. Even if the effects of these changes on world carbon dioxide production are not actually visible, they will at least have the undeniable advantage of reducing oil consumption. Yet, in this field too, an examination of the facts reveals that often accepted ideas are far removed from reality.

10.2 ENERGY OUTLOOK

In 1960, there were 45 billion tonnes of established oil reserves, corresponding to 32 years annual consumption at the time, such that it was possible to imagine at the time that 32 years later, in 1992, they would have been used up. But in 1994, despite the quantities of oil consumed since 1960, the same approach indicates that the planet has 135 billion tonnes of established reserves, the equivalent of 45 years of consumption at the current extraction rate [10]! What is more, real reserves are estimated at three times the amount of established reserves.

In other words, the more time passes, the more the problem of shortages is deferred, contrary to the dominant fears, particularly after the two oil crises of 1973 and 1979. There are two reasons for this. The first is that prospecting by oil companies has led to the discovery of new deposits, and technical progress has substantially increased the amount of oil that can be recovered from existing deposits (as, for example, in the North Sea, which produces far more than predicted 10 years ago). In 1995, the International Energy Agency again revised significantly upwards its forecasts on world-wide oil production, estimating the figures at 4.6 billion tonnes per year in 2010 instead of 3.4, due to a reassessment of the potential of countries that were not members of OPEC, for which a decline in production had initially been predicted.

The second reason is that contrary to all expectations, world-wide consumption has remained practically unchanged for 20 years. In 1993, world-wide oil consumption equalled 3.1 billion tonnes, against 3.3 in 1979 and 2.9 in 1973. Today, consumption is almost identical to the level of 20 years ago whereas prior to 1973 it had doubled every seven years. This remarkable stabilisation is the result of energy-saving measures set in motion under the influence of the sudden oil price rises in the 1970s. It should be added that such price rises are now a thing of the past, since the real problem of oil-producing countries is now most of the time keeping the price of crude oil at around $18 or $20 per barrel, or one-third of the price reached in 1980, in real value. Admittedly, nothing can guarantee that the oil market will not experience other temporary tensions. But today's production capacities exceed demand, even without Iraq (potentially one of the world's great oil producers). Contrary to appearances, the fact that more than 60% of world-wide reserves are concentrated in the Middle East is not a risk factor, but on the contrary a guarantee of stability for the planet. As it is unthinkable that the planet could do without oil from the Middle East, it is clear that any threat of disruption in supplies will meet with a swift reaction from the developed world, including military action should this be necessary.

This is what happened in 1991 as soon as Iraq invaded Kuwait. And it would happen again, since the same causes produce the same effects, if risks of the same nature were to occur again in the future. Actually, the fact that most of the world's oil is located in one region, on sparsely-populated desert land as well, is an advantage for the planet. This is even more true for developing countries as they therefore have access to cheap oil, whereas developed countries could, if necessary, pay more for it. The situation would be quite different if oil reserves were scattered throughout the globe or concentrated in highly populated countries, and thus at their mercy. Whether we like it or not, it is the balance of the whole planet and peace that are at stake and that requires the presence of American Marines in the Persian Gulf.

However, even if there is doubtless no need to worry about the next quarter of a century, fewer and fewer large oil deposits are being discovered and fossil oil reserves are not eternal. A distant day will come when the reserves will no longer be able to satisfy demand. But other energy sources will then be available to replace them. Established reserves of natural gas, which can easily be used by road vehicles, represent more than 60 years of consumption of the product at current rates and there are enough coal reserves for more than two centuries, not to mention enormous deposits of bituminous schist that also exist. It is possible to create energy from any of these products. Plant products such as sugar cane and rapeseed can also be used to this end. When these substitutions need to be used, it will mean an increase in the cost of fuel. But fuel users in most European countries are already used to paying three to five times the current international market price of their fuel through taxes, and it is obvious that when they are confronted with the price increases, the economies of the day will be able to meet them. In other words, there is no risk of fuel shortages on any human timescale.

Finally, it has to be hoped that electricity storage techniques will progress, making this means of propulsion more competitive, especially for urban travel.

Of course, if all the Chinese were to acquire a car tomorrow, world-wide oil reserves would be incapable of meeting the demand. But this is impossible and things will not happen in this way. There will be a gradual increase in demand, and it is certain that when the time comes, appropriate solutions will be found to deal with a problem that today could seem unsolvable.

10.3 NOISE POLLUTION

Before closing this chapter on some of the effects of road traffic on the environment, the problem of noise pollution must be discussed as it is actually more difficult than that of air pollution, even if significant progress has also been made in recent years and if more is planned for the near future.

Vehicle noise emission standards have been considerably tightened in the last two decades and modern vehicle engines are now relatively quiet. More specifically, the noise level of private cars is four times lower today than it was in 1970, and the authorised noise level has been reduced from 82 decibels to 74. It is significant to note that whenever a noisy car is heard, it is almost always an old model.

Progress has been even more remarkable for lorries. A heavy goods vehicle that complies with 1990 European Community standards produces noise equivalent to only one-fifteenth of that of a vehicle from the 1960s or 1970s (84 decibels instead of 97) and this figure was halved again in 1995. In other words, a modern lorry is no noisier than a car from the 1970s! However, special mention should be made of two-wheeled motor vehicles, which are particularly noisy when they are badly tuned or have been tampered with, although they remain, fortunately, an exception among motorized road vehicles that only confirms the general rule.

Nevertheless, if considerable progress has been achieved in the last two decades to make engines quieter, it has a limit. As in all areas, there comes a time when more and more money must be spent to obtain smaller and smaller results, and it is getting to the point where it will no longer be reasonable to justify trying to decrease noise emission standards in engines, particularly as the problem is now elsewhere.

Due to technical progress, engines have ceased in many cases to be the primary cause of noise caused by traffic. This now comes from either the rolling noise the vehicle makes on the road surface or the whistling noises that accompany high-speed driving. For the latter problem, progress in aerodynamics has significantly improved the situation. It is now the problem of the rolling noise the vehicle makes when it exceeds a certain speed that predominates. The contact of the tyres with the road surface inevitably creates a certain amount of rolling noise and efforts must be made to reduce it.

Road-building companies have set themselves to the task and have introduced road surfaces aimed at maximal noise reduction, especially those using "draining coatings," which are porous and offer the additional advantage of absorbing rain water, thereby greatly improving visibility when raining as the water is not projected by the vehicles as they move. Recent technical achievements towards noise reduction have been considerable, and the initiative must now come from those who are responsible for the road networks because these road surfaces are more expensive than traditional ones. The additional cost is, however, fully justified in many areas as some of them—which amongst other things use reprocessed tyre particles in their composition, a nice way of giving them back to the environment—are extremely efficient in limiting traffic noise.

The large tyre manufacturers have also led research programmes in conjunction with the road industry, which have notably resulted in modern tyre treads being irregular, despite appearances, in order to eliminate noise resonance.

Such efforts will allow a reduction in driving noise, but it is obviously impossible to eliminate it altogether. That is why reduction of traffic noise "at its source" must be added to by other means that aim at limiting its spreading. Techniques now exist that allow closed spaces to be completely insulated from external noise, by reinforcing or changing the windows that are, in any case, kept closed most of the time in oceanic climates. The cost of doing so is relatively low, and it is all the more surprising to note that in certain countries few of the occupants of buildings situated in noisy areas have installed double-glazed windows although no one can deny the health disadvantages linked to the existence of high levels of noise.

To the various measures used to combat noise should be added the building of new roads in cuttings; the installation of acoustic screening between traffic lanes and buildings, which has become increasingly common in large urban areas; or even the partial or total covering of certain sections. In this respect, the underground motorways mentioned earlier obviously give an ideal solution, but they can only be used in exceptional cases.

With this last exception of entirely covered roads, the battle against traffic noise will never be completely won. But much progress has already been made. More can still be accomplished in order to reduce this inevitable disadvantage of road transport to a strict minimum. Lowering speeds limit, "calm" driving, and automatic transmission vehicles can help. There is ample room for improvement, as shown, among others, by Japanese towns that, by combining all possible kinds of action, have often achieved impressive results.

Before closing this chapter on the harmful effects of traffic, it would perhaps be useful to make a few final remarks on air pollution as this is the subject that now holds the attention, above all, in many countries in Western Europe.

10.4 SPECIAL GEOGRAPHIC LOCATIONS

On the whole, air pollution problems are similar for most West European countries. The average concentrations of the different products and their fluctuations in time are relatively close. But there are a limited number of cities situated in the Mediterranean basin that are exceptions as they combine abundant sunshine and particular geographic conditions that sometimes result in the air stagnating for long periods of time. The main towns concerned are Milan and various other Italian towns and, even more particularly, Athens.

Concentrations of sulphur dioxide, nitrogen dioxide, dust, and ozone are all much higher than in other places [5]:

- An annual average of 53 $\mu g/m^3$ of sulphur dioxide in Milan and 80 in Athens, as opposed to 10 to 30 in other West European cities.
- An annual average of 143 $\mu g/m^3$ of nitrogen dioxide in Milan and 120 in Athens, against 30 to 70 in general.
- An annual average of 93 $\mu g/m^3$ of dust in Milan and 104 in Athens, against 20 to 50 in general.
- Finally, the maximum level of ozone per hour once reached 392 $\mu g/m^3$ in Athens in 1990, whereas it very rarely exceeds 250 in the other European cities.

Nevertheless, it is not possible in the present state of knowledge on the subject to distinguish among the different sources that go to make up the pollution in the towns concerned. Italian experiments prohibiting driving of even-numbered cars on even-numbered days and vice versa (*targhe alterno*) produced no results despite a decrease in traffic, and the National Research Council (CNR) on air quality in Milan concluded that "if studies had been carried out prior to taking the decisions, our country would have avoided ineffectual measures such as traffic restrictions."

Things are therefore not simple. It is safe to say that catalytic exhaust systems will lead to an improvement, but this can only be clearly established if all other activities—factories, power stations, and so forth—also make efforts at the same time.

Some propose that these particular towns should be subject to a specific set of standards in the future, which can apply either to vehicles or to fuel, as further restrictions would appear to be increasingly difficult to justify in other areas in the present state of knowledge. Nevertheless, the present atmosphere in Brussels is toward issuing extremely costly new Europe-wide regulations for engines and fuels without any real reason, as the general situation in Western Europe regarding air pollution is overall very satisfactory. The total cost of the forecast new regulations is estimated to be 5 to 7 billion ECU per year, a striking example of waste. Attention should better be paid in future not to again tightening standards for engines, but to making sure that they are actually respected by the vehicles on the roads, as recent studies have shown that most pollution is created by a small minority of badly tuned vehicles. According to some estimates, 20% of the vehicles in circulation produce 80% of pollution. In some cases, it has been shown that one badly tuned old vehicle can emit as many pollutants as 40 vehicles that comply with current standards.

Likewise, it must be emphasised that it is in the public interest to encourage the purchase of new cars and the corresponding replacement of older ones, which are by far the biggest polluters. Finally, it is important to underline that everyone who wishes can contribute to reducing emissions. "Calm" driving reduces the volume of emissions by one-quarter compared to "ordinary" driving.

10.5 EPIDEMIOLOGICAL STUDIES

Epidemiological studies aim to identify the effects of different situations on health, not by studying their influence on isolated individuals but by bringing to light statistical relationships that can only become clear with large samples of the population. Such studies are common on the other side of the Atlantic Ocean and are becoming more and more popular in Europe as concerns air pollution.

One of the most significant and recent of such studies was completed in Paris in 1994. It was christened "ERPURS" [11] and aimed to identify any existing correlation between the content of different products (SO_2, NO_2, dust, ozone) in the air and other factors, such as the number of consultations and hospitalisations for a respiratory illness, for asthma attacks, and so forth. Data gathered over six years (from 1987 to 1992) for ERPURS revealed certain correlations that, like all correlations, do not necessarily mean that a cause-and-effect relationship exists considering all the different parameters that can be involved. The study found that the number of respiratory-related hospitalisations for people over 65 was 8.7% higher when the ozone concentration reached 103 μg/m^3 during eight hours than when the ozone concentration was 3 μg/m^3, the content on the least polluted days. But the margin of error is considerable, as it extends from 0.7% to 17.6%, for a confidence interval of 95%. It must be added that there were no more than 30 days when the average ozone concentrations exceeded 100 μg/m^3 for six hours in Paris during those six years, so that the impact on the total number of hospitalisations during the entire period (2,922 days) is extremely limited.

Finally, and above all, the difficulties inherent to such studies derive from the fact that it is a most delicate matter to decide which data to attribute to climatic factors (temperature and barometric pressure) and which to air pollution as the two are very closely linked, the latter being, by far, a secondary one. But, if such results of epidemiological studies are in fact confirmed, the question is to know what conclusions to draw from them.

10.6 TWO APPROACHES TO HEALTH QUESTIONS

As we have seen previously, there are two possible approaches to health issues. The first, traditional, approach holds that whenever there is a health risk, all measures should be taken to avoid it, even if its probability is very low. This is the *principle of precaution*. The second approach evaluates the possible impact on health and the cost of the corresponding preventive measures. This is the principle of *rationalisation of economic choices*. Some people may find this "cost-effectiveness" approach somewhat shocking. But it is, in fact, the only justifiable approach when public health issues are at stake. This is because the community's resources are not unlimited and a choice must be made as to the areas where they would be most effective (i.e., where they avoid the most illnesses or save the most human lives).

Yet, curious as it may seem, the WHO seems unaware of this possible approach to the question, which explains why such disproportionate attention is given to air pollution problems in comparison with other public health issues. Doctors in WHO workgroups make recommendations concerning the concentrations of different products so that there is no effect whatsoever, *even minor*, on the population. But their role stops there. Actions are taken based on such recommendations that force the automobile industry, the oil industry and, in the end, the community to spend sums that represent billions of ECUs each year on a European level, without this expenditure ever having been placed in the context of what benefits could be expected from it from a health standpoint.

If the WHO doctors had been asked if this was the best possible use for the money in this respect, their answer would doubtless have been negative, considering how small the stakes are in comparison with other areas of public health. But in such cases, the WHO acts as consultant, not the payer, no more so, for that matter, than the international and national administrations that set the regulations to follow.

Staying within the field of transport, the difference in approach as far as road accidents are concerned is striking. Earlier in this chapter we have seen that in order to save one year of human life, the United States spent an average of 100 times more on the environment than on road safety or other public health sectors! It is no different in Europe. It is to remedy this sort of inconsistency, which goes far beyond the field of transport, that the United States has tried in the past to adopt very important legislation, which would doubtless have made drastic changes to the approach to environmental and health problems on the other side of the Atlantic Ocean.

During a debate on the status of the Environmental Protection Agency (EPA) in 1993, Senator Bennett Johnson introduced an amendment that specified that in the future, any proposed measure to protect the environment should be based on a cost-effectiveness study that would balance and quantify both the expenses involved and the benefits to be gained for the community. The amendment was adopted by 95 votes to 3. Public opinion polls showed that 83% of Americans approved of the idea that risk analysis methods should be used to identify the most serious environmental problems, and that public money should be allocated accordingly. On 28th February 1995, after long debates, the House of Representatives adopted a complete text based on these principles [12], requesting that in the future the different federal agencies develop their regulatory proposals on the basis of cost-benefit analysis and not on the basis of health or safety criteria that were not financially quantified. Unfortunately, it does not seem that this text will be passed as a law in the near future.

But such an approach would also be needed in Europe, for it must be pointed out that expenditure by the car and oil industries in favour of air quality (through catalytic exhaust systems, restructuring of refineries, research studies, etc.) can be estimated at nearly 10 billion ECUs per year on a European Union level and such costs are evidently passed on to the user (that is, to the community).

One very curious way often used to assess the "cost" of pollution must also be mentioned. In the absence of real data on the cost of pollution, which would be assessed mainly from the actual impact on health (i.e., the possible number of deaths, consultations, or hospitalisations that are caused by pollution, which can only be very low given the conditions that prevail in Europe), the "Avoidance Cost" theory stipulates that the cost of pollution is none other than the cost industry must pay to comply with standards fixed by the authorities. The absurdity of this approach is immediately obvious. The stricter the standards, the higher the "cost" of pollution, and vice versa. If inaccessible standards are set, the "cost" becomes infinite even if the real cost (i.e., the harm actually caused by pollution) is non-existent or very low. Most surprisingly, despite its being impossible to defend, the "avoidance cost" approach, which is nothing other than a tautology, is widespread and taken most seriously.

It must be added that whenever vehicle emission standards are set, there is opposition between backers of the "principle of precaution" theory, which automatically attributes an infinite cost to any impact on health, however small, and those who support the economic approach. The former believe that emissions should be kept as low as possible, independent of the cost. The latter hold that standards should be as low as *reasonably* acceptable (i.e., they should be set with cost-effectiveness in mind), because any ECU spent needlessly in this area only limits the resources of other areas, where it could be of more benefit to the community and the general interest. As French professor Claude Allegre rightly says, "The precaution principle is just absurd. Every human activity bears with it a part of risk. A society that refuses to accept it is doomed to death, for only death is without risk."

10.7 PUBLIC OPINION AND AIR POLLUTION

Whereas the level of air pollution is practically identical in all the different countries of Western Europe, with certain exceptions that have already been mentioned, the general public's perception of air pollution varies enormously.

The proportion of those who consider that "air pollution in large towns is increasing significantly" is 17% in the Netherlands, 21% in Germany, 55% in Italy, 60% in France, and 64% in Great Britain, even though it is actually decreasing everywhere and, with the exception of certain Mediterranean towns, evolutions are very similar from one country to another. In other words, the information level, or, to be more exact, the disinformation level, is extremely variable depending on the country. [13].

There is an explanation for this surprising state of affairs. As we have seen, pollution phenomena are very complex. A multitude of products is involved, with completely different characteristics, effects, and ways of developing, and it is obviously absolutely impossible for the general public to understand such a complex subject. Faced with a strong decrease in visible evidence (fumes, odours, dust), the public has to rely on the information provided by the media. But the problem is the same for them. With the exception of highly trained chemists who have devoted a great amount of time to the field, journalists quite naturally find it no easier to make the distinction between nitrogen monoxide and nitrogen dioxide, the different categories of particles, volatile organic compounds, carbon monoxide and carbon dioxide, ozone, and so forth. This is why, in fact, as they are unable to formulate their own opinion, journalists must mainly rely on public material and official institutions to assess pollution problems. And here there are tremendous differences among European countries. Angela Merkel, the German Minister of the Environment, made the following declaration during the Berlin Congress on the greenhouse effect in March 1995: "*It is wrong to say that the car plays a major role in air pollution.*"

But this attitude is far from being shared by all, and many administrative and political figures in different European countries simply reproduce, or even amplify, the most widespread of opinions that illogically claims that the air we breathe is more and more polluted. Numerous reports published by diverse national and international institutions, theoretically the most credible sources, give air pollution an image that is far removed from reality, as those who write the reports are themselves victims of generally accepted ideas and, knowingly or unknowingly, have lost their professional objectivity.

10.7.1 A Surprising Report

There is a concrete example that helps to illustrate this assertion. The exceptionally high percentage of Britons who are convinced, against every obviousness, that the air in their towns is more and more polluted can be explained by a series of official reports, each more alarmist than the next. The last of them, which the media naturally broadcast far and wide, is a voluminous report published by the Royal Commission on Environmental Pollution in October 1994, that reiterates all the usual errors on the subject [13].

The report presents growth in mobility as a catastrophe, inevitably leading to road network congestion. As far as the problems of pollution are concerned, it gives no mention whatsoever of the marked improvement in air quality for most pollutants in Great Britain as elsewhere, which can only improve with the increasingly stricter standards that apply to every new vehicle placed on the market. It is quite an achievement to write a 345-page report on the connection between transport and the environment without ever mentioning the only thing that really counts, which is the evolution in the quality of the air that the British people breathe. Yet everyone knows that the classic English smog has disappeared and that numerous animal species that had not been seen for more than a century have reappeared in London parks.

The great majority of the Royal Commission's members were doctors and specialists in ecology, but there were no representatives from the world of transport.

The report registered the changes that are and will become necessary in standards for new vehicles coming onto the market, but did not draw the conclusions, which has been and will obviously be a drastic reduction in pollutant emissions and thus improved air quality for Britons as for other Europeans. It is no surprise that the conclusions, completely removed from reality, were based on the following assumption: "pollutants emitted by vehicles are the primary cause of the bad air quality that harms human health, vegetation and buildings" and "even allowing for technical improvements in vehicles, the consequences of the expected growth in traffic would be unacceptable in terms of pollutant emissions, noise, depletion of natural resources and the deterioration in peoples' physical constitution."

Of course, these assumptions were false, as air quality is better now than it has been for over a century in the towns of Great Britain, and technical improvements have been far more rapid than growth in traffic, which is now very moderate (total traffic volume even stagnated in Great Britain from 1991 to 1994) and is even sometimes negative in the centres of urban areas, while technical progress has reduced emissions by factors that vary from 4 to 20 depending on the product. The consequences of the Royal Commission's doomsday approach can be found in the 110 recommendations that are systematically hostile to road transport, one of the main ones being that taxes on fuel should be progressively increased in a view to *doubling* fuel prices compared to other products by the year 2005, and that the British government should take firm action to achieve similar increases on a European Community level, given that the objective set for 2005 should only be the first stage of the process!

Following the same logic, the report recommends an increase in the proportion of passenger kilometres to be provided by public transport from 12% in 1993 to 20% in 2005, and to 30% in 2020, an increase in tonne kilometres from 6.5% in 1993 to 10% in 2000, and to 20% in 2010, and, inversely, that the proportion of journeys made by car should be lowered from 65% in urban areas to 60% in 2000 and 50% in 2020. What the report appears to forget is that it is the users who decide on the means of transport and not a hypothetical central power.

Finally, what is even more serious is that the Commission recommends that, allowing for exceptions, no new roads or motorways should be built and that all planned spending for this sector should be reduced by half to the benefit of rail transport. If followed, these recommendations will progressively paralyse traffic in Great Britain and give credence to the theory that road transport leads to blocking the situation, which is clearly the intended aim. They could also result in a substantial increase in pollution as it is all the higher when traffic does not flow freely.

It is perfectly understandable that such a firm stance, especially held by a Royal Commission, had considerable repercussions in the United Kingdom and influenced the government, which immediately reduced the already limited number of road credits available. Documents of this nature, obviously ideological but presented as scientific, are probably at the source of the very pessimistic but entirely mistaken idea the British have about air quality in their towns.

The situation is hardly any different in France where, in the place of the Royal Commission, reports published by medical institutions or official environmental departments, and amplified by the media and the political powers, have succeeded in convincing a very large majority of the population of the existence of serious pollution problems at the very time when all types of pollution are receding.

The two examples above show to what point public opinion depends entirely on the information with which it is supplied, and not on its own evaluation of the situation.

If this needs confirming, study of a recent French public opinion poll gives further proof [14]. In response to the question: "Are you personally affected by air pollution?," 52% of the French questioned in 1993 answered to the affirmative. It might be thought that these people were inhabitants of large towns, but this was not the case. The proportion of affirmative responses was 57% in towns with more than 100,000 inhabitants, 48% in towns with 20,000 to 100,000 inhabitants, 47% in towns of less than 20,000 inhabitants, and 45% in rural areas. In other words, the proportion of people who say they are personally affected by air pollution is not very different in villages of 200 inhabitants situated in the mountains of central France where human-created pollution clearly does not exist, from the proportion of those who live in the largest French towns . . . Minds have clearly become more intoxicated than lungs.

10.8 EXTERNAL COSTS OF ENVIRONMENTAL POLLUTION

10.8.1 Biased Evaluations

Another reason should be added to explain why pollution is given so much attention in so many countries, even at European level, and this is that there are pressure groups who find it in their interest to emphasise the disadvantages of road traffic, either real or imagined.

These groups recently developed the theory of "external costs" of traffic, which aims at quantifying the negative effects not accounted for by what is paid by road users through costs and taxes and which are considered to be "disguised subsidies" although no one actually pays them. As we have seen with freight transport, the theory of external costs attaches the utmost importance to problems of pollution.

The most recent study carried out on behalf of the Union Internationale des Chemins de Fer (UIC) [15] and mentioned previously in other chapters, estimates the external costs in Western Europe attributable to all road traffic at 36 billion ECUs per year for air pollution, 33 billion for its contribution to the greenhouse effect, and 33 billion also for noise, or more than 100 billion ECUs for these three issues, roughly equivalent to the gross national products of Portugal and Greece combined!

In fact, as we have seen, the effects of air pollution on health that can be attributed to traffic in most Western European countries are so low that it is impossible to assign a cost of any significance to them compared with other public health issues, unless of course it is based on the tautological theory of avoidance cost.

As for the contribution of traffic to the greenhouse effect, no one can honestly declare anything whatsoever with certainty on this subject, except that road traffic plays a minor role, so that if the above figures were accepted, it would be necessary to close all traditional thermal power stations as they are the principal source of carbon dioxide production in the developed countries.

As far as noise is concerned, no one can deny that it has a cost that must be evaluated. This task is easier in this area. The cost of soundproofing a home, an apartment, or an office is already known, and it is therefore easy to calculate the cost of eliminating noise, at least for the closed spaces in which most people spend most of their time, as well as the amount that those concerned would be willing to pay for it.

Some studies [16] using this approach estimated that the external cost of traffic noise amounts to an average of 0.15% to 0.20% of the gross national product, which, when extrapolated to all of Western Europe, would give a figure of 9 to 12 billion ECUs.

In summary, there is nothing near the 100 billion ECUs mentioned above. In fact, it is not difficult to see that the figures given under cover of so many "scientific" studies are hardly credible at all, especially since they never mention the positive factors of road traffic—its contribution to economic growth, its influence on regional planning, the battle against the draining of rural population, a response to people's need for space, the improvement in their quality of life, the struggle against increasing property prices, its positive impact on the cost of living, and so forth—and it is difficult to imagine that such positive factors do not largely exceed the above-mentioned negative ones.

10.8.2 Ecotax

There is a lot of talk on the European level about creating an "ecotax" in order to reduce CO_2 emissions. But, in order to reduce world-wide production of CO_2 by road vehicles, a tax on its production (an ecotax) is not an effective means because if it were to obtain significant results, the rate would have to be so high that it would be unbearable for the European economy. According to the International Energy Agency, even a tax on carbon of \$300 per tonne, which would increase European fuel prices by 40%, would only reduce emissions by 8% in 2010 compared with 1990 [9]. It will be possible to obtain positive results only by using other methods, such as the car manufacturers making sure that their vehicles will consume less fuel in the future. In other words, it is by direct action at the source and not by the roundabout route of taxation that it will be possible to be really effective in this area, if this is actually the objective sought after.

10.8.3 A Swollen Question

In summary, it is clear that air pollution is presently fashionable in Western Europe. As in every other period in time, human beings probably need to have something to be frightened about. Nevertheless, the fear that many people have of outside air pollution dangers cannot be justified, as proved by a recent report by the French "Academie des Sciences," the highest scientific authority in the country: "In France, active smoking is responsible for one million life-years lost each year and passive smoking for ten thousand. Road accidents correspond to a loss of about 250,000 life-years. By comparison, estimates of outdoor air pollution vary from one to a few hundred life-years lost, if it is considered that the some hundreds of people who die during pollution peaks decease a few weeks or a few months ahead of what would have happened otherwise. . . . These data help to evaluate the sanitary risk linked to transport related outdoor air pollution, which is not justifying the fright created in the public by the release of recent studies results."

One of the reasons for the misunderstandings that are dominating air pollution matters is to be found in the fact that the people in charge of the three main sides of the question—pollutant emissions; pollutant concentrations in the atmosphere, and medical consequences—belong to three distinct fields of activities. Their specialties are entirely different. They don't speak the same languages and are unable to understand each other. As it often happens in our modern societies, no one is covering the whole of the subject, with the result that huge amounts of money are wasted in the name of public health. The European Union is showing in this circumstance a complete lack of basic economic knowledge.

Considerable progress has already been made. Air quality is, on the whole, purer in most Western European towns than it has been for a century. In addition, technical improvements in vehicles are developing faster and faster and vehicles are progressively being replaced by others that pollute far less. Except for unforeseeable incidents, the picture is very reassuring as to the quality of the air that the coming generation will breathe, also taking into consideration the improvement achieved in industries and for heating devices.

The situation is already different from that which is widely imagined. The organisation that performed the epidemiological study for the Paris region mentioned above [11] noted that Paris inhabitants are those in France who have the longest life spans, that mortality due to respiratory disease is statistically lower than the national average, and perhaps even more significantly, the same mortality rate decreased by 10% from 1982 to 1989 [17]. Even if a cause-and-effect relationship is not to be established, the least that can be said is that this is an evolution that hardly complies with the theory of a deterioration of the quality of air and that there is no reason to alarm the population.

In Paris, lichen, which is particularly sensitive to pollution and which had disappeared from the trees on avenues and boulevards in the 19th century, has returned in large quantities since 1990. The Swiss Federal Institute for Forest Research recently admitted publicly that it had made a mistake concerning acid rains and that it had wrongly sounded the alert at the beginning of the 1980s. One of its directors stated with rare frankness: "At that time, we ceased working as scientists. Normally, we would have given more importance to the arguments contradicting our assertions. Actually, our trees grow up to 20% faster than at the beginning of the century and, they are 2 to 3 metres taller at 50 years (. . .)" [18]

To conclude, it is indisputable that the dangers linked to air pollution have been considerably reduced almost everywhere in comparison to what they were a few decades ago in Europe. They will be reduced even further in the future by means of continual technological progress and vehicle replacements, and if nothing unforeseen occurs, everything points to the fact that such dangers, already extremely low, will soon be a thing of the past over almost all of Europe.

It should be added that, in 1996, some scientists from the Water and Forest European Institute complained that trees were now in too good health, growing too rapidly . . .

References

[1] Joumard, R., and R. Vidon, *Evolution des émissions de polluants,* TEC (Transport, Environnement, Circulation), n° 129, Paris 1995.

[2] World Health Organisation, *Air Quality Guidelines for Europe,* Geneva, 1987.

[3] OEST, French Ministry of Equipment, *Evolution des externalités des transports,* Paris, 1995.

[4] Harvard Center for Risk Analysis, *Five Hundred Life Saving Interventions and Their Cost Effectiveness,* Harvard, MA, 1994.

[5] AIRPARIF, *La pollution dans vingt villes européennes,* Paris, 1995.

[6] Revue, "Pollution atmosphérique," *Numéro spécial Ozone & Santé,* Paris, Avril, 1994.

[7] Department of Health, *Asthma and Outdoor Air Pollution,* HMSO, London, 1995.

[8] Départment Fédéral de l'environnement, des forêts, et des sites, *Lettre de la section "Protection de l'air,"* Bern, 1995.

[9] International Energy Agency, *World Energy Outlook,* Paris, 1994.

[10] British Petroleum, *BP Annual World Energy Review,* London, 1995.

[11] Gerondeau, Christian, *L'énergie à revendre,* Ed J.C. Lattès, Paris, 1983.

[12] Observatoire régional de la Santé, *Impact de la pollution atmosphérique urbaine sur la santé en Ile-de-France 1987–1992* Paris, 1994.

[13] House of Representatives, *Act HR1022, 104th Congress, First session* Washington, 1995.

[14] Union Routière de France, SOFRES *Surveys 1993–1996,* Paris, 1996.

[15] Royal Commission on Environmental Pollution 18th report, *Transport and Environment,* HMSO London, 1994.

[16] A report by IWW and INFRAS, *External Effects of Transports,* Union Internationale des chemins de fer, Paris, 1995.

[17] INSEE-OEST, *Les comptes des transports en France en 1993,* Paris, 1994.

[18] Observatoire régional de la santé, *La mortalité en Ile-de-France en 1988–1990,* Paris, 1994.

CHAPTER 11
▼▼▼

THE CAR: THE REASONS FOR ITS SUCCESS

11.1 A STEADY PROGRESSION

The history of the car does not go back just 50 years. Europe had 10,000 cars in 1900, 300,000 in 1914, 4 million in 1930, and almost 8 million in 1939. These quantities were not negligible, but, contrary to the United States, which took the lead in this field, it was only in the second half of the 20th century that the age of the car really took hold in the Old World: 6 million private cars in 1950 in Western Europe, 22 million in 1960, 63 million in 1970, 104 million in 1980, 140 million in 1990, and approximately 150 million in 1993.

Nevertheless, the appearances can be misleading: the figures are in fact levelling off, as there were 16 million more automobiles between 1950 and 1960, 41 million between 1960 and 1970, 41 million more between 1970 and 1980, and 36 million between 1980 and 1990, and it can be assumed that growth between 1990 and 2000 will be even slower.

11.1.1 The Age of Maturity

Its childhood and adolescence over, the car has now entered in Western Europe into its age of maturity, which implies improved perspectives for the traffic situation.

This slowdown is more pronounced in countries that have already reached a high level of motorisation. There are still large differences from one Western European country to another in terms of the vehicle/inhabitant ratio, although these differences are tending to decrease over the years. In 1995, Greece had only 180 cars per 1,000 inhabitants, Portugal and Spain 300 per 1,000 inhabitants. But most of the other countries are relatively alike in this respect, and count between 350 to 500 private cars per 1,000 inhabitants. The Western European average is currently a little more than 400 cars per 1,000 inhabitants, which is already considerable in that it represents slightly more than one car per household, since the average household consists of 2.7 people.

Within just a few decades, the car has thus become accessible to all social classes in almost all West European countries, and more than four-fifths of Europeans live in a household possessing at least one car. Owning two or more vehicles is no longer an exception, because almost 30 out of every 100 households with a car are in this category. The individual vehicle is gradually taking the place of the family car, as all members of the household—spouses, adult children, and so forth—benefits from the advantages of driving their own cars.

It is therefore wrong for some to say that the car is the least "social" means of transport because it is now, in the etymological sense of the term, the most social of them all. What was only a dream for most Western Europeans a few decades ago has become reality. It now remains to be seen why the car was, and continues to be, so popular and why Europeans freely devote such a large part of their budget—one-eighth on average—to their car.

11.1.2 Rational Behaviour

One of the most generally accepted ideas is the notion that Europeans are irrational as far as their cars are concerned. For no logical reason, they would apparently be ready to sacrifice everything for them, to spend considerable and unjustified amounts of money, and generally lose common sense. Such reasoning is extremely pessimistic, to say the least, regarding the mental state of our contemporaries. It would mean that the majority of them had to some extent gone mad. But given that Europeans are no different in this respect from the world's other inhabitants, be they Americans, Australians, Japanese, and so forth, the theory seems less likely. The desire to own and use a car is equally strong throughout the world, even if geographic or fiscal circumstances lead to some differences in levels of motorisation and types of vehicles possessed at equal levels of income. In developing countries, one of the first things those who emerge from poverty do is buy a car, just like our parents in the 1950s, 1960s, or 1970s. There is no reason to be worried about the mental health of our European compatriots: they do not suffer from a specific form of mental illness. If they are so enthusiastic about buying and using four-wheeled vehicles, there must be other reasons for this.

There are, of course, many reasons. They all stem from the fact that the car is an individual transport vehicle, bringing unprecedented freedom, meaning that it can leave from anywhere and go anywhere at any moment and without problems of having to switch to other means of transport on the way. What is more, cars are now far more powerful, more reliable, and more comfortable, as there has been constant technical progress, even though the first cars had essentially the same basic characteristics as they do today. Finally, a car can be driven by practically all adults and the combination of higher living standards and lower acquisition costs, whether for new or (even more so) for used cars, have made them accessible to almost everyone in developed countries.

More specifically, the principal reasons for the car's success can be expressed in terms of freedom, time saving, flexibility, ease of use, attractiveness, and low cost. But there is one particular reason that now predominates.

11.2 THE LACK OF AN ALTERNATIVE

The main reason why the car has become indispensable in today's society is perhaps the most obvious, but at the same time the least known. The changes in use of land and space on the one hand, and the types of trips on the other, have been such in the last few decades that there is now little alternative to the car for a great majority of trips taking place in normal day-to-day life.

The penetration of the car into Western society has led to sweeping changes in land use in urban, suburban, and even rural areas. Housing, shops, jobs, leisure centres, and all activities in general are now spread over vast areas rather than being concentrated in a few specific parts of the country.

Likewise, except for certain inhabitants of a few central areas, the structure of trips has completely changed due to the ease provided by the car. The average distance between the home and the workplace has almost doubled in two decades. Shopping in small local shops has been replaced to a great extent by the use of supermarkets and shopping centres, much farther from the home in distance but not in access time. Friendships can be established or continued with people or families living kilometres or tens of kilometres away, instead of those living in the same neighbourhood. Sports are no longer played in the vicinity of the home, assuming this was possible, but in a club several kilometres away. Weekends have become times when previously unheard of numbers of people travel to the country, the mountains, or the seaside, tens or hundreds of kilometres from home. All these tendencies towards dispersal, both in terms of land use and travel, explain why the average distances travelled by West Europeans are ten times higher today than 40 years ago. Before the Industrial Age, the number of daily trips per inhabitant is estimated at two, almost always on foot. Today, the figure is about 3.2, of which only one is on foot. If very short trips, taken on foot or, more rarely, by bicycle, are excluded, our contemporaries travel on average long enough distances per trip and therefore have to rely on motorised transport.

This is not at all surprising considering the new opportunities offered by the car and the changes in use of land and space outlined above. This last point explains why today's trips are not only much longer in distance but also differ far more widely as to their departure points and destinations. Public transport can only provide coverage for a small part of these trips, particularly those towards or inside city centres whose relative importance is generally decreasing or at best levelling. In all European towns, the great majority of movements do not now concern the centres, but intersuburban or peripheral travel. The result is that in practice, except for very short distances, there is rarely a choice between means of transport and the car has usually become an absolute necessity, rather in the same way that for thousands of years our ancestors relied only on walking.

The comparison between the car and walking is not, for that matter, as strange as it may appear at first sight. Studies made in large Third World countries, where the great majority of the population has hardly any access to motorised means of transport, have shown not only that the level of mobility was much lower, but also that the length of trips on foot were much longer than those in developed countries, where the average duration is about 10 minutes. This is the case, for example, in Algeria and Turkey, where the average trip time on foot would appear to be about 20 minutes, which is precisely about the same as the average car trip in Western countries, on the understanding that the surface area covered in the same time (and therefore the scope of activities) are obviously far smaller in the first case than in the second and that the overall economic productivity is reduced accordingly. It has equally been seen that in a town such as Guandzou in China, where the bicycle is the dominant means of transport, the corresponding average trip time was also 20 minutes, which appears to be characteristic to individual means of transport, the areas accessible in this lapse of time being greater than by foot, without coming anywhere near those made possible by the car.

11.2.1 A Striking Example

Different studies have been carried out in order to estimate the proportion of trips using motorised transport that could in practice only be undertaken by car. The most far-reaching of these studies may be those carried out in the Netherlands [1]. They began by noting that 40% of all Dutch citizens lived in towns with no railway or underground train station. They then calculated that approximately half of the kilometres travelled by the inhabitants of the Netherlands were between places with no means of public transport linking them. Going even further, they showed that suitable means of public transport only existed for 22% of the kilometres travelled by car, with this percentage amounting to 30% for usual trips (home to work, for example) and only 11% for nonregular ones. In other words, in the most densely populated country in Europe, with one of the best public transport networks, there is no credible alternative for about 80% of the kilometres travelled by car.

This situation results directly from the fact that for 80% of trips made in Holland, the ratio between the time required to make a trip door to door using public transport and that by car is more than 2, the average being 3.2 for the whole of the country. As a result, the proportion of Dutch inhabitants who use public transport to commute to work does not exceed 10%. Finally, the studies showed that even a very active urban policy, implying, for example, that offices should be built as often as possible in the vicinity of railway or underground stations, would have no great impact on the situation.

Of course, what holds true for Holland also generally holds, *mutatis mutandis,* for the other European countries. The survey on home-to-work commuting carried out in 1994 for the Union Routière de France in the four most populated West European countries [2] indirectly confirmed the results of the Dutch specialists. It showed that among those who commute to work daily by car, 70% had never used public transport for this trip. As it is highly likely that their car had been unavailable for one reason or another on at least one occasion, the conclusion seems clear: if they had never used public transport at all, it was because there was none allowing them to reach their workplace conveniently.

The recent changes in the geography of trips are therefore such that, except for very short distances that can be travelled on foot or, more rarely, by bicycle, the use of the car is indispensable for most movements, as, for most people, public transport is only a credible alternative in a limited number of cases, usually when travelling to and within large town centres, where it unquestionably plays an essential role.

In addition, even when accessible public transport links exist, the use of the car could nonetheless be necessary for a number of other reasons. The first to consider is the adaptation of the means of transport to the needs of the traveller; in other words, its convenience. In numerous cases, this element of convenience can only be fulfilled by the car. For transporting luggage, going shopping, dropping a child off at school, going to visit a friend on the way home, and so forth, the use of the car is often actually imperative even if accessible public transport exists. A second reason is linked to the way travel is spread out over 24 hours of the day or night and every day of the year. Public transport is by its nature unavailable during part of these 24 hours, and it is often reduced during another part for economic reasons. Even if the trip to be made is on a well-served public transport route, the use of the car can become necessary when at least one part of the trip will take place at a time when public transport is not in service or is too infrequent.

In summary, the combination of restrictions linked to the geographic location of departure points and destinations, convenience with regard to specific needs, and the time of day the trip is made, proves that the commonly held notion that means of transport are interchangeable is mistaken. In all countries, the proportion of "captive" car trips is very high. This helps explain why the Dutch study cited above ended with the final conclusion that, even if all Dutch cities were endowed with the best possible public transport networks-underground railways, trams, buses-and even if the (impossible) task of building railway stations in all cities, towns, and villages were undertaken, the proportion of kilometres travelled by car would only decrease by 5%.

A recent report by the Foundation for Motoring and the Environment of the Royal Automobile Club of Great Britain on car dependency also reaches the conclusion that the possibilities of substituting another means of transport for the car are, in practice, extremely limited [3].

It must for that matter be noted that if the majority of car users do not in practice have access to other forms of motorised transport, the situation is the same for most of those who use public transport. They often have no choice as to their means of transport, either because they do not have access to a car, they do not have a driving licence, have no access to parking facilities, or for a host of other reasons. To borrow the vocabulary of transport specialists, public transport users, like car users, are in their large majority "captives" of the means of transport they use, which means that all the debates on the possibilities of substitution among means of transport are usually irrelevant as they are not based on analysis of the true facts. The success of the car and the continuing growth in the market are therefore of no surprise, as it has often become indispensable to own a car due to the changes in use of land and space.

However, it should not be assumed that car users feel restricted by the fact that they have no other alternative but their vehicle. This is not the case since most of the time, even when they do have another option, our European compatriots still prefer their car, for reasons that are particularly clear after studying trip times.

11.3 THE CAR AND TIMESAVING

Thanks to the ease with which it transports its users from door to door, without breaks, without waiting, and without too much walking, the car is an exceptional time-saver in most situations compared to walking or public transport, even when the latter is available.

Numerous studies carried out both nationally and locally have proved this many times. The survey conducted in 1994, mentioned above, in the four most populated countries of Western Europe (Germany, France, the United Kingdom, and Italy) on home-to-work commuting is particularly revealing in this respect [2]. First of all, it shows an extraordinary similarity of habit across borders, although urban structures, geographical conditions, and transport networks appear very dissimilar from one country to another at first glance. If those who work at home or walk to their place of employment are excluded, the similarities are quite stunning:

78% of the active population using a means of mechanised transport go to work by car in France, 80% in Great Britain, 73% in Germany, and 78% in Italy. The proportion of those using public transport is 16% in France, 13% in Great Britain, 12% in Germany, and 12% in Italy. The only notable difference concerns the use of the bicycle, which is used by 10% of the active population in Germany against 2 to 4% in the other three countries.

But the similarities do not stop there. They also concern travel times. Whereas the active population of Europe that commutes using public transport spends an average of 38 minutes door-to-door getting to work, those who drive spend an average of only 19 minutes, average trip times being 18 minutes in France, 17 in Great Britain, 17 in Italy, and 25 in Germany (which is the only country to differ somewhat from the others on this point, for reasons that would be interesting to clarify). These commuting times, confirmed by national surveys, are obviously remarkably low, and much shorter than usually imagined. Only 10% of European workers who use a car take more than 30 minutes to get to their workplace! It is also striking to note that in the United States, the average home-to-work commute by car is exactly the same as in Western Europe—19 minutes—as if there were some kind of universal constant [3].

Some specialists have in fact suggested that travel time is an invariable, and that those who travel choose their destinations in order to stay within a constant "time budget" for transport. This is probably true in part, especially with respect to individual transport means: walking, two-wheeled vehicles, and cars. But this theory of a time-budget constant is largely disproved by the observation that on the one hand, average daily overall travel times vary from one urban centre to another, and (particularly) on the other, that they depend on the means of transport used.

In fact, two very different categories of trip must be distinguished. The first have a "compelled" destination and a "forced" means of transport, and those who travel have to accept long trip times if necessary. This is the case for certain trips to and from work in large urban areas when it is impossible to use a car. This is, for instance, the case for those who go to work by public transport in the Paris region as they take an average of almost an hour (53 minutes) to get to their workplace and the same for the return trip, this considerable amount of time obviously reducing the quality of life for those concerned. But such commuters have no choice, especially when the job market is difficult, and they are obliged to accept this constraint. And it must also be noted that for those who live in the distant suburbs and go to work in Paris by public rail transport, the average commuting time reaches on average 1 hour 10 minutes from door to door and sometimes much more [4].

However, most trips do not belong to this category because their destinations and means of transport are not "compelled." Whether it is to go shopping, play sports, or visit friends, our contemporaries obviously choose destinations that will not force them to travel too far, and choose transport means accordingly. In fact, in most cases they make sure that travel time does not exceed about 20 minutes or even considerably less, which, allowing for exceptions, usually implies the use of an individual means of transport: walking, two-wheeled vehicles, or cars. The designers of suburban shopping centres are well aware of this, as they know that they cannot attract customers unless the access time is generally shorter than 20 minutes. All in all, experience shows that the time allocated for transport in daily life averages no more than one hour in modern societies—except for the minority having to resort to long, compelled trips. In fact, if the theory of the time-budget constant is partly true, it can evidently only be applied to those not having to suffer from this kind of trips.

Whatever the case, this theory should not lead to the conclusion that it would be useless to invest in transport networks on the pretext that the time devoted every day to transport by our contemporaries hardly varies. All appropriate improvements to transport will result in an increase of possible destinations within a given time budget, thereby improving the working and productivity of the economy on the one hand and the opportunities and the quality of life for the populations concerned on the other. This is particularly important as the great majority of trips are "non-compelled." In a region such as the Paris one, the total number of trips to work using public transport, and thus compelled, amount to 2.3 million per weekday out of a daily total of 33.2 million, of which 21.7 are motorised, and this even excludes nonworking days when they are practically non-existent. And this is an extreme case due to the dimensions of this region with 11 million inhabitants.

11.3.1 Thirty Minutes Saved per Trip

For similar destinations, the time saved by car users is considerable. To calculate it, the European survey mentioned above asked people who used their cars daily to commute to work and who had already tried to use public transport—it was seen that this was the case for 30% of them—how much time it had taken them to reach the same destination. The average reply was 49 minutes, instead of 19, which means that all things being equal, use of the car saves its users about a half-hour per trip.

In other words, even when a public transport alternative exists, the car is still usually chosen by those who have access to it. Who would want to lose a half-hour of transport in the morning and the same in the evening without a good reason, especially when this precious hour per day is clearly part of one's personal life?

Of course, in some rare cases where the destination is the centre of a large urban area with good rail connections, the use of public transport can be quicker than the car. But when such situations exist, they are very rare when taken as a percentage of all trips. In most situations, the car saves time for all those who have the possibility of using it, since it provides door-to-door transport without breaks, and this is the main reason for its success.

The situation is even the same in the Paris region, the most densely populated in Europe: the difference between average trip times by car as opposed to public transport is, on average, 9 minutes in favour of the car for trips within Paris, 14 minutes for trips between the city of Paris and its suburbs, and 25 minutes for trips from suburb to suburb. On the whole, the average time required to travel by car in the Paris region, regardless of the motive, is 22 minutes, whereas the time needed using public transport is 46 minutes, or more than double [5].

On a European level, the average car trip takes approximately 20 minutes, which, for 680 million daily movements, equals about 230 million hours. Contrary to what is sometimes stated, this time is not "lost" but "spent" in travel because the car allows a considerable amount of time to be saved when compared to other means of transport.

11.3.2 Ignorance of the Facts

It would be reasonable to assume that the considerable advantages that the car offers its users in terms of trip time saved would be well recognised by public opinion and decision-makers. Curiously, this is not the case.

As we have seen, when the French public is asked how much time it takes them to commute to work by car, the response is 18 minutes. But when the same people are asked how much time, in their opinion, it takes other French people to commute to work by car, the average reply is 38 minutes, or twice the real figure [2]. In big cities, the gap between ideas and facts is even greater. Whereas the average length of time it takes for inhabitants of the Paris region to commute to work by car is 27 minutes, the public thinks it is 1 hour 20 minutes, or *three times* the real figure. Inhabitants of the Paris region also think that those who use public transport to commute to work get there faster than those who use the car, although it actually takes commuters an average of 53 minutes in the first case and only half as much in the second [2]. Although the car is an extraordinary timesaving tool, the opposite idea prevails!

The situation is most probably the same in the other countries. Our contemporaries, intoxicated by a flood of negative information about the traffic situation, are not really aware of the time that is saved in most cases by using the car and how much it improves their quality of life, although in fact they confirm this every day through their behaviour, which is a veritable plebiscite in favour of the car. It is perfectly understandable that many European transport ministers declare sincerely and in good faith, but in utter ignorance of the facts, that public transport should be aided as much as possible to put an end to the drivers' nightmare of being blocked in traffic jams. Yet, with a few exceptions, even those who face traffic jams daily have far shorter travel times than those making the same trip by public transport. This ignorance of the facts is undoubtedly largely responsible for the mistakes that have been made nearly everywhere in the field of transport. It is impossible to elaborate a sound transport policy without knowing the facts. And this is rarely the case, because door-to-door trip times most often go unmentioned in official studies and reports, even though they are the fundamental criterion that should guide decisions as they are the best measurement of services provided to the user.

11.3.3 Time Is Money

For given departure points and destinations, individuals save a considerable amount of time by using the car and this obviously has a quantifiable economic and financial value. Numerous studies have shown how much our fellow citizens were prepared to pay to save one hour of transport when they had a choice between two means of transport: one faster but more costly, the other slower but cheaper. These studies revealed that on average, the price is high and, logically, more or less in line with the hourly wage of the country in question.

In most countries of Western Europe, the average value attributed to time savings is between 5 and 10 ECUs per hour, obviously with very great differences (for example, depending on whether it concerns senior executives travelling for business purposes or members of other social categories travelling for personal reasons). In fact, there is not *one* value to be attributed to time, but many values, which can vary from 1 to 10, and even vary greatly for the same person, depending on the circumstances. This is especially clear when toll financing is considered. In particular, there is a fundamental difference in behaviour between those who must pay tolls out of their own pocket and those who can claim back the toll from their company on expenses. The introduction of toll infrastructures in urban areas is beginning to give a better understanding of this phenomenon [6].

For a country and *a fortiori* for a continent, the time saved by the car is considerable, not only for the individual but for the entire population. In fact, the average number of trips made daily in Western Europe is currently about 1,200 million, of which 680 million are by car, 400 million on foot (or, less often, by bicycle), and 120 million by public transport, which gives an idea of the time and the money saved by the community given our land and space use and our trip patterns through the use of the car and its corresponding impact on the economic efficiency of our societies and the quality of life of our contemporaries. Of course, if the car was non-existent, land use and trip patterns would be different. But the above-mentioned approach is nevertheless interesting. The high value that individuals attach to their time can also help explain why traffic volume is only slightly affected in the short term by variations in fuel prices, a fact that never ceases to amaze. Of course, the main reason for this low elasticity of demand is due in most cases to the lack of alternatives to the car. But it can also be explained by the fact that even if a choice exists, the time saved by the use of the automobile is considerable and its value usually largely exceeds the marginal cost of its use.

In general, user sensitivity to price increases is limited: to use the usual formula, the long-term elasticity of car traffic does not exceed -0.25 to -0.30. That of goods transport is still lower, between −0.06 and −0.07 [7]. The main explanation for these low values is that for most trips there is no realistic alternative to the car or the truck. A recent survey showed that 86% of French people agree with the idea that: "L'automobile, on ne peut s'en passer" (we cannot do without the car) [2].

Governments have known this for a long time and are well aware that taxing fuel is one of the easiest ways of collecting money for public finances, which are always in need of funds, although excessive taxation presents high disadvantages especially suffered by the underprivileged social classes and inhabitants of rural and distant suburban areas, who need to travel relatively long distances.

However, in addition to these quantitative reasons explaining why our fellow citizens rely increasingly on their cars, there are others that are more qualitative in nature.

11.4 THE CAR AND FREEDOM

Our contemporaries give freedom as the first reason for using their cars. A French survey showed that 88% of car owners consider their car "an important part of their personal freedom." There is nothing surprising in this, considering the multitude of new activities that car ownership has made accessible: the possibility of widening relationships, leisure activities, places to shop, the chance to discover new places and new landscapes, to go on holiday easily to previously unknown regions and countries, and even possibilities of considerably expanding the choice of jobs.

One figure illustrates the sweeping changes brought about by the use of the car. Whereas walking for 20 minutes means covering a distance of 2 km at the most, driving a car for the same period of time usually means covering about 10 km in an urban area, thereby multiplying by 25 the accessible area, or even more in the suburbs or in rural areas! The idea of mobility is actually indissociable from liberty, as being deprived of liberty precisely means imprisonment (that is, immobility).

Ease of access to new activities explains the increase in mobility brought about by motorisation. Studies conducted in Norway have shown that the average number of trips per person changed from 2.4 per day in households without a car to 3.4 in households with, increasing to 4 when there were two or more cars, and that, in addition, the destinations were then more distant and more diverse [1]. This led some people to state [3]:

The fact is that those who have a car can adopt a completely different lifestyle from those who do not have access to one. It is a lifestyle charac-terised by living in a low population density area, a high level of activity, greater freedom for daily tasks, and the capacity to respond spontaneously to social and leisure opportunities whenever they present themselves. From most standpoints, it is a superior lifestyle.

11.4.1 The Car and Convenience

We have already mentioned the notion of convenience, which covers the fact that the car not only transports the driver but also one or more passengers and, if necessary, numerous purchases, packages, and boxes, both in everyday circumstances and during more exceptional weekend and holiday travel.

It also covers the flexibility characterised by use of the car:

- Flexibility in schedules: The car means that the time of departure can be chosen freely and changed at will, without having to think about fixed timetables.
- Flexibility in routes: They can vary according to traffic conditions or be adapted to make a detour to drop someone off, to stop to make a purchase, or pay someone a private or business call.
- Flexibility of destination: The car has the unique characteristic of being able to transport its users either to the shop 800m from home or to the other end of the country (or even the continent).

On reflection, this is really something quite extraordinary. This is what explains that the car was so exceptionally popular as soon as it was introduced, and that it still inspires wonder in those who have access to it for the first time. But something strange happens as people get used to anything. Very quickly, the cars' possibilities are taken for granted by those who benefit from them.

What is abnormal is considered normal, and vice versa. What is abnormal is being able to commute in 19 minutes door-to-door to a place of work located 12 km away, which is the European average; it is being able to leave home and in less than an hour arrive in the country to visit friends or relatives, with the children, perhaps the grandchildren, the luggage, some food, a few presents, the dog, and so on, without it being tiring and in the most comfortable conditions. This is abnormal in the etymological sense of the term, as the great majority of the inhabitants of the planet do not have these possibilities, any more than those who came before us, even if they were kings or emperors and the most powerful people in the world.

What is normal, in the absence of specific tolls, is that the dimensions of the transport system cannot always be designed to deal with rush-hour peak traffic flows or weekend or holiday departures, as this would be an undeniable waste of resources, and that at certain times and in certain places there will therefore be slow traffic and congestion. But human nature is such that we think things are normal when they are not, and abnormal when they are.

11.5 THE CAR AND ATTRACTIVENESS, PRIVACY, AND SAFETY

For most Europeans, using a car is perceived to varying degrees as a pleasure. According to a recent study [8], 82% of European drivers say they like driving.

Over 80% of French drivers say that one of the things that they appreciate most about driving a car is the discovery of new landscapes and the possibility of having easy access to nature, the car being the simplest way of getting into the country. It is interesting to note, however, that the pleasure of speed is less common: only 26% of French drivers say they enjoy driving fast [2].

Being protected from bad weather and having a radio, and possibly air conditioning (and now a telephone), adds to the attractiveness of the car. The time needed to travel by car is perceived as shorter than an equivalent trip on foot or by public transport. Many studies have shown that walking and waiting were unconsciously estimated by our contemporaries as being two to three times longer than their actual duration as a result of their relative unpleasantness.

It is unlikely that the car will be any less attractive to the coming generations. According to a recent survey carried out amongst 11- to 24-year-olds in the Paris region [9], 50% used cars and liked them, whereas 40% did not use them and regretted it. The percentages were quite different for public transport: 48% used it and liked it, but 42% used it and did not like it. And yet this region has one of the best public transport networks that exist.

11.5.1 Privacy and Safety

The car gives its users privacy that by definition cannot be found in public transport, and can to a certain extent even be considered an extension of the home. It is a well-known fact those who use a car to drive home after a day's work consider the work day over as soon as they get into their cars, whereas those who use public transport have the impression that the work day is not really over until they get home.

It can be added that especially at night, the car is felt in many European towns to be safer than public transport, which is unfortunately plagued by malicious acts, making users apprehensive. The actual or believed unsafety of public transport in some countries or cities is becoming an extremely serious matter and explains part of their patronage decrease.

The danger of a road accident is feared much less than a criminal attack. It must be said that, paradoxically, the car is not necessarily less safe regarding road accidents than public transport in the case of urban travel. In fact, in urban areas, most accident victims are not drivers, but pedestrians or users of two-wheeled vehicles. According to a recent Danish study, the risk is in fact higher for users of public transport than for car users, due to the part of the trip made on foot to and from the public transport route. The death rate is 0.45 per hundred million kilometres travelled by car , but 13.60 for pedestrians, themselves being endangered by vehicle traffic [10].

11.5.2 The Car and its Costs

When evaluating the cost of their cars, users have a tendency to consider only the marginal expenditure involved. They even usually tend to count only fuel purchase, which obviously has no comparison to the overall cost, which includes depreciation on the car, insurance, parking, maintenance, and so forth that together often add up to six times the price of fuel purchase in European conditions. But in fact, this attitude is not at all illogical. If a person decides, for any number of reasons, to purchase a car, then insure, house, and maintain it, it would be absurd if he did not use it, and it is therefore normal to take only the marginal cost of use into account when deciding on a means of transport.

The decision to purchase a car, and the fact that on average European households devote 12% of their budgets to it, can obviously only be explained by the fact that all the savings made (in terms of time and money, convenience, and quality of life) outweigh the amount of money spent. No one has ever forced anyone to buy a car and to use it.

11.6 GAINS FOR THE COMMUNITY

However, it is not only the individual standpoint that must be considered. The advantages to the community as a whole are even more important, given that nearly all individuals profit from the considerable advantages offered by the car. It would therefore be highly unlikely that the result for the community should not be positive. Of course, road traffic gives rise to negative effects that must not be forgotten and must be fought against. But on top of the individual advantages outlined above, there are other positive effects for the community.

11.6.1 Land Use and Living Space

On the whole, the car has a considerable, positive influence on land use, both in urban and in rural areas. Its penetration into society has increased by 10, 100, or even more, the area that can be used for housing, shops, factories, offices, and facilities of all kinds, and this has led to several different consequences.

In some countries, certain of these consequences are negative. Cars, roads, and road transport have led to the possible urbanisation of considerable amounts of space, and this encouraged the anarchic development of building works in the absence of consistent urban planning policies and gave birth to what the French call the "moth-eaten" effect, where former country areas are haphazardly dotted with new buildings. But this has not been the case everywhere. Several European countries have managed to avoid this kind of disorder by adopting sound land-use control policies, whilst still benefiting from the advantages of the car. England, the Nether-lands, Sweden, Germany, and others are good examples.

But alongside these potentially negative aspects, the penetration of the car has had other, eminently positive, effects. By opening vast areas to urbanisation, it has been possible to avoid crowding of buildings, allocating them far more space and making them more attractive, whether it be for individual homes, blocks of flats, offices, workshops, factories, shops, leisure centres, or many other types of activities. Cramped and overpopulated housing has been replaced for most Europeans by individual houses with gardens or small blocks of flats, obviously preferable to the huge high-rise variety long recommended by urban developers, whose adverse effects need no comment. Badly designed offices with less than $10m^2$ per employee have given way to modern units with an average of 20 to $30m^2$ per person, equipped to make work more efficient and pleasant. These changes also hold for workshops, factories, and sports, and leisure centres.

The urban population of many European countries has doubled within a few decades as a result of the rural exodus and demographic growth. It is clear that the majority of this population can no longer live in compact town centres but, on the contrary, have to live and work in the suburbs and surrounding regions where the availability of space has become an essential part of the quality of life. All public opinion polls show that the great majority of the inhabitants are happy to live, and particularly bring up their children, in these areas, even though their lifestyle is quite different from those of the inhabitants of traditional town centres. In the Paris region, three-quarters of suburbanites declare that they would not want to live in the city of Paris itself, any financial considerations aside, despite the attractiveness of the French capital [2].

Of course, people living on the outskirts do not normally have the benefit of a lively town centre, but they have other advantages: calm; greenery; the absence of congestion if the road network is satisfactory; easy access to all services, businesses, and activities within a few minutes; the possibility of owning a home at a reasonable price, which would be impossible in the town centre; and so forth. It is another lifestyle that has appeared, dependent on use of the car, and has gradually become the most common in Europe: "Suburbia" gives its inhabitants a quality of life with which the great majority is satisfied, surprising as this may seem to some. Around most European towns, this outward-spreading movement has taken an original form: it has allowed the rebirth of thousands of old villages whose populations have begun to increase after more than a century of decline. Whereas since the start of the industrial era people have migrated from the country to the town, the opposite is now happening. The phenomenon has important repercussions. By substituting regions of remote towns or isolated villages with vast, unified transport zones, the car has become an essential factor in the productivity of Western societies, as experience has constantly shown that this latter one is in direct relation to the size of the labour pool.

Finally, the complete population drain from the vast regions of the European continent that are the furthest away from towns was only avoided thanks to the car. Who would accept to live all year round in a remote country area if, in addition to television and other modern means of telecommunications, they did not have the possibility of a car to take them at will to the closest town with all its services?

11.6.2 The Car and the Cost of Living

The increasing access to cars has had another positive impact on the community: its influence on the cost of living. Since the car opened vast spaces to urbanisation, it has played a determining role in the moderation of land prices and consequently those of buying or renting houses and building in general. It is impossible to imagine what these would be if the entire urban population was concentrated in a few limited areas, as would otherwise be the case. Roads and cars are the primary weapons in the struggle against high land prices. As the World Bank has noted: "High urban densities are usually associated with the disadvantage of high housing costs and a low level of residential space per person" [11].

It was not a coincidence that the first hypermarkets appeared with the first dual carriageways in the early 1960s. Without the car they would never have existed and Europeans would still be making do with their local shops, which may be pleasant and friendly but whose prices for everyday products are often over a third higher, if not more, than those offered by more modern types of shops.

In allowing competition to develop, the car has played a major role in raising living standards, and it is not surprising that the great majority of Europeans use it to do their weekly shopping, often in modern suburban shopping centres but sometimes also in town centres (in different proportions depending on the country).

11.6.3 The Car and Employment

As we have seen, the car provides a living for millions of European households working in many different professions that depend on it either completely or in part, such as the steel, glass, plastic, electronics, and textile industries; equipment manufacturers; tyre manufacturers; car manufacturers; garages,; the oil industry; the road industry; motorway companies; insurance companies; public-work companies; and so forth—so many it makes the head spin! Without these activities, the European economy would be unrecognisable. It used to be said: "When the building industry goes well, everything goes well." In many ways, today it could be said: "When the car industry goes well, everything goes well," as it plays such a central role in modern economies.

The effects of the vast changes brought about by the penetration of the car into society concern many sectors of the economy in one way or another. Amongst many others, one particular one should be mentioned: tourism and leisure activities, which are extremely dependent on the car and represent almost 10% of all European jobs.

An Invention That Changed the World, and Europe as Well

The car has developed so quickly and taken such a dominant role in our transport system because, on the whole, it provides high-level services to society, both in terms of the quality of life of its members and the workings of the economy. Without necessarily realising it, our society has organised itself around the car during the last four decades thanks to both industrial progress—which has continually produced better and more reliable vehicles at a lower cost, making them accessible to the great majority of the population instead of just to a privileged few—and the more or less continual development of road and motorway networks.

Considering the changes in geography and life-style discussed above, the rate of motorisation will continue to expand. In the United States, it has now reached almost 700 private vehicles per 1,000 inhabitants, consisting of 600 cars and about 100 pickup type vehicles. Less than 10% of households have no vehicle, 33% have one, 38% have two and 19% have three or more. On average, there are 1.75 vehicles per household, or exactly one for each driving licence holder, whereas in Europe the number of individual vehicles—150 million—is still lower than the number of drivers (around 180 million).

There is no reason why Europe should not follow the same general trend, even though the structure and density of Europe's large urban centres will to a certain extent limit, at equal rates of income, the number of cars. In a country such as France, the Paris region has one-third fewer cars per inhabitant than the rural areas, even though the latter are much less wealthy. But certain European countries such as Germany in its former West German section, Italy, and Switzerland have already reached the level of 500 cars per 1,000 inhabitants.

In summary, it is reasonable to expect an increase of about 50% in the number of cars in Western Europe in the next 20 years, which will very gradually, at an average rate of 2% per year, bring the total number of vehicles to a maximum of about 600 per 1,000 inhabitants. This does not necessarily mean that the distances travelled will increase in the same proportion, as second vehicles travel less than the others. They also travel mostly outside rush hours and outside town centres, as witnessed by the forecasts for evolution in urban transport in Europe. And they will be helped in the near future by the development of "intelligent transport" features

11.7 INTELLIGENT TRANSPORT

11.7.1 Introduction

The use of telematics—electronics, telecommunications, computerisation—in the field of transport is one of the greatest innovations in this sector since the introduction of the car a century ago or the motorway about 60 years ago. This innovation is in the process of giving birth to what is now usually known under the general term of *intelligent transport,* which particularly (although not exclusively) concerns road transport.

This is a very recent development as it only started at the end of the 1980s and the beginning of the 1990s, taking place almost simultaneously in the three main poles of the developed world: North America, Western Europe, and Japan.

In Western Europe, the European manufacturers launched the PROMETHEUS research programme (Programme for a European Traffic system with Highest Efficiency and Unprecedented Safety) in 1987, in the framework of the "EUREKA" process and with backing from the European Community, which is aimed at developing systems to improve road vehicle efficiency and safety. This programme ended in October 1994, after expenditure amounting to 0.8 billion ECUs. In 1988, the European Commission launched the DRIVE programme (Dedicated Road Infrastructures for Vehicle Safety in Europe), whose actions associate at least two partners belonging to Member States. DRIVE I (1989–1991) and DRIVE II (1992–1995) represented overall expenditure of 0.5 billion ECUs, and a new phase is now in progress, particularly aimed at optimising the interoperability of services provided to road users throughout the different European Union countries.

In 1991, the ERTICO organisation (European Road Transport Telematics Implementation Co-ordination Organisation) was founded in Brussels, grouping together about 30 industrial firms and private and public sector organisations working in the field of transport, particularly including car manufacturers. Finally, mention should be made of the creation, also in 1991, of a Technical Committee for European Standarisation, "Road Transport and Telematics," which is subdivided into 13 work groups aimed at ensuring that each different country does not develop processes and techniques that are incompatible with the others.

In the United States, IVHS America (Intelligent Vehicle/Highway Society of America) was founded in 1990 and became ITS America (Intelligent Transportation Society of America) in 1994. It groups together all the different actors from the private and public sector together with universities. The Federal Administration made the development of intelligent transport one of the priorities of the Intermodal Surface Transportation Efficiency Act (ISTEA) in 1991, and increasingly large sums are allocated to its financing, rising from 2 million dollars in 1989 to 356 million in 1996.

In Japan, the economic group VICS (Vehicle Information Communication System) was also created in 1991, and is particularly concerned with the communication of information to drivers, in this country where over a milllion vehicles are already equipped with on-board navigation aid systems. The year 1994 was marked by the creation of VERTIS (Vehicle, Road and Traffic Intelligent Society), which groups together experts from universities, national research organisations, and the private sector.

Since 1994, a world congress is held every year, with each of the three continents being responsible in turn for its organisation, via ERTICO, VERTIS, and ITS America, the first three having taken place, respectively, in Paris, Yokohama, and Orlando, and the fourth one being held in Berlin in 1997.

The products, functions, or services that fall within the scope of "intelligent transport" are now extremely numerous. ERTICO has identified six different sectors, 25 functions, and 130 subfunctions, whereas ITS America has defined 29 distinct products and services.

However, generally speaking, it is possible to group most of the activities that participate in "intelligent transport" under six main headings, which sometimes overlap:

- Road safety;
- Traffic management;
- Motorist information;
- Remote toll system;
- Fleet management;
- Automatic motorways.

11.7.2 Road Safety

Improvements to road safety through the use of telematics have mainly been sought in two different areas, the first concerning vehicles alone and the second concerning traffic management and user information.

The first has been the object of much research within the framework of the European programme, PROMETHEUS. But it must be admitted that in spite of the efforts made, this has not yet given many results in terms of road safety that can be applied to the vehicles currently on the road. The fruits of this research will only be forthcoming in the longer term.

By nature, the process of vehicle design and development is very long. It is therefore not in the least abnormal that it takes time to transfer research results to new vehicles. The first practical fallouts should be on the market around 2000.

Areas of research include improvements to vision at night and in fog (infrared projectors and image reproduction), reductions in accidental risk between vehicles (anticollision radars and intelligent speed control systems), short-distance communication between vehicles and road infrastructures based on "remote toll" equipment, and systems for monitoring trajectories to avoid swerving caused by drowsiness. Many adjustments will still be necessary before such systems can be marketed with a sufficient level of reliability for there to be no doubt whatsoever as to their contribution in terms of safety, which in the medium and long term could be important. In the shorter term, progress in road safety linked to intelligent transport systems will come from the development of traffic management techniques and user information.

11.7.3 Traffic Management

The main objective of traffic management is to make the best possible use of existing roads in terms of capacity and free traffic flow, whether it be for traditional urban road networks or for express roads (roads with limited access) and motorways.

In traditional urban sites, it is particularly aimed at optimising free traffic flow by regulating traffic lights. The first control systems used were relatively simple, with, for example, the introduction of "green waves" allowing the user not to have to stop on certain one-way routes.

But considerable progress has been made over the past two or three decades as a result of permanent analysis of traffic flow, speed, and lane occupancy data, enabling expert systems to make optimal decisions at all times regarding traffic lights, either within the framework of overall, preestablished programmes, or on the level of each particular crossroads. Such control systems, backed up by coverage by television cameras, which is particularly useful for prompt processing of incidents by traffic control centres, led to a significant capacity increase on the networks concerned and now cover increasingly wide areas of most of Europe's large urban zones, even if many suburbs are yet to be properly equipped.

Whilst it is true that much has been done in Europe regarding traditional urban networks, this is not the case elsewhere: traffic management techniques are only just starting to be applied to the expressways and motorways that crisscross the large European urban areas. Until very recently, these networks were practically left to themselves, with the authorities concerned remaining mainly passive in the face of problems of congestion and users rightly feeling that they were abandoned to their fate as soon as they used such roads.

Even access regulation techniques aimed at limiting, when necessary, the number of vehicles that enter express networks at a given interchange, have been used very little in Europe compared with the United States, where in California, for example, hundreds of access points are equipped in this way (900 out of 1,200).

The interest of this practice is twofold: firstly, it enables traffic on the motorway to be maintained at a level close to maximum capacity, therefore avoiding or limiting congestion and increasing traffic flows and speeds; and secondly, it helps coming vehicles to join the motorway's main traffic stream more easily. Many experiments conducted in the United States have given extremely positive results, with a reduction in motorway trip times varying from 20% to 48%, a corresponding increase in speed of 16% to 62%, an increase in flows of 17% to 25%, and a decrease in accident rates of 15% to 50% [12]. The effectiveness of access regulation systems has therefore been proved, at least on networks that meet the conditions for their implementation, which could not always be easy in very densely populated urban areas or where there are large crisscrossed networks that are difficult to monitor entirely.

In Europe, such control systems are nonetheless under study and are beginning to be adopted in England, the Netherlands, France, and other countries, sometimes by improving on experiments that had already been attempted several decades ago.

But it is also possible to act not on accesses to motorways, but on the main traffic stream, as is the case, for example, in Germany, in the Munich area, where variable message signs (V.M.S.) are used to give information to users, particularly concerning recommended speeds taking into account traffic density, with the aim to limit "stop and go" problems. Very satisfactory results have been obtained, particularly with a reduction of 39% in accidents causing injuries and an increase of capacity of 5 to 8%. Similar experiments are spreading out in a number of European countries.

This example shows that informing users, with a view to changing their behaviour is one of the key factors in the implementation of efficient management for expressways and motorways networks.

11.7.4 User Information

In order to provide users with relevant information, the first stage obviously consists in knowing what is going on.

Data Collection

This is why in a number of large European towns not only traditional road networks but also express networks, are progressively being equipped with detectors capable of gathering data on the three key issues concerning traffic: flow, speed, and density of occupancy. It should be pointed out that this equipment is relatively expensive, which explains why it is still the exception and not the rule. But certain regions of Europe are now making up for this deficiency with high-performance systems. Mention can be made of the "IPER" and "SIRIUS" systems, which have been introduced progressively since 1994 on most motorways in the Paris region, with loop sensors installed about every 500m. Now, 330 km of motorway are equipped with nearly 3,000 sensors that collect 400,000 items of information per second, and the remaining 240 km will be equipped within about three years.

Analysis of Congestion

The first result of the introduction of such systems is not necessarily that which may be expected. It comes from the fact that it is at last possible to analyse the way in which the motorway networks really work on the basis of reliable facts, and particularly to measure the scale and evolution of problems of congestion both in differed and in real time. In most cases it is shown that such problems are less serious than imagined. Generally speaking, congestion on the radial motorways of the large European towns only concerns 2 to 3 hours per day in each direction, whereas the traffic is in fact often almost constant for about 15 hours per day. The very large number of nonworking or semiworking days must also be taken into account. The overall result in average speed is surprisingly very high and the volume of additional time that can be attributed to problems of congestion compared with an acceptable reference speed (60km/h, for instance) is relatively low. Even on the *Boulevard Périphérique,* the inner Paris ringroad, which has by far the heaviest traffic in Europe, the average speed reaches 53 km/h, which has to be compared with the maximum allowed speed of 80 km/h, and this in spite of a record daily traffic flow of about 30,000 vehicles per lane!

The statistics obtained are only just beginning to be handled, but they already shed a very new light on the way in which the European motorway networks work. Official positions stating that they are subject to permanent congestion just proves to be wrong and will now be able to be relativised, and serious investment errors, such as the ORLYVAL light railway between Paris and Orly Airport, whose attendance was a third of that forecast, could be avoided.

It must be said that the Paris region motorway network is unique in Europe. Not only is it relatively long with its 660 km of motorways, but it has no equivalent in terms of traffic density. Out of the about 250 km in Western Europe where average daily traffic exceeds 150,000 vehicles, about 110 are to be found in the Paris area, including almost all of the 70 km with an average daily traffic of more than 200,000 vehicles, the latter taking place on 8-lane motorways (2×4), with some limited stretches of 10 lanes (2×5) or even 12 lanes (4×3). In the centre of the region, daily traffic per lane is thus between 25,000 and 30,000 vehicles. This is explained by the fact that the Paris region has about 11 million inhabitants in a very limited area, a situation that is found in no other place in Western Europe, except in London. But, contrary to Paris, the London region has no motorway network, with the exception of the M25 motorway ringroad, located well on the outskirts and some incomplete radial links, whereas the Paris area has three motorway ringroads, including the inner "Boulevard Périphérique," and about eight radial motorways. It is therefore not surprising that the density of motorway traffic in the Paris region has no match elsewhere in urban areas in Europe, where a level of 100,000 to 130,000 vehicles per day is usually a maximum, instead of the double.

It is most interesting to note that the IPER and SIRIUS monitoring systems are showing that the "additional time" spent on the motorway network in the Paris area, in comparison with a "reference speed" of 60 km/h, does not seem to exceed about 50 million vehicle hours per year [13]. Even if this amount appears considerable in itself, it is quite limited when translated into monetary terms. If, for instance, the average monetary value of one vehicle hour is estimated at 15 ECUs, the value of the additional time spent due to problems of congestion amounts to 750 million ECUs, which is no more than 0.07% of French GNP. It should be added that it is estimated that 80% of all French traffic congestion problems take place in the Paris area.

Due to the fact that traffic levels and traffic density encountered on the Paris motorway network are not matched anywhere else in Europe, it is fairly safe to assume that the additional time spent due to congestion in the Paris area represents a fair proportion of the additional time spent on the entire West European motorway network, as surprising as this may be. Only when similar data for other networks is available will it be possible to check this hypothesis precisely.

In reality, time differences compared with a free-flowing traffic situation mainly occur on roads other than express roads and motorways. They are due to a *lack* of motorways, and certainly not to their existence.

But the main reason for installing a costly traffic data monitoring system is obviously not to gather statistical data. One of the main aims is to be able to inform the users, which is particularly done by two means. The first consists of installing variable message signs, visible by all the users concerned, at key points throughout the network. The second consists in communicating with certain users only, either before departure or on board their vehicle.

Variable Message Signs

Variable message signs can provide road users with a certain amount of useful information in real time. As we have seen in the case of Munich, they can display a recommended speed and thus help to make traffic smoother. They can also inform users of traffic jams taking place either daily or due to specific incidents (accident, breakdown, etc.) One of the most interesting uses to be noted is that existing in the Paris region, which alone has more variable message signs than the rest of Europe put together, in the scope of the project mentioned above whose cost exceeds 150 million ECUs. The 400 existing variable message signs inform users of the trip time to the next exits or to main points along the motorways they use, on a permanently updated basis. Experience has shown that travel times indicated are remarkably reliable and this use of the system, which has been in service since 1995 and 1996 on the initiative of the City of Paris (whereas it was not initially planned), was met with almost unanimous approval and has significantly changed the perception that the road users now have of the network. For the first time, they no longer feel almost left to their own means whilst driving. Whether the information is positive or negative, at least they know what to expect. Even if they are caught in a traffic jam, they are more patient because they have been informed.

Information given on estimated trip times has a second major advantage. There are three different categories of variable message signs. Some are located on motorway network bifurcations. Others are located outside the motorway network, at access points. Finally, others are located in main traffic stream sections.

The first two types of variable message signs enable users to change their behaviour regarding travel decisions. If they are informed that a given destination will require 15 minutes by one route and 25 by another, they will obviously choose the first, even if they usually use the second. If they see that the motorway network is blocked, by an accident, for example, they will avoid getting caught in the "trap" by staying on the traditional road network. A certain number of users can therefore change their normal behaviour thanks to the information given. It is possible that 2% of users change their routes in this way in the Paris region since the introduction of the signs giving estimated trip times. The percentage may seem low, but it is enough to improve things significantly, and the economic return of the SIRIUS network has been estimated at between 83 and 121%, even without the access regulation systems, which are planned to be the next step to be put in operation [14].

The following stage will be informing certain road users, either before their departure or on board their vehicles.

Information Before Departure

In the first case, the information can be found either in particular places equipped with terminals, such as business or shopping centres, or everywhere, for example through the INTERNET network. This is the case in the Paris region, with the "SYTADIN" server, which is updated every five minutes (http//www.club-internet.fr/sytadin). In addition, specialised portable "CARMINAT" terminals will soon be available in this region.

Information on Board Vehicles

But it is particularly the second case, communicating with users on board their vehicles, that is likely to have the greatest success in the future, not to mention the traditional or specialised radio stations. In the very short term, users will be able to receive information concerning traffic conditions on the network that they are using or planning to use, in real time and on board their vehicle. Several devices are already operational in various places in Europe, and vehicles with the appropriate equipment are now on the market (CARMINAT by Renault; TRAFFIC MASTER), or will be in the immediate future (INF-FLUX by Peugeot; EUROSCOUT).

As an example, the CARMINAT system, which was tested by 2,000 drivers as of 1995 in the Paris region and along the Paris-London corridor and the Lyon-Stuttgart corridor, comprises four types of terminals:

1. A voice information terminal, which receives all the information available in the zone through which the vehicle is travelling, but filters it according to instructions from the user who indicates the trip planned;

2. A graphical information terminal, which supplies simplified maps of the road networks on a colour screen, which can be adjusted to the scale required by the driver;
3. A graphical information and positioning terminal, which shows the vehicle's position to within a few tens of metres using the global positioning system (GPS) satellite localisation system;
4. A dynamic route guidance terminal, which calculates and proposes the best route, in real time, according to information received, particularly regarding traffic densities.

What may have been considered sheer utopianism just a few years ago is now part of our immediate future.

Those who have experienced driving with such aids have been able to appreciate the astonishing progress they represent. Whatever the destination, drivers no longer need to work out their route, even to the most out-of-the-way suburb. They are constantly informed of their exact position, whether they should go straight on, turn right, and so forth. On the level 4 models, traffic conditions are also analysed on a permanent basis and taken into account to optimise the choice of route at all times.

For this to be possible, certain conditions must of course be met. Firstly, the road network must be entirely mapped and information digitized, this being in the final stages in 1997 for most West European countries.

But in order to advance and enter the user guidance phase, it is necessary to have a precise indication of the vehicle's position, which means that a number of sensors and map-matching devices have to be installed aboard the vehicle and coupled with the GPS system.

Finally, if the choice of routes is to be optimised in relation with the traffic, a system must be available to analyse traffic conditions on a permanent basis in order to be able to supply trip times throughout the network, in real time, by means of radio beacons. At the present time, only a minority of European towns are programmed to be equipped in this way, for cost reasons.

In a few years from now, an ever-increasing number of vehicles on Europe's roads will be equipped with devices providing accurate maps of all Europe's road networks, informing drivers on a permanent basis of their position and, in a limited number of places, on the traffic conditions in order to help them to make the best possible decisions regarding routes to take, public parking spaces available, and so forth.

Incident Processing

Improvements in processing incidents is one of the main objectives of the traffic management and user information programmes. Even though they are tending to decrease, various types of incidents (breakdowns, collisions, serious accidents) are nonetheless at the origin of a significant percentage of time lost on the road networks, most particularly in urban areas. Estimates for the Paris region reach about 40%. If these figures are to be reduced, the efficient systems need to be introduced to process incidents.

Curiously, the first difficulty to overcome is the actual detection of the incident. Until recently, the only way to know that an incident had occurred was to note, usually after several minutes had gone by, that there was a traffic jam. In other words, there was no information in real time.

Fortunately, things are now changing very rapidly in this respect with the simultaneous appearance of at least two means of instant incident detection:

- Permanent analysis of data provided by sensors (loop detectors) for those roadways that are equipped with them;
- Automatic, permanent analysis of images received by the television cameras covering the network. This is the case, for example, on a stretch of the A8 motorway that serves the region of Nice, in France, which is successfully equipped with a system of this nature, part of a broader project called "MIGRA-ZUR," which *instantly* detects any abnormal event, thereby considerably improving the competent services' response times and enabling users to be informed immediately, either by means of variable message signs or the motorway radio.

Experiments conducted in the United States have given the following results for incident clearance time [12]:

- Decrease in wrecker (breakdown lorry) response time: 5–7 minutes;
- Decrease for stalls (breakdowns) (which represent 84% of service calls): 8 minutes;
- Decrease in travel times: 10%–42%;
- Decrease in fatalities: 10% in urban areas.

This last point is especially important, as a number of fatalities occur in follow-up accidents.

It is also possible to imagine that in the future, drivers themselves will be able to use automatic devices to warn freeway management centres (motorway traffic control centres) of any incidents they may have witnessed, for instance through systems such as "ADAMS," which is currently being tested in France.

American specialists consider that it should be possible to reduce congestion due to incidents by 50 to 60% overall, with a profit/cost ratio of about 10 to 1 [14].

11.7.5 Remote Toll Systems

Remote toll systems and their scope of application will be developed in the following chapter.

11.7.6 Freight and Fleet Management

Telematics are a top priority for road transport professionals who are subject to very harsh competition and see these systems as a means of improving their productivity. Unlike the individual or "general public" user who simply uses the products offered, professionals must develop their own means to satisfy their particular needs. For instance, the large taxi companies have introduced intelligent telematic systems to handle customer calls more efficiently.

Those responsible for bus networks are progressively equipping their vehicles with positioning and distress call systems, particularly for use in case of attack. More generally, the new techniques improve management of public transport services, and provide better service and more information for users.

As for road transport companies, they have been using on-board telecommunications systems for some time already: trucks are usually equipped with radio-telephones enabling the driver to stay in touch with his company and are systematically equipped with CB radio, an unrivalled tool for this profession both in terms of usefulness and conviviality. Fleet management systems using satellite communications have also been developed.

Finally, mention must be made of various projects that are being undertaken in Europe to test the use of GSM radio-telephones as a means for these different applications: distress calls, information on board vehicles, automatic toll payment, freight and fleet management, and so forth.

11.7.7 Automatic Motorways

The aim of the "automatic motorway" would be to take over the vehicles as soon as they enter the motorway, thereby relieving motorists of their responsibility as drivers.

The concept is not new: as soon as motorists have given their destination, all of the vehicle's movements would be governed by powerful computer systems.

The automatic motorway should be able to solve problems of capacity and safety and problems of autonomy and even pollution if they are used only by electrical vehicles, recharged by induction whilst running!

To have a clearer picture, let us imagine that vehicles are driving at 108 km/h, or 30 m/s at a distance of 30m from each other. At a given point on the road, one vehicle will pass per second, or 3,600 vehicles per hour; that is, nearly double the maximal flow of a motorway lane. Drivers will, in perfect safety conditions, have broken the road capacity barrier—if there is sufficient capacity at the arrival points to absorb the extra flow.

In fact, the automatic motorway is aimed at multiplying traffic flow by ten rather than by two. Vehicles would be driven with a distance of 3m between them, in bunches of a few units.

Is this a dream? The automatic motorway is on the list of ITS America's systems, and the federal state allocates significant sums to finance it: 18.7 million dollars are shown in the 1996 provisional budget, and it is then planned to spend 300 million dollars over a five-year period, with the ambition of opening a demonstration site as soon as possible, perhaps as soon as 1997.

This ambitious programme is somewhat similar to the moon exploration programme that mobilised much national fervour in the United States in the 1960s, but it is far more complex in that it brings into play tens of millions of vehicles and not just one single one, meaning that a successful conclusion is very uncertain, even in the very long term.

Actually, all vehicles would have to be equipped, which would pose an acute transition problem, and there would have to be almost 100% reliability if serious accidents were to be avoided, thus making it appear to be a very remote goal.

In Europe, the PROMETHEUS programme has led to the development of "cooperative driving" devices, including the autonomous intelligent cruise control (AICC) or a system for following white strips, which make vehicles' movements interdependent and prefigures the possible coming of the automatic motorway, in the very long term.

11.7.8 Conclusion

Following this description of *intelligent transport* systems, an essential question must be asked. To what extent will they help to improve the performance of road infrastructures?

For the traditional urban road network, the reply is straightforward. Without traffic lights and the intelligent devices that are now used to manage them, streets and boulevards could not operate at current traffic levels. In comparison to a nonequipped network, the gains in capacity and traffic speeds are therefore considerable. But such networks are now coming near to their limit in towns that are equipped with the most modern expert devices. A given traffic lane cannot handle more than a certain number of vehicles per hour of "green light." Gains still to be made are more and more limited in the European towns that already benefit from the most "intelligent" systems. On the other hand, in other towns and suburbs much still remains to be done.

As we have seen, the situation is different for the express road network, which is only at the beginning of its "intelligent" operating. But it is important not to be under too many illusions. Possible gains in hourly capacity to be made by implementing these techniques will be limited in scope—probably about 10 to 20% depending on the case—which is a lot and little at the same time. This could be particularly true in the crisscross networks of large urban areas, where it is more difficult to act than on isolated sections only. The most obvious benefits will be more regarding traffic speeds and driving comfort than capacity.

This is why the Japanese are right to consider that an *intelligent transport* policy must be comprised of two parts: on the one hand, an increase in capacity and traffic speeds on existing roads by introducing telematic techniques, but also, on the other hand, physical improvements to infrastructures by creating new roads or by increasing the capacity of existing ones [15]. Amongst the most intelligent measures to be implemented in urban areas can also be found the addition of extra lanes by reducing the width of each lane, together with the use of hard shoulders.

Telematic techniques have their limits. In other words, although they are of the greatest interest, they can under no circumstances replace a physical increase in infrastructures when this is necessary and possible, as this can add to network capacity and improve traffic flow far more significantly.

References

[1] Bovy; Van der Waard; Baanders, *Substitution of Travel Between Car and Public Transport*, Rijkswaterstaat Dutch Ministry of Transport, Rotterdam, 1991.

[2] Union Routière de France, SOFRES, *1993–1997 Surveys*, Paris, 1997.

[3] RAC Foundation for Motoring and the Environment, *Car Dependancy*, London, 1995.

[4] U.S. Department of Transport (FHWA), *Urban Travel Patterns 1990 Nationwide Personal Transportation Survey*, Washington, 1992.

[5] Préfecture de la Région Ile-de-France, *1991–1992 Enquête Générale de Transport*, Paris, 1995.

[6] Piron, V., *A propos du prix du temps dans le calcul des coûts de transport*, Etudes Foncières n° 69, Paris, 1995.

[7] Netherlands Organization for Applied Scientific Research TNO, *New hope for tomorrow, Part II*, Den Hagen, 1995.

[8] Europcar—Interrent. *Pan European Motorist Report*, Boulogne Billancourt, France, 1994.

[9] Groupement des autorités responsibles des transports (GART), *Planète Jeune Survey*, Paris, 1996.

[10] Elbek, B., *Impact of transport modes on society and fiscal indirect policy*, Niels-Bohr Institute, Copenhagen, 1995.

[11] The World Bank, *Sustainable Transport*, Washington, D.C., 1996.

[12] FHWA, U.S. Department of Transport, *Intelligent Transportation Infrastructure Benefits: Expected and Experienced*, Washington, January 1996.

[13] Benkadi, R., M. Deniau, and C. Gerondeau, *Le temps additionnel passé sur les autoroutes de la Région Ile-de-France*, Union Routière de France, Paris, 1997.

[14] Frybourg, M., and J. Orselli, *Evaluation monétaire de l'information sur les panneaux à messages variables du système SIRIUS*, Journal TEC n° 137, July–August 1996, Paris.

[15] ITS Japan-Highway Industry Development Organization, *ITS Data Book*, Tokyo, 1995.

CHAPTER 12
▼▼▼

URBAN TRANSPORT: CENTRES AND SUBURBS

12.1 URBAN EVOLUTION

The 17 countries that make up Western Europe, of which 15 now belong to the European Union, have 380 million inhabitants, spread out over an area of 3,600,000 square kilometres, making the western isthmus of the Eurasian continent one of the most densely populated parts of the planet, with population density exceeding 200 inhabitants per square kilometre in Great Britain, Benelux, Germany, and Italy.

The great majority of Europeans now live in or near towns. The progress made in agricultural productivity has been such that only a small percentage of the population is needed to feed the entire Continent, with enough left over to export abroad.

12.1.1 Very Different Towns

European towns are extremely diverse from one country to another and even within the same country, ranging from small towns with a few thousand inhabitants to large urban centres with ten million or more. Size is not the only difference. Some towns are very compact, others are sprawled out. Geographic situations vary greatly as well: some are located in the middle of vast, far-reaching plains, others along the coast or nestled in the mountains. In certain countries with a long tradition of controlled urban development, public authorities control land use, either by rules and regulations or because they are the owners, whereas in others there is a complete lack of legislation and disorder prevails. The role of town centres also differs from place to place. In certain countries they are full of life and animation with permanent inhabitants, in others they are almost exclusively reserved for office buildings and certain shops, and elsewhere they are more or less run down.

12.1.2 Similar Evolution

These different situations are reflected in questions of transport, which are specific to each city. However, despite the differences that characterise the evolution of the thousands of European towns, there are also numerous points of similarity. The increasing tendency to spread out is the first among them.

A very strong link has always existed between the available mode of transport and the way urban structures develop. For thousands of years, walking was practically the only form of transport and so towns tended to be limited to a few hundred metres, or a few kilometres for the largest of them. The first photographs of large towns, taken in the 19th century, show streets crowded with pedestrians, as can be seen today in the Third World towns. Several different forms of transport appeared successively in the 19th century, bringing about a first series of changes in urban structures in Europe. In the first half of that century, horse-drawn omnibus networks appeared. At the same time, the first steam train lines began to run, which, for the first time in the history of humanity enabled people to leave the town centres if they wished and live further away, where life was less expensive, whilst still continuing to participate in their daily activities. London was the first city where this was seen, to the great admiration of the French press, which could not help making the comparison with Paris. The journal *La Nature* published the following in 1863: "In this way, many workers can leave the centre of London and go and live in less expensive areas. Think how useful this would be in Paris, where rents are killing the working classes"!

The second half of the 19th century saw the arrival of new modes of transport, with the first tram lines (originally drawn by horses), then the first underground railway line in London in 1863 (the Metropolitan Railway, which ran on steam), then the first underground railway line to run on electricity (again in London) in 1894. This gave the signal for the creation at the turn of the century of metropolitan railway lines in several large European cities—Berlin, Budapest, Paris, Hamburg, Glasgow—although they were still limited in number due to the cost of such structures. These networks were mainly underground, despite the peremptory remarks made by those who declared at the time that their contemporaries would never accept underground travel.

During the first half of the 20th century, suburban railway lines and, to a lesser extent, bus lines, had the strongest influence on changes in urban development, since they helped to create and expand the suburbs surrounding large towns. The increased use of the bicycle also participated in these changes by allowing homes to be built within a range of several kilometres from railway stations, and in this way also contributed to the spreading movement that had begun in the 19th century.

12.1.3 Increased Spreading

But these changes were nothing compared to the revolution to come in the second half of the 20th century, caused by the double phenomenon of the explosion in car ownership and the creation of urban and suburban motorways and expressways. As we have seen, it is now possible to cover considerable distances in just a few minutes, allowing housing, offices, factories, warehouses, shops, and other activities to be located tens of kilometres away from the old centre. Furthermore, whereas railway lines only provide access to areas close to stations, this is not the case for motorways and expressways. From their interchanges, most if not all of the outer suburban areas become open to urbanisation, as the car, contrary to the train, can continue its trip without having to change to another form of transport to travel on the ordinary road network. A 10-minute walk from a railway station serves an area of only 2 km^2. Ten minutes in a car from a motorway interchange may serve about 200 km^2!

Without people always realising it, land use patterns have completely changed in the last century and a half. Densely populated towns were first followed by large urban areas, with the creation of suburbs. These large urban areas are being succeeded, since about 20 years ago, by what can be called "living and employment basins" or "transport basins" covering an area of 30 or 40 km radius around the old town centre. In countries with a low or medium population density, these "basins" are separated from each other by rural areas with very few inhabitants. A map of the region densities looks rather like a leopard skin, with the living basins as the spots, the rest being the "deep country," or nearly deserted areas, only used for agricultural or ecological purposes (Figure 13).

But in densely populated countries with tightly knit urban networks, the main towns' living basins often join one another, or even sometimes share the same territory. It is possible to live in the suburbs of Brussels and work in the outskirts of Antwerp, to live close to Amsterdam and work in The Hague, and so forth. A vast continuum has thus been created in what is now a large part of West European territory.

12.1.4 The Diminution of Centres

Everywhere in Europe, this unprecedented spread of towns has decreased the weight of their central areas, ranging from welcome reliefs in housing and job densities to major declines due to a massive departure of inhabitants and shops, and even jobs. From 1970 to 1980, towns such as Antwerp, Birmingham, and Hamburg lost 8% of their population, whereas the figure reached 11% in Paris and 15% in Rotterdam, Copenhagen, or Liverpool, which decreased from 867,000 inhabitants in 1937 to 450,000 in 1991 [1]. From 1970 to 1990, Zurich lost 13% of its inhabitants, London 17%, and Helsinki 26%. From 1981 to 1993, Turin alone lost 170,000 inhabitants. What is more, these global figures do not really reflect how much more deeply this decrease affected the actual cores of these cities, even if for some of them the decline has now either slowed or stopped, as in London and Paris today.

Sometimes not only city centres but also the surrounding suburbs have witnessed a decline in their populations to the profit of more easily accessible outlying areas. It must be added that in many countries, the upper classes generally prefer to live far from centres, in a natural environment, and abandon the central parts of the urban areas to less wealthy categories of residents or to offices or shops, whereas in others, the attraction of living in the city centre remains strong for part of the population, thus splitting European towns into two distinct categories in this respect, the first being far more numerous than the second.

These changes have sometimes been the same for jobs, and many town centres have registered decreases in employment opportunities varying from 3 to 25% over 10 years, although this is not a general trend.

The situation is more varied for shops and stores. In many countries, the tendency towards spreading has been even more marked. While the decrease in the number of inhabitants and jobs in town centres continued, easily accessible, ultramodern shopping centres with vast parking facilities appeared on the outskirts of the urban areas, with France having taken the lead in that direction as the most "Americanized" European country in that respect. Some of these centres are spread out and customers must cover hundreds of metres to go from one store to another, but others are compact and, besides hypermarkets and large supermarkets, also include large numbers of specialised shops. They therefore provide their clients with a wide variety of products and services under excellent conditions and often at quite low prices, thus recreating a central function. It can be said that the modern shopping centres are reproducing a miniature town, where the user has access to everything she requires: insurance, travel agencies, banks, and so forth.

The phenomenon is similar to what already exists on a large scale in the United States, were there are no less than two hundred "edge cities," which have grown up on the outskirts of large urban areas and are in fact spontaneous new towns, with the major difference, however, that historic American centres have often fallen victim to decay, which is fortunately not usually the case in Europe. In other words, American towns do have centres, but they are not in the centre of the towns, which explains the confusion of Europeans who look for them there. It should be stressed again that the fact that American towns do not have the traditional centres that go to make up the charm of many European towns obviously comes from the fact that they are so recent.

As in Europe, the spread of numerous activities—business, jobs, and so forth—towards the outskirts of urban areas has had beneficial side effects as far as transport is concerned by making jobs closer to home, a goal that had long been sought after by most urban planners, and by reducing commuting times, enabling certain people to write: *"Suburbanisation is not the problem, but the solution"* [2]. It must be added that contrary to what is often said, there is no proof that the social life in low-density areas is less rich than that in dense ones, due to the existence of clubs, sports facilities, the number of meeting opportunities for adults and children, and so forth. In fact, there is no reliable study on the subject.

The only European countries that succeeded in slowing somewhat this decentralisation of shopping activities are those which, like Germany, implemented restrictive urban policies with regard to shops and stores, but this can give way to other kinds of disadvantages. In some cities, the historic town centre merely becomes an immense shopping and office zone and is devoid of life once the shops and offices close at night, as there are no permanent residents to bring it to life. It has been said as a joke that the only inhabitants who remain in the pedestrian precincts in certain town centres in the evening are the caretakers watching over closed shops and empty office buildings, as in Munich.

It must be added that the tendency to create outlying shopping centres and more generally to spread out activities, is even more marked when there are road and motorway ring roads that can drain tens or hundreds of thousands of potential customers within 20 minutes, who have easier access and better parking conditions than in traditional town centres. The construction of ring roads or bypass means that several points along the route can have a vocation to become centres. European cities can thus be classified into several categories, according to whether they have complete ring roads, incomplete ring roads, or no ring road or bypass at all, obliging traffic to converge on the town centre and making traffic problems much more difficult to solve. These differences have an important effect on travel patterns as ring roads completely change traffic flows.

But to some degree, all European urban areas are confronted with the general phenomenon of the spread in activities and lower density. This phenomenon of course has direct consequences on transport demand because if transport networks contribute towards shaping urban land use, this in turn dictates the demand for transport.

12.2 A SPREAD-OUT DEMAND FOR TRANSPORT

As we have seen in the preceding chapters, the recent demand trend for transport is, first of all, characterised by its physical growth, which is directly linked to the way activities are spreading outwards from the centre, and mobility is consequently increasing. In a country such as France, the average distance between the home and the workplace increased by 56% between 1975 and 1990 [3]. The length of other trips has also increased, as the car gradually replaced walking, buses, and two-wheeled vehicles. This has also happened in the other countries of Europe. The average distance between the home and the workplace was approximately 11 or 12 km as the crow flies in the 1980s in West Germany, France, Finland, Great Britain, The Netherlands, and so forth [4], with very high variation depending on occupation and sex. In France, for an average distance of 11.3 km from the home to the workplace in 1990, commuting distance was 10.8 km for male blue-collar workers, 11.3 km for white-collar employees, 22.4 km for technicians and engineers, and 26.9 km for executives, whereas women commuted, on average, half those distances, in part because of stronger family-related constraints [3].

But it is quite remarkable to note that because of the development in the use of the car, the increases in distances travelled (whatever the motive of the trips) were not accompanied by a corresponding increase in average trip times, which alone can truly measure the quality of service rendered and the impact on quality of life, and remain remarkably stable, contrary to public belief.

In summary, the combination of geographic spreading and the growth in car numbers and road networks explains that in all European urban areas, and *a fortiori* in their living basins, the car is now used for the great majority of motorised trips. The proportion varies from 90% or more in small towns to 66% in the Paris region and 62% in the London region, which are both extreme cases due to their high populations. In other words, these two cases excepted, the proportion of motorised daily trips by public transport in European urban areas is usually between only 10 and 25%, and trips by car account for 75 to 90%. The proportion of public transport is obviously higher when the destination is the town centre, as this is where it is the most efficient, especially for home-to-work commuting.

But now, everywhere in Europe, trips within central areas of urban centres, or to them, are a small minority compared with movements in the suburbs. In France, a study of trips in 24 of the largest urban areas showed that only 16% of them were internal to the centre, 20% between the centre and the suburbs, and 64% from suburb to suburb. If only motorised travel is considered, the proportions are 8%, 26%, and 66%, respectively [5]. In the Paris region, out of 22 million motorised daily trips, 3 million are internal to the city of Paris, 4 million take place between Paris and the suburbs, and 15 million (68%) take place between one suburb and another. The pattern is the same in almost all European cities. In addition, the only category of trips that is still increasing is generally the last, whereas movements within or to town centres normally vary very little, when they are not decreasing. In the Paris region, four million new trips from suburb to suburb are forecast for the coming years, and no increase in the other two categories of movements. Nevertheless, as travel from suburb to suburb is by nature more diffuse, less attention is focused on it than on those internal to the centre or between centre and suburb, which are naturally more concentrated.

Thus, despite the considerable disparities that exist among European towns, there are often striking similarities with respect to transport patterns, and this enables an understanding of the policies they usually follow.

12.3 TRANSPORT POLICIES FOR TOWN CENTRES

These policies differ, of course, according to whether they are aimed at the town centres or the suburbs. Faced with a loss of inhabitants, jobs, shopping facilities, and other activities that have often affected centres of the European cities, together with a deterioration in their living environment, most of them have tried to react in two different ways: by improving both their accessibility and their environment.

Of course, the policies implemented are extremely diverse, not only according to geographic constraints but also depending on financial means available and the regulatory power held by existing municipal, regional, and national institutions. The range of situations is extremely wide, with certain cities giving an example of what can be done by combining volontarist policies based on strong regulatory powers and powerful financial mode, whereas others have neither and are more or less obliged to let things take their course. Nevertheless, in all towns of a certain size, accessibility to the centre has to rely on both public transport and the car in varying proportions.

12.3.1 Public Transport for Town Centres

Public transport situations are very different. Certain urban areas inherited "own-site" (or "nonintersecting") networks from previous generations; that is, transport networks that are sheltered from traffic congestion as they have separate right of way. These can be railway lines, underground railway lines, trams, or own site buses. Some of these networks are limited, whereas others are so developed that their further extension would be difficult to justify. Other urban areas, on the other hand, possess very few public transport infrastructures, or even none at all, and would like to construct them insofar as this is possible. The great difficulty resides in the fact that it is very difficult to find intermediate solutions between the bus (very inexpensive as far as infrastructures are concerned, but usually at the mercy of general traffic conditions) and the own-site underground railways, trains, or trams that are protected from congestion but which generally provide too much capacity compared to needs and are very expensive to build.

This is why much effort is currently being made to find intermediate solutions. Technically, these range from the traditional tram to the tram with tyres, as well as "guided" buses or buses that can run either on an external electricity feed (like trolley buses) or with a normal engine. "Light" public transport of this sort is planned by many European towns. Also of importance are the own-site bus lines that are beginning to appear and can often provide the same or better service at a much lower cost than the other modes of transport that need a specific infrastructure. Is it not true that the traffic on certain own-site bus routes reaches 20,000 passengers per hour in several towns in South America? One of such bus lines exists in the Paris area, with around 30,000 passengers per day (Trans-Val de Marne).

Mention can also be made of the French "SK" continuous transport system that will soon be in operation at Charles de Gaulle Airport in Paris and can be suitable for relatively short links.

Whatever the technology used, it is desirable for public transport to have, when possible, its own site, distinct from the road used by cars, for all or part of the route. European cities differ enormously in this respect. Some, which planned their urban development long ago, have wide boulevards at their disposal in their outskirts, where it is relatively inexpensive to install complete or partial own-site public transport routes to be used by buses, trams, or even metros or railways. In such cases, or where historical or geographical circumstances have left free spaces (for instance, along old railway lines or river banks), it is only in the most central part of the town where it may be necessary to create underground infrastructures, which would therefore be limited in length. And even this is not necessarily indispensable, since trams or buses can locally join the general road traffic.

But other towns are not able to do this because their urban fabric is practically continuous, and the only possible solution is to create a rail public transport network that is under ground for all or most of its route. The cost of creating such underground networks is so high that they can only be built where vast financial means are available. Their cost is in the range of 50 to 100 million ECUs per kilometre and it is impossible to expect them to be financially profitable for reasons that will be explained below, whereas their capacity, which can reach 30,000 to 50,000 passengers per hour and per direction (sometimes even more), is almost always in no proportion whatsoever to needs, as these rarely exceed a few thousand passengers. This explains why it has long been said that the construction of an underground railway network is only justified in Europe for towns of over a million inhabitants. (The World Bank even set this limit at 5 million people for developing countries.)

But this "rule" is not at all systematic. Certain urban areas in Europe with several million inhabitants would justify the construction of underground railway networks but do not have them yet, either because they are located in a country with a relatively low gross domestic product or because the political authorities have not yet had sufficient will to find the corresponding financial means. In other countries, on the contrary, specific financial resources allow towns with populations well below one million inhabitants to create one or several underground railway lines. But this is far from being frequent due to the high cost of building this type of infrastructure. Nevertheless, the trend in Europe is towards the construction of new networks—either light transport or regular undergrounds—in a growing number of cities. In 1996, there are 31 regular underground railway networks (metros) in operation in Western Europe [6] and far more light transport ones.

These light transports—trams, own-site buses, and so forth—can cost less than regular undergrounds when there is not too much construction work involved, with costs per kilometre, for example, in the range of 20 to 40 million ECUs, which can justify their creation in urban areas with a few hundred thousand inhabitants. In France, the aim today is to try to decrease the cost to under 10 million ECUs per kilometre. In order to decrease investment costs, some European towns are also currently trying to use existing railway lines, to be used by trams capable of travelling at high speeds for long-distance suburban travel. In other places (that is, in the great majority of towns where the population is lower than 200 to 300,000 inhabitants) only the traditional bus is possible and realistic, with possibly some improvements and restructuring in certain places to give them, for example, among other things, the right of way at cross-roads.

12.3.2 Road Accessibility for Town Centres

To improve accessibility to central parts of urban areas, it is not enough to build, when possible, good public transport networks. It is just as necessary, and often more so, to be able to reach the historic centre easily by car as many professional, commercial, and residential activities depend on its use, particularly as old town centres are now in competition with outlying areas where it is often easier to drive and park. If the traditional centre does not want to decline in the face of this competition from the outlying areas, it must also be accessible by car to a large part (often the majority) of its residents and users. It must not be forgotten that cars also bring life.

This is all the more important because, as we have seen, the possibilities of substitution among modes of transport are limited: the car is practically indispensable to a number of users, especially those who come from areas that are not densely populated and therefore, by nature, have limited public transport services. It is also the case for those who do not want to abandon individual transport because it saves them considerable amounts of time, and for the large numbers of people who use their car during the day for professional reasons. It must be emphasised that intermodality (i.e., using several successive modes of transport), can only be a stopgap as far as service is concerned, even if it is sometimes necessary in the largest cities. Intermodality is by nature subject to breaks between transport modes, in addition to waiting and walking, which, except in special cases, can only make travel long and uncomfortable. For this reason, Europeans logically choose unimodality whenever they can, and not intermodality. In France, 92.1% of home-to-work trips are made using a single mode of transport, including walking, 5.3% by two modes of transport, and 2.6% by three or more modes [7]. This is easily understandable. In the first case, the average trip time is 18 minutes; in the second, 45 minutes; and in the third, over 72 minutes.

This is why "park and ride" type solutions must only be considered as a last resort, and in practice can only be a real—and limited—success in a very few large "megalopoles."

As in the case of public transport, the existing road networks and the possibilities of creating new high-capacity roads to give access to the central part of an urban area are extremely variable from one European town to another. For some, good urban planning policies or favourable geographic conditions have reserved the space needed for construction at a relatively low cost. For others, however, new urban roads would be extremely expensive or impossible to construct on the surface at present due to opposition from inhabitants living in the areas in question. In such cases, historic town centres will see their relative importance within the urban area diminish, sometimes to the point of becoming marginal. Some towns, especially those on the Mediterranean that were unable to create the road structures necessary for easy access to their historic centres, have seen them decline, deserted by their inhabitants, shops, and other activities, and are now obliged to implement policies to "reconquer" them. In others, such as London, their economic development itself is somewhat handicapped by traffic problems and transport problems in general. A number of European cities, by giving public transport too high a priority and restricting or forbidding car access to their centres, ran into trouble, with inhabitants leaving and shopping activities decreasing and deteriorating.

Fortunately, due to considerable efforts made over the last few decades, very many European cities do have satisfactory road networks allowing, amongst other purposes, easy access to their centres. These centres are sometimes surrounded by a small-size ring road that distributes traffic coming from outside and protects them by avoiding unnecessary entrance from those who do not need to enter, thus considerably alleviating inside traffic flow.

It must be added that if they were not remodelled in the 19th century with the construction of large boulevards, or destroyed during the Wars, the historical centres of European towns traditionally only reserve a very small part of their land surfaces to roads and streets. The corresponding percentages are sometimes only just over 10%, a ratio that was well adapted to walking but is completely insufficient to enable the use of the car, for which it can be considered that a level of about 25% is necessary. The phenomenon is the same in many developing countries, and explains why towns such as Mexico City, Buenos-Aires, Seoul, Bangkok, and so forth are saturated with three times fewer vehicles than in most European towns, at least in the absence of a network of high-capacity motorways.

This is why the very large urban areas in developing countries, which will be the world largest in population terms in the 21st century, need to plan as soon as possible their future transport networks and especially to purchase, as of now, the stretches of land necessary to enable them to criss-cross their present outskirts with corridors where they could be able to introduce both motorways and own-site transport systems at the appropriate moment. A grid of about 3-km intervals between such corridors, each being 80m wide could be a reasonable choice and cover only 5% of the land [8].

12.3.3 Parking in Town Centres

It is not enough to have access to centres; cars also need to be able to park there. The number of vehicles that can travel to a central area is directly linked to parking capacity, its accessibility, and its turnover. Two contradictory pitfalls are to be avoided in this respect. The first is that of insufficient parking spaces, which often characterises old town centres and lowers accessibility. The second is that of too many parking spaces, which results in congestion on the network providing access to the centre, especially during rush hours. In fact, three types of needs must be distinguished as far as parking is concerned.

The first concerns residents. Certain categories of the population, such as the elderly or certain students, do not need a car, especially when efficient public transport networks exist. But this is far from being the general rule, and it is necessary to plan a sufficient number of residential parking spaces in order to maintain a balanced population in central areas, especially for households with children. The prohibitive cost of building underground car parks—usually from 25,000 to 40,000 ECUs per space—often makes it impossible to systematically eliminate residents' parking at the surface in the old quarters. It should be added that the fact that residents can park their cars easily is not always sufficient a reason to guarantee that town centres will be inhabited by a large, diversified population as in certain countries the attraction of the individual house and, more generally speaking, suburban housing that is closer to nature, is too great.

The second type of need is linked to commercial and professional activities, for which an appropriate number of parking spaces must be calculated on the understanding that paying parking spaces result in a high vehicle turnover in town centres, therefore ensuring an optimum use of available spaces. Everybody knows the expression "no parking, no business," even if for some shops and in the centre of large towns there can be partial exceptions.

The third type of need is linked to home-to-work commuting. The proportion of people who commute by car is obviously directly linked to the number of parking spaces available for them. This is the need many European towns are focusing on. They must take into account the fact that street parking spaces are paying, as this makes it practically impossible for those who do not have a reserved parking space to use their car to commute to work. For this reason, most European towns require a minimum number of off-road parking spaces to be created whenever office buildings are built, providing a very sizeable advantage to those allowed to use them. But some have adopted the opposite policy in order to discourage use of the car, and have set a very strict ceiling on the number of parking spaces that office building promoters are authorised to construct. And it is true only parking can presently regulate demand, since for almost all trips except those aiming at the very centre of a limited number of large cities, experience has shown that the car is the quickest mode of transport, the most comfortable, and therefore the most attractive.

No general rules can be set in this matter, and optimum decisions depend on the size and geography of the towns and the capacity of the road networks serving the areas in question. But it must not be forgotten that any change from the car towards public transport results in an increase in commuting times for those who have to change, even if it does alleviate traffic for those who continue to use their car. As the OECD has rightly observed [9]: "It is not easy to make the majority of employees accept transport conditions that are not as good as before." It might be added that it is clearly best to make sure that the game is worth the candle before taking such action.

This, together with the risks that housing, offices, shops, and so forth will move to the outlying areas where parking generally poses no problem, implies that careful thought must be given when making decisions. Each particular situation has its own constraints for achieving balance and optimisation. The decisions to be made are obviously not the same in the case of the centre of an urban area with several million inhabitants with a mediocre road network, or a town with a few hundred thousand inhabitants with a satisfactory motorway network, for which there is no valid reason to prevent the majority of the workers from making the most of the considerable advantages offered by the use of the car, in timesaving and therefore in quality of life.

12.3.4 Traffic Calming

Parking policies in town centres can be different, but there is nonetheless one issue on which practically all European towns agree. Policies for restructuring the street network to improve the way in which it is used by its various kinds of users are, with differing degrees of importance, gradually being implemented everywhere. For too long, policies were aimed at one objective alone, which was to ease road vehicle traffic and parking as much as possible. Roadways were widened and pavements made narrower, when they were not completely taken over by cars parked upon them.

In many European town centres, another vision of things is being introduced in the form of "traffic calming" policies. When affordable, parking is wholly or partially removed from streets to underground or elevated car parks. Pedestrians are given more space, either by enlarging the pavements or by reserving certain streets or quarters of the town for them, or by creating mixed or semipedestrian malls where only limited traffic is allowed. Public transport is being given priority along some main routes. In Italy, for instance, there are 40 cities with limited traffic areas. When circumstances allow it, even two-wheeled vehicles are regaining rights they lost long ago.

It must be noted nevertheless that the total ban on cars is not a solution. Three or four decades ago the fashion was for total segregation, following theories established between the two Wars, which particularly entailed the creation of elevated areas for pedestrians in the new districts, with the car being confined to a lower level, both for traffic and parking. The idea was doubtless appealing, but except in one or two cases, the results turned out to be catastrophic. In several places attempts are made today to reintroduce the car in such pedestrian areas, which had become veritable "no man's lands" at night. The car may have certain disadvantages, but, as underlined earlier, it does also bring life.

There is also a new approach towards the roads that remain accessible to cars. Whereas in the past the different types of urban roads (streets, avenues, boulevards, etc.) were not differentiated and were used at the same time for long-, medium-, and short-distance travel, the present idea is to organise the roads into a hierarchy. The road network is usually split into four categories according to whether their function is traffic flow, distribution, access, or strictly residential. The roads and streets are then dealt with differently. The first type is equipped to drain large quantities of vehicles at relatively high speeds, whereas at the opposite end of the scale everything is done to ensure that the car remains as discreet as possible and drives at slow speeds so that pedestrians and possibly cyclists are given real priority. There are many ways to obtain such results—roundabouts, twist-and-turn obstacles, cul-de-sacs, narrowed roads, changes in road surface, and so forth. Speed limits must also be different according to the role attributed to each road category. But road hierarchy policies, which can lead to quite high restructuring costs, can only be implemented progressively as part of a consistent strategy to find the right balance between the different modes of transport—walking, public transport, the car, and, possibly, the bicycle.

The principles of this kind of network hierarchy policy do not only apply to town centres, but are just as valid for the suburbs, especially residential areas. Some countries have even created limited areas where the car is only just tolerated and is limited to speeds of about 10 km/h, thus giving a very high degree of safety for pedestrians and cyclists. Such zones were invented and are now widespread in the Netherlands, where they are known as "Woonerfs" or "cocoon areas," and it can only be wished that they will continue to spread to other places.

12.3.5 Bicycles

There are considerable differences between countries as far as bicycles are concerned. In most of Europe, the bicycle has disappeared as a mode of transport and is only used as a free-time activity. But there are exceptions. In some countries, especially Germany, Denmark, Switzerland, and particularly the Netherlands, the bicycle occupies an important place in the field of transport. Two to four percent of the French, the British, or the Italians go to work daily by bicycle, but the proportion reaches 10% in Germany and 32% in the Netherlands!

A more in-depth analysis reveals that the use of the bicycle overlaps with walking, public transport, and use of the car, for trips of about 1 to 6 km, which in their absence represent a significant proportion of the number of car trips even if, in travelled distance, they obviously represent only a very small fraction.

The question is whether the experience of the above-mentioned countries can be transferred to others. Obviously, it cannot be in places where topography is too varied to use the bicycle comfortably for everyday use, thus eliminating a large proportion of European cities. In the rare towns in the Netherlands that are not completely flat, the bicycle is little used. Moreover, massive use of the bicycle in urban areas requires specific arrangements for obvious reasons of safety and convenience. These have always existed in the Netherlands, where a far-seeing urban policy gave birth to a network outside city centres consisting of wide corridors with enough room to make specific bicycle lanes and routes for public transport and still leave enough space for cars. Unfortunately, the situation is very different in many other countries of Europe, especially the Mediterranean ones, which do not have the same traditions, meaning that bicycles are usually forced to fend for themselves on narrow, heavily used roads, with the obvious adverse consequences in terms of comfort and safety.

Therefore, even if the use of bicycles should be encouraged, especially in medium-sized towns, it is probable that its use will remain modest in most European towns compared to the success it has in the Netherlands and, to a lesser degree, in some other European countries. It has to be added that in some cities with very dense public transport networks, there is no real need nor room for an additional transport means. In Paris, the creation in 1996 and 1997 of reserved lanes for cyclists in the main arteries just resulted in an increase in traffic jams. According to surveys, 70% of the almost negligible number of cyclists using the lanes would have used public transport rather than cars if they had not chosen the bicycle, and 20% would have walked [13].

It is important to realise that whatever the case may be, the bicycle or walking can by definition only be used for short trips. Even when they may concern a significant percentage of trips, their possible development can therefore only have a slight influence on the number of kilometres travelled by motorised transport modes.

12.4 TRANSPORT POLICIES FOR SUBURBAN AREAS

12.4.1 A Near Monopoly for the Car

Transport problems in the suburbs are usually quite different from those in city centres. The car is so dominant that except for very short trips that can be made on foot or perhaps by bicycle, it has a near monopoly in most West European countries whenever it is a question of travelling from suburb to suburb, especially along bypass or ring road routes. This is not in the least surprising. Densities for this kind of trip are far too low to justify the creation of independent, own-site public transport lines—underground railways, trams, or even buses using reserved lanes—if they do not already exist. This is because away from centres, average traffic demand decreases drastically.

Admittedly, inhabitants of suburban areas often think that if "suitable" modes of public transport existed, they would be sure to use them. But, on taking a closer look, it is found that the term "suitable" often has a very specific meaning in their eyes. They actually want a mode of "public" transport that would pick them up at their doorstep, would drop them off right at their destination, at any time of day or night, without any waiting or any transfers, in good, comfortable conditions. Without realising it, they are in fact redefining individual transport and in particular that by car. It is in fact impossible to create public transport networks in the suburbs, and even less so in the outer suburbs, that correspond to the wishes expressed above for the simple reason that there is usually only one person who leaves one point for another at a given moment in time. According to a report on urban transport from the World Bank [10]: "There is no example in the world of a rail ring route that performs well, as the passengers are too scattered." This is easy to understand. If the average population density of a suburban district is 20 times lower than a central district, exchange between two areas with an equivalent surface area will be *400 times* lower, all else being equal.

It must be stated that contrary to popular opinion, there is nothing shocking about the fact that the average number of occupants per car is very low and rarely exceeds one or two people. It is the direct result of the above observation, which explains why there has been such limited success from efforts to establish car-pools, even though they should be encouraged whenever the circumstances allow it. An experiment carried out in the Netherlands in 1995 that consisted in reserving a motorway lane for vehicles using a "car-pool" system was an obvious failure. Today, the car is above all a mode of individual transport, and if it is built with a capacity of 4 to 5 occupants instead of 1 or 2, this is only because there is hardly any extra cost in doing so, and that it can be very useful once every so often to be able to make use of four or five seats.

For the great majority of inhabitants of the inner and outer suburbs, the need to use a car is not a disadvantage under the present economic conditions in Europe. Quite logically, it is in these areas that most households with two, even three or more cars, can be found, so that each adult family member has access to one.

12.4.2 The Minorities

Nevertheless, two categories of the population do not fit this framework. The first consists of children and adolescents who do not yet have their driving licence. There are various different solutions for their movements: their parents, public transport if such is available, special school buses, and finally, light, two-wheeled vehicles for adolescents, which then often pose difficult safety problems. The first solution, in particular when the children are dropped off at school by a parent or neighbour, is developing very rapidly in Western Europe.

The second category is the minority of the population that does not have a car, either because they cannot afford it or because they cannot or do not want to drive, which is often the case with the elderly, although more and more often, these do have a driving licence and continue driving much longer than before, even though Europe is not yet in the same situation as America where only 10% of households do not have a car.

Many of these people can, however, use the car as passengers in the vehicle of a family member or friend, although some do not have this option. Nevertheless, the relatively small number of people concerned, together with their low mobility, does not justify traditional, permanent, frequent public transport networks for their benefit, as these would be condemned to running empty most of the time. This is a real problem, and a growing number of communities are trying to find imaginative solutions such as operating minibus services with flexible itineraries or that travel on request, or distributing "taxi coupons" to the persons concerned, which is often easier and far cheaper than operating permanent public transport networks, and with a higher quality of service. A quick, obviously theoretical, calculation shows that an urban area with one million inhabitants that devotes 150 million ECUs per year to operating its public transport system could, for the same amount, pay for a trip in a taxi costing 7 ECUs for 100,000 people, or 10% of its population, all age groups included, every working day of the year.

It would be contrary to the European tradition of solidarity if efforts were not made to find a solution for those otherwise condemned to isolation because they do not have access to a car, especially since the numbers of adults in question are decreasing with the gradual disappearance of the generations that did not know to drive. Fortunately, experience also shows that people who cannot or do not want to own a car make a spontaneous effort to live close to a mode of public transport or in central parts of urban areas.

It must be added that some European countries (Sweden, for example) have mastered their suburban planning to such an extent that most new collective housing is built near suburban railway stations, giving the residents immediate access to rapid and comfortable public transport. But such a result presupposes a certain number of conditions that do not exist in most European countries, particularly concerning sufficient control over land use, which is out of the question when there are a number of local authorities competing with each other to attract housing, office buildings, shops, and all kinds of other activities. It must be added that, overall, the measures taken in Sweden do not stop people from using the car for most of their needs, and that the majority of Swedish people nevertheless live in individual homes.

12.4.3 Suburban Road Networks

Generally speaking, only the car is capable of responding to the great majority of the travel needs of inhabitants in outer suburban areas, either as drivers or passengers. It is therefore necessary to create or develop the roads needed to ensure proper traffic flow, and consequently provide a smooth-running economy and a satisfactory quality of life for the inhabitants. As a general rule, the task is far from impossible in the suburbs and even less so in the outer suburban areas, where abundant space is available for road building.

Of course, far more precautions must be taken now than in the past to ensure that new roads do as little harm as possible to the environment, by accepting the corresponding additional costs. But physically, the capacity of motorways and expressways is considerable, so that except for the centres of the largest urban areas, they can continuously and definitively satisfy all road transport needs as long as they are constructed with the proper dimensions. In other words, there is no problem of "sustainability." In many cities, it is not rare to see a motorway with three lanes in each direction used by 110,000 cars per day, thus transporting over 160,000 people, as well as 15,000 commercial vehicles transporting several thousands tonnes of freight. In very large urban areas, even higher figures are often reached, with daily traffic in certain exceptional cases amounting to 16 times the peak hour traffic. In such situations, average annual daily traffic on six lane (2 x 3) motorways can exceed 150,000 vehicles per day. On the south part of the Paris Boulevard Périphérique, it even goes up to 180,000! Overall, the European record is being held by the Paris region where, on two jointly parallel motorways with three lanes each way (A6a and A6b motorways) total traffic reaches nearly 300,000 vehicles per day! Transport studies, which traditionally comprise four phases—trip generation, distribution, modal split, and traffic assignment—allow specialists to calculate quite accurately for each agglomeration the optimum size of motorway and expressway networks necessary to deal with present and future traffic flow and to plan them in consequence.

Hundreds of medium and large European towns have already succeeded in eliminating serious traffic problems outside central areas thanks to proper public works, when they have been capable of implementing an appropriate road investment programme. Due to the huge capacity of motorways, congestion is not inevitable. Even in the Paris region with its 11 million inhabitants, studies have shown that it was perfectly possible to deal with future road demands in a sustainable way through an acceptable, financeable investment programme [11], considering that a very good public transport network is already in place, mainly adapted for access to the city central area and travel within it. Admittedly, in the absence of congestion tolls, the Paris region, as is the case for all the large cities in Europe, has significant traffic jams during rush hours. But, as we have seen, the cost of the additional time spent due to them is actually low in comparison to the overall turnover of the road transport system.

In fact, overall, as in the other countries in Europe and contrary to widespread opinion, the transport situation has not deteriorated in France in recent years. From 1981 to 1994, the average trip time, all modes of transport taken together, remained at 17 minutes, whereas the "time budget" devoted by the French on average each day for travelling was slightly reduced, from 57 to 54 minutes. As travelled distances were increased by 40% between these two dates, the average speed increased on the other hand from 19 to 26 km/h on a national level [12]. Yet, in France as elsewhere, most of the population lives in urban areas or on their outskirts.

But more and more often, the real obstacle that hinders necessary road projects is psychological and political. As we have seen, a large part of the population as well as political decision-makers assume that building new, additional roads or increasing the capacity of existing roads cannot possibly satisfy new demand.

According to an International Public Transport Union (UITP) opinion poll, 50% of the European population considers that it is the roads themselves that create traffic, and only 50% believe that new roads would allow better driving conditions. In the Paris region, only 40% share the latter belief, whereas 60% consider the opposite to be true [13]. Everyone has a spontaneous tendency to project the high traffic growth rates of the past few decades into the future and imagine that there is no solution and that "we are heading for a brick wall." This is only true for the cities that have obviously underinvested in their road systems. The difference is striking, for example, between Athens, with almost no motorways, and Barcelona, with its superb network, which completely changed for the best traffic conditions in the city. The difference is also striking between Paris, which has a high-density motorway network, and London, which lacks one.

12.4.4 Four Positive Factors

Several positive factors show that there is no need to be pessimistic about the future if the right decisions are made, even if, locally, new infrastructures can awaken a latent demand that was not satisfied previously.

The first essential point is based on the fact that traffic demand cannot grow indefinitely. As we have seen, 80% of those who use a motorised form of transport to commute to work use the car in the large countries of Europe. This percentage will obviously not rise to 160%! During rush hours, the majority of European workers are already behind the wheel. Admittedly, the average distances travelled can still increase somewhat, thus leading to an increase in traffic. But from now on, it can only be a question of moderate and "manageable" increase because, fortunately, no one can drive two cars at the same time, and we have seen that average travel times remained surprisingly stable.

The second factor, which has already been emphasised, is that demand for new trips is closely linked to geographic changes in the population, jobs, and other activities: it is spreading outwards and is continually moving towards outer urban areas where it is easier to increase road capacity. In central parts of West Europeans towns and urban areas, travel needs are consequently often tending to stagnate or even decrease, both for road traffic and public transport. Trips are not generated spontaneously and are more a consequence of where people live and work rather than of transport network capacity. It is most significant that road traffic has been steady for 15 years in the city of Paris proper; that it decreased by 6% in the centre of Frankfurt between 1988 and 1994, and by 5% in the centre of Hamburg between 1988 and 1993; and that it has also recently decreased in the centres of Copenhagen, Munich, Milan, Lyons, Bordeaux, Lille, Toulouse, and so forth. Many other European towns are subject to the same trends, particularly as new routes have been created to bypass the centres and inner traffic flows have been controlled by good parking management. This is an extremely important point. *Traffic is no longer increasing in the centre of large European cities. Traffic flow there is now steady and is often decreasing.* A balance has progressively been found between the places people live and work and the way they travel, as well as among the different mode of transport. In town centres, the worst is usually over. Yet public opinion is rarely conscious of this new situation.

In certain European town centres, traffic speed has even stopped decreasing, and sometimes slightly increases. In the centre of Paris, it rose from 17 km/h in 1988 to 18.5 km/h in 1992 [14]. For French town centres overall, it increased from 20.3 km/h in 1981 to 20.7 km/h in 1994 for trips within the centres [15]. The improvement was even more spectacular in Madrid, with 21 km/h in 1988 and 26 km/h in 1994 [16]. In inner London, between 1988 and 1994 the average speed increased from 18.8 km/h to 20.2 km/h(+7%) in peak morning traffic, from 21.4 km/h to 22.1 km/h(+3%) in off-peak periods, and from 18.3 km/h to 19.6 km/h(+7%) in the peak evening period [17]. Even though there was a very slight deterioration in the very heart of London during the same period, the overall evolution is positive. In London as in Paris, the results were partly influenced by the introduction of "red routes" regulations, which improved traffic flow on certain main roads.

The similarity of speeds on streets in urban areas in Paris, London, Madrid, or elsewhere, reaching about 20 km/h, calls for another remark, as these speeds are very different from the average trip speeds on expressways and motorways, which are far higher.

On the motorway with the heaviest traffic in the Paris Region—the *Boulevard Périphérique*—the average speed is 53 km/h. It is even far higher still on the other motorways. On most urban motorway type infrastructures, there are really only two different types of driving conditions: slow traffic during peak hours and very smooth traffic for the great majority of the time.

This observation explains how a large number of European urban areas work. They consist in "islands" with an area of a few square kilometres, with traditional streets and roads where it is practically impossible to drive at high speed whatever the time of day, which are bordered by motorways where, except in peak periods, the traffic normally flows in excellent conditions, at high speeds and with a considerable capacity, given that the "peak" periods vary in duration depending on the towns (but are often far shorter than is imagined). In fact, it is the duration of the peak periods that is the right criteria with which to appreciate traffic situations. Only urban areas that do not have this "criss-crossing" of expressways or motorways obviously have great traffic problems and have a much more pessimistic view of road transport than the others.

It should be said that, contrary to the United States, which defined a coherent planning policy for its urban road networks about 40 years ago [18], there was obviously no equivalent in Europe where each country acted independently from the others. Certain countries developed policies on the subject very early on, as France, [19], but others did not, so that if geographical and economic discrepancies are also taken into consideration, very different situations prevail today.

It has to be added that the existence of transport networks providing the unicity of large urban areas is a very important factor in terms of productivity. Certain studies have shown that the productivity of "megalopoles" was usually 20 to 40% higher than for the rest of the national territory due to the size of their job market [20].

Another positive factor concerns the spread of trips throughout the day. Those that are presently developing are less concentrated in certain times of the day than existing trips. New movements are usually for personal matters, leisure activities, shopping, and so forth, they often use the household's second or third car, they can easily be made outside rush hours, and the driver has more easily the choice of their destination. Trips to and from work now account for less than a quarter of total daily trips. On the basis that most road networks are built to accommodate rush-hour commuting needs, they can obviously allow traffic to flow smoothly and freely the rest of the time. The growth in work-at-home jobs may also contribute to this positive trend.

A final positive factor is linked to progressive improvement in existing road capacities. This can be the result, in many cases, of an increase in the number of lanes—if necessary by the partial or total elimination of the hard shoulder, replacing it with an additional traffic lane, which can significantly increase the capacity of existing motorways. That was the case in 1996 in the Netherlands with the A28 motorway, where the experiment was, according to the local press, a "complete triumph" [21]. If necessary, such an addition can justify a reduction in the width of traffic lanes, which optimises the use of existing roadways whilst also reducing emissions of pollutants by improving traffic flow. But increases in the capacity of road networks can also be the result of the implementation of technical equipment.

The installation of "intelligent" technology to control traffic lights in dense urban environments, which takes into account traffic density at every given moment and reacts in consequence, can often increase capacity by 20 to 30%, as witnessed by the inextricable traffic jams that arise when the equipment breaks down.

As seen in the previous chapter, an increase in capacity and flowing conditions can also be expected on the expressway and motorway network, following the implementation of "intelligent" techniques.

Finally, a curious phenomenon must be mentioned that has been noted in the United States: Motorway lane capacity is growing all by itself with time. Whereas it consisted there of a maximum of around 2,000 vehicles per hour and per lane in 1985 for speeds of approximately 60 km/h, it has reached 2,200 vehicles per hour in 1994 for speeds of around 90 km/h, and it is considered that it will increase to 2,400 vehicles per hour in the year 2000, for a "natural" increase in capacity by 20% in 15 years, with much higher travelling speeds [22]!

This is probably the result of three factors: the growing similarity in the technical achievements of vehicles, which are all powerful enough today to merge into traffic without difficulty; the great uniformity of speeds on American roads, which obviously favours an even flow of dense traffic and is particularly favourable to safety conditions; and finally, the changes in the behaviour of drivers in high-density traffic.

The same can be found in Europe. The Paris ring road, the *Boulevard Périphérique*, increased the capacity of its three-lane southern section from 6,080 vehicles per hour in 1979 to 6,690 in 1994, an increase of approximately 10%, and saturation speed equally increased during the same period [23].

At any rate, the experience of the last few years does not show a general worsening in traffic conditions in Europe, even if there are local problems for which action must be taken. In Great Britain itself, the national average car trip has varied little in 16 years, increasing from 18 minutes in 1976 to 20 in 1992 [24], while average speed increased from 22 mph to 26 [25]. In French provincial towns, which have generally had the advantage of considerable road improvement work, the trend is even towards an improvement in trip durations (Figure 8).

The spread over a wider suburban area and the extension of road networks explains these surprising results, which clearly show, if needed, that roads do not create congestion.

But the existence of these different positive factors cannot be serve as a pretext to conclude that it is not worthwhile to undertake new road projects or increase the capacity of existing networks. The medium term gains that can be hoped to be achieved through possible improvements in traffic management are limited and can only be a temporary remedy if demand increases significantly. Only the construction of new roads of sufficient capacity or the enlargement of existing roads will then stop the situation from degenerating. In fact, all is the matter of competition between the increase in traffic, now moderate and spread out, and road capacity. Contrary to what is frequently stated, and for the reasons mentioned above, there is no reason to think that this competition should be lost. An objective analysis of the present situation and the forecasts for evolution in traffic usually lead to the opposite conclusion.

Every kilometre of motorway constructed or enlarged thus represents thousands of hours saved and/or an increase in the opportunities for exchanges and activities offered to individuals and companies. Every kilometre of motorway that is prevented from being constructed results on the other hand in thousands of hours being lost and/or in restrictions on opportunities for exchanges, and therefore has negative effects on the quality of life and the running of the economy.

It is not a coincidence if urban motorways, when well-designed, often have a very high return from an economic point of view, and are therefore one of the best possible investments for the community, and that on the contrary much time and money is wasted if they are not built.

Nevertheless, in certain European countries, the resistance from residents living in areas where new road projects are planned is so strong that any real expansion of the road network is presently practically impossible to implement. These countries are moving towards a significant decline in economic efficiency together with a decrease in the quality of life of their inhabitants due to inevitable road congestion and restrictions on movement and the resulting loss of opportunities, which will often affect some of the exact people who are today opposing the needed infrastructures.

It must be added that many decision-makers and opinion-makers work and sometimes live in town centres, and often have no idea of how the great majority of their fellow citizens live, and are ignorant of the fact that their activities are almost exclusively located in the suburbs or outer suburban areas. It is for this reason that some regions, such as Paris, currently devote about two-thirds of their transport investment resources to the construction of new underground and railway lines in the city centre, where demand is decreasing, and not to the construction of outer suburban motorways, where needs are growing constantly, even if certain major road works are there in progress.

12.5 PUBLIC TRANSPORT FINANCING

From a financial point of view, public transport infrastructures and road infrastructures are very different.

Public transport infrastructures can practically never be self-financing. Nearly always, operations for these transport networks are in deficit themselves, obviously leaving no margin for infrastructure financing should it be necessary.

12.5.1 Public Transport Operations Financing

The percentage of operating expenditure covered by fare revenues varies greatly from one country to another and even within one country. According to the Janes'

Urban Transport report, the coverage rate in 1995 was 96% in Dublin; 79% in London; 75% in Madrid; 62% in Lisbon; 52% in Copenhagen; 45% in Frankfurt; 40% in Vienna; 33% in Brussels, Paris, and Stockholm; 27% in Amsterdam and Athens; and 10% in Rome. This is very different from other areas of economic activity and calls for investigation into the causes. Why are users not asked to pay the "true cost" of their trip by public transport and why are network operations and investments so often highly subsidised in one way or another?

Several answers are possible, and they are not exclusive one from the other. First of all, in most towns the competent authorities hesitate to raise public transport fares because it is reputedly used by the poorest social classes. Without being entirely untrue, this statement should sometimes be qualified. Of course, there are residents in all cities who do not have access to a car and must therefore use public transport over large distances when necessary. But in large urban areas with good public transport networks, the choice of mode of transport is often linked to the characteristics of the trip—its point of departure and destination—rather than the social category of the person travelling. Not only the poorer social classes are found among users of public transport networks, but also many executives and employees who could pay much higher prices than those normally paid, but who do not use their cars, either because they do not have a parking space or because they do not wish to. In many cases in Western Europe, such users are even in the majority [26]. This is less true in small and medium-sized towns, which have only bus services and where parking is more readily available.

Another reason for the low fares generally applied to public transport stems from the fact that, allowing for exceptions, users have long, tiring door-to-door trips and that, despite all the efforts that have been made, passengers often need to transfer, wait, and walk relatively long distances. It is difficult to ask a high price for a service that is essentially of relatively low quality by itself.

High subsidies are also granted with the often-expressed desire to influence users towards using public transport instead of the car. However, international comparisons have not revealed any link between the amount of operating subsidies granted to public transport and the proportion of trips they carry out, which generally tends to decrease with time as more and more people have access to cars. Some studies have shown, on the other hand, that the network operating costs increased in proportion to increases in subsidies due to management inefficiencies [27].

There is one final, paradoxical issue that must be mentioned. The existence of high subsidies for suburban rail transport encourages the residential development of areas located at long distances from the main town centre, and experience shows that it is these residents who use the car the most! In other words, it is not impossible that one of the consequences of high subsidies to public transport may be in some cases an increase in road traffic, an assumption that has led executive directors close to the German Social Democrat Party (the Friedrich-Ebert Foundation), for instance, to recommend the elimination of subsidies to any form of transport.

In summary, it is striking to note the enormous differences between the different European countries' policies on public transport financing for both operations and infrastructure investments. They appear to show that there is plenty of room to manoeuvre for those who wish to reduce the public financing burden.

The Exception: United Kingdom and London

The high coverage rate for operating costs obtained by the British authorities in the London area indicates that, at least for the very large cities with extensive public transport networks and high numbers of users, operating accounts can come near to being balanced. It must be said that the policy followed in Great Britain since 1985, introducing legislation to "deregulate" public transport, has resulted in large savings in operating costs and has consequently reduced the need for public financing. It has also resulted in an increase in minibus lines. They are less costly than traditional buses and now account for 13% of kilometres provided, against 1% previously. Outside London, overall employee productivity rose by 34%, and operating costs, excluding depreciation, decreased by 45% per vehicle kilometre. The percentage of households having access to a bus service running at least every 15 minutes rose from 30% to 40% in seven years [25]. As we have seen previously (Chapter 7), the results achieved in London itself were particularly spectacular in terms of user service and reductions in government spending. The experiment in London proved to be more successful than in other British towns as the new system was based on concessioning on the bus network in the framework of competition *for* the market, with strict conditions attached, and not on opening competition *in* the market as elsewhere in Great Britain. The reduction in the burden on public finances is manifestly far more a question of better public transport management, as this enabled the amount of subsidies to buses in London to be divided by 7 in 10 years while improving service quality and without unusual fare increases, than of policies systematically restricting the use of the car, which can only have limited effects in financial terms for public transport, as the markets of the two transport modes are different. It is not surprising that the Tory government was considering in 1996 privatizing the underground itself, which could bring in a lot of money—maybe more than 10 billion pounds—due to the property value of the tracks, the yards, the stations, etc. This would make the London "tube" probably the only financially profitable metro system in the world.

It must be added that the overall market for urban transport, which is by nature mainly dependent on the volume of activity in the centres of urban areas, is in stagnation or decreasing in many places in Europe, and that it is illusory to try to widely increase public transport clientele by "reconquering" that of the car, as is often suggested. Certain among the more clear-sighted managers of public transport companies are now aware of this. This is, for example, the case for the President of the RATP (Paris Public Transport Authority) who stated in the newspaper *Le Monde* in February 1996:

> *We are suffering directly from the effects of the change in behaviour of the French population. As is proved by the good road traffic conditions in the inner-city of Paris, it is not because there has been a transfer from public transport to the car that our clientele has decreased. Our company must adopt a policy of restrictions, and we have chosen to decrease our investment expenditure and to postpone a certain number of our investment projects.*

The British example questions all those in charge of public transport in Europe. Aren't they too frequently overspending and asking for too much from the taxpayer rather than the user?

12.5.2 Public Transport Infrastructure Financing

Decisions on tariffs and investment are thus essentially both political and social. Each community has to decide whether it wishes to open the market to competition (if so, in which framework) and to what extent it will subsidise existing public transport networks. It is responsible for calculating whether the creation or development of new own-site lines (underground railways, trams on rails or tyres, buses on reserved lanes, etc.) constitutes the best possible use of taxpayers' money or not. These decisions should take into account the nature and the scope of demand, the existing networks, and, above all, the amount of financial resources available. In most countries, it is very difficult to free the necessary credits to construct new own-site lines, since the costs are very high, although they can vary depending on the technical solution retained. For this reason, central authorities often subsidise communities that undertake projects of this nature, as in Germany where numerous large urban centres were able to be equipped with high-performance public transport networks. Eleven German towns now have underground or urban railway networks and 20 have tram networks due to a special fund for urban transport created in 1967. The fund, however, did not prevent public transport modal share from receding from 65% in 1960 to 15% in 1995, despite 50 billion DM investment funding.

But there are also some countries that have developed original solutions to financing problems. This is the case in France, where a law took effect in 1972 creating a specific *"Transport Payment"* tax (*versement transport*) on salaries, designed to participate in financing not only the operating costs of public transport networks, but also, if necessary, their investments. The tax can reach 2% of the total salary, thus representing considerable sums. This legislation provided the means to construct underground rail networks in Lille, Lyons, Marseilles (1 million inhabitants) and Toulouse (600,000 inhabitants); together with traditional tram networks in Nantes, Rouen, Strasbourg, and Saint-Étienne; and trams with tyres, which are planned in Clermont-Ferrand, Le Mans, and possibly in Montpellier, Orléans, and Bordeaux. In different ways, Germany and France thus built numerous own-site public transport networks, which is not the case for all the other nations of the continent. Spain, Italy, and many others have recently taken steps in this direction or have plans to do so. For instance, Italy decided in 1995 and 1996 to subsidy more than 20 new public transport schemes.

Contrary to other European countries, the risk today in a country like France is, paradoxically, that unjustified projects may be undertaken, since the money collected through the "transport payment" tax can only be used to finance public transport and nothing else. It is well-known that any revenues "earmarked " for a particular use risk being more or less wasted. While the development of underground railway networks or trams in the above-mentioned towns was often justified and long overdue, the decision to build underground railway (metro) lines in certain French towns with 300,000 inhabitants, (as Rennes), where hardly 10% of residents use public transport to commute to work, is clearly a waste.

The case is the same for the new sections of underground and railway currently under construction in the centre of Paris, although it already has the densest network in the world and the number of users is decreasing (5% fewer passengers in the Paris *Métro* from 1990 to 1994) as a result of the stabilisation in population and a decrease in the number of jobs. When high-capacity, own-site networks already exist, it is unjustified to extend them indefinitely, considering the magnitude of the sums in question and the absence of economic justification. Furthermore, financial profitability, even in terms of operating costs, often does not exist and any new extension usually results in an increase in future operational deficits.

Public transport plays an irreplaceable, undeniable role in large towns. But faced with a limited clientele eroded by changes in urban structures and the development of the car, the extension of the networks cannot be an end in itself. There is a point at which it reaches its limit, which is that of the optimum use of the community's financial resources. In this field as in all others, one of the primary obligations of a "public service" is to avoid weighing too heavily on these resources. But with reservations for a reasonable use of the available funds, the "transport payment" tax can be one solution for financing public transport in large European urban areas, where high investment would appear to be necessary to make up for an obvious lack of infrastructures inherited from previous generations and when traditional financing methods are found to be inappropriate.

It is particularly significant that in June 1996, the Corporation of London, which manages the district of the city, proposed that the local companies should pay a voluntary tax designed to finance investments in public transport that are needed to ensure the smooth running of the business district where 250,000 mostly highly qualified people work daily, in an area of 2 km^2. For its advocates, this measure is essential to reinforce the London financial centre, which explains why

Artech House, Inc. BOSTON • LONDON

As a buyer of Artech House technical and professional books, you are invited to receive the latest information on our new and forthcoming titles. To be included on our mailing list, fill in the address details below, noting your areas of interest, and return to one of the locations listed on the back of this card. We look forward to your reply.

Name: _____

Position: _____

Company: _____

Address: _____

_____

Telephone: _____

Fax: _____

E-Mail Address: _____

Please indicate your areas of interest:

- Radar
- Microwave
- Optoelectronics
- Remote Sensing
- Computer Science
- Computer Systems & Architecture

- ☐ Software Engineering
- ☐ Signal Processing
- ☐ Solid-State Technology & Devices
- ☐ Antennas
- ☐ Telecommunications Engineering

- ☐ Telecommunications Management
- ☐ Technology Management & Professional Development
- ☐ Other

Thank You!

the British Employers' Federation and the London Chamber of Commerce are in favour of it [28].

It must finally be mentioned that although public transport networks are indispensable, it is not at all sure that on average public transport travel costs the community or the user less than transport by car. In Copenhagen (1,200,000 inhabitants), calculations showed that the average cost per passenger kilometre was 1.20 kroner for trips by bus or by tram, and only 0.80 kroner by car, when time was not taken into account. If time is considered, the figures rise to 2.20 and 1.30 kroner, respectively [29]. In the Paris region, with its 11 million inhabitants, the figures published by the regional prefecture are the following: the average cost to the community per passenger kilometre, if trip time is not taken into account, is 1.91 francs by car (including negative externalities, which, as we have seen, are decreasing) and 1.27 francs by public transport. But if the trip time is taken into account, the figures rise to 5.30 francs by car and 5.75 francs by public transport, which makes the latter more expensive for the community [30]. One of the reasons is that car drivers drive their vehicles for nothing. It must immediately be added that these are only averages for the whole of the region and that the situation is obviously very different depending on geographical location, with public transport having the advantage in dense areas, and the car for suburban movements where the costs per passenger for public transport are on the contrary very high.

12.6 URBAN ROAD FINANCING

In terms of financial profitability, the contrast between public transport and urban road networks is clear, under the conditions prevailing in most of Europe. While the former practically never covers its operating costs, and even less its investment expenditure, urban roads almost always earn more for the public finances than they cost.

Except for some rare exceptions, the profits that public authorities, particularly the national state, gain from the existence of urban road networks do not come from tolls, but from the numerous taxes which all countries impose on the purchase, possession, and use of road vehicles.

12.6.1 The Numerous Car Taxes

Practices vary greatly in this respect from one country to another, not to mention that car manufacturers do not apply the same prices excluding tax in each country, as they are usually much lower in countries without a national car industry where competition is fiercer than in others, as well as in countries where the currency is undervalued.

Differences in taxes are visible, first of all, when vehicles are purchased. V.A.T. rates range from 14% to 38%, depending on the country. In addition, in at least five countries (Denmark, Greece, the Netherlands, Norway, and Finland), special taxes are added to the V.A.T, which can be extremely high, so that the purchase price of a new vehicle in one country of the European Union can be double that in another. The Danes, who have one of the highest purchase taxes in Europe pay twice as much as the Germans for the same vehicle!

Most countries also have a mode of annual taxation in the form of a road tax disc vignette and, once more, the levels also vary widely. According to the European of Conference Ministers of Transport, these taxes range from 20 to 300 ECUs for a recent, two-litre vehicle. The Netherlands and Austria have the highest of these taxes, and Greece, Sweden, and Italy the lowest. The basis of assessment is also very different from one country to another: the complicated "fiscal horsepower" in France, the weight of the vehicle in the Netherlands, the number of engine litres in Germany, whereas in Great Britain the tax is the same for all vehicles.

Finally, there is a third large tax category linked to vehicle use and which is the heaviest in Europe—fuel tax. Here as well, great differences exist from one Western European country to another, although the recent trend is for them to converge at the high end of the scale and for disparities among countries to be less marked than for taxes linked to the purchase and possession of vehicles, although the treatment of diesel fuel and petrol fuel is subject to significant variations from one country to another.

It is surprising to note the extreme variety of ways in which buying, owning, and using a vehicle can be taxed. One comparative study carried out in 1989 on an average category of vehicle travelling 15,000 km per year showed at the time that the total taxation was, on average, 0.07 ECU per kilometre travelled in Western Europe, but that this figure ranged, depending on the country, from 0.14 ECU per kilometre in Denmark to 0.03 ECU in Germany, even though these are neighbouring countries [1]!

But in all the countries, the total amount of money paid to governments by cars and road transport vehicles is much higher than that which is allocated to road network management (administration, police, etc.) and road works. This is evident, first of all, on an overall level. According to International Road Federation (I.R.F.) statistics, total road spending in Western Europe, including expenditure on infrastructure and running costs, was 71 billion ECUs in 1992, whereas the revenues linked to the different taxes on purchasing, possessing, and using road vehicles was estimated at 154 billion ECUs, or more than double [31]. This is also true at the urban level. It has been estimated that in France, urban traffic brought in 60 billion francs per year to the national and local governments through V.A.T., road disc, and petrol taxes, whereas they only devoted 17 billion francs towards urban network construction and maintenance, and about the same amount to operating costs (especially the police), leaving the public finances with a considerable profit when taken overall.

Even if detailed figures are often not available, it is common knowledge that, unlike public transport users, car users supply the public finances with considerable sums of money, which could finance, usually with no difficulty whatsoever, not only maintenance and operating of the urban road networks they use but also investments in extensions when necessary. The car's apparently surprising ability to produce considerable financial resources was explained in the preceding chapter: It is due to the many advantages the car offers its users, especially in terms of time saved, which explain why users are prepared to pay relatively high sums of money to purchase and use a car. It is just a question of efficiency. It must be emphasised that it is quite legitimate to draw the parallel between what users pay and what is spent in favour of them. This reasoning is definitely used for the other modes of transport. Whether payment is made by purchasing a plane or train ticket, or by purchasing and using a car (for instance, on buying fuel), obviously changes nothing for the traveller. It is always a question of comparing an expenditure with a service rendered.

Faced with the general problems of balancing public finances, the faculty of road traffic to provide resources is such that governments increasingly consider asking users to contribute, on top of the many taxes they already pay, to the financing of road works through another form of fee, the road toll, which can also be justified for other reasons. Tolls can be planned and implemented under two forms: tolls specific to particular projects and tolls for a whole geographic area. A third form has recently been added to the two previous ones: the shadow toll.

12.6.2 Specific Tolls

The financing of particular projects by exacting tolls from their users is an age-old practice and was especially frequent in the Middle Ages at the entrances to towns and at river crossings.

As far as modern road networks are concerned, this mode of financing has been used either for expensive, one-off projects such as bridges or tunnels, or, on a much larger scale, for nation-wide intercity motorway networks. On this point, Europe is divided into two groups: the larger group has up until now created its intercity motorway networks by only using budget allocations, whereas the other has used tolls to finance totally or in part construction works and maintenance. The latter group includes Italy (the first country to adopt this technique), France, Spain, Portugal, Greece, as well as the former Yugoslavian states. As we have seen, toll roads allowed certain countries to significantly increase the numbers of kilometres of intercity motorways and this rapid progression is still continuing today, whereas countries that have not used tolls often have a much lower rate of road network expansion due to budgetary restrictions.

Following this observation, the idea has recently developed that certain projects in towns or outer urban areas could also be subject to tolls, thereby financing themselves in whole or in part through revenues from users. There is, however, one particular difficulty specific to urban areas. Unless there is a natural obstacle to cross, most projects are undertaken in areas where there already are other competing routes free of tolls, and which will remain so in the foreseeable future, so that this "unfair" competition limits the *financial* profitability of projects. This one is much lower than the *economic* return of these same projects for the community, the latter taking into account the amount of time saved, not only by those using the future toll roads but also by those who will keep using the existing network, where traffic conditions will be improved, or where additional users will find room.

In other words, the financial profitability of such projects will often be quite low, which more often than not requires and justifies aid in one form or another from the public authorities when the private sector is entrusted with constructing and operating the projects. This is the case, for example, for the Lyons northern ring road, which is currently under construction and is financed at least 25% by the public sector—therefore saving it three-quarters of the investment cost anyway. The Prado-Carénage Tunnel in Marseilles, mainly financed by private funds and opened in 1993, has a satisfactory number of users and confirms the validity of the principle of private financing for road construction in certain circumstances, in contrast to almost all public transport projects. So does the motorway A14 west of Paris, opened at the end of 1996 and largely underground. Of course, it would almost always be better, from an economic point of view, to operate the new infrastructures without tolls. However, it is better to have roads with tolls than no roads.

12.6.3 Shadow Tolls and Other Private Road Financings

Already described in Chapter 4, shadow tolls have many advantages for financing specific works—even if the word *toll* is somewhat misleading. They enable infrastructures to be financed by the private sector, thus taking advantage of its efficiency at all levels. They do not lead to the diversion of traffic inherent to traditional tolls. There are no additional costs for collection, as it is simply necessary to count the number of vehicles using the road. They can be used on existing infrastructures that need improvements and not only on new roads. They can also be used in urban areas. Last but not least, there is no problem of acceptance by public opinion, as there is no extra cost to road users.

Admittedly, the public authorities must then repay, each year, those responsible for the design, financing, and building of the infrastructures and who are in charge of the operating (on a DBFO system). But, as already explained, building or improving road infrastructures brings important additional revenues to the public finances from two different sources. Firstly, revenues are generated from fuel taxes coming from the additional trips that the infrastructure allows. Even when they are in a minority compared with the overall traffic on the new road, they do nonetheless exist. Secondly, there are the additional revenues resulting from the fact that a road infrastructure has positive effects on the economy, and therefore on tax revenues of various kinds. According to recent studies, the total tax revenues resulting in this way may exceed in Europe the amount paid for shadow tolls, meaning that this system of financing would be a great advantage from all points of view [32]. When relating to road building, the use is to calculate an economic return, or a financial one if real tolls are levied. The notion of fiscal return also seems worth a close examination.

A somewhat different way of involving private financing into road building has been adopted by Germany. The private bodies that are providing funds and building the road are repaid on a 15-year basis, without any reference to traffic volumes but accordingly to an agreement providing them an appropriate return on their investment.

12.6.4 Generalised Urban Tolls

There is another type of urban toll, the generalised toll, that does not concern a specific structure but an entire geographic area. In order to drive inside it, the user must pay a toll, either as a flat fee or in relation to the distance travelled. From a theoretical viewpoint, a generalised urban toll is justified when traffic demand exceeds supply since it leads to a decrease in congestion, thus improving traffic flowing to the benefit of the community. There is a second possible justification, which is by no mode a contradiction of the first: it allows money to be raised (for instance, to finance new road infrastructures).

A generalised toll is easy to imagine in principle but is impossible to implement today in most large urban areas with the payment collection methods currently available. At present, only one European country, Norway, uses this system. Since 1990, after two other cities, Oslo has required a 1.5-ECU entry toll to the city centre for private vehicles and a 3-ECU toll for trucks, the money raised being expressly reserved for road network improvement. It must nonetheless be emphasised that the geographic circumstances of the Norwegian capital are extremely favourable, as the city centre has only 19 points of entry, and as there is enough space and relatively little traffic, on account of its population (500,000 inhabitants), to make the installation of tollbooths physically possible. But this would not be the case today in many other European cities, as the examination of usual toll techniques demonstrates.

12.6.5 Changing Techniques

The technique usually used on toll motorways in country areas consists of barriers. This equipment, however, has the major disadvantage of requiring a considerable surface area. On the A6 motorway in France, at the Villefranche toll barrier north of Lyons, no less than 6 hectares of land are taken up by the 31 toll lanes, and yet peak traffic there is much lower than along many urban European motorways.

Electronic payment requires far fewer lanes than the present toll barriers, because it is estimated that each lane could debit with usual technical devices at least 1,000 vehicles per hour instead of 250. In many large European cities, however, even a reduced number of toll barriers would be impossible to install, even with latest technology, because there is simply not enough physical space.

But toll "barriers" are no longer necessary. Vehicle identification technology exists that does not require toll barriers, but consists of emitting-receiving beacons, fixed on frames, that "question" the vehicle as it passes.

There will then remain the question of the political decision to oblige all vehicles wishing to travel in the areas covered by the generalised tolls to be equipped with the necessary mode of identification and that of setting the corresponding tariffs. Even if in theory this is the most suitable solution in certain cases, it will obviously not be easy to implement all over a continent, unless automatic video reading of licence plates becomes sufficiently reliable in the future to avoid any fraud.

The city of Melbourne, Australia, has taken up this last option. In June 1995, Melbourne granted a private consortium the concession of a motorway toll bypass at a cost of 1.2 billions ECUs, on which tolls will be collected in two ways. Drivers will, first of all, be encouraged to buy emitting-receiving badges, allowing them to be identified whatever their speed, and debit their accounts automatically according to the distance travelled. Vehicles not equipped in this way will be allowed to use the motorway, but the vehicle will be photographed and the bill sent to the owner after identification of the vehicle. It must be pointed out that the State of Victoria, where Melbourne is located, is ahead in this field because of its successful efforts to increase road safety. In their fight against speeding, these particularly led to the development of excellent licence-plate reading technology that permits immediate identification of the owner through constantly updated files (see Chapter 1). In a subsequent stage, all vehicles registered in the State of Victoria are due to be equipped with emitting-receiving identification technology, a sort of modern-day licence plate. There can be no doubt that this evolution is inevitable and will progressively enable toll collection to be extended in Australia and elsewhere. For instance, a similar system is currently being introduced in Toronto.

As far as Europe is concerned, in mid 1995 the Dutch Transport Minister announced that the Dutch government wished to introduce a system of electronic tolls on the Randstadt Motorways in 2001 after consultations on a European level. Tolls would be collected near Amsterdam during morning rush hours with the aim of reducing traffic jams. It is needless to say that many problems must be solved before this project can be implemented, if only for foreign tourists' vehicles. It must be added that studies carried out on behalf of the confederation of Dutch employers [33] came to the conclusion that these traffic reduction measures would be both useless and harmful to national competitiveness. It should be added that the Dutch government also decided in 1996 to launch a large investment program to enlarge existing motorways, the aim being to eliminate most traffic jams by 2005.

Of course, doing away with traffic jams by introducing electronic tolls is tempting. But the advantages are probably less obvious than imagined, as the scale of congestion, and therefore its cost, are generally lower than is thought, and as there could be some negative side effects, such as diverting traffic and increasing congestion elsewhere.

Nevertheless, it is not impossible that in the medium term—perhaps 10 to 15 years—all European vehicles will be equipped with multifunction "electronic chips" for identification, maybe toll collection for driving and parking, vehicle spotting in case of theft, detailed descriptions of the vehicle and its equipment, the vehicle's maintenance record, and other uses still to be imagined.

12.6.6 Paying Parking

In the meantime, and without forgetting fuel taxes, another form of urban toll has been in existence for many decades in most European cities: paying parking. This is often a deterrent since in many large urban areas, it reaches or exceeds the equivalent of 2 ECUs per hour, which means that whenever the car is parked for more than a few hours, the amount can be considerable and much higher than sums usually considered for urban tolls. Of course, the deterrent does not affect those who have a free parking space at their destination. But the latter are often a minority in town centres, such that in many European towns, policies requiring paying parking are a very effective, if not perfect, traffic regulation tool. The Germans have even given it a name: "*Parkraumbewirtschaftung*." It is needless to say that it is, of course, very important that the enforcement of the measure should be well organised—which is not the case everywhere in Europe—maybe with the help of up-to-date electronic technology.

12.6.7 The Future

As for future urban tolls, everything will depend on the circumstances. In many European cities, traffic has stopped getting worse in central areas, especially since demand has stabilised, urban structures have changed, and progress has been made on road use and traffic flow control, notably through parking policies. The usefulness of creating generalised urban tolls will need to be carefully considered by weighing the advantages against the disadvantages. This type of toll programme is only justified, in theory, when heavy congestion exists, and it has been seen that these situations are rare in time and space for most urban areas and can be considered to represent only a very small percentage of trips at the level of a country.

Nevertheless, urban tolls in certain areas and at certain times of day will perhaps develop in Europe and progress with improvements in technology, which limit its extension at the present time and exclude the largest urban areas of the continent. Perhaps one day in the future will it be possible to drive at any time of the day, any day of the year without meeting any traffic jams. This dream could come true if the toll's level is properly set and modulated. Towns would then only be distinguished by their toll prices, not by their traffic conditions. However, there is no certainty about this at the present time.

When speaking about congestion tolls, one paradox must be mentioned. It would seem sensible that the setting up of such tolls would result in a decrease in demand and thus in traffic volumes. It is the opposite. This is due to the peculiar shape of the relation between traffic volumes and travel speeds and has nothing to do with what happens in a water pipe. Let us take for instance a motorway. When the number of vehicles arriving on a given stretch is low, speeds are high—maybe 100 km/h, if allowed. If this number increases, average speeds tend to progressively decrease, down to a speed that could be in the range of 60 to 80 km/h. But, if the number of arriving vehicles continue to increase, bottlenecks will appear, and, suddenly, average speed will fall down sharply, *as will traffic flow* (i.e., the number of vehicles per hour getting through the motorway).

So, the absence of proper tolls results in a *decrease* in traffic flows, not an increase. This can be checked, for instance, on the radial motorways leading to Paris. During morning rush hours there is *less* traffic per hour on them at Paris gates level in the direction going towards Paris than during off peak hours, this being due to an excess of arriving cars, which creates bottlenecks and long queues. If proper tolls were implemented, the number of cars trying to reach Paris would decrease at the beginning and no traffic jam would appear, this resulting in an *increase* of traffic volumes actually reaching Paris!

This can be easily explained. When an excess of vehicles try to drive at the same time on motorways or streets, they create bottlenecks and as a consequence give birth to important delays, which deter later on a number of potential road users to take their car or truck. If proper congestion tolling was set up, such bottleneck would not happen, travel times would consequently be shorter, and a number of potential road users that were deterred from driving would take the wheel. It is not sure that all those who recommend congestion tolls realise that such a practice would in fact increase car use and not the reverse. This is due to the fact that in the absence of tolling by money, another form of tolling exists anyway. It is tolling by wasted time.

It must be added that if this practice were implemented, the revenues collected would be sizeable, leading to a "virtuous circle." Political logic and the high economic return of many road projects suggest that the sums received should be reinvested towards improving the road network and not towards competing modes of transport or other uses.

However these are not short- or even medium-term perspectives for the Continent's large towns where there is not yet the possibility of implementing tolls on a large scale. For the time being, road financing will continue to rely on the usual budgetary processes.

In conclusion, thanks to the efforts of past generations, and those made in the road sector in the last three or four decades in many countries and towns, it would appear that in most cases urban transport in Europe is working far better than is usually imagined, even if, in a number of places, this is not the case today due to insufficient investments. Around 80% of motorised urban trips are made by car, often in very satisfactory conditions, and on average with very short travel times. With the help in large cities of underground or other public transport networks, the future of the European urban transport is usually "sustainable," which is not necessarily the case in other parts of the world where problems are presently of a completely different nature and magnitude.

References

[1] Salomon, I., P. Bovy, and J.P. Orfeuil, *A Billion Trips a Day*, Kulwer Academic Publishers, Dordrecht/Boston/London, 1993.

[2] Joël Garreau, *Edge City, Life on the New Frontier*, Anchor Books, New York, 1991.

[3] Orfeuil, J.P., *Espaces de vie, espaces de travail, quinze ans d'évolution*, Inrets, Arcueil France, 1995.

[4] Salomon, I., P. Bovy, and J.P. Orfeuil, *A Billion Trips a Day*, Kulwer Academic Publishers, Dordrecht/Boston/London, 1993.

[5] Benoit, J.M., and P. Benoit, *La France qui bouge*, Ed Romillat, Paris, 1995.

[6] Hinkel, W.J., K. Treiber, and G. Valenta, *Underground Railways—Yesterday, Today, Tomorrow*, Compress Verlag, Vienna, 1994.

[7] INSEE-INRETS, *Enquête Générale Transports 1993–1994*, Paris, 1996.

[8] Gerondeau, C., *What can be done about road safety?*, April 1996, Transport Seminar, The World Bank, Washington, 1996.

[9] OECD, *Managing congestion and road traffic demand*, Paris, 1994.

[10] The World Bank, *Urban Transport*, Washington, 1986.

[11] Gerondeau, C., *Les Transports en France*, Transports actualités, Paris, 1994.

[12] INSEE-INRETS, *Enquête Générale Transports 1993–1994*, Paris, 1996.

[13] Union Routière de France, SOFRES, *1992–1996 Surveys*, Paris, 1996.

[14] Gerondeau, C., *Les Transports en France*, Transports Actualités, Paris, 1994.

[15] INSEE-INRETS, *Enquête Générale Transports 1993–1994*, Paris, 1996.

[16] Association Espanola de la Carretera, *Velocidad in Madrid*, Madrid, 1996.

[17] The Department of Transport, *Traffic speeds in Inner London* HMSO, London 1995.

[18] AASHO, *A policy on arterial highways in urban areas*, Washington, 1961.

[19] Gerondeau, C., *La conception des réseaux routiers urbains*, Ministère des Travaux Publics, Paris, June 1963.

[20] Prud'homme, R., *La productivité des mégalopoles*, Courrier du CNRS n° 82, Paris, 1996.

[21] De Telegraaf, *Spits-Proef Groot Success*, 29 June 1996, Den Hagen.

[22] May, A.D., *Traffic management from theory to practice: past, present and future*, Transportation Research Board, 73rd Annual meeting, Washington, D.C., 1994.

[23] Cohen, S., *La circulation sur le boulevard périphérique*, Revue RTS n° 47, INRETS, Arcueil 1995.

[24] The Department of Transport, *National Travel Survey 1991–1993, Transport Statistics Report*, HMSO, London, 1995.

[25] Department of Transport, *Transport, the Way Forward*, HMSO London, 1996.

[26] The World Bank, *Proceedings of the Urban Transport Policy Seminar for Countries of the Former Soviet Union*, Washington, 1995.

[27] Salomon, I., P. Bovy, and J.P. Orfeuil, *A Billion Trips a Day*, Kluwer Academic Publishers, Dordrecht/Boston/London, 1993.

[28] La Vie du Rail n° 2551, 19 June 1996, Paris.

[29] *Nordic Road Transport in the Europe of Tomorrow*, The Danish Road Association, Holte, 1993.

[30] Préfecture d'Ile-de-France, *Les Transports de voyageurs de l'Ile-de-France*, Paris, 1994.

[31] Dieckmann, A., *Towards More Rational Transport Policies in Europe*, Die Deutsche Bibliothek, CIV, Cologne, 1995.

[32] R. Prud'homme, *Le financement des routes par des capitaux privés*, L'OEIL Université de Paris XII, Créteil, 1996.

[33] *New Hope for Tomorrow, Part II*, Netherlands Organization for Applied Scientific Research, TNO, The Hague, 1995.

CHAPTER 13
▼▼▼

CONCLUSION

A number of readers may well have found themselves often sceptical or incredulous when reading the preceding chapters. To be truthful, even their author had to carry out numerous checks as, to use a common expression, truth can be stranger than fiction. Nonetheless, all the facts and figures cited can be verified. The sources are indicated, and most come from official national or international institutions.

Why are the conclusions reached after an objective analysis of the facts so far removed from generally accepted ideas? There are three answers to this question. Appearances are misleading. Existing statistics misrepresent the facts. The balance of power is not equal between pressure groups.

13.1 MISLEADING APPEARANCES

About 20 ideas were outlined in the introduction of this book that are obviously mistaken. Nonetheless they are almost unanimously accepted by public opinion. For many of them the reason for this paradox is quite simple: appearances do not match reality.

When a motorway full of cars and trucks can be seen, side by side, with a railway or canal with practically no traffic, the obvious reaction is to conclude that the motorway must be relieved by transferring part of its activity to the other means of transport. This idea makes "good sense" and , according to a recent opinion poll, is shared by 92% of opinion leaders in France [1] and doubtless by at least as many in the other European countries!

As we have seen, this "good sense" is at the heart of the transport policies followed by the various European bodies concerned and by many countries. It is nevertheless clear this idea is not valid in the least because the vehicles using the motorway come from widespread departure points and travel to destinations that are no less so, only driving very temporarily on the same infrastructure, whereas the railway or waterway can only conveniently serve links between a very small number of departure points and destinations. But this is neither immediately perceptible nor easy to explain. Similarly, even though this is the truth, how is it possible to make people accept that road traffic in cities is not relieved by the creation of underground railway lines?

This is certainly one of the most obvious of the "misleading appearances" that troubles the perception of transport problems in Europe. But there are many others.

Some are related to traffic congestion. Attention is quite naturally focused on the negative aspects (traffic jams) and not the positive ones (free-flowing traffic). All studies show that the great majority of car or truck trips are astonishingly short and therefore meet no traffic jams. But the advantage obtained—the brevity of trip times—is not physically perceptible. On the contrary a traffic jam can be seen especially on motorways, where every study shows that congestion phenomena are particularly limited when compared with free-flowing situations due to their very high capacity. The advantages are in the domain of the invisible; the disadvantages are immediately visible. This is another answer to the question posed. Everyone speaks of the time "lost" due to congestion. Nobody mentions the time *saved* in relation to other means of transport on the countless trips when there is none and even when there is some. It is therefore in all good faith that the great majority of Europeans have a pessimistic vision of traffic conditions and are convinced that they are bad, even if personally they usually travel without experiencing any serious problems. As for those who are really the victims of frequent traffic jams, it is even harder to explain to them that their case is not the general rule.

This pessimistic vision concerns the past and the future alike. Whereas traffic volume has long been stabilised in most European town centres or is even decreasing, nine out of ten Europeans are convinced that it continues to increase. Whereas there is nothing to indicate that there is a general deterioration of traffic conditions in Europe and that many positive factors are at work, the great majority of people are convinced that the road network is heading towards a more or less complete standstill because they hear every day of the traffic jams, which characterise the central parts of large urban areas in rush hours, and a few times a year of the congestion that results from weekend or summer holiday traffic, on which it would obviously be absurd to base the calculations of the dimensions of infrastructures. Yet, even in the densely populated parts of the main European towns, speed is now stabilised or even slightly increasing, whether it be in London, Paris, Madrid, or many other cities.

The fact that appearances are misleading also concerns heavy goods vehicles. Their difference in mass naturally leads to an exaggeration of the disadvantages that they can present. Everybody thinks that trucks are the cause of traffic jams, even if the latter mainly take place when they are not on the roads, and that they are responsible for a very large portion of accidents, even if they are actually only involved in a limited proportion of them.

Regarding buses, instinct leads us to compare the street area they need per passenger with that of a car, and therefore attribute to them a better efficiency. However, this is usually a wrong criteria. What counts is the quality of the service provided to the user, which is mainly expressed by door-to-door travel time. If space use were the right criteria, it would also be justified to replace family homes and their gardens by high-rise buildings, on the grounds that they use too much space.

The economic side is also affected. Whereas railways cost taxpayers considerable amounts of money throughout Europe, a recent opinion poll carried out in the whole of Europe on behalf of the International Road Transport Union (I.R.U.) [2] showed that 65% of the Europeans who gave their opinion consider that the railways are a more economical means of transporting freight than the road! It is true that appearances are in favour of the train, which only needs one driver for a large number of wagons, and not of the road, which needs one for every truck.

Several such other misleading appearances may finally be cited.

For instance, urban areas are nearly always confused with city centres, whereas the latter no longer represent the living and working environment of the majority of the inhabitants.

Traffic flow of undergrounds and railways is believed to be necessarily higher than that of motorways, although except in certain circumstances, the opposite is true, whether it be for passengers or for freight.

Tunnels are instinctively thought to be more dangerous than surface routes, whereas it is the contrary.

The list of misleading appearances could, of course, be continued still further. But the examples given above are sufficient to show how often they arise in the field of transport and how difficult it is to fight against them, as all who have tried to do so quickly realised. For the good faith of most of those who profess these ideas that are taken for granted cannot be doubted. It is always extremely difficult to bring victory to rationality when faced with an argument that appears to make good sense. The only way to do so is to make the true facts known. But to have any chance whatsoever of succeeding, these facts must be available, which often is not the case today.

13.2 FAULTY STATISTICS

The lack of available proper data is due to the fact that there is no appropriate statistical approach. Surprising as it may seem, on many points the methods used are the same now at the end of the 20th century as in the middle of the last century. They simply add meaningless physical units and are incapable of answering the most basic questions properly: What is the share of transport in the economy? What percentage of transport is provided by each of the different means? How much does each means of transport cost or earn for the public finances? What proportion of trips is hindered by traffic congestion and what proportion is not? What is the average length of time each of the different categories of trips takes (i.e., the quality of the service) and how is it evolving? Is the situation getting better or worse? What are the external costs and advantages? And so forth.

According to each case, the data is either absent or, even worse, misleading. Yet it would be easy, for a number of them, to remedy the current situation in the short term. Of course, this would mean abandoning methods that have been mistakenly used for over a century, but the change is necessary.

Contrary to what may be supposed, this is not a problem that ought to interest only statisticians. Only the current flaws in the statistics system allow so many false ideas to circulate freely without being questioned: congestion dominates the road network, the situation is getting constantly worse, it is possible to transfer road traffic to other means of transport, public transport is necessarily less costly than individual transport, the aeroplane is always more expensive than the train, combined transport can relieve road traffic, and so forth.

As long as the reasoning and the conclusions of national and international institutions and decision-makers are based on assumptions and not on facts, progress will be impossible. There is a corpus of ideas today in the transport sector that is accepted by the public and by nearly all the media and the decision-makers, which has the dual characteristic of being coherent and being false.

If proper statistics existed to answer the basic questions mentioned above, they would immediately reveal that the ideas that predominate today contradict reality. Appendix A presents some suggestions for establishing significant statistics. The author proposes them without too many illusions, even if he has managed to start a movement in his own country [3], but the institutions involved are usually slow to change their habits. So, even the most basic data will probably not be available for a long time, thereby allowing the most mistaken ideas to proliferate and the heaviest decisions to be made in consequence. It is not even necessary to innovate systematically as examples do exist, at least in certain areas, of transport statistics presented in a valid way in certain countries, as in the United States (see pp. 309 and 310).

The setting up of statistics enabling a true assessment of the transport situation in Europe is an absolute priority and the preliminary to any kind of consistent policy. This is the only way to put an end to the controversies and lack of understanding that permeate this sector of activity. If those in charge could sort out this problem, it would be the most useful thing they could do. It is impossible to deal efficiently with an issue when the most basic data is unknown or disguised. In other words:

"Give me good statistics and I will give you a good policy." Today, transport policies in Europe largely rely on senseless statistics—and are consequently themselves largely senseless.

13.3 IMBALANCE BETWEEN PRESSURE GROUPS

But statistics are obviously not the only problem. The respective importance of the different pressure groups also plays an essential role. Once again, commonly held ideas do not correspond to reality. There is often mention of a "powerful road lobby," and yet this does not exist.

Of course, a car "lobby" does exist in the American sense of the word, in that the industry is organised to defend its own interests. In the same way, there is a trucking companies lobby, an oil industry lobby, and so forth. But contrary to what everyone seems to imagine, there is no "road lobby" with a mission to defend and promote road transport as a whole, to define its role and its advantages compared to those of its competitors, to justify why investment has to be made in its favour, and so forth.

This curious paradox is due to the very nature of the road transport system, which is comprised of many different professions, independently exercising different functions and trades and in no way organised between themselves to defend their common interests.

It could be assumed that the car industry, with its enormous economic power and industrial importance, would have become massively involved in this issue. But this has not yet happened, at least in Europe. If there is any doubt about this, the best way to be convinced is to ask the Continent's different car manufacturers their opinion about the road programmes. Such a question would usually only meet with sheer perplexity. Among the tens of thousands of engineers who work for the car industry and its suppliers throughout Europe, almost none have been given the mission of thinking about this problem, and practically no car industry manager has ever expressed a real opinion on what should be done for the road network on which the vehicles he produces are to drive. It is almost as if, for the railways, those in charge of rolling stock had no contact whatsoever with those dealing with the railway lines and were uninterested in them.

In truth, until recently this had not been a problem for the car industry, which had confidence in the authorities in charge of the road network, and their sales did not seem affected by any possible deficiencies in it. But will things remain this way if heavy congestion was to develop in the large towns and on the major routes of the Continent to such an extent that driving becomes increasingly difficult and unpleasant, and if there is a spreading out in policies systematically hostile to the use of the car? At a time when the car is increasingly singled out in Europe in environmental issues, for its place in the town, and generally within society, the question becomes even more pertinent. Perhaps a day will come when the car industry and its related sectors will judge that promoting the road network and the road transport system as a whole is their responsibility, because their medium and long term future depends on it, as does the image of the industry in the eyes of the public. Perhaps they will become organised in consequence, which would actually require very few resources in relation to what is at stake.

For its part, the road-building industry continues to plead its case, of course, in order to obtain enough credits to satisfy needs. But in taking up its own cause, it is obviously suspect when it proclaims to defend the general interest, even if it is true that road investment is one of the most cost-effective for the community and represents only a few percentage points of the total cost of the road transport system, most of which concerns the acquisition and running of vehicles and is therefore paid for by users. In addition, the large road-building companies often belong to large public works groups, which also have the national railway companies as their customers and are therefore obliged to be cautious.

Government civil servants in charge of roads are forced by nature to remain somewhat reserved on the matter. There are also the road trucking companies that defend their specific interests. As for the other road-related sectors—the oil industry, insurance companies, garages, and so forth—they are largely absent from the transport debate unless they are directly concerned in a specific issue.

Thus, by nature, the road transport system has no unity, and has neither a clearly defined doctrine nor, obviously, any promotional policy worthy of the name. It is the story of the Horatii and the Curiatii. It is telling that the International Road Federation, the institution in charge of uniting and promoting this sector, has a total of three executives in Geneva to take care of half of the globe, and does not have a single full-time representative in Brussels! In such circumstances, it is not surprising that the importance of pressure groups in the transport sector is the opposite of the weight that the different means of transport have in the economy and that public authorities' lending is often to transport modes that are in the minority and in deficit, but that know how to plead their cause.

For, contrary to the road sector, its main competitors are organised. The International Union of Railways (UIC) employs more than a hundred people in Paris, not to mention the Community of European Railways (CCFE), with close to 20 people, in Brussels, or the permanent representative offices of the main national railway companies in the same town, or any of the many other international railway institutions. Public transport is also well represented in Brussels through well-staffed bodies like the Union Internationale des Transports Publics, not to speak of the numerous "green" pressure groups dealing with the subject, which are, on principle, hostile to the road and in favor of public transport.

If the railways have often succeeded up until now in making their point of view prevail, it is for a number of converging reasons. The first is related to the structure of the railway system. It consists, with the recent exception of the United Kingdom, of companies that integrate most of the functions that in the road sector are divided up among many different entities. They are responsible for infrastructure, rolling stock, energy supplies, business policy, personnel management, and so forth. In other words, these companies' business is *transport*, which is not the case for car manufacturers, road builders, garage owners, the oil industry or, of course, each isolated driver or even automobile clubs. For their part, road freight or passenger transport is carried out by tens of thousands of companies, most of which have enough difficulties balancing their accounts not to have much time and money left over to devote to a collective cause.

The second reason is the most important. Everything stems from the nationalisation of the railway companies that took place in Europe, depending on the country, immediately before or immediately after the Second World War. Nationalisation created a blood relationship between the governments and their railway companies. The national governments were officially entrusted with the administrative supervision of the railway companies, but it worked the reverse way. The railway companies had hundreds of high-level engineers and executives, and the few civil servants in charge of the sector within the ministries could not counterbalance them. Without undue difficulty, the railway companies convinced the states to adopt their point of view and a large part of government administrations then became more or less hostile to the road.

The national governments, *de facto* managers of the railways, found themselves judge and judged on transport policy. Each minister of transport was a sort of company chairman, forced to devote a large amount of time to the railways—setting salaries, choosing investments, naming managers, dealing with labour difficulties, and so forth—whereas road transport grew without receiving any special attention and without resorting to government involvement, except for infrastructure.

In addition, the railways offered, and still offer, excellent career opportunities to state civil servants and even politicians in a certain number of countries, and it is therefore easy to understand why the "supervisory authority" failed to function in the way it was designed. This is the origin of the confusion that is often made in Europe between public companies (i.e., the railway) and public service. The private sector (i.e., the road) is said to represent exclusively private interests, even if it provides 90% of each country's and the Continent's transport needs and thus constitutes, in the etymological sense of the term, the core of the "public service" (i.e., the service of the public).

In such conditions, it is not surprising that railways have always been favoured by governments, thus explaining the huge levels of subsidies that were, and still are, granted for investment and/or operating costs.

The idea is sometimes put forward that the sentimental attachment of Europeans to their railways weighted in their favour when transport policies were at stake on the European continent, as almost every family counts one or several railway employees among its members or former members. But the situation was the same on the other side of the Atlantic, where the railway played an even more important role than it did in Europe by helping to "conquer" the West, giving birth to a myth documented in so many films and songs. However, intercity passenger trains have all but disappeared in North America without this giving any particular problems. As soon as the trains ceased to be profitable, they gave way to cars, aeroplanes, and buses, despite the regrets voiced by certain people. The American tradition precluded the possibility of state intervention, which, in Europe, has created enormous financial deficits to such an extent that they have become unbearable.

A third and final reason why the rail lobby is so powerful is closely linked to the other two reasons. Unlike the private sector, and due to their status as national companies, until now the railways have never had to balance their accounts. When deficits run into the tens of billions of ECUs on a European level, the costs linked to a few promotional activities are hardly of any importance. It is also easy to find "experts" who are ready to approve your views, even if they are as fanciful as they usually are, for instance, in the field of railway traffic forecasting or road "external cost" evaluation. Consequently, numerous representatives of the railways and public transport can always be found in the various work groups, committees, meetings, seminars, and conventions dealing with transport. And these representatives systematically dominate the debates, if only because there is generally no one opposite them to defend another point of view, as the road and air transport sectors, which have to balance their accounts, have practically left them the monopoly of thought and action. It is simply a question of balance of power.

Despite their wish to remain independent, the decision-making institutions are nonetheless inevitably swayed by a single way of thinking, defining what is "politically correct." The problem is that they hear only one side of the story. The result of this situation is that without always realising it, national governments and international institutions finance a means of transport that is used to continually asking them to increase the amount of money they grant, and will even sometimes go so far as to accuse them of not doing their "duty" when the sums granted are insufficient in their eyes—as if "duty" were something that does not concern those who benefit from public financing, but those who grant the funds.

Most European railway networks consider that a massive state participation, particularly for the financing of infrastructures, is their *right*.

The only exception to this rule is to be found nowadays in Great Britain. Inspired by the principles that have now been adopted practically everywhere in the world except in continental Europe, it considers that there is no reason to treat the railways any differently than other sectors of activity, and that there is no "right" on principle to subsidies, which does not stop certain services being subsidised for social reasons if this appears justified. The privatisation process that the British have just carried through with this approach resulted in British Railways being split into more than 80 separate companies and was crowned with exceptional success, contrary to the forecasts of its many detractors. Generally offering an improvement in the service rendered together with a drastic reduction in the burden on public finances due to privatization, it is certain that it gives food for deep thought for the other European countries. But this is now the only exception in Europe. Everywhere else, the weight of the railway companies, which have remained more or less monolithic, is still considerable even if there have been some limited changes.

It must be added that there is an exceptionally active lobby formed by the railway equipment manufacturing companies, this for an obvious reason. Their only clients are public companies, meaning in fact national governments or local communities. They therefore depend on them entirely for their business, or even their survival, contrary to car and truck manufacturers whose clients are private persons or companies, but not the public authorities. It is therefore easy to understand why lobbying from the first group is incomparably more active than from the second. This is doubtless an important factor in explaining the transport policy implemented in Europe, as is the political power of railway workers unions, counting hundreds of thousands of members Continent wide.

13.4 SURPRISING ASSERTIONS

Overall, this situation has led to some surprising results, of which succeeding in making everyone think that there was a "road lobby" worthy of the name to defend private interests against the defenders of public interest is not the least of them. But this is not the main point. More essential is the fact that on the eve of the 21st century, the European Continent is not yet aware of the real situation of its transport sector. The issue is not to know whether entire regions of Europe's territory can live without the railway, but to realise that they already do. Of course, there is still a dense network of railway lines practically everywhere, but except for the suburban lines serving large urban areas and on certain major routes, they now have hardly any significant traffic, which explains, in part, the enormous losses they generate, the other cause being the very high costs linked to outdated statutes and poor management. This ignorance of reality, or the refusal to see it, explains why many decision-makers in all good faith do not have a correct view of the subject. The result is that many assertions that defy common sense are deeply rooted in public opinion, in the media, and in the minds of decision-makers, so that those who denounce them are considered to be partial or slightly out of their minds, even though they are only trying to defend the general interest. They will not all be reiterated here as they have been listed at the beginning of this work.

Overall, the combination of the facts that, as far as transport is concerned, appearances are often misleading, that the most significant statistics are senseless or deceitful, and that the balance of power between the different modes of transport is completely unequal, gives the surprising results shown previously.

Otherwise, how can you explain that a sector of activity that does not even cover half of its costs has succeeded in making believe that its principal competitor does not pay its true costs, whereas everyone knows that this competitor is taxed so much that it is one of the primary sources of revenue for the European States?

In particular, how can you explain the prevailing notion that, unlike train users, road users do not pay for the infrastructure they use, whereas in fact the situation is exactly the opposite, as in total road users pay far more through fuel taxes than the public authorities spend on roads, and all the railway companies are highly subsidised in one form or another [4]?

How can you explain the lasting idea that the "external costs" of the road are considerable and ever-growing, whereas any objective examination of the facts leads to the conclusion that most of them are limited with respect to road transport turnover and are undeniably decreasing significantly?

How can you explain that for questions of transport, unlike all other sectors of the economy, meaningless physical units are almost always used and that the financial aspects of the issue are systematically veiled from sight?

How can you explain that road goods transport is sometimes criticised for being too inexpensive, whereas in all other sectors of the economy people are delighted when competition succeeds in lowering costs and that the latter is precisely the cause of productivity gains and the corresponding drop in prices registered in the road transport sector?

How can you explain the widespread idea that road network congestion is the rule, whereas it is only an exception as shown by the average duration of car trips, which is surprisingly short and has not shown any tendency to increase even though the distances travelled are increasing, and by the success of "just in time" practices, which are a perfect demonstration of the reliability of the road network?

How can you explain that, when congestion does exist, the recommended solution is often not to increase road capacity, as common sense and sound economic practice would usually dictate, but to create a general taxation of road use, which, unless tariffs are prohibitively high, would have no major effect on traffic volume?

How can you explain the fashion for "intermodality," which is necessarily complicated and expensive, whereas almost all Europeans have selected unimodality, or simplicity and savings? Today, 92% of home-to-work trips taking place in France use one means of transport only, with an average trip time of 18 minutes, 5% use two means of transport with an average trip time of 45 minutes and 3% use three means of transport or more, with trip times exceeding 70 minutes [5].

How can you explain the persistence of the legend according to which it is possible to transfer passenger or freight traffic from the road onto the railway whereas, unless artificial restrictions are imposed, there is not one example of a significant result in the world, because the markets and their scales are different? How would it be particularly possible to relieve road traffic—3,000 billion vehicle kilometres per year in Western Europe—by developing rail freight traffic (14 billion vehicle kilometres)?

How can you explain that three entirely different sets of rules exist in Europe in the area of transport, completely contradicting the principles of free competition, as air transport must pay all its costs, the road should be increasingly taxed, and rail transport has the "right" to be subsidised for its infrastructure and often operations in proportions unheard of elsewhere, enabling it to set its tariffs in most cases without any reference to its overall costs, whereas in all three cases they supply the same needs: transport of people or goods?

How can you explain the almost unbelievable fact that the European Union, which works effectively in all areas to promote free competition, accepts the fact that on the eve of the year 2000 it is still forbidden in many European countries, either by law or *de facto*, to create intercity coach lines for the sole reason that the railways' monopoly must be protected, whilst at the same time rightly imposing a complete opening up of the European skies?

Finally, how can you explain that whereas the road provides 90% of the transport of people and freight in Europe and is profit-making and developing, the projected European programmes for major construction works allocate about 90% of the proposed financing to the railways, which cost all the governments of Western Europe colossal amounts of money as, according to statistics from the International Union of Railways (UIC) itself, cumulative losses reached 300 billion ECUs over the past ten years and that, not only the road but also air transport are practically ignored, thereby encouraging loss-makers and penalising those who make a profit?

A few decades from now, those studying the economic history of this period will probably struggle to explain these contradictions.

And yet, overall, the European transport system works well.

Thanks to economic progress, which has given rise to an increase in the numbers of cars and road vehicles for goods transport, and thanks to the efforts of most public authorities in the development of road networks, free-flowing traffic prevails over congestion, even if the latter is obviously higher in the countries and towns that have invested less in their road networks. There is no reason to be pessimistic for the future if an appropriate effort is granted in their favour. But it has to be, which is today far from being sure everywhere.

As for air transport, it is more and more efficient and democratic thanks to the policy of free market competition introduced with the impetus of the European Union. It is, of course, important to ensure that it is not a victim of its own success, which means that there must be a marked improvement in air traffic management, but this is by no means impossible.

In truth, for many European countries, the most difficult problems are now mainly in three sectors, and they are of a financial nature.

First of all, the railways must adjust their activities and expenditure to market possibilities. The problem is social, as very large staff reductions are inevitable, and financial, as the states can no longer support the burden of the deficit. To deal with these two aspects of the problem, the best solution is to offer the railway employees large sums of money so that those who wish to do so accept to leave, and then to open the network to concessions granted to private companies. This has been achieved in Great Britain with remarkable success, but nowhere else in Europe.

The second problem concerns urban public transport. In most European countries, the financial burden is becoming excessive in this field, too, due to defects in network management and tariffs being too low. The solution is to be found both in improvements in management, if possible within the scope of strict concession agreements, and in an increase in tariffs even if, generally speaking, this can only be done progressively. But it can also be found by introducing certain targeted measures enabling the most underprivileged people to travel more easily, particularly those who do not have access to a car. It can be cheaper, more efficient, and fairer for the public authorities to concentrate their efforts on those who are really in need rather than to disperse them throughout the whole population.

A third very negative point must be added to this list of problems. As seen in Chapter 10, tighter and tighter regulations are compelling the motor and the oil industries to spend ever-increasing amounts of money to fight pollution even though it is already disappearing. This is wasting billions of ECUs each year for almost nothing, at the user's expense.

13.5 A FEW COMMON-SENSE FACTS

Sooner or later, the facts always win. These can be summarised in a few simple proposals.

If users of land transport freely choose road transport, it is because it offers them a certain number of advantages. And if the immense majority of fellow citizens and firms find road transport advantageous, it is quite sure that except for a few marginal cases, it is also advantageous for the community.

The car is an extraordinary key to freedom and quality of life. Due to its capacity to reduce door-to-door trip times considerably, it allows people to increase their activities and has opened up previously non-existent choices, either for the location and type of residence, the workplace, personal relationships, sports activities, shopping places, and so forth. It is for these reasons that the car is chosen, not only by Europeans but by all the other inhabitants of the planet who can afford it.

Above all, it has allowed everybody to have at their disposal unprecedented areas of land for their housing and other activities at a much lower cost than in traditional towns, which is perhaps the most important advantage offered by the car and roads. At the same time, the car is a key to economic efficiency. It has given all activities the chance to have access to far greater horizons than ever before. By increasing the size of markets, it is a catalyst for exchange and competition in business, work, tourism, and many other areas.

The transport of freight by road is one of the fundamental cornerstones of modern economic activity. Its flexibility and productivity are outstanding compared to those of its older competitors. Progress on vehicles, on the road network, and in carriers companies has been so great that according to some estimates, a sizeable part of the postwar productivity gains in Western Europe has been due to the fact that modern industry can now count on road transport [6].

Road transport's physically perceptible disadvantages should not lead to the assumption that its advantages, less visible by nature, are of any less importance.

Of course, it would be absurd to deny the existence of harmful effects linked to the use of road vehicles. But in areas such as air pollution, they are now often grossly exaggerated. In fact, the problem is now being solved, as remarkable progress has been made by vehicle manufacturers, not to mention those made by fixed pollution sources (industry and heating). Why should air quality be the only area where technological progress does not yield results, even though traffic is now increasing only very slowly and has already stabilised in central urban areas where most of the real problems can occur?

European and national policies on traffic and vehicles can, on the other hand, have only very limited effects on the global production of carbon dioxide and consequently on its possible impact on the greenhouse effect due to the perspective of considerable increases in carbon dioxide production by Third World countries, against which the developed world can do very little.

However, one appalling problem remains, to which far too little attention is paid. Road accidents, which are still responsible for nearly 50,000 deaths each year in Western Europe, are too often accepted as inevitable, with insufficient resources devoted to their prevention compared with what is at stake. For too many, road deaths are of no or little interest. Yet one of the surest solutions for reducing the number of accidents would be, among other things, to increase credits granted to roads, in order to create dual carriageways, to plan and equip existing roads, and to systematically implement traffic-calming policies, rather than promoting the delusion that road traffic can be transferred towards other means of transport in the name of road safety.

Most of the time the congestion of the road network is not inevitable. Of all road trips taking place in Europe, those hindered by heavy traffic are now a minority. When there is sufficient demand, there is nothing, in most cases, to stop road investment from meeting the new needs, if necessary underground in the cores of large cities. All other sectors of economic activity function this way. It is all the more justified as the costs of meeting the additional demand can be covered through existing taxes or even through those that the new infrastructure will bring, and as the growth in traffic has now become sustainable practically everywhere in Western Europe, as it is very moderate or even non-existent in certain places. In cases where it would be unrealistic and unjustified to increase road network capacity to satisfy potential demand without adding tolls to the existing taxes, it will perhaps be suitable, once the techniques become fully functional, to use them locally to regulate traffic and in addition gather funds, which could then logically be used to improve the road system. But increasing levies on traffic has no economic justification except in this small number of special cases, such as rush hours in large urban areas and would, on the contrary, have elsewhere serious social and economic consequences.

For the transport of both passengers and freight, it is the user who chooses the means of transport, and not the authorities. The market decides, and that is why it would be unrealistic to think that the increase in road traffic, which is a result of economic development and moves in tandem with it, could be influenced without harm in any significant way by government decisions.

The same goes for air traffic, whose success is a direct result of its efficiency and the advantages it brings to its users, for passengers as well as for freight transport.

In fact, transport policy leads to other far-reaching questions. Should people be forced to be happy against their wishes? Unfortunately, for some people the answer would appear to be positive. Does a majority of the population prefer to live in an individual home? It "would be better" if they lived in flats. Do they prefer shopping in large shopping centres on the outskirts of town? It "would be better" if they did their shopping in the local shops or in the town centre. Do they prefer working in offices spread throughout the suburbs? It "would be better" if they were grouped together in town centres. Do they prefer using the car for most of their trips? It "would be better" if they used the other means of transport. And so forth.

Such a manner of seeing things is eminently dangerous, because it puts the very principles of democracy in the balance. All studies show that those who select the behaviours described above are happy to do so. And there are objective reasons for this. It is pleasant to have plentiful living space and a garden, especially for a family with children; it is logical to wish to pay 25 to 30% less on shopping bills; it is understandable to prefer to work in an easily accessible place rather than in one that is not; there is nothing surprising about choosing the means of transport that saves the most time and is also the most comfortable.

Individually, some people may make other choices, such as living in the town centre, going shopping on foot, and giving up their car. Nevertheless, it is obvious that such solutions cannot be generalised and can only be open to an often privileged minority, unaware of how most of its other fellow citizens live.

But above all, what justification is there for dictating these choices to those who do not want to follow them? Drive-in McDonald's restaurants recently appeared in Europe where, *horresco referens*, as in the United States, it is possible to buy a hamburger and french fries and eat them without leaving the car. Few European readers of this book will probably be tempted to try this culinary experience. But if such drive-in restaurants exist, it is because there are people who think otherwise, and that is their right.

What justification is there, *a fortiori*, to force those who spend 20 minutes daily commuting to work to use alternative means of transport that, as all studies show, take an average of 30 minutes longer per trip when they actually exist, and would make them lose an hour of their lives every day, even if there are of course exceptions? Saving time on transport means the possibility of more happiness and a better quality of life.

What justification is there, except for a very small minority of cases, to make those who quite logically prefer to use their car feel guilty about it, other than that yesterday was the golden era and that any human invention that is so overwhelmingly popular can only be bad?

Of course, nobody denies that it is necessary, especially in town centres, to readjust the balance among means of transport if this has not already been done, moderate the use of the car on surface streets if necessary to restore the quality of living, and offer other choices when this is possible. It would also be wrong not to take the necessary steps to help those who do not have access to cars to enable them to travel wherever they live. European town centres are an irreplaceable heritage and everything must be done to protect them, make them more beautiful, and hand them on to future generations, whilst remaining conscious of the fact that today they are not in the least representative of the living environment of the great majority of the population and that solutions that are valid for them cannot by transposed elsewhere. It would also be absurd to advocate an absence of any planning in land use as it is, on the contrary, essential whenever possible if it is well thought out.

As this book has amply shown, the problem comes from the point that the facts are usually badly known. Those who are required to make decisions in the field of transport obviously do so in all good faith, but often without having been correctly informed of the true situation. Sometimes, they do not even really have any choice. There is then the risk that decisions are made based on ideological apriorisms.

But ideology should have no place in transport policy. Transport is an important aspect of daily life and plays an essential role in the running of the economy. Means of transport, such as cars, two-wheeled vehicles, public transport, trucks, trains, aeroplanes, ships, and so forth are only tools and should be considered as such, without assigning them with an ideological "value"—either positive or negative— as is too often the case in Europe. The things that count are services rendered, which includes first of all trip duration, which although essential is almost always omitted, and the financial side of the issue, as one of first the duties of any public or private service is to not squander public resources, any unjustified expenditure being paid for elsewhere in one way or another, through poverty, unemployment, or exclusion. It must be recalled that undue public spending is one of the main causes of high unemployment, the worst plague of most continental European countries today. Moreover, in many of these nations, public subsidies to rail and public transport are close to or in excess of 1% of the national product. Transport is one of the main fields in which Europe has to reassess its policy.

It is a question of making the best possible decisions objectively and on the basis of facts and not opinions, for the quality of life of our contemporaries and the efficiency of society. All that really counts is the happiness of the people and the proper functioning of the economy, which is one of its conditions.

References

[1] Union Routière de France, BVA survey, *Les leaders d'opinion et la route,* July 1996, Paris.
[2] International Road Transport Union (IRU), MIS *Survey About Transport* Geneva, 1996.
[3] Rexecode, *L'analyse économique du secteur des transports de marchandises,* Paris, 1996.
[4] Dieckmann, A., *Towards More Rational Transport Policies in Europe,* Die Deutsche Bibliothek, CIV, Cologne, 1995.
[5] INSEE-INRETS, *Enquête Générale de transport 1993–1994,* Paris, 1996.
[6] Souley, H., *L'effet de la dérégulation de 1986 du transport routier de marchandises sur les prix et les flux,* DEA, Ecole Nationale des Ponts & Chaussées, Paris, 1996.

APPENDIX A
▼▼▼

SUGGESTIONS FOR STATISTICS

Obviously, it is impossible to treat any subject without knowing it well, which presupposes that statistics and indicators capable of describing it must exist. Yet, in the transport sector, elementary data is often lacking and everyone is consequently led to rely on their own opinions or, most often, on generally accepted ideas which rarely correspond to the way things really are. Even worse, the statistics that are usually used often misrepresent reality.

The absence of statistics and valid indicators is not only an issue for specialists. It is serious because it leads governments and international entities to make wrong decisions. It is therefore necessary to fundamentally reform the statistical approach to transport in Europe. In some cases, it can be reformed rapidly using existing data; in others, the essential data is still missing and must be collected.

At least four areas can be distinguished. They are not necessarily exhaustive and they correspond to the elementary questions that, surprisingly, still remain unanswered:

- What is the weight of transport within the economy?
- What are the weights of the different modes of transport?
- What is the financial position of the different modes of transport?
- How do the different modes of transport function?

A.1 THE WEIGHT OF TRANSPORT IN THE ECONOMY

As has been seen, almost all the published national and international data on the weight of the transport sector within the economy only take into account the specific companies that are "statistically" in the transport business (railways, air transport, road transport). This strictly formal approach tends to mask the fact that modern economies devote 15 to 20% of their activity, not 5%, to the transport of people and freight. Obviously, as in North America, the economic approach should predominate because it is the only one that reveals the reality of the situation; the traditional statistical approach gives an entirely mistaken idea of the weight of the "transport function" within economic activity.

A.2 THE RESPECTIVE WEIGHTS OF THE DIFFERENT MODES OF TRANSPORT

A.2.1 Freight Transport

As we have seen, statistics on the transport of freight in Europe rely almost exclusively on the use of tonne kilometres, units that are entirely meaningless whenever a comparison is made between anything other than the transport of identical products under identical conditions. It has been seen that the economic value of a tonne kilometre could vary from one to one hundred, or even more.

As is the case in all other sectors of the economy that abandoned the cumbersome "Gosplan-type" units long ago, only the comparison between turnover figures (i.e., what is paid by the customer) can allow us to validly compare the different modes of transport in an economic sense. All use of tonne kilometres should be banished as misleading.

Access to the turnover figures of the different modes of transport is not an insurmountable problem. Turnover is obviously readily available for transport companies (rail, air, road, river, sea transport, etc.). Freight transport costs by private fleets or by individuals possessing their own vehicles can be estimated.

Therefore, nothing stands in the way of abandoning the tonne kilometre, which brings together facts that have nothing to do with each other, and replacing it with monetary units, the only ones that can measure what counts (i.e., the value of the service rendered to the people and the community).

It must be emphasised that the use of the vehicle kilometre, a physical unit, is also worthwhile. It is the only unit that makes sense when we speak of network congestion and of possible transfers from one mode of transport towards another. For the transport of freight, things are relatively simple. It is possible to convert the activity of the different modes of transport in *truck units* (TUs) and in *truck-kilometre units* (TKUs), keeping in mind that the average rail freight wagon load is generally equal in Western Europe to that of a heavy, high-load truck when empty travel is accounted for. The adoption of the truck unit is justified by the fact that road transport is by far the dominant mode. To tackle the problems of road congestion, it is possible to convert the TU into a "private car unit" (PCU), by adopting, for example, a rule stating that 1 TU = 2 PCUs. The adoption of the TU and the TKU to measure the physical aspect of goods transport would not pose any particular problem since data on journeys and tonnages are available in all countries for all modes of transport. The publication of TKUs would thus complement the use of turnover figures. Unlike the tonne kilometre, it would give a realistic image of the physical aspect of freight transport and would also make it possible to monitor changes in time of markets prices per unit of transport.

A.2.2 Passenger Transport

The transport of passengers could be partly measured in the same way as the transport of freight, and partly differently.

As for the transport of freight, only the turnover figures of the different modes of transport can translate their true economic weight. For some (air transport or railway transport, in particular), turnover figures are available even they are usually nowhere compared. For automobile transport, there are generally no turnover figures in the proper sense, except for taxis. One must then consider the figures consisting of the amount users spend to acquire and use their vehicles, on the principle that all spending on the part of the beneficiary of a good or service is obviously the other side of a turnover figure for a supplier, or of a taxation.

The corresponding data, classified under the category "users' spending," exist in most countries. The turnover figures of the different modes of transport of people can therefore be collected and compared in each country and can be added to obtain a European total.

However, things are not the same for the physical measurement of the transport of people. Unlike tonne kilometres, which are entirely heterogeneous, "passenger kilometres" do have a certain meaning. If one tonne of a given product is not equivalent to one tonne of another product, a person is always a person. Even if the journey of one aeroplane passenger over a distance of 1,000 km is obviously not the same thing as the journey of 100 underground railway users over a distance of 10 km, experience shows that the price of transporting one person over a distance of 1 km varies relatively not too much—from one to three, for example—from one mode of transport to another. This is especially due to the fact that the automobile is the dominant means of transport in Western Europe, and the other modes of transport cannot set prices that differ too much from the price of travel in a private car. The use of the passenger kilometre can therefore be allowed despite its limited validity.

Finally, as is the case for freight, the use of vehicle kilometres should complete the panoply of tools used to measure the transport of people. The conversion from passenger kilometres to vehicle kilometres is made by using the average occupancy rates of the vehicles, which are an essential indicator that should be monitored for the different modes of transport.

All this data is generally available or accessible in each country so that, as for freight, there is no objection to the rapid reform of European statistics on passenger transport in order to give a more accurate image of the situation.

A.3 THE FINANCIAL POSITION OF THE DIFFERENT MODES

In order to judge any economic activity, it is also essential to know its financial aspects (e.g., revenues and expenses). The final balance of each mode of transport *vis-à-vis* the public authorities is a particularly essential management indicator, albeit not the only one, but it rarely shows up in published statistical documents.

For road transport (cars and commercial vehicles), the calculation is rather simple, as the products of the different taxes are known. The amount of State spending on networks and their operations is also readily available. The different figures should be classified by categories of vehicles and geographic zones (rural zones, urban zones, etc.).

However, the situation is usually different for railways, since State aid in many countries is given under very different forms (subsidies, advances, contributions, reimbursements, loan guarantees, etc.), which are extremely confusing. Nonetheless, a general calculation can be made of the annual State resources devoted to railways and the way they are attributed to the two categories of traffic (freight, passengers), themselves subdivided into other large categories (long-distance passenger lines, regional lines, suburban passenger lines; block trains, individual freight wagons, combined transport for freight). Some countries have already done this and it is the least that can be expected.

The real financial flow between the State and the different modes of transport, which should constitute an essential element of any transport policy, could thus be collected or developed within each country and then gathered at the European level. It is, however, currently absent from most national and international statistics, so that anyone looking for these essential data is confronted by severe difficulties, and many decisions are made without knowing them.

A.4 FUNCTIONING

In transport as in other areas, the quality of the service rendered to the user is an essential evaluation criterion. It should be permanently monitored. The quality of service rendered can be evaluated primarily by the normal travel time and by the proportion of travel that takes longer than the norm.

For railways and air transport, this data is known. The proportion of trains or aeroplanes that are 5, 15, 30 minutes, and so forth behind schedule is an essential indicator. It is monitored daily, or almost daily, by the managers of the companies concerned.

The principal problem is with the road network. There is an almost complete absence of data on the quality of service rendered, allowing all manner of hypotheses, especially the most negative kind, to circulate unconstrained as to the way the road network functions. This fundamental absence is very serious because it is precisely on the basis of postulates that contradict reality that numerous national and international decisions are made. It is not easy to fill the gap. As simple as it may be to know the proportion of trains or aeroplanes that arrive behind schedule and by how much, it is just as difficult to answer the same question for car and lorry traffic.

Three ways of facing this difficulty can be envisioned. The first consists in surveys of drivers carried in the home or in companies, the second in studies carried out on the road, and the third in using available traffic data (average speed, flow, density) for the few networks equipped with a sufficient number of measuring instruments. This book will not undertake to describe the different approaches in detail, especially since it is largely unexplored territory.

Nevertheless, it can be stated that home surveys could, at a very low cost, allow one to have at least an idea of the way the essential characteristics of a particularly important kind of travel are changing from year to year: for instance, home-to-work commuting. In addition to the traditional transport surveys, a few questions asked within "omnibus surveys" carried out periodically by polling institutes would make it possible to obtain precise, fundamental data at a low cost, such as distribution of travel among the different modes of transport and average travel times for each one. It would permit one to see the way these fundamental data are changing with time, indicating whether the situation is stable, improving, or deteriorating, as these are essential indicators of the quality of life on the Continent.

Without prejudice to other approaches, such could be the first European Union procedure for rationally evaluating the way the European transport system works. Likewise, travel times for intercity travel could be monitored from year to year, especially with the participation of transport companies.

The second approach could consist in studies carried out on the road by questioning users on their travel and, particularly, on the congestion they encounter. Contrary to the first approach, this one would require large resources and could thus apply only to particular cases (for instance, on toll motorways).

The third approach, easier to implement, resides in the analysis of existing data, particularly that which applies to traffic volumes and, wherever they are known, speeds, in order to estimate the conditions under which the network functions. This last approach should enable one to detect the true extent of congestion or, more often, its absence.

The existence in the Paris region of a motorway traffic monitoring system (SIRIUS), which is unique in Europe, is beginning to allow there, as in some other European cities, a permanent and precise knowledge of traffic conditions, which appear to be very different—and far better—than usually thought.

We can only emphasise yet again how imperative it is to set up indicators that enable the evaluation of the way the road transport system really works since it is the one that responds to most of the transport needs of the continent.

In conclusion, it appears that a renewed statistical approach of transport is needed.

On the following pages, there are two abstracts from the American national transport statistics related to expenditure and revenues (turnover) and vehicle-miles (see Figures A.1 and A.2).

US WAY OF PRESENTING TRANSPORT STATISTICS
Expenditures and revenues ($ millions) - 1990

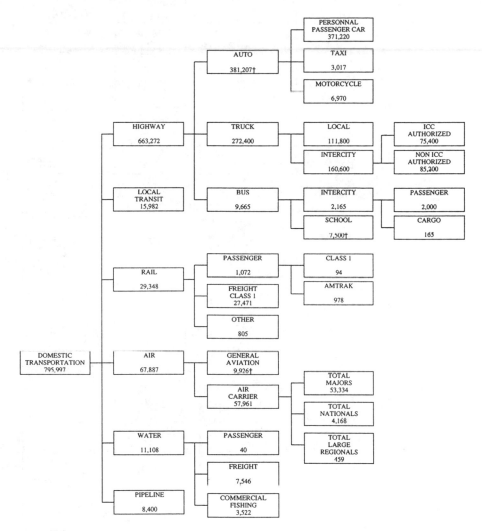

† Represents Expenditures

Figure A.1 American national transport statistics related to turnovers. (*Source:* National Transportation Statistics. U.S. Department of Transportation Annual Report 1990.)

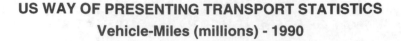

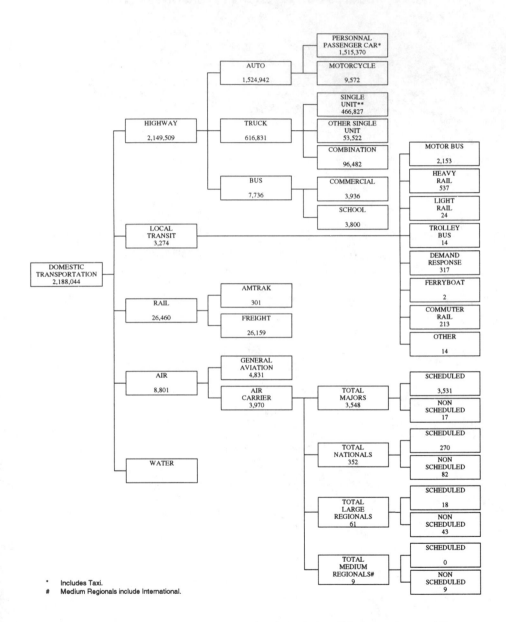

Figure A.2 American national transport statistics related to vehicle-miles. (*Source:* National Transportation Statistics. U.S. Department of Transportation Annual Report 1990.)

APPENDIX B

▼▼▼

TUNNELS RESERVED FOR LIGHT VEHICLES SUMMARY AND CONCLUSIONS*

After more than 30 work meetings with the participation of over 60 people, the members of the Inter-Departmental Safety Commission, created to examine the construction of a two-level low-gauge 10-km tunnel for the A86 motorway, reached a set of unanimous conclusions.

The first concerns the feasibility of the project. On condition that a certain number of measures would be implemented that would not strongly increase the investment and operating costs of the project, the conclusion was reached that a project of this nature was not only feasible but that it would offer its users a particularly high level of safety so that, from this viewpoint, there was no obstacle to its realisation.

In order to achieve this, the Commission drew up a certain number of recommendations and requests, the most important of which are the following:

---

*The Inter-Departmental Safety Commission of the Ministries of Equipment, Housing and Transport, and of the Interior, Paris, June 1992.

---

1. Traffic in the future structure should be permanently controlled, especially by regulating entry and exit flows in order to avoid congestion in normal circumstances. In addition to safety benefits, the users of the structure would have the added advantage of a guaranteed journey time, an innovation of utmost importance in the urban environment.
2. Specific devices should allow permanent speed control throughout the structure so that strict compliance with the speed limit—70 km/h is proposed—would be ensured.
3. The roadway of the principal structure should be three lanes wide between interchanges and two lanes wide at interchange levels to provide room for incoming traffic. Between two successive interchanges, the third lane could serve either as an emergency shoulder or an exchange lane. Although the choice between the two options is not urgent and could be deferred for several years, it appears that from the standpoint of the capacity offered, the second solution is distinctly preferable to the first. The capacity of the structure would then be intermediary between that of a four-lane motorway and a six-lane motorway. In addition, available knowledge leads one to think that the second option is also superior to the first in terms of safety.
4. The recommended size for the principal tunnel is the following:

- A width of 9.60m at 1m from the ground, implying that the internal diameter of the structure would be approximately 10m;
- An internal height of 2.55m, allowing the passage of vehicles at least 2m high.

Constraints on width, necessary to build three traffic lanes in good safety conditions, and constraints on height, necessary to allow vehicles of satisfactory size to use the tunnel, do thus converge to produce a consistent design compatible with present-day technical boring capacities.

It has to be added that the proposed size of the structure is such that it is expected that most users would not have a negative reaction when driving through the tunnel.

5. The upper and lower parts of the tunnel are large enough to allow the installation of an effective ventilation system that could also remove smoke from the structure in case of vehicle fires. Surface ventilation and air-removal stations will be spaced an average of 1,600m apart at the surface, which leads to an average distance of 3,200m between two successive air-removal stations.
6. The two levels should possess an automatic accident detection system allowing any stopped or excessively slowing vehicle to be spotted immediately.

The system would thus permit the management to immediately take the required operating decisions and would also allow breakdown and rescue services to be immediately dispatched if need be.

7. When breakdowns or accidents occur, two cases can be distinguished.

Incidents that are not serious will be dealt with by the concessionary breakdown and emergency services; the latter's equipment and qualifications will have to comply with strict standards.

In serious cases, which will be infrequent, an innovative system will be set up. Traffic will be stopped not only at the traffic level concerned by the accident but also on the other traffic level. The result is that emergency services will possess an "emergency structure," which can be used, if necessary, to get to the scene of the emergency or to evacuate persons in difficulty through stairways placed every 400m between the two levels.

In addition, nine wells are projected, which will give specialised emergency services the possibility of entering the structure from the surface in addition to the usual means of entry, for added caution.

* * *

All these systems, if implemented, will offer an unprecedented level of safety in France and probably even abroad, for the following reasons:

- The structure will be of the motorway type (i.e., no pedestrians or bicycles will be allowed). Access to the structure will be controlled and no intersections or head-on collision risks will exist.
- Structures of this type are particularly safe and have much lower accident rates than traditional roads.
- The structure will be an underground one, and experience shows that this kind of structure is safer than surface ones, especially because of the heightened level of user attention, the absence of bad weather, and the steady visibility.
- The structure will be forbidden to heavy vehicles, which are involved in a sizeable proportion of serious accidents.
- Speeds will be constantly checked and speeding will consequently be almost eliminated.
- The many steps organised for emergency and other aid will be unprecedented in comparison to other underground structures.

For such reasons, it is possible to state that if the Commission's recommendations are adopted, the number of accidents in the structure will be exceptionally low and their consequences limited.

It has been possible to estimate the number of lives saved due to the realisation of the structure at more than two per year and the number of injuries at more than fifty, compared to what would happen if vehicles that will use the underground structure had continued to drive on the traditional surface roads.

* * *

Finally, it should be noted that most of the conclusions emanating from the Commission work could, if adapted to local situations, be adopted for other, similar low-gauge underground structures currently in the planning stages in the Paris region or elsewhere.

Christian Gerondeau
Chairman, Union Routière de France

▼▼▼

FIGURES AND COMMENTARIES

Figure 1

EVOLUTION OF PASSENGER TRAFFIC IN WESTERN EUROPE

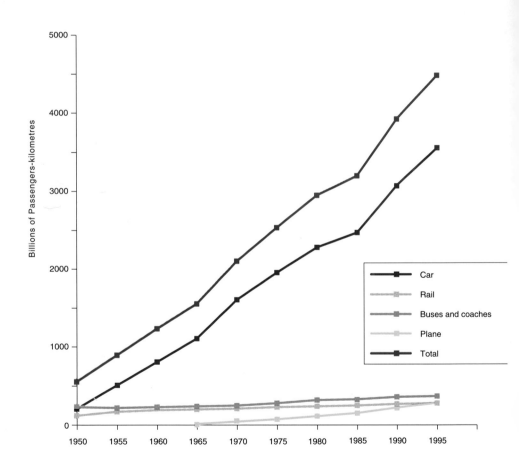

Sources : European Conference of Ministers of Transport (E.C.M.T.), Air Inter, others.

Figure 1
The Explosion

The last four decades have been marked by an explosion in the mobility of Europeans. As their standard of living has improved, they have increased the distances they travel by a factor of eight.

This revolution in lifestyles is principally due to the car, which is now accessible to the great majority of households.

On the other hand, the overall figures of numbers of people using the railways, intercity coaches, and buses has hardly varied.

Air transport, for its part, has recently experienced the most rapid growth, to such a point that domestic European air traffic now exceeds that of rail in terms of kilometres travelled, not to speak of turnover.

Figure 2

GROWTH IN NUMBER OF ROAD VEHICLES
(Western Europe, United States of America)

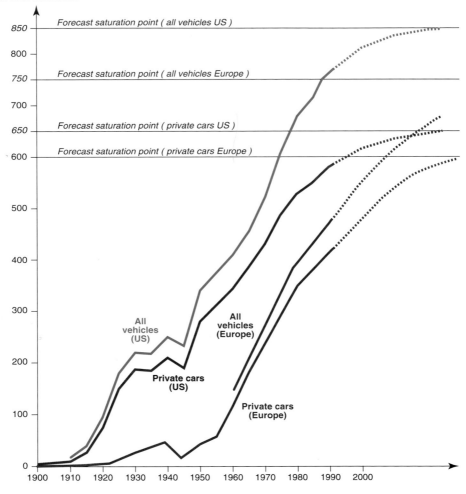

Sources : *Facts and Figures, Motor Vehicles Manufacturers Association (US) and others.*

Figure 2
Limits to Growth

The development of car and road transport in Europe, for both private and commercial use, has globally followed U.S. trends, with a time lag of about 20 years. There is nothing that suggests that this tendency will change in the future even if the forecast vehicle number saturation levels are somewhat lower in Europe due to the urban layout differences on the two continents.

This observation provides two important lessons.

The first concerns the inevitable increase in the number of vehicles expected in Europe over the years to come. This is a consequence on the one hand of the trend towards having two or more cars per household, reflecting the changed attitude towards the car (which has become a personal vehicle rather than a family vehicle), and on the other of an increase in the number of commercial vehicles and heavy goods vehicles.

The second lesson relates to the fact that this increase is going to be limited in the future, since the forecast saturation level corresponds to an average growth in vehicle numbers of about 50% in 20 years and even less in some countries. As a result, there is no reason to worry about a never-ending increase in the number of vehicles, and even less about the volume of traffic, since the additional cars are supplementary vehicles that will be on the road less than the others.

Furthermore, in urban areas the new traffic will occur primarily in the outlying areas of cities because of the decentralised nature of modern urban development, with the increase in traffic therefore being spread over a wide area.

The bulk of the increase in traffic volume, therefore, has already been achieved in dense areas. Except in a limited number of cases, the increases to come will be moderate and manageable as long as the necessary road investment and management improvement are made. Investing in the road does not equate, as is sometimes claimed, to throwing money down a bottomless pit but, rather, to responding to the needs of individuals and the community, in a clear-sighted manner.

Figure 3

NUMBER OF TRIPS
PER DAY PER PERSON

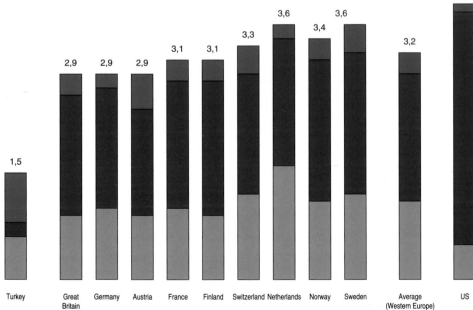

Sources : *A billion trips a day and updates; Nationwide Personal Transportation Survey (US).*

Figure 3
Great Similarities

Overall, the average number of trips per day per person reveals great similarities throughout the various countries of Western Europe. The trips are not an end in themselves but are linked to the pace of daily activities: work, study, shopping, visiting, leisure pursuits, and so forth. Where lifestyles are identical, the number of trips varies relatively little and can only increase within small limits once the bulk of households has access to cars.

In any case, the vast majority of trips are made using individual means of transport (on foot, two-wheeled vehicles, and cars).

In the United States, the private car responds even more to the bulk of transport needs; walking, two-wheeled vehicles, and to a greater extent public transport represent a very small share even though the statistics shown here concern only urban areas.

The situation is clearly different in a country like Turkey, where lifestyles are different and the car not yet very widespread.

Figure 4

EVOLUTION OF TRIPS BY CAR
IN WEST GERMANY

**Number of daily trips
by car per inhabitant**

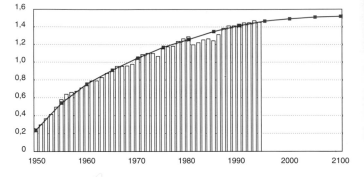

**Average distance
per trip by car**

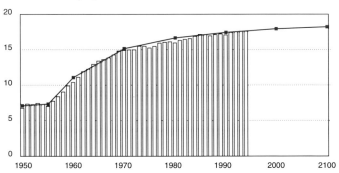

**Average distance covered
by car per day and
per inhabitant**

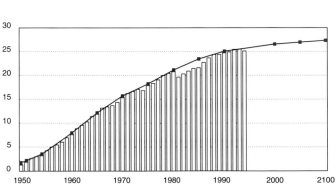

Source : B.V.M. (D.I.V.).

Figure 4
Sustainable Development Henceforward

With approximately 500 cars per 1,000 inhabitants, West Germany has one of the highest car ownership rates in continental Europe.

So, henceforth, the growth in car numbers there will be very moderate since most households already have at least one car and many have two or more. Therefore, the number of trips per day by car per inhabitant is now only increasing very moderately, whereas between 1950 and 1980 it was multiplied by six.

The same development can be observed for the average distance of trips by car; at around 18 km, this corresponds to average trip times of about 20 minutes.

There is no cause for surprise, therefore, that overall the average distance covered by car per day per inhabitant can in the future increase only very moderately. The same phenomenon will be seen for overall distances covered, in a country where the population is stabilised.

Figure 5

MODES OF TRANSPORT USED BY WEST EUROPEANS TO GO TO WORK

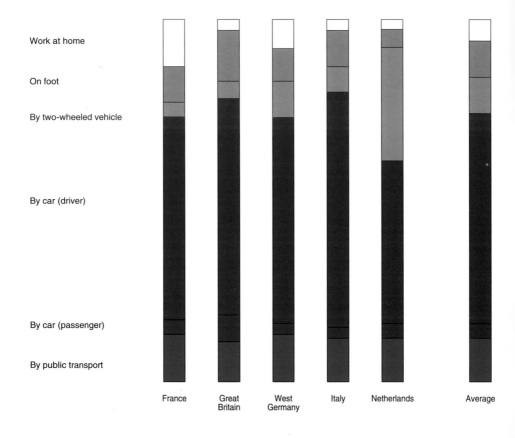

Source : U.R.F. / Sofres Surveys, 1994.

Figure 5
The Prevalence of the Car

There are strong similarities in the travel decisions made by Europeans, and getting to work is no exception in spite of the differences to be found in transport systems and in city layouts.

Among those who use motorised transport, about 80% use the car and only 15% public transport.

The Netherlands must be singled out for its intensive use of the bicycle, which for short trips replaces the car and, to a lesser extent, public transport and walking. However, the very specific Dutch geography and urban layout largely explain this exception.

These are, of course, national averages and the proportion of journeys made using public transport is higher in large urban regions, although it remains the minority.

Figure 6

REASONS FOR CHOOSING THE CAR
TRIP TIME COMPARISONS
BETWEEN HOME AND WORK

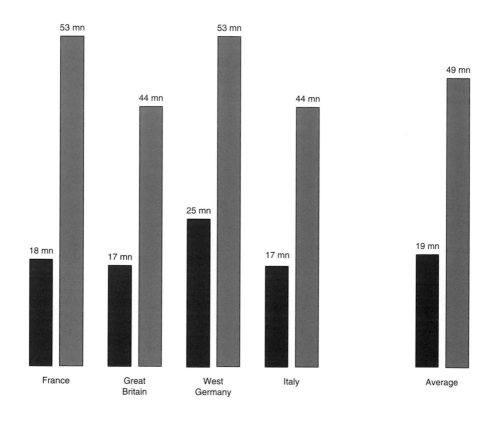

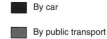
By car

By public transport

Source : U.R.F. / Sofres Surveys, 1994.

Figure 6
A One-Hour Saving

Because of its ability to transport passengers from door to door without having to wait or change transport, the car is almost always much faster than public transport. In this regard as well, the similarities among European countries are striking.

On average, car users take 19 minutes to reach their place of work and public transport users 38 minutes (i.e., twice as long). What is more, these statistics do not concern the same trips. When habitual car users who have already tried using public transport are asked how long their trip took, their responses average 49 minutes. In other words, for them, using a car saves them 30 minutes per trip, an hour a day. For some, it can be less. But for many others, it is much more still.

This is the principal reason for the car's success. For given destinations, it allows substantial time savings. On the other hand, in a given time period, it provides access to a substantially increased number of destinations and, hence, activities.

In both cases, it is a vital factor of quality of life and economic efficiency, which explains why it is so largely endorsed by people all over Europe.

The time savings that the car provides is an essential factor that is often entirely forgotten or underestimated in transport-related decision-making, whereas taking into account the quality of the service rendered (i.e., above all the duration of the trip), should be the most important criterion for the choice in social terms. It is most important to weigh up all the consequences, including the negative ones, before considering taking measures to reduce the use of cars. Such measures are only justified in very limited cases.

Figure 7

PROPORTION OF EUROPEANS STATING
THAT THEY DO NOT USUALLY ENCOUNTER
MANY TRAFFIC JAMS ON THE WAY TO WORK

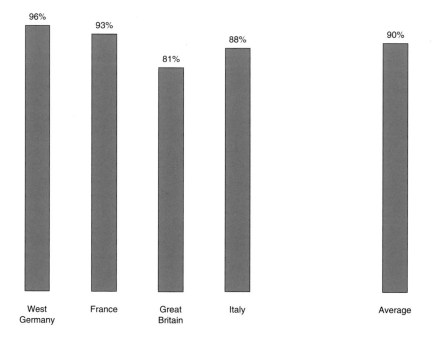

West Germany	France	Great Britain	Italy		Average
96%	93%	81%	88%		90%

Source : U.R.F. / Sofres Surveys, 1994.

Figure 7
Fluidity and Congestion

The brevity of car trips shown above may cause surprise since public opinion is almost unaware of it. When French people are asked to estimate the average time of trips by car between home and work made by their compatriots, they estimate around 38 minutes whereas in reality it is 18 minutes, roughly half the time. For the Paris region, the difference is even greater since the estimate is 1 hour 20 minutes whereas the real average trip time is 27 minutes, a third of the time! The same type of replies are given in other European countries and elsewhere: The car's effectiveness is always underestimated.

Even if there are some differences between European countries, probably related to differences in urban layouts and in road investments, the brevity of car trips is, nevertheless, confirmed by numerous corroborating surveys. It is also confirmed by the fact that, among Europeans who go to work by car, the proportion of those who state that they usually encounter many traffic jams is surprisingly small and does not exceed 10% on average. Furthermore, these are trips principally made at rush hour.

Even if a minority of commuters encounter traffic jams on an everyday basis, the generally accepted vision of road networks being saturated most of the time is contrary to the truth.

Figure 8

STABILITY OF TRIP TIMES
BY CAR OVER TIME

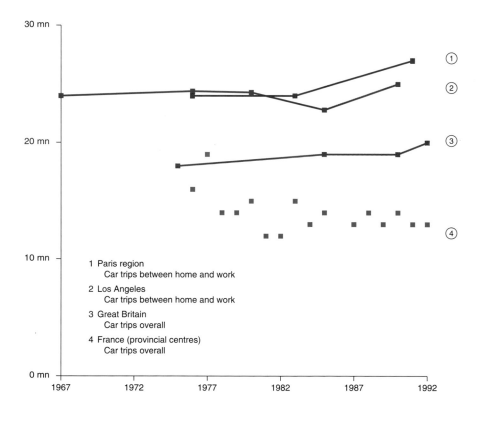

1 Paris region
   Car trips between home and work

2 Los Angeles
   Car trips between home and work

3 Great Britain
   Car trips overall

4 France (provincial centres)
   Car trips overall

Sources : (1) General Transport Surveys, Paris Region.
(2) National Censuses and other surveys (US).
(3) National Travel Surveys (GB).
(4) Transports Urbains (French urban transport periodical), n° 84.

Figure 8
Limited Variations

The table opposite is rich in information. It first shows that, as could be expected, average car trip times grow longer as the size of the urban region increases: 27 minutes for trips between home and work in Paris (11 million inhabitants) and 25 minutes in Los Angeles (14 million inhabitants). The average is 20 minutes for the whole of Great Britain, and about 14 minutes for French provincial centres, all purposes combined.

Nevertheless, whatever the size of the urban regions, such trip times are very short in comparison with those on public transport and are not far from an average of 20 minutes.

The second piece of information concerns the small variations in these trip times over the years:

- Los Angeles: 24 minutes in 1967, 25 in 1990;
- Paris: 24 minutes in 1976, 27 in 1991;
- Great Britain: 18 minutes in 1975, 20 in 1992.

In French provincial centres, where there has been a great deal of road development work, the situation is likely to have improved slightly over recent years.

As average trip distances have very greatly increased over recent decades, this stability of duration reveals that average trip speeds have likewise sharply increased, notably because of the development of journeys in suburban areas where traffic flows better. It is therefore paradoxical and mistaken to talk of an overall increase in congestion. It is just the opposite.

The third piece of information given in the table opposite relates to the fact that inadequacy of investment in roads nevertheless leads to a relative deterioration of the situation, as may be shown the recent figures for the Paris region, even if road's performance nonetheless remains very high overall.

Figure 9

AREAS EASILY ACCESSIBLE
BY ROAD AND BY RAIL

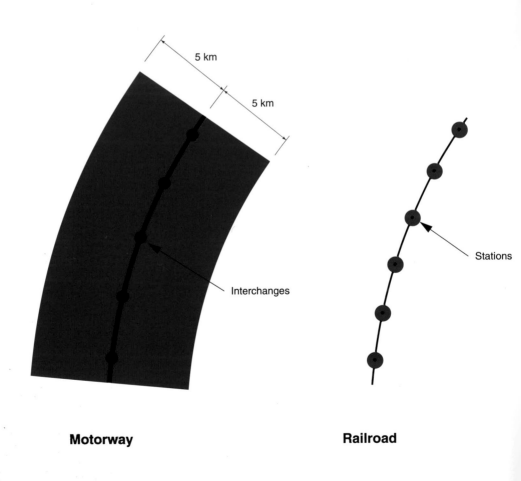

Motorway   **Railroad**

Figure 9
The Real Difference

It is sometimes difficult to understand the profound difference in nature between a road and a railway, as they are similar when examined on a map. The difference comes from the fact that the car can offer door-to-door transport. The result is that the urban or suburban area served in a few minutes by an expressway from its interchanges is a strip several kilometres wide, whereas that covered in the same lapse of time from a train station is usually a circle a few hundred metres in radius because of the slow speed of walking.

Being a few kilometres away from a motorway means practically being on it. Being a few kilometres away from a station means being nowhere, except by using several successive means of transport, which is usually a long, hard, and costly solution. Consequently, public transport is only well-adapted to serving high-density central areas.

As far as ring links are concerned, as they are between areas with average or low overall densities, it is hardly surprising that the World Bank noted, "nowhere in the world is there a ring railway network that is profitable, because the travellers are too spread out." On the opposite, road ringroads, are very well-suited to this kind of low-density area and have heavy traffic.

Mutatis mutandis, what is true for passengers regarding the road ability to provide door-to-door transport is just as true for freight, and this explains the success of road transport for goods.

Figure 10

GASOLINE CONSUMPTION VERSUS URBAN DENSITY

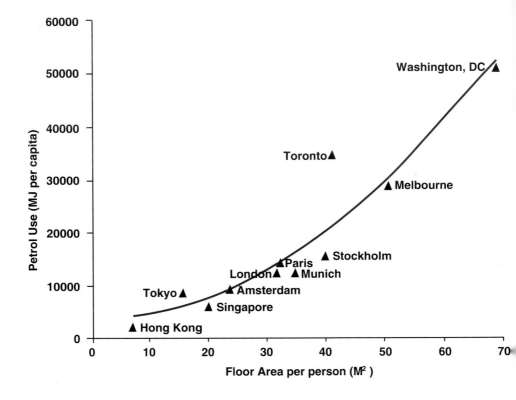

Source: Sustainable Transport, World Bank 1996

Figure 10
Considerable Benefits

As they give easy access to vast areas, roads, and even more so motorways, enable the inhabitants of the regions concerned to have large living spaces at their disposal at low cost. As a result, they can purchase or rent larger homes, often in a more enjoyable environment, than would be possible in towns that do not benefit from these transport networks.

In this respect, the World Bank has established a direct relationship between the volume of fuel consumed, which indicates the level of the use of the car, and the residential space per person, adding that "high urban densities with relatively lower fuel use are usually associated with the disadvantages of high housing costs and a low level of residential space per person."

The relationship is extremely strong because 89% of the difference in the fuel consumption per inhabitant is explained in statistical terms by the area of dwelling space available per person. This is a considerable positive external effect of the use of the car and the road, which completely changes the quality of life for the populations concerned.

Figure 11

DISTRIBUTION OF FREIGHT TRANSPORTATION
IN WESTERN EUROPE ACCORDING TO
VARIOUS CRITERIA
(1993)

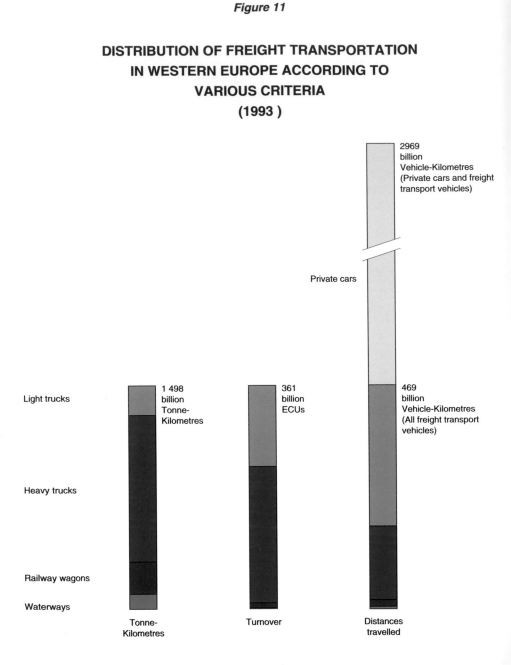

Sources : - ECMT and estimates by the author (tonne-kilometres)
- International Union of Railways and estimates by the author (turnover)
- International Union of Railways and O.E.C.D. (distances).

Figure 11
Meaningless Units of Measure

The unit of measure universally adopted in Europe to compare the different modes of freight transport is the *tonne kilometre*. This measure, however, has no meaning either in economics or in the physical world. The value of transporting one tonne over one kilometre can vary by a factor of between one and a hundred or more depending on the product being transported (e.g., fruit or minerals), the distance travelled, packing conditions, the transport mode, delivery times, and so forth. The turnover of the different modes of transport (i.e., the sums that users pay for them) is the only significant reflection of the economic reality of the service rendered and has no connection with tonne kilometres.

The same is true on the physical level: The occupancy of the transport networks depends on distances travelled, not on the weight of the loads transported. A hundred delivery vans carrying 250 kilos each obviously create more congestion than one heavy truck carrying 25 tonnes, although in tonne kilometres they are equal. This is why only *vehicle kilometres* have meaning in the measurement of the physical occupancy of the networks, and not tonne kilometres.

Because of the use of meaningless units, the various modes of freight transport do not at all have the weight attributed to them by official statistics used in Europe as in other parts of the world.

The railways do not deal with 18% of freight transport in Europe, but with less than 3% from an economic point of view. They count for less than 1% of the transport networks' occupancy (14 billion kilometres travelled each year by rail freight wagons, as against nearly 3,000 billion by all road vehicles taken together).

Even if rail traffic or the traffic on inland waterways were to double, which is not a realistic assumption, there would be no perceptible impact on road traffic. No "balancing" among land modes of transportation is therefore possible. Only the road can relieve the road.

Figure 12

FRENCH ROAD TRANSPORT SYSTEM
TURNOVER FOR 1993
(In billions of francs)

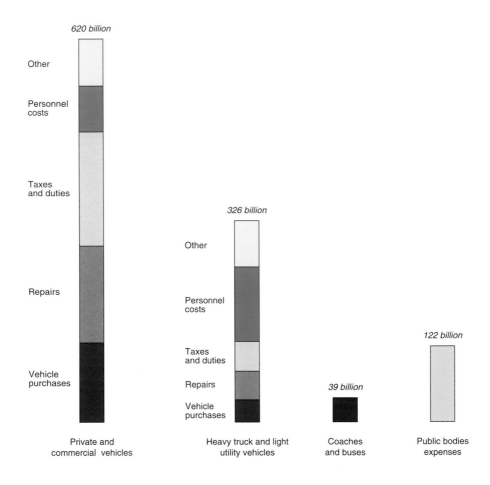

Source : Insee - Oest, French national transport accounts, 1993.

Figure 12
Fifteen Percent of the GDP

In France, as elsewhere in Europe, the community devotes around 15% of the gross domestic product (GDP) to the transportation by road of people and freight.

A myriad of businesses and services are directly concerned: the steel industry, the oil industry, chemicals, textiles and electronics, the automobile industry, component manufacturers, tyre manufacturers, garages, service stations, long-distance hauliers, logistics companies, driving schools, road builders, the police and other forces of order, government departments, coach and bus companies, insurance companies, and so forth.

Together, these activities represent more than 10% of jobs in Europe and therefore provide a great deal of employment.

Road transport is both indispensable to modern economies and is, in many respects, their number one sector of activity.

Figure 13

ROADS AND GEOGRAPHY

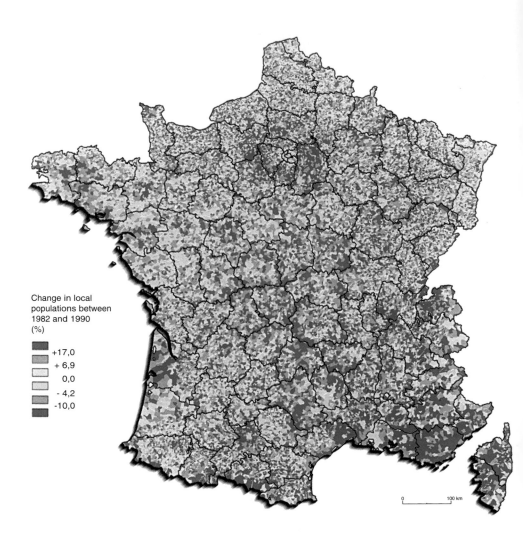

Change in local
populations between
1982 and 1990
(%)

+17,0
+ 6,9
0,0
- 4,2
-10,0

0   100 km

POPULATION CHANGE 1982 TO 1990

Source : Atlas of France, Population, Documentation Française (Reclus, 1995).

Figure 13
An Historic Revolution

From the beginning of the industrial era, the facts were simple: The European countryside was being deserted in favour of towns, and many people still remain convinced in this belief, which indeed corresponded to reality even 15 or 20 years ago.

However, with the spread of the car and the expansion of road freight transport, the situation changed suddenly and thoroughly. Now it is possible to live 20 or 30 km away from a town while still participating in its activities and benefiting from its services. Towns have been succeeded by conurbations. Conurbations in turn have been succeeded by huge "living and employment basins," which cover the majority of the territory of Western Europe. The result is that tens of thousands of villages have been revived and are again seeing their population grow, as French geographers, like those of the other countries, have discovered with amazement.

In France, nearly 7,000 communes, of which the populations had been diminishing since the beginning of the 19th century, suddenly began gaining population between the censuses of 1982 and 1990, in the frame of the new "living and employment basins" whose boundaries are curiously not far from those of the "départements" created by Napoleon, for which the reference was a half-day journey by horse instead of half an hour today by car.

On the other hand, the population in overly dense town centres has stabilised or more often decreased. Overall, a better population distribution has resulted, improving the quality of life of the majority of Europeans, who wish to have more space at their disposal. This is a positive side effect of the spread of the car and of road freight transport, which, furthermore, increases the productivity of modern economies for they allow the creation of much larger employment basins than was possible before.

Figure 14

METROROUTE
CROSS-SECTION

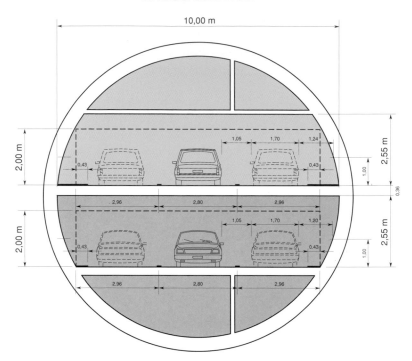

Source : *Commission Interministérielle de Sécurité (july 1992)*
(French Interdepartmental Safety Commission).

REAL-SIZE MODEL (Near Orleans)

Source : *Société COFIROUTE.*

Figure 14
The Invention of the Century

It was in France that, in 1987, the idea arose of applying technical progress in tunnelling to the creation of an entirely new breed of road tunnels. Whereas traditionally road tunnels have been accessible to heavy vehicles and have therefore had a ceiling height of more than 5m, the suggested innovation was to restrict these new tunnels, or *metroroutes,* to vehicles with a maximum height of about 2m, which represent 90% of road traffic in urban areas at rush hour. In dense urban areas, it is more judicious to make cars travel underground rather than lorries.

In a tunnel bored 10m in interior diameter, there is then room to put two levels with three lanes each, one above the other, instead of having, as is usually the case, a single two-lane road.

In addition, these tunnels offer numerous advantages from an environmental point of view: no visual disturbance of the scenery, no noise pollution, and the spacing of air ventilation outlets more than 3 km apart thanks to the regularity of traffic speeds (which will limit polluting emissions) and to technical advances in car construction.

However, the chief environmental benefit of these tunnels is rather that, thanks to their capacity, they will greatly alleviate the existing surface traffic. This will allow implementation of traffic reduction and safety policies, which will benefit the local population, pedestrians, two-wheeled vehicles, and buses and, in a much more general manner, will contribute to a better living environment.

As the most striking invention for dense urban environment since the underground railway at the end of the 19th century, it responds to similar concerns and needs.

The construction of a life-size model near the town of Orléans has proved the relevance of the project.

Figure 15

INSERTION OF METROROUTES
IN AN URBAN ENVIRONMENT

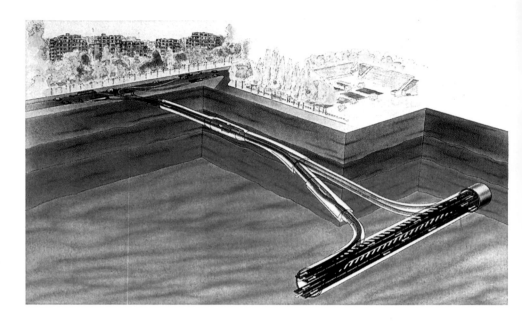

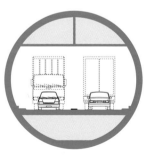

Conventional 2-lane tunnel
Ceiling height : more than 5 m
Inside diameter : 10 m

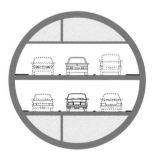

6-lane metroroute
Ceiling height : 2,55 m
Inside diameter : 10 m

Source : Société COFIROUTE.

Figure 15
Easy Insertion

It is often very difficult, if not impossible, to create traditional tunnels in a dense urban environment. The entries and exits require considerable amounts of land and produce bulky, unsightly structures since they have to allow for trucks.

The connections to the metroroutes can, on the contrary, be constructed almost anywhere since they will be identical to the entries and exits to underground car parks. They are therefore far more discrete because they are only accessible to vehicles of a limited height.

It should be added that, in the central parts of urban areas, most goods deliveries are made by light goods vehicles that will also be able to use the metroroutes, and not by heavy trucks.

At the price of a limited diameter increase, metroroutes could also be used by specifically designed light public transport vehicles and, at the same time, answer private and public transport needs.

Figure 16

PLANNED METROROUTES IN PARIS AREA

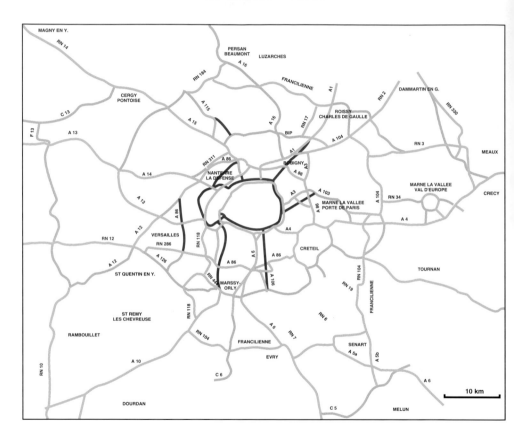

Motorways in use

Planned regular motorways

Planned underground
motorways (metroroutes)

Source: Schéma Directeur d'Aménagement et d'Urbanisme de la Région Ile de France (1993)

Figure 16
More than 100 Kilometres of Metroroutes

The Paris region's urban planning and development schedule for 2015, officially adopted in 1994, has planned more than 100 km of underground reduced-gauge metroroutes, which together represent a far more ambitious project than the Channel Tunnel. The first of them is due to come into service around 2002 in the western part of the region, to complete the A86 bypass motorway with a 10-km stretch beneath the town of Versailles. The necessary permits were finally granted in December 1995, and work is commencing in 1997. The figure opposite shows the section that is furthest to the west. Another much shorter section is also planned in the short term in the northwest, close to Paris.

On completion of the entire works, the Paris region will then be able to provide its residents and visitors with substantially altered traffic conditions in its central areas, with guaranteed journey times for those who use the toll metroroutes, in itself a revolution made possible by the control of entry flows with the tariffs being adjusted according to demand if necessary.

However, it is impossible at present to form an opinion on the rate at which the whole project will be implemented. Paradoxically, traffic conditions in the central part of the Paris area are much better than is generally imagined due to an already well-developed motorway network and do not seem to be deteriorating for now. The result is that the tolls collected would not be sufficient to finance alone the construction of the metroroutes.

But the most important thing was to make a start, in order to have a prototype section capable of demonstrating the feasibility and the advantages of this innovative concept.

Figure 17

LONDON POTENTIAL
METROROUTE NETWORK

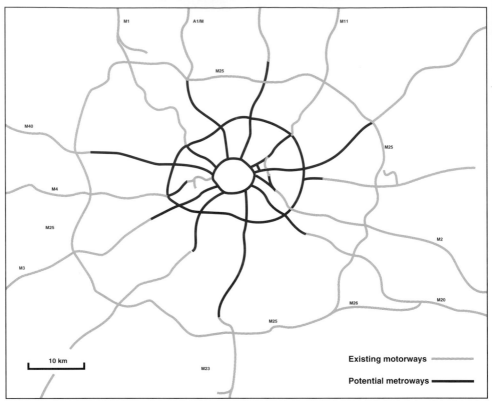

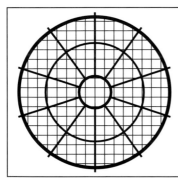

A HYPOTHETICAL STRATEGIC
ROAD NETWORK FOR LONDON

Source : a transport strategy
for London (1996) :
UK Government Office for London
and Department of Transport

Figure 17
An Ideal Network for London?

Contrary to Paris, Western Europes's other megacity, London's motorway network is not very developed. It only has one ring road motorway (M25), which is very much on the outskirts as it is on average 25 kilometres from the historical centre, and a few embryonic radial urban motorways. Paris, on the other hand, has three almost complete motorway ring roads and about ten high-capacity radial urban motorways, not to mention an important network of boulevards and dual carriageways. For this reason, a network of metroroutes, maybe as shown in the draft outline in the figure opposite, would be even more justified in London than in the French capital and would probably merit being studied. A world city deserves it.

Such a network would be in line with the British government report published in 1996 under the title "A transport strategy for London," which outlined the ideal motorway plan considered necessary for the smooth running of the economy of London's urban area.

Finally, such a project would be fitting to the historical tradition of the country, which was the remakable forerunner in the 19th century in the field of underground transport with the first Thames crossing, followed later on by the "Tube." Are "Metroroutes" anything other than "Car-tubes"?

Figure 18

PLANNED STOCKHOLM UNDERGROUND ROAD NETWORK

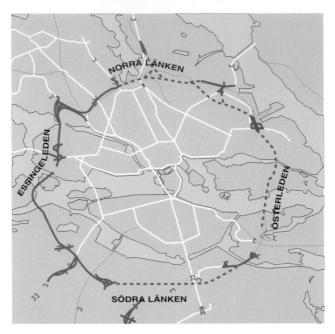

Source: Swedish National Road Administration

Figure 18
A Lost Opportunity

At the beginining of the 1990s, the Swedish government and the city of Stockholm launched a remarkable transport scheme called the "DENNIS PACKAGE," which is evenly split between public transport and road infrastructures.

As part of this project, the latter were to benefit from the completion of two bypasses, one on the western Stockholm outskirts and the other a ringroad close to the historical center. The missing stretch of the central ringroad was to be constructed underground as opposed to to the existing western part, which was constructed on the surface 20 years ago.

The works were to be gigantic, as the planned tunnels were designed to handle all categories of vehicles, including heavy trucks, as is shown in the photograph of the life-size model on the opposite page. Although the length of the ringroad still to be built does not exceed 14 kilometres, the boring of about 45 kilometres of tunnels was planned, since they would have been one-way only and structures linking them to the surface were also to be counted. The financing was to come from tolls, paid by those using the tunnels and every car and truck entering Stockholm, which would have had to contribute to this scheme dedicated to alleviating the traffic in the city and thus improving the environment.

Works began in 1996, and everything was settled when, in February 1997, a new government, using a law initially aimed at protecting Laponia in northern Sweden, stopped everything on an environmental pretext. The fact that the planned structure was almost entirely underground shows the extremes that those who are opposed on principle to any type of road (even when favorable to the environment) will go to prevent new road construction. At the beginning of March 1997, it seemed most unlikely that works have any chance of resuming in the near future. This leaves France alone in Europe in the construction of underground city motorways.

Maybe someday the remarkable "DENNIS PACKAGE" will have to be relaunched with the far less expensive *metroroute* technique. Actually, as the western part of the ringroad already exists and can largely divert heavy traffic, it is not clear why the missing part should necessarily be designed to accept heavy vehicles. Doing so would, in fact, roughly triple the cost.

Figure 19

MOTORWAY'S ROLE IN URBAN AREAS

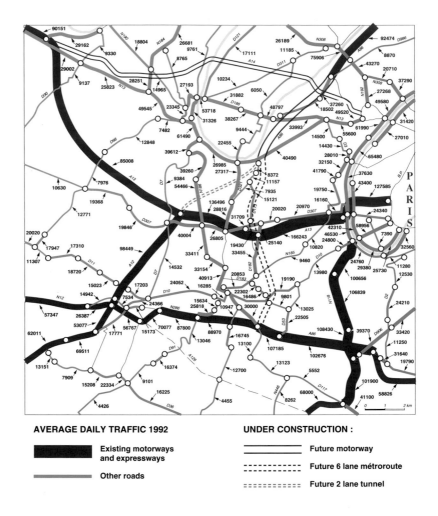

AVERAGE DAILY TRAFFIC 1992

Existing motorways and expressways

Other roads

UNDER CONSTRUCTION :

Future motorway

Future 6 lane métroroute

Future 2 lane tunnel

Sources : Traffic map 1992. Arterial Network. Hauts de Seine and Yvelines Prefectures.

Figure 19
Traffic Draining

When a village is blocked with traffic coming from outside and not concerning it, everybody usually agrees that it is useful to build a bypass to allow its inhabitants to return to peace and quiet and their former quality of life.

The problem is the same for large urban areas. In order to decrease the volume of traffic crossing through their different areas and districts, new capacities capable of absorbing a maximum of traffic must be created. The main way of achieving this is to build motorways, as there can be no possible comparison between their capacity and that of traditional roads. A motorway with three lanes each way can absorb 150,000 and even in exceptional cases up to 180,000 vehicles per day in urban areas, compared to, generally speaking, 30,000 to 40,000 for a traditional boulevard and far less still for a normal street or road.

This is being implemented in the western part of the Paris region shown opposite. It can be clearly seen that in areas where there are already motorways, the local streets and roads are not overloaded, whereas when there is a lack of high-capacity infrastructures, the local streets and roads are congested with very heavy traffic, to the detriment of the local inhabitants.

It is to remedy this situation that two new motorways were planned, one (A14) on an east-west route and the other (A86) on a north-south route, designed to bring significant relief to the local streets and roads, which are congested at present and run parallel to their routes. A14 opened at the end of 1996.

On the condition that the necessary investments are made by creating new motorways or by increasing the capacity of existing ones, it is possible and justified, except in the centres of large urban areas, to answer all the demand for traffic to the benefit of the inhabitants' quality of life and the smooth running of the economy. It is a question of adjusting supply and demand.

The good news is that the demand is now only slightly increasing in most West European countries and that it is even stabilised in the central parts of most urban areas and their vicinity, meaning that the problem can be solved, if necessary by creating underground infrastructures of the *metroroute* type, as is the case here for part of the A86 motorway.

Figure 20

TRAFFIC INTENSITY
IN THE NETHERLANDS IN 1994

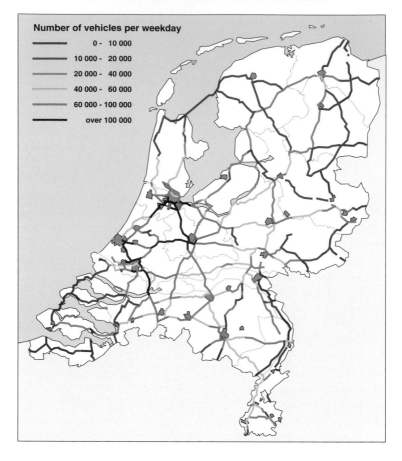

Source: National Road Census

Figure 20
A Solvable Problem

Even in the Netherlands, which is the country with the highest population in Europe, there are few motorway sections where traffic exceeds 100,000 vehicles per day, and these are all located in urban or suburban areas.

This is a general rule. In the whole of Western Europe, there are not more than about 200 kilometres of interurban motorway sections where the average traffic exceeds 80,000 vehicles per day. It is generally accepted that the maximum capacity of an interurban motorway is 50,000 vehicles per day for two lanes each way, 80,000 for three lanes each way, and 110,000 for four lanes each way. But the average traffic on interurban motorways in Europe is less than 30,000 vehicles per day.

The result is that there is reserve capacity on all European interurban motorways, on the one condition that some of them should be progressively widened by adding additional lanes up to four each way, as and when justified, and that there is no reason for them to be saturated, except for a few weekend or holiday migrations, which is clearly acceptable.

In urban areas, the capacities are far higher, due to more intensive use and a better spreading of journeys throughout the day. In the Paris region the figures are sometimes over 100,000 vehicles per day for two lanes each way, 150,000 for three lanes each way and 200,000 for four lanes each way.

But these are exceptional figures for Europe. Overall, even in urban areas, there are very few sections that exceed 100,000 vehicles per day. It is therefore possible to meet demand except in the centre of certain cities, on the condition that reasonable investments are made in road networks, in addition to "intelligent" management techniques.

Figure 21

GOVERNMENT EXPENSES AND REVENUES
AS CONCERNS THE ROAD

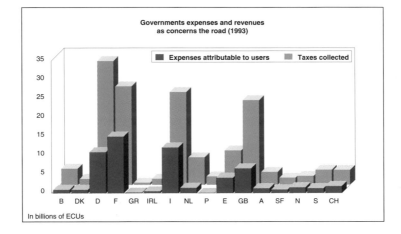

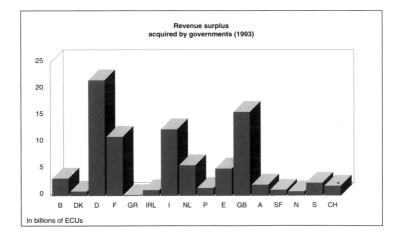

Source : O.I.C.A. (World car manufacturers association)

Figure 21
A "Milch Cow"

In all the countries of Europe, the various taxes and duties that are imposed on the purchase, possession, and use of road transport vehicles exceed by a large margin the financial expenditures made in their favour by national and local governments.

All together, the revenues collected in 1995 came to 167 billion ECUs and expenditure to 57 billion, which leaves a considerable surplus of more than 100 billion ECUs for Western Europe as a whole.

This ability of road transport to provide such high revenues—accepted, furthermore, whether they like it or not, by road users—relates directly to the substantial advantages that users gain from using it, which are linked to its door-to-door ability. This is, therefore, proof of the scope of the services it provides as much as to individuals and companies as to the community as a whole.

High taxes on road transport, which are usually the rule in Europe, do not exist, however, without serious drawbacks, both for the economy as a whole since they inflate the price of all products and socially, since they hit hardest those with modest incomes, in particular those in rural and suburban areas who by nature have the longest distances to travel.

Figure 22

COVERAGE OF RUNNING COSTS
OF URBAN PUBLIC TRANSPORT
BY RECEIPTS IN 1993

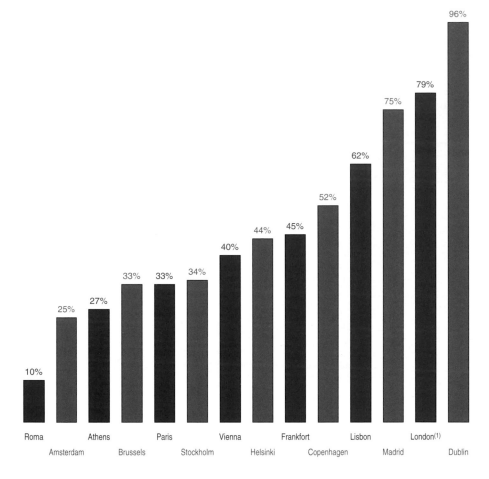

(1) including depreciation.

Source : Janes' Urban Transport, cited in the "Citizens' network" European Commission Green Paper.

Figure 22
Considerable Disparities

There is currently almost no European city where receipts from public transport users cover the running costs of the system, not to mention the large capital investments that many of them are undertaking.

This situation stems from several factors: stagnation or reduction in customers due to competition from cars and changes in urban land use, the "labour intensive" nature of public transport, and the deliberate granting of subsidies or specific financing to take into account the social side of public transport.

However, the extreme disparity in the networks' level of expenditure coverage is particularly striking given that no link has ever been established between the level of subsidies received and the volume of passenger traffic on the network. On the other hand, productivity seems to be higher whenever the size of subsidies is limited. Proof of this can be seen in the recent remarkable example of London, which, by granting a concession on its bus network to the private sector, has succeeded not only in improving the quality of service but at the same time in dividing the amount of subsidies by seven in 10 years.

Moreover, the fact that fares on certain routes are set substantially below their cost is not without drawbacks since it can result in the artificial development of long-distance journeys.

It is in fact largely for historical reasons that in countries similar in all other respects, the weight of urban public transport subsidies sometimes varies by a factor of one to three, if not more. This is without doubt one of the areas where there are the greatest possible margins of variation in conceivable policies.

Figure 23

RAILWAYS :
COVERAGE OF OPERATION COSTS
AND INTEREST CHARGES BY RECEIPTS
Year 1992

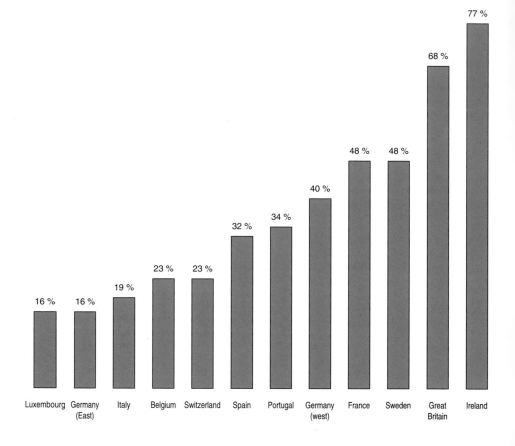

Source : *International Railway Statistics : International Union of Railways (U.I.C.).*

Figure 23
A Unique Case

The extent of public subsidies to the railways in Europe reaches levels unequalled in other sectors of the economy. This situation is the direct result of the nationalisations carried out around the time of World War II, which allowed the railways to escape the laws of the market, and today poses especially difficult financial problems for all European countries.

However, as is the case for urban transport, the extent of the use of public finances to balance the accounts is extremely variable. Reforms have been initiated nearly everywhere, but they differ fundamentally in their goals and means. Some are sharply reducing the charge on the public finances, whereas others are perpetuating the current state of affairs or making only partial changes.

In fact, only Great Britain seems to be in the process of really solving the problem. The total privatisation of the network by granting concessions to a large number of independent companies will lead in the short term, as for the London buses, to a drastic reduction in the burden to taxpayers and will improve nevertheless the offer and the quality of service wherever this is judged necessary. It is significant to note that there are no longer any British political parties that consider making a serious challenge to this revolutionary reform. But Great Britain, which is only putting into practice principles that are now in force throughout the world by returning the management of the railway networks to the private sector whilst retaining the overall control of the system, is still completely isolated in Europe with such a policy.

Nevertheless, all European governments have to agree that it is no longer possible to continue the past situation in light of the widespread general constraints rightly imposed on public finances.

Figure 24

DISPARITY OF TREATMENT
OF THE DIFFERENT MODES OF TRANSPORT
IN 1992

ROAD	AIR	RAIL
(Government surpluses)		(Government contributions)

97 billion ECUs

- 40 billion ECUs

Sources : International Road Federation
International Union of Railways.

Figure 24
A Huge Inconsistency

In Europe, the different modes of transport are subjected to very different rules of play.

Airlines must balance their accounts while covering almost all costs related to their business, including airport charges and air traffic control expenses. European Union directives forbid states to subsidise them except in extraordinary circumstances.

As we have seen, the road sector, through numerous taxes and levies, provides governments with much more, overall, than it costs them.

The opposite is true for the railways, which, with the encouragement of European Community authorities, benefit from substantial subsidies for their capital investment not to speak of the ones they receive for their operations' costs.

The existence of three totally different rules of play, although the services in question all respond to the same function—transport of people and freight—has no real justification, and the arguments that are often put forward to defend the contrary do not stand up to analysis, as the differences in the rules are too great.

Figure 25

COMPARISON OF INFRASTRUCTURE EXPENSES
FOR ROAD AND RAIL
1975 - 1989

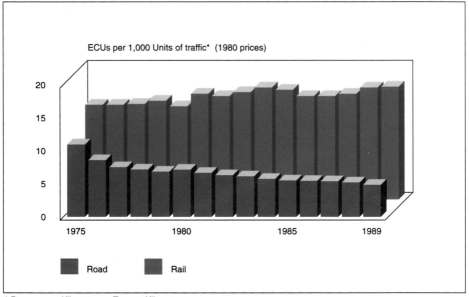

ECUs per 1,000 Units of traffic* (1980 prices)

Road   Rail

* Passengers-Kilometres + Tonnes-Kilometres

Source : European Conférence of Ministers of Transport (E.C.M.T.).

Figure 25
Unequal Treatment

When measured in terms of traffic handled, capital investment in rail has not stopped growing over recent years in spite of the deficits recorded, whereas the opposite is true for the road in spite of the money it earns. This is the consequence of the marked preference shown by the European governments and Community and international authorities for rail transport.

It must be stressed that the graph opposite, developed from data expressed in passenger kilometres and tonne kilometres, only very partially reflects reality, which is still far more favourable to the railways than indicated when taking into account the actual figures (i.e., the financial turnovers).

Figure 26

DEVELOPMENT OF BUS AND COACH
JOURNEYS FROM 1970 TO 1990
(In billions of passenger-kilometres)

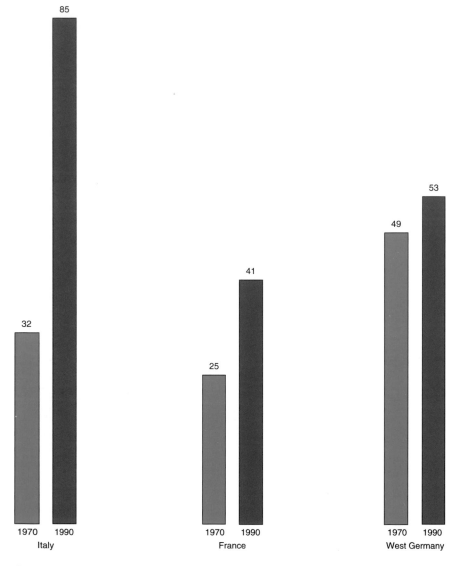

Source : *European Conference of Ministers of Transport (E.C.M.T.); Transport Evolution 1970-1990.*

Figure 26
A Situation Difficult to Explain

On the issue of coaches, European countries can be divided into two categories. The first permits free establishment of regular intercity lines. The second forbids it, either in theory or in fact, to protect the railway monopoly, except for some local lines. The development of traffic is clearly very different in the two cases.

Many countries that belong in the first category have experienced a very rapid development of this mode of transport. Italy has a lot of long-distance intercity coach lines that interconnect all the large towns and that use the motorway system.

Much cheaper to buy or operate than the railway, the coach is a particularly economical form of transport for which an important potential clientele exists. One role of the coach, among others, is to supplement the main railway lines on intercity links with limited or moderate traffic, at a lower cost.

On the eve of the 21st century and at a time when European regulations are rightly imposing the complete opening of the skies to competition among airlines, continuing the ban on coach lines in a large number of West European countries and the past inaction of the Community authorities in this field constitute one of the surprising inconsistencies in Europe's transport policy, as well as proof of the power of the railway companies.

Figure 27

THE EUROPEAN ARCHIPELAGO
THE TRUE MAP OF "TRANSPORT EUROPE"

0   100 km

Figure 27
Europe Is Not America

As far as transport is concerned, Europe—unlike the United States—is an archipelago and not a continent.

When a border separates two cities or two regions, experience shows that exchanges of people or freight between them are five to ten times lower than if they were located in the same country.

The result is that traffic crossing borders is very low compared with that within each country.

This "border effect" should decrease with time, but it will always remain a substantial factor on a continent that possesses more than 20 languages and where the centuries have so clearly differentiated national mentalities and habits. It will probably require decades for the coefficient of reduction to drop below about four.

This basic statement applies as much to the road as to air or rail transport.

Figure 28

PARIS-BRUSSELS LINK
MOTORWAY TRAFFIC

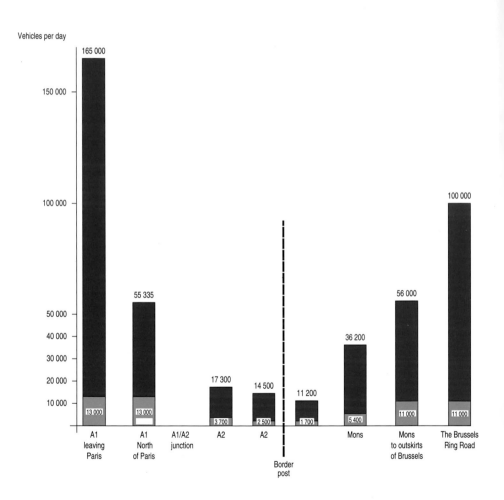

Figure 28
The "Border Effect" and the Road

Those driving from Paris to Brussels encounter highly variable traffic conditions during their journey.

Upon leaving Paris, the traffic on the A1 motorway reaches 165,000 vehicles per day, which makes it one of the most heavily travelled in Europe.

After passing the Roissy-Charles-de-Gaulle Airport, the traffic stabilises for more than 120 km at around 50,000 vehicles per day.

However, the bulk of this traffic heads to northern France, not to Belgium. Once the motorist leaves the A1 to take the A2, which goes to the Belgian border and on to Brussels, the traffic drops by three-quarters and the motorway is little used. The phenomenon is then strictly symmetrical for the last part of the journey.

What makes this striking is that the border between France and Belgium is located in one of the most densely populated regions of Europe, and, what is more, the two sides are inhabited for once by the same peoples, speaking the same language but in two different countries.

Figure 29

MAIN AIR LINKS
IN WESTERN EUROPE
(more than 1 million passengers - 1994)

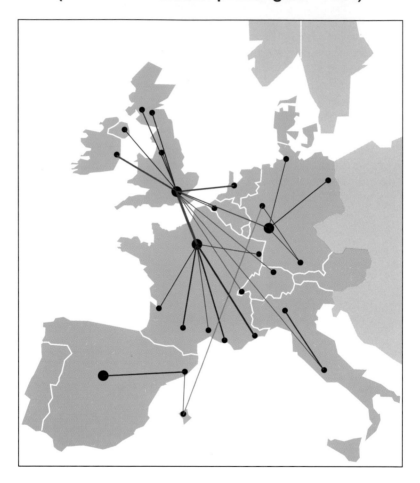

Domestic links ———————
Regular international links ———————
Charter link ———————

1 mm = 3 billion passengers

Source: AIR INTER (AIR FRANCE GROUP)

Figure 29
The "Border Effect" and Air Transport

If one excludes links with Great Britain, the relative importance of which is partly explained by the fact that it is an island, all the scheduled air routes that recorded traffic in excess of one million passengers in 1994 were domestic routes in various countries, and not international ones between countries.

It would clearly be completely different if it were not for the *border effect*. Munich is the same distance from Paris as Marseilles and has many more inhabitants. Yet the air traffic between Paris and Munich is 10 times lower than between Paris and Marseilles.

In 1995, air traffic decreased between London and Paris and between London and Brussels, due to the arrival on the market of the railway link EUROSTAR through the Channel tunnel. It will decrease further when the new British rail line between London and the tunnel begins operating, around 2003.

But these are exceptions. Due to the border effect, there is no other international link with heavy traffic in the distance bracket suitable for high-speed trains.

Figure 30

1988 PASSENGER RAIL TRAFFIC

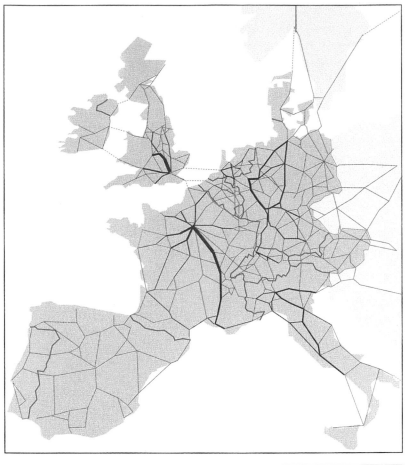

RAIL TRAFFIC
1988 Analysis

Journeys of more than 80 KM

1,000,000 travellers per year

25,000,000 travellers per year

0   600 km

Source: Traffic and Profitability of the Western European High-Speed Train network (1993)

European Commission and Community of European Railways INRETS - INTRAPLAN

Figure 30
The "Border Effect" and the Train

A rapid look at the map opposite is enough to see that rail transport is no different from other modes of transport when it comes to the respective volume of national and international traffic. Just as for air transport, the passenger market is above all domestic, which explains why the traffic recorded at borders is still extremely low most of the time and destined to remain so.

Figure 31

PASSENGER RAIL TRAFFIC FORECASTS FOR 2010

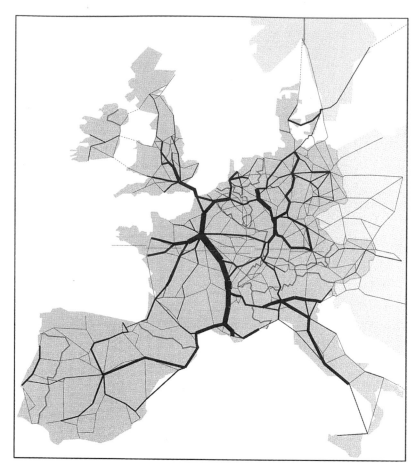

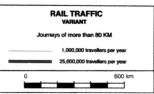

Source: Traffic and Profitability of the Western European High-Speed Train network (1993)
European Commission and Community of European Railways INRETS - INTRAPLAN

Figure 31
Unrealistic Expectations

The map opposite shows the official traffic forecasts for 2010, on which the European "major projects" for the railways are based. One glance is enough to see that although these forecasts were drawn up by well-known research organisations, they are completely fanciful and have not the slightest chance of ever being achieved.

How can it seriously be imagined that the traffic between Barcelona in Spain and Perpignan in France will one day be equal to current traffic between Paris and Lyons, on the most heavily travelled route in Europe (see Figure 30), and reach 16 million passengers, or more than five times the real 1995 traffic aboard the trains through the Channel Tunnel, which links the heart of England to the economic heart of Europe? To reach such conclusions, it must be supposed that the *border effect* will disappear and, furthermore, that the high-speed train will take away a huge slice of traffic not only from the air route between Paris and Madrid—although the "high-speed" train journey would take seven hours—but also from the motorway that runs parallel to the railway. Experience has shown such hypotheses to be unrealistic. As the president of the Spanish railway company (Renfe) declared: "There is no traffic between Barcelona and the French border to justify a high-speed train. The bulk of travellers can be found between Madrid, Saragossa, and Barcelona."

The same can be said for all the other international rail traffic forecasts shown opposite.

For those who may doubt this, it should be remembered that similar forecasts announced that there would be 15 million passengers on the "Eurostar" rail link between London and the continent in the first year of operations and that there were in fact 3 million. The absence of serious counter-research is a real problem in Europe in this field, as it leads to huge wastes of taxpayers' money.

Figure 32

THE GOLDEN STAR OF INTERNATIONAL RAILWAYS

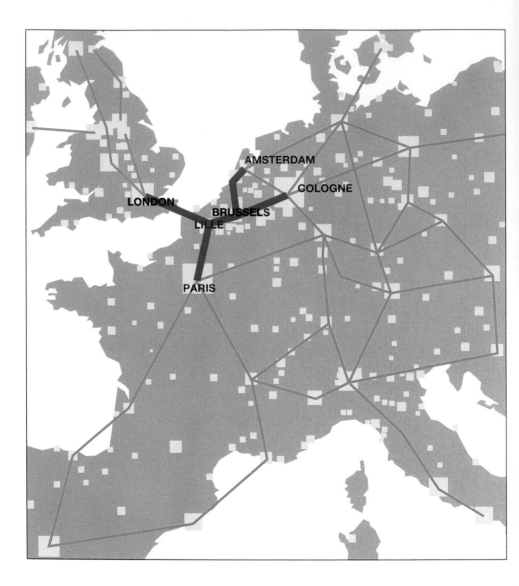

Figure 32
An Ideal Geographical Situation

There is only one area in Europe where, in spite of the *border effect,* it is possible to count on sizeable international traffic on high-speed train lines. It is the "Golden Star," the points of which extend to London, Paris, Amsterdam, and Cologne, around the nodes of Lille and Brussels.

This area's dimensions and density are perfectly suited to the potential offered by the high-speed train. When all the new line work is finished, journeys between the cities concerned will be made in unbelievably short times: 2 hours 30 minutes from London to Paris, 2 hours 5 minutes from London to Brussels, 1 hour 20 minutes from Paris to Brussels, 1 hour 40 minutes from Brussels to Amsterdam and from Brussels to Cologne, and so forth. Moreover, the comfort offered by high-speed trains is unbeatable.

Once completed, however, this network will have cost huge sums to both the taxpayers of the countries concerned and to the financiers of the Channel Tunnel, with no hope of sizeable returns.

Figure 33

THE GREAT SWISS TUNNELS

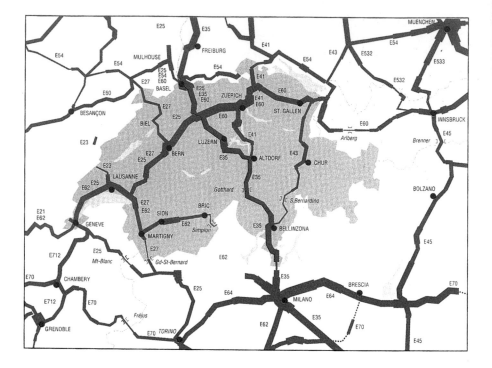

Source: *International Road Census383*

Year 1990

Figure 33
An Astounding Project

Contrary to widespread public opinion, heavy goods vehicle traffic crossing the Alps is very low compared with that which exists on the domestic motorways of the various countries of Europe. Switzerland is no exception to the rule. The heavy goods vehicle traffic in transit between Italy and Germany is minor compared with the traffic inside Switzerland itself, and this makes it impossible to understand the Swiss people's decision to construct two rail tunnels covering more than 100 km in all, at an initial cost representing one and a half times the cost of the Channel Tunnel. The estimated traffic is insignificant and the tunnels will do nothing to actually alter the possible congestion of Swiss roads.

However, there is no certainty that this unjustifiable project will see the light of day. A referendum can cancel what a previous referendum has decided and Switzerland has a reputation for knowing how to do its sums.

It suffices to note that implementing this project would be at least the equivalent for the 6 million Swiss population of what would have been the cost for the 120 million French and English populations of boring 30 Channel Tunnels...

Figure 34

THE GREAT SEA CROSSINGS

Figure 34
Three Projects of Titanic Proportions

By the end of the century there will be several new links of extraordinary proportions that will attach islands and a peninsula to the European continent, from which they have been isolated for thousands of years.

The Channel Tunnel is the first of these. Financed solely through private funding and brought into service progressively as from the end of 1994, it is composed of two rail lines that can be used not only by passenger or freight trains, but also by shuttles that carry cars, trucks, and buses from one side of the Channel to the other. A huge technical achievement, it is also an enormous financial disaster: Its construction costs and operational expenses have far exceeded initial forecasts, whereas its revenues have been considerably beneath estimates because of increased competition and fare decreases from ferries and air transport, which have shown substantial improvements in productivity that were not anticipated by the project's promoters, and because of fanciful traffic forecasts.

Denmark has embarked on the construction of three enormous projects that will together exceed the scope of the Channel Tunnel. These three structures will link Zealand, the island on which Copenhagen is located, to the rest of Denmark, to Sweden, and to Germany, respectively. Unlike the Channel Tunnel, these structures include roadways as well as railways and are combinations of bridges and tunnels. The first of them, well under way, will open in 1997; the second, on which work has just begun, in 2000; while the timetable for the third has not yet been set and will probably come much later.

To complete this programme of European large-scale works, there will only be one more project to achieve: a bridge of unprecedented scale across the Straits of Messina linking Sicily with Italy.

Figure 35

COMPARATIVE TRAFFIC LEVELS FOR A MOTORWAY AND A CANAL

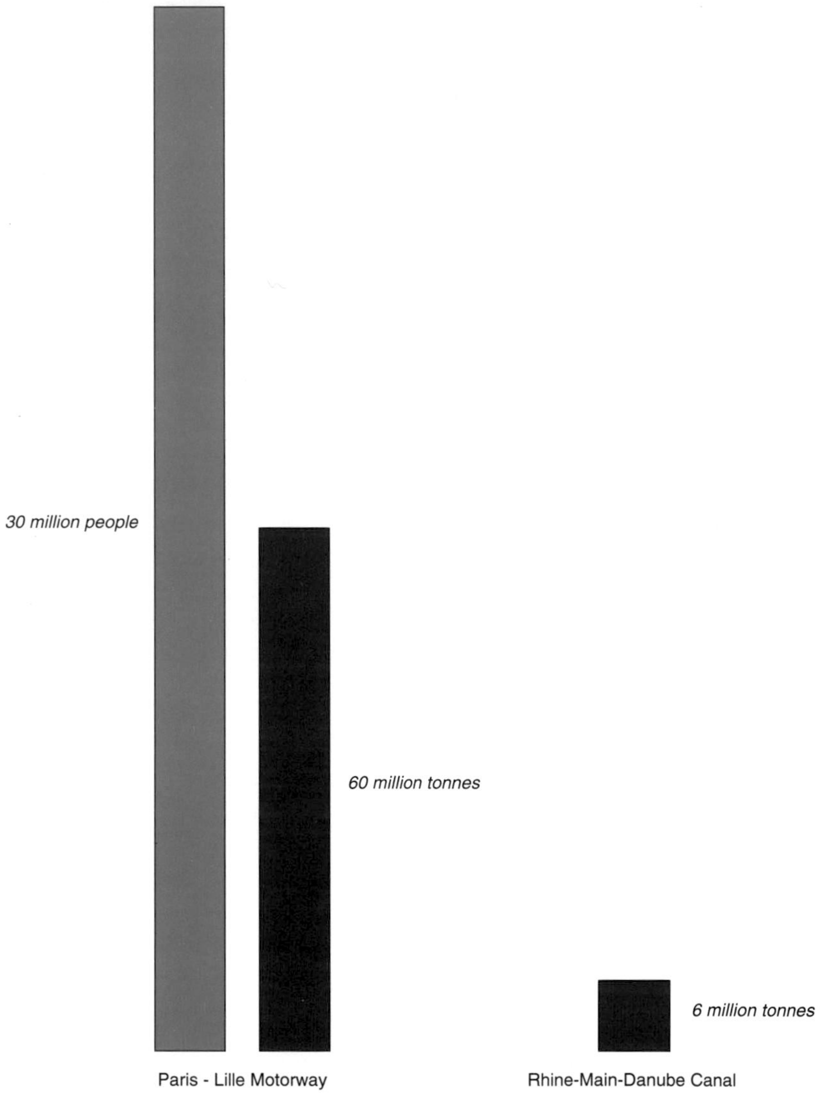

30 million people

60 million tonnes

6 million tonnes

Paris - Lille Motorway

Rhine-Main-Danube Canal

Source : Motorway companies' statistics, German press.

Figure 35
The Rhine-Main-Danube Canal

Existing waterways should obviously be used when possible for transporting those products for which they are particularly suited, such as heavy freight able to support long journey times. However, competition from other forms of transport, in particular road transport, makes it extremely hard to contemplate the construction of new waterways.

The graph opposite shows that traffic on the canal linking the Rhine and Danube basins, which has just been completed after several decades of construction work, represents only a small fraction of freight transported by a typical European motorway. It had been dubbed by a former German Transport Minister as "the silliest project since Babel's Tower." It should also be added that freight traffic represents only a part of the activities of the motorway, which obviously also cover passenger transport, and that wide-gauge canals are far more expensive to build than motorways for a comparable number of kilometres.

Furthermore, as products transported by waterway are dense and not bulky, they cannot be considered to relieve road traffic.

The average value per tonne of freight transported by waterway is also very low, which means that high tariffs cannot be applied and explains the very limited turnover for river navigation, as well as the complete lack of economic potential for waterway construction projects at the dawn of the 21st century.

Finally, it should be stressed that when there are numerous locks to be crossed through, the time and corresponding costs of the journeys along a canal become prohibitive, contrary to the use of natural waterways.

It is therefore all the more surprising that certain countries, such as France, have decided to launch the construction of new wide-gauge canals.

Figure 36

EVOLUTION IN UNITARY EMISSIONS
OF POLLUTANTS FROM NEW VEHICLES

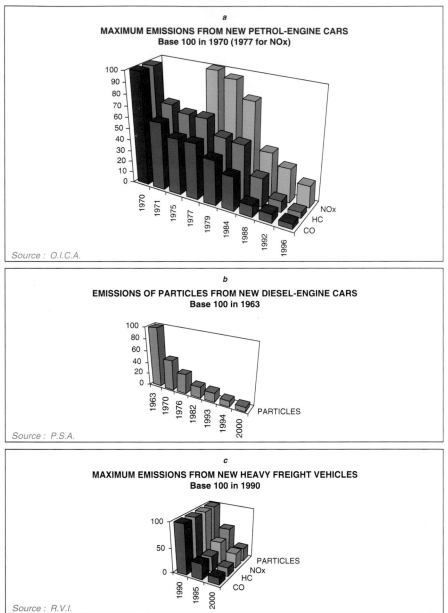

a

MAXIMUM EMISSIONS FROM NEW PETROL-ENGINE CARS
Base 100 in 1970 (1977 for NOx)

Source : O.I.C.A.

b

EMISSIONS OF PARTICLES FROM NEW DIESEL-ENGINE CARS
Base 100 in 1963

Source : P.S.A.

c

MAXIMUM EMISSIONS FROM NEW HEAVY FREIGHT VEHICLES
Base 100 in 1990

Source : R.V.I.

Figure 36
Major Technical Changes

All road vehicles, including petrol- and diesel-powered cars and heavy goods vehicles, have entered into a process leading to a drastic reduction in the emission of pollutants.

Unitary quantities of pollutants emitted have been (and/or will be) divided by factors ranging from three to forty or more, depending on the types of vehicles and the products. This cannot be compared with the evolution in traffic volume, as it is increasing by an average of only 2 to 3% per year, and is usually even stable or decreasing in European town centres where most pollution-related problems may arise.

As in past years, car and lorry manufacturers and the oil industry are continuing to spend billions of ECUs every year, thereby completely changing air pollution problems, which except for unforeseen circumstances will most probably soon be a thing of the past in the majority of Western European countries.

Figure 37

EVOLUTION OF AIR POLLUTION IN PARIS

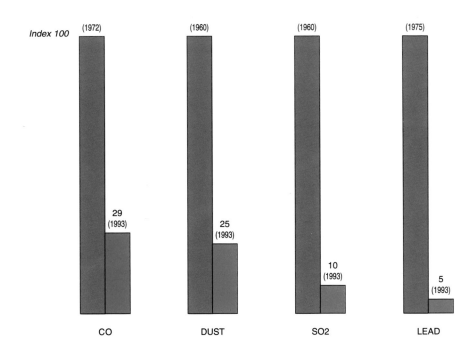

Source : A.I.R.P.A.R.I.F.

Figure 37
A Widely Unknown Improvement

A spectacular improvement in the quality of air has already been recorded in most European towns with regard to a large number of pollutant products, particularly those that presented the most risks in the past.

This progress is not only due to improvements in vehicles but also to efforts made in the housing and industrial sectors.

The consequences of this spectacular improvement in the quality of air can be seen in vegetable and animal life.

Many bird species that had disappeared from London parks have now returned, and the trees on the Paris boulevards are once again covered with lichens, an excellent indicator of pollution levels, which had not been seen in the French capital since as long ago as 1880!

Figure 38

EVOLUTION OF THE CONCENTRATION
OF SULPHUR DIOXIDE (SO2)
IN LONDON SINCE 1930

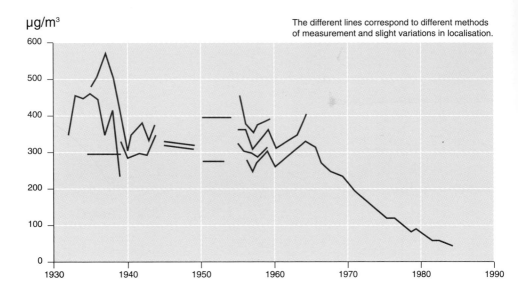

Source : *Asthma and outdoor air pollution (1995).*
Department of Heath (U.K.).

Figure 38
Smog Is a Thing of the Past

From the days of Charles Dickens, every year London suffered from its all too famous smog, a mixture of fog, smoke fumes, and sulphur dioxide that caused hundreds, or even thousands, of deaths as in the dramatic 1952 episode, with hourly concentrations probably exceeding 5,000 µg/m³, which caused 4,000 deaths.

Everything has changed since then, following the 1956 Clean Air Act, and smog has disappeared. The average annual concentration has fallen from 400 µg/m³ to 30 in 1992, and, as for most European towns, it is no longer possible to actually diagnose major health problems linked to the presence of sulphur dioxide in the atmosphere today.

Figure 39

AVERAGE ANNUAL OZONE (O3) LEVELS
IN A SELECTION OF EUROPEAN CITIES
(Station with the highest reading)

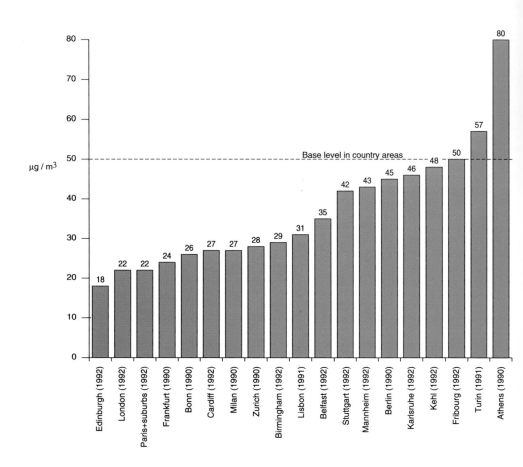

Source : A.I.R.P.A.R.I.F.

Figure 39
Town and Country

An unusual phenomenon occurs in the case of ozone, in that levels are lower in towns than in the country.

For example, the average annual concentration in Paris or in London is two and a half times lower than in most country areas. This can be explained by the fact that cars produce a gas—nitrogen monoxide—that destroys ozone on contact so that the lowest readings are found along the busiest routes. Paradoxically, if ozone is proved to be toxic at any level of concentration, as certain studies would seem to imply, risks would therefore be lower in towns.

There is, of course, the phenomenon of "peaking" that usually takes place several times a year for a few hours, but even during these periods the highest levels are usually to be found on the outskirts of towns or even in rural areas.

Moreover, the peak levels reached during a few hours per year in most Western European towns rarely exceed 250 µg/m³, whereas the average *annual* concentration is nearly 400 µg/m³ in a town such as Mexico City (i.e., 20 times more than in London or Paris). Generally speaking, Western European countries can be considered as safe areas as far as ozone risks are concerned.

Figure 40

EVOLUTION IN CONCENTRATION OF OZONE
IN THE CENTRE OF LONDON

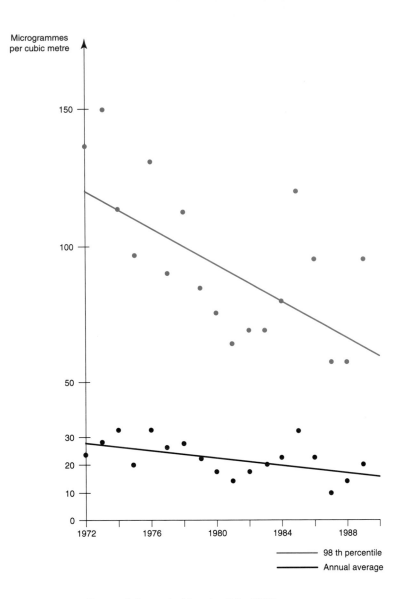

Source : *Asthma and outdoor air pollution (1995).*
Department of Heath (U.K.).

Figure 40
Ozone Decreasing Trend

Few countries or towns have long-term data at their disposal concerning observations of ozone levels. However, as for most other products and despite certain statements to the contrary, the existing data show a downward trend.

It is difficult to prove this by analysing results covering only a short period because there are important variations from one year to the next due to the climatic fluctuations that characterise Western Europe.

The figures given opposite regarding London are most probably very close to results that could have been collected in Paris or other Western European towns, which, unfortunately, do not have statistics that go back so far in time.

Consequently, it would be most unwise to jump to the conclusion that road traffic has increased peak ozone levels especially as towns that have introduced traffic restrictions during peak ozone pollution levels have not registered any significant changes in them.

Figure 41

COMPARISON OF EMISSIONS AND CONCENTRATIONS
OF NITROGEN DIOXIDE IN GREAT BRITAIN

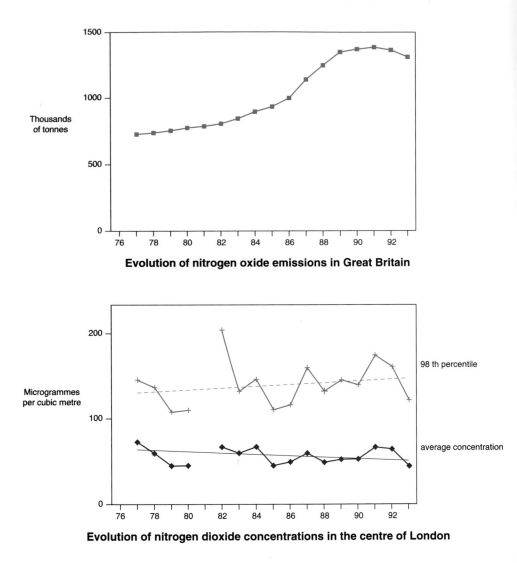

Evolution of nitrogen oxide emissions in Great Britain

Evolution of nitrogen dioxide concentrations in the centre of London

Source : *Asthma and outdoor air pollution (1995).*
Department of Heath (U.K.).

Figure 41
Emission and Immission

The figure opposite illustrates one of the most common errors encountered in the field of air pollution. Pollution concentrations are often confused with the quantity of products emitted in the atmosphere whereas, for quite simple reasons, there is usually no connection between the two.

The graph opposite shows clearly that quantities of nitrogen oxides emitted in Great Britain doubled between 1977 and 1991 whereas there was a *reduction* in average concentration—which scientists call "immission"—in the atmosphere of central London during the same period.

One of the most obvious explanations for this apparent paradox is that traffic is increasing mainly in suburban and country areas, where the products emitted are often immediately diluted, and not in the middle of towns. Confusing emissions and immissions gives an untrue picture of the situation. The only important factor, which is often not even mentioned, is the quality of the air breathed and not the overall quantities of products emitted throughout a territory, as these are of no significance from a health standpoint.

It should also be added that emissions are now decreasing as far as nitrogen dioxide is concerned, due to technical advances for vehicles, and that this decrease will be even more significant in the coming years, as and when old vehicles are replaced by new quite pollution-free ones.

Figure 42

AVERAGE ANNUAL NITROGEN DIOXIDE (NO2) LEVELS
IN A SELECTION OF EUROPEAN CITIES
(Station with the highest reading)

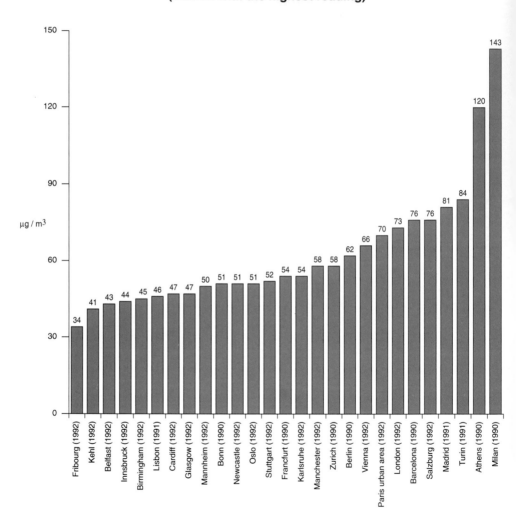

Source : A.I.R.P.A.R.I.F.

Figure 42
Two Exceptions

A great majority of European towns have very low concentrations of nitrogen dioxide, which will probably be gradually reduced even further in the coming years with the significant decrease in emissions from new vehicles.

The only exceptions are certain towns in southern Europe for which the problem is more complex due to geographical or climatic specificities. One solution for these towns, at least in part, may be to distribute fuel with special characteristics if the problem cannot be solved by treating other sources of pollution such as factories.

Figure 43

PROCESS OF ESTABLISHING
AIR QUALITY NORMS
THE EXAMPLE OF NITROGEN DIOXIDE (NO2)

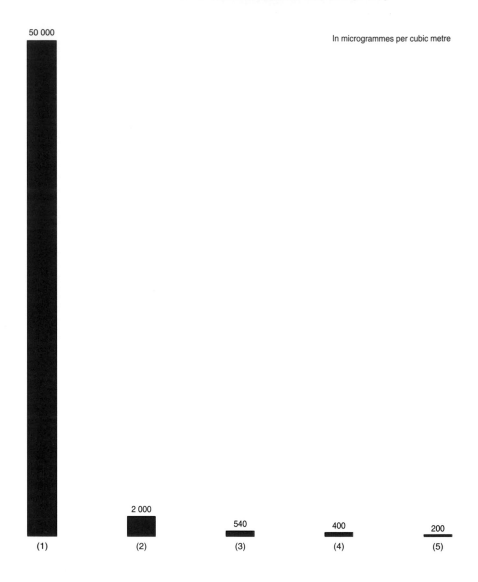

In microgrammes per cubic metre

Source : Air Quality Guidelines for Europe; World Health Organization; European Community Directives.

Figure 43
The Principle of Precaution

It is particularly interesting to study the way in which air quality norms are established, as shown by the example of nitrogen dioxide (NO2), one of the main gases issued from motor traffic. The process begins with the World Health Organisation whose work can be summarised as follows:

1. There have been acute cases of bronchitis and pneumonia, given a concentration of NO2 of 50,000 µg/m^3 and over.
2. Concentrations of 2,000 µg/m^3 are frequently recorded in the home when gas appliances are used in the kitchen, "without there appearing to be any long term effect on health."
3. Asthmatics undertaking physical exercise in the presence of concentrations of 540 µg/m^3 registered slight physiological changes to the lungs that were "not necessarily significant."
4. In accordance with the "principle of precaution," it is recommended not to exceed hourly concentrations of 400 µg/m^3.
5. As an extra safety measure, the European authorities decided to divide the level recommended by the World Health Organisation by two, also adding that this limit should not be exceeded for more than 2% of the time during the year. The result of this process is that the European norm for the quality of air represents a tenth of the level that many housewives breathe in daily in their kitchens, with no known side effects.

Such caution is quite remarkable, but it should be noted, in addition, that all towns in most European countries already respected the European norms even before the introduction of catalytic exhaust systems, even though one of the main aims of this measure is to reduce emissions of nitrogen oxides at the price of a substantial increase in the cost of vehicles and in their fuel consumption.

Figure 44

PETROL CONSUMPTION AND LEUKAEMIA
IN THE NETHERLANDS

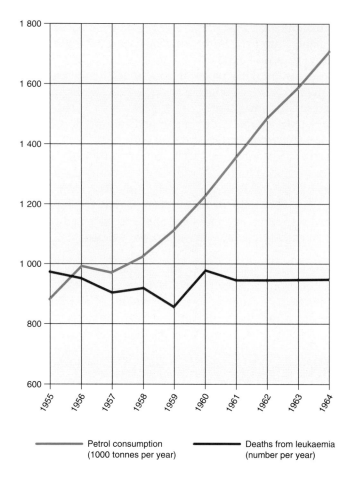

Petrol consumption
(1000 tonnes per year)

Deaths from leukaemia
(number per year)

Source : Concawe.

Figure 44
Traffic and Cancer

Studies carried out in the Netherlands and later confirmed by observations in 19 other countries were unable to establish any relation between the increase in fuel use and the frequency of cases of leukaemia subsequently diagnosed.

No evidence was found to prove that concentrations of hydrocarbons in the air, particularly benzene, had a significant impact on health due to the extremely low level of concentrations present in the open air in European countries, which is decreasing even further with current progress in eliminating vehicle pollutants.

Figure 45

THE OPINION OF WESTERN EUROPEANS ON THE EVOLUTION OF POLLUTION IN LARGE TOWNS

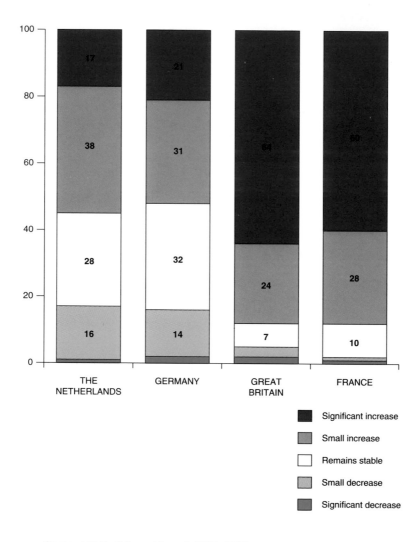

Source : U.R.F. - Sofres opinion polls (1994 - 1995).

Figure 45
Poisoning of the Mind

Air pollution phenomena are very similar in the Netherlands, Germany, Great Britain, and France.

However, national opinion of them diverges completely: 60% of the French and 64% of the English consider that air pollution is increasing significantly, but the figure falls to 17% in the Netherlands and 21% in Germany.

This surprising difference can easily be explained. At a time when it has become practically impossible for individuals to gauge by themselves the level of air pollution due to considerable progress made over several decades in the fields of industry, urban heating systems, and vehicles, public opinion must rely on the media for information.

As air pollution is an extremely complex and sensitive subject, the media must in turn rely on experts' reports, particularly those issued by official bodies. The publication of biased or badly presented reports with insufficient information to counterbalance their arguments sparked off extremely violent campaigns in Great Britain and France, which managed to misrepresent the facts and create a situation of collective psychosis. Whereas the overall quality of air continues to improve, public opinion is now convinced of the contrary. The situation is very different in Germany and the Netherlands where the facts are seen in a less negative light, probably due to more balanced information sources.

It has to be added that the link between external air pollution and health events is far from clear. A comprehensive study on asthma commissioned by the British Department of Health recently came to the following conclusion:

> "Distribution of asthma in England and Wales has little in common with the regional spread of major pollutant elements (...) Hospital admission and death rates show no clear geographical tendency and would appear to depend more on the characteristics of the health-care system than on environmental factors."

The same study came to the conclusion that,

> "There is no proof that asthma is more frequent in urban areas than in the country. There has been an increase in asthma in the last thirty years, but it is improbable that this is a result of changes in air pollution."

In France, the frequency of deaths due to respiratory illnesses in Paris is lower than the national average. Moreover, the frequency decreased by 10% from 1982 to 1989.

Figure 46

EVOLUTION OF ESTABLISHED OIL RESERVES

145 billion
tonnes

45 billion
tonnes

1960	1994
32 years' consumption	45 years' consumption

Source : B.P. Statistical Review of World Energy (1995).

Figure 46
A Receding Horizon

The risk of depleting oil reserves is one of the arguments often used against cars and road transport to justify limiting their use.

Examination of the facts reveals a very different situation from that which is most often imagined. In 1960, established oil reserves amounted to 45 billion tonnes of oil, corresponding to 32 years' consumption at that time. Thirty-four years later, in 1992, reserves were three times higher and represented 45 years' consumption at the current rate, in spite of the amounts of oil extracted in the meantime.

In other words, new discoveries, together with progress in oil-extraction techniques, are continually deferring depletion of reserves, and this is likely to continue to be the case for quite some time as probable reserves are estimated at three times more than established reserves.

We have now entered a long period in which supply will exceed demand. Oil-producing countries are well aware of this as they are having great difficulty in avoiding the collapse of oil prices, which are already at a very low level. The fact that most oil reserves are located in a few Middle East desert countries is an added safety factor as things would clearly be far more difficult if they were in the midst of heavily populated areas.

Even though temporary problems may arise, the time when it will really be necessary to use other sources of energy is not yet foreseeable. Substitute sources of energy will be more expensive but they are nevertheless available, and some of them are extremely abundant.

Figure 47

SPEED LIMIT EFFICIENCY

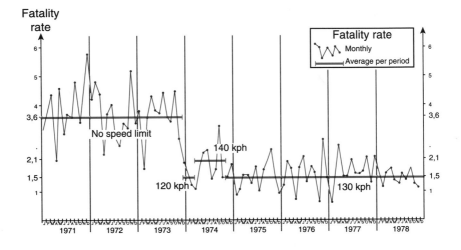

Source: French Ministry of Equipment - Direction of Road Safety

Figure 47
Immediate, Lasting Effects

The introduction of a speed limit on French motorways on 1st December 1973 was a particularly striking confirmation of the results obtained by the many experiments carried out worldwide, which all came to the same conclusions.

Whereas the death rate was 3.6 in the absence of a speed limit, it suddenly dropped to 1.5 (i.e. 2.4 times less) and has never returned to its previous level. Between December 1973 and October 1974 the changes in the legally authorised level had direct effects on the accident level, before French law finally fixed the maximum authorised speed limit at 130 km.p.h. for motorways in country areas, where it still is today.

It is easy to understand why no subsequent French government has ever considered questioning the existence of speed limits.

Since then, progress made in the area of infrastrustures, vehicles, and driver behaviour has resulted in the continuing decrease in the frequency of accidents. The death rate is at about 0.5 in 1996 (i.e., 7 times less than 1972!) and continues to decrease regularly at the rate of about 5% per year, offering a high level of safety for motorway journeys.

The existence of speed limits on almost all the European road networks is one of the main reasons for the decrease in the number of deaths in Western Europe from approximately 75,000 per year in 1970 to 45,000 today. In the same period, traffic has almost doubled. However, with such a horrendous figure, not to mention the countless injured, road accidents remain one of the worst scourges of our time. This fact is too often met with indifference.

Figure 48

EVOLUTION OF ACCIDENTS AND RANDOM BREATH TESTING IN AUSTRALIA

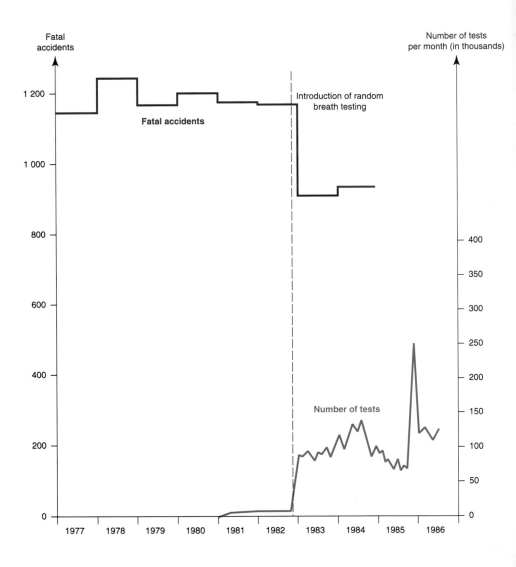

Source : New South Wales, Road safety.

Figure 48
"You Can't Drink and Drive"

There are at least ten ways of having an almost immediate significant effect on accident rates. One of the most effective is performing more alcohol tests on drivers when needed. The table opposite concerns New South Wales, Australia, on the other side of the world from Europe, and shows that a sufficient number of tests can lead to a highly significant drop in accident figures. This has been shown not only in Australia, but in France too, where the introduction of random breath testing in 1978 led to a major reduction in accidents and where drivers underwent a real change of behaviour. However, the effect was only temporary as controls were insufficient at that time.

It has been proved since, mainly in the northern European countries, that this method really works in bringing down the level of accidents, in particular the especially tragic ones that take place on Saturday evenings.

In France, the reduction in the authorised level of alcohol in the blood to 0.5 grams per litre in 1995 also appears to have had very positive results, and this measure should be adopted as soon as possible by those countries that have not yet done so.

Figure 49

THE EFFECT OF THE USE OF DAYTIME RUNNING LIGHTS
ACCORDING TO THE LATITUDE

Percentage reduction in daytime accidents
involving several vehicles

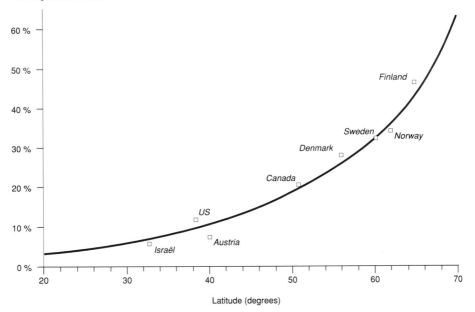

Latitude (degrees)

Source : M. Koornstra, Dutch Road Safety Research Institute (S.W.O.V.).

Figure 49
A Simple, Effective Measure?

Northern countries were the first to make the use of dipped headlights compulsory at all times and even in full daylight, with a very positive impact on road safety.

Various other European countries followed suit, such as Austria in the west or Poland and Hungary in the east, either on an experimental or a permanent basis, apparently with equally positive results.

Since 1990 in Canada, a country in which the majority of the population lives at the same latitude as central Europe, special lights come on automatically in new cars when the engine is started, thanks to a simple electrical connection. The positive impact on the reduction in total accidents is estimated at about 5%.

Subject to confirmation and further study of advantages and disadvantages, this could be one of the simplest and most effective measures for significantly reducing road accidents. A study commissioned by the European Commission should allow for a definite opinion to be reached on the subject and could lead to a recommendation being made to all its member countries.

Figure 50

EVOLUTION OF ROAD ACCIDENTS IN AUSTRALIA
(State of Victoria)

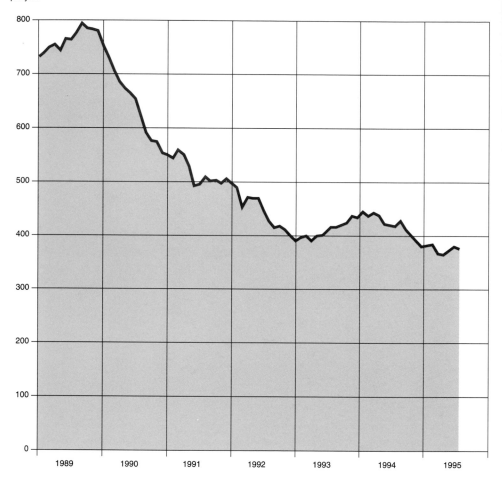

Number
of deaths
per year

Source : *Transport Accident Commission (Melbourne).*

Figure 50
Preventing Is Better Than Not Curing

In 1989, those responsible for compulsory motor insurance in the State of Victoria, Australia, decided to appropriate 3% of premiums received to the prevention of accidents, instead of to compensation. The percentage may seem small, but in absolute terms the sums involved were considerable. On a European scale, 3 percent of compulsory insurance premiums—which are only half of total car premiums—would represent about one billion ECUs per year.

With the sums made available in this way, it was possible to organise exceptionally dense coverage for information campaigns and to purchase the large quantities of ultramodern equipment that had always been lacking for the police force.

A year later, the number of victims killed had fallen by more than 20% and car insurance companies, therefore, made large profits. The share of compulsory insurance premiums appropriated to the prevention of accidents was then increased to 8%, which would correspond to an annual allowance of about 2.5 billion ECUs in Europe, and part of this was appropriated to safety improvements on the road network itself.

At the end of 1992, after the policy had been in practice for three years, the number of fatal accidents had been halved and has not increased since, which is a result without precedent worldwide. Proof has thus been given that it is possible to obtain results in the short term that were thought to be unattainable until now and that it is essential to change the approach to most road safety policies throughout the world that consist in finding the money when it is too late, attempting to compensate for accidents instead of trying to avoiding them.

As far as road safety is concerned, the attitude of today's society is both absurd and deeply guilty.

Figure 51

THE PARIS REGIONAL
RAPID TRANSIT NETWORK (RER)

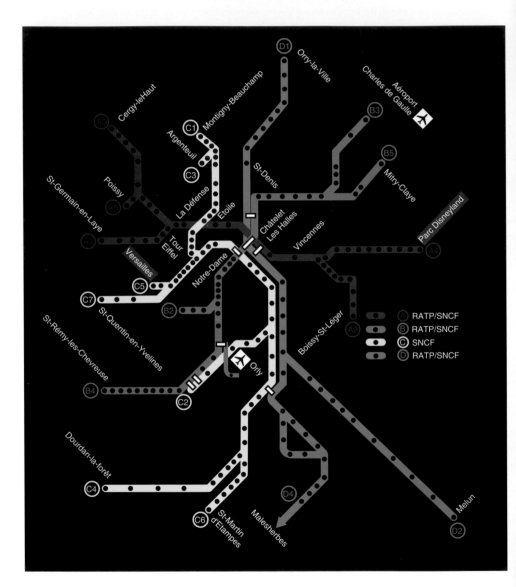

Figure 51
A Powerful Network

Until recently, the different railway lines that served the Paris Region suburbs all stopped in outlying railway stations and were not linked to each other. In 1971, the author of this book, who was adviser to the French prime minister at that time, thought up the plan shown opposite and had it adopted by the French government in 1972. It came into being over the following quarter of a century.

At the present time, 20 suburban lines, split into 4 networks (A, B, C, D), have access to the centre of Paris and are linked to suburban lines on the opposite side. This has led to significant changes in transport conditions for a large number of the region's inhabitants.

The Paris Regional Express Network [*Réseau Express Régional* (RER)] is one of the most effective in the world and has become an essential factor in the region's unity, as it is possible to travel very rapidly from one extremity to another in comfortable conditions. This helps to create a vast job market that benefits companies and workers alike, even if a majority of the region's inhabitants are using their car to go to work.

More than 160 suburban railway stations are now served by the RER, which also counts 22 stations in the city of Paris itself, including seven that play a major role, as they are very well connected to the urban undergound network, the *metro*. The main one is the central *hub* station, Châtelet-les-Halles with its seven tracks located in the very heart of Paris.

Figure 52

SPEED SPACE-TIME DIAGRAM
ON THE PARIS RINGROAD

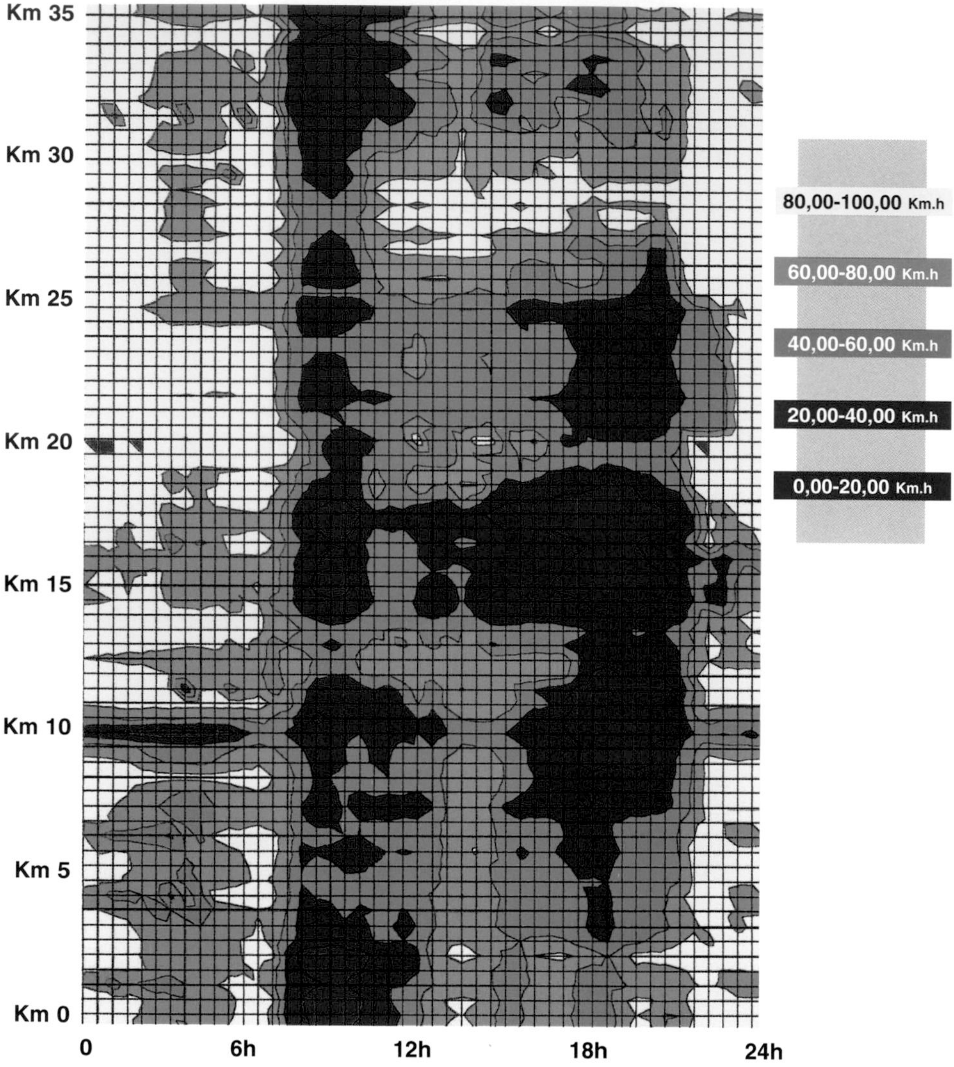

Source: Union Routiere de France

Figure 52
A Very Clear Cartography

Until recently, it was difficult to obtain a true picture of traffic conditions on motorway and express roads. This is no longer the case when they are equipped with detectors capable of providing ongoing data on the three key issues involved (i.e., traffic flow, average speed, and roadway occupancy by vehicles).

It therefore becomes possible to represent, in a simple manner, the evolution of traffic conditions during a given day on a given motorway stretch. The figure opposite corresponds to a working day in June 1996, on the outside roadway of the Paris Region inner motorway (the Boulevard Périphérique, 35 km long).

The places and times corresponding to the most difficult traffic conditions (less than 20 km.p.h.) or very heavy traffic (from 20 to 40 km.p.h.) can be seen immediately. They particularly concern the southern section of the motorway, which has only three lanes each way, compared with four lanes each way in the west, north, and east sections.

It must, however, be noted that the average speed over the whole year is 53 km.p.h., which is quite high. And yet this is, by far, the road with the heaviest traffic in Europe, with daily flow reaching about 30,000 vehicles per lane. Due to the considerable capacity they offer, motorways and express roads actually function much better than is generally imagined, even in urban areas. The main problems arise when such roads do not exist.

This type of graphical representation means that it is possible to see at a glance what the traffic situation has been for a given day or period. This can now be drawn up daily for most of the motorways in the Paris region.

List of Figures

INDEX

The Artech House Mobile Communications Series

John Walker, Series Editor

For further informatin on these and other Artech House titles, contact:

Artech House
685 Canton Street
Norwood, MA 02062
617-769-9750
Fax: 617-769-6334
Telex: 951-659
email: artech@artech-house.com

Artech House
Portland House, Stag Place
London SW1E 5XA England
+44 (0) 171-973-8077
Fax: +44 (0) 171-630-0166
Telex: 951-659
email: artech-uk@artech-house.com

WWW: http://www.artech-house.com

Learning Resources
Centre